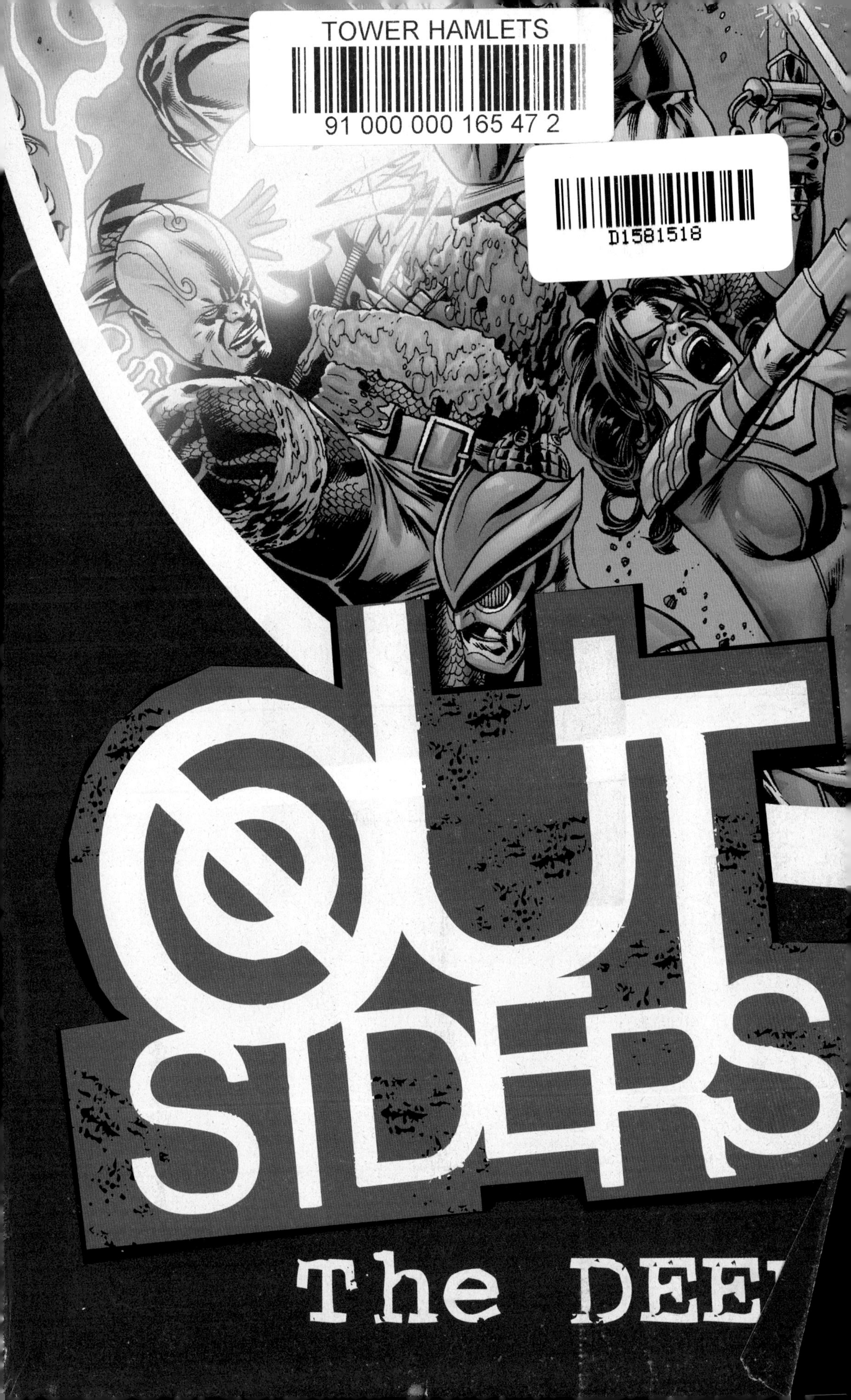
OUT-
SIDERS
The DEE

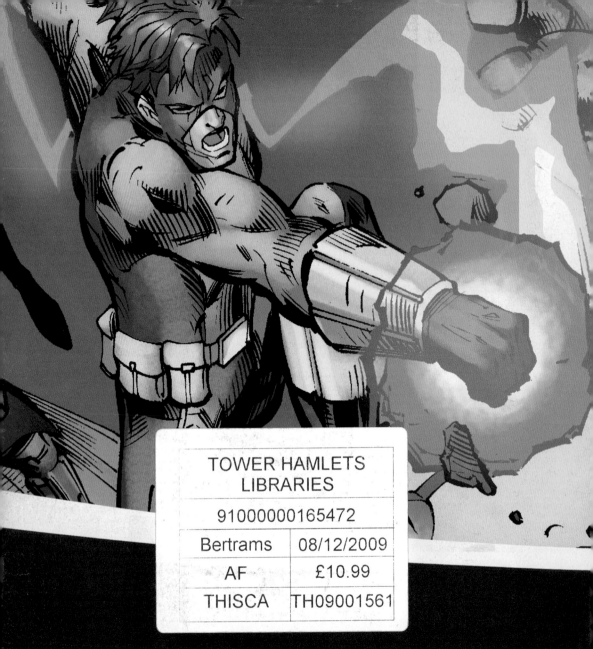

DAN DIDIO SVP – EXECUTIVE EDITOR **MIKE MARTS MICHAEL SIGLAIN** EDITORS – ORIGINAL SERIES
JANELLE SIEGEL HARVEY RICHARDS ASSISTANT EDITORS – ORIGINAL SERIES **GEORG BREWER** VP – DESIGN & DC DIRECT CREATIVE
BOB HARRAS GROUP EDITOR – COLLECTED EDITIONS **SCOTT NYBAKKEN** EDITOR **ROBBIN BROSTERMAN** DESIGN DIRECTOR – BOOKS

DC COMICS
PAUL LEVITZ PRESIDENT & PUBLISHER **RICHARD BRUNING** SVP-CREATIVE DIRECTOR
PATRICK CALDON EVP – FINANCE & OPERATIONS **AMY GENKINS** SVP – BUSINESS & LEGAL AFFAIRS
JIM LEE EDITORIAL DIRECTOR – WILDSTORM **GREGORY NOVECK** SVP – CREATIVE AFFAIRS
STEVE ROTTERDAM SVP – SALES & MARKETING **CHERYL RUBIN** SVP – BRAND MANAGEMENT

Cover art by Lee Garbett and Trevor Scott. Cover color by Brian Reber.

THE OUTSIDERS: THE DEEP
Published by DC Comics. Cover and compilation. Copyright © 2009 DC Comics. All Rights Reserved.
Originally published in single magazine form in BATMAN AND THE OUTSIDERS SPECIAL 1 and THE OUTSIDERS 15-20.
Copyright © 2009 DC Comics. All Rights Reserved. All characters, their distinctive likenesses and related elements featured
in this publication are trademarks of DC Comics. The stories, characters and incidents featured in this publication are entirely fictional.
DC Comics does not read or accept unsolicited submissions of ideas, stories or artwork.

DC Comics, 1700 Broadway, New York, NY 10019
A Warner Bros. Entertainment Company
Printed by World Color Press, Inc.
St-Romuald, QC, Canada 10/14/09. First Printing.
ISBN: 978-1-4012-2502-5

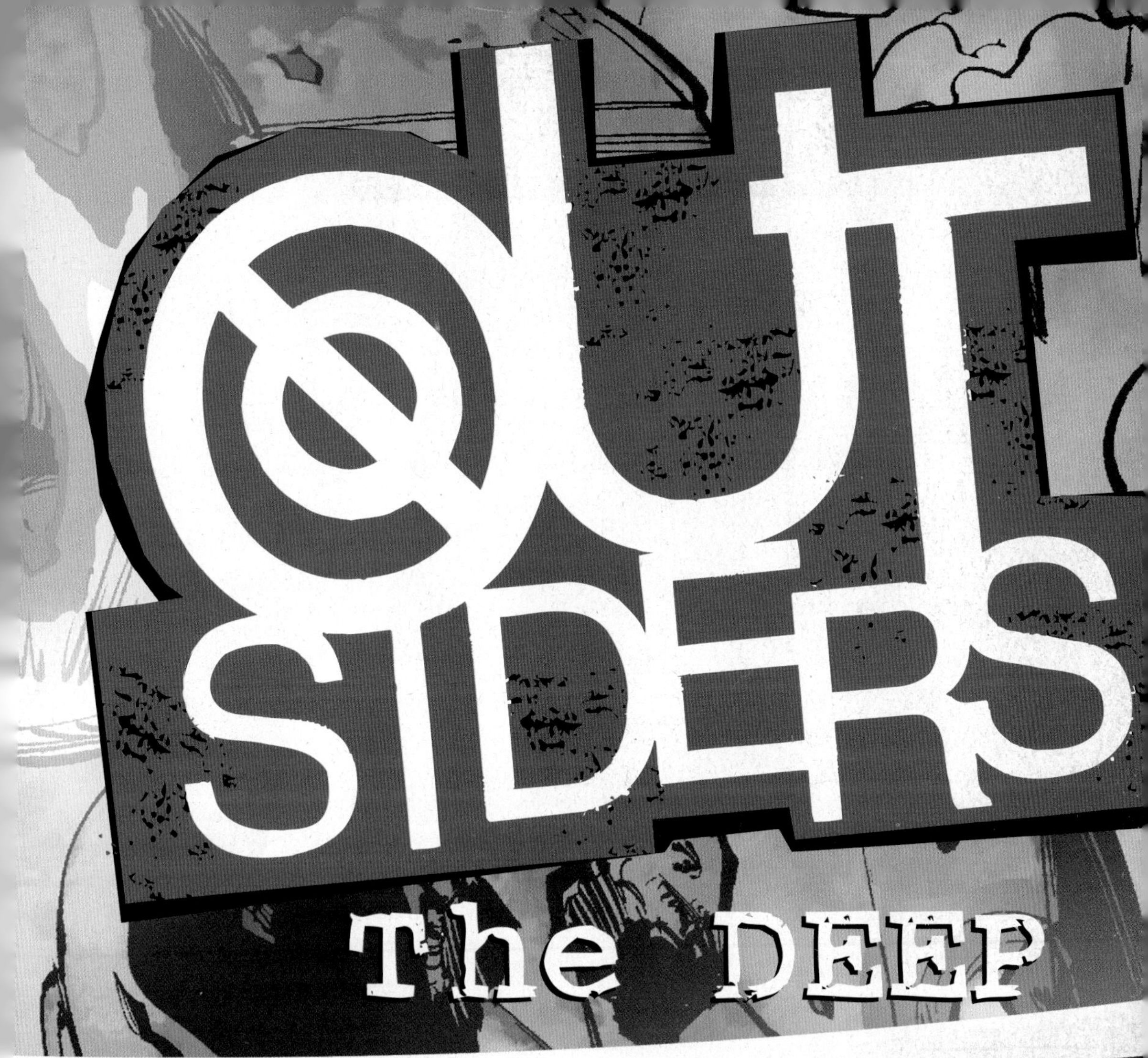

OUTSIDERS
The DEEP

WRITTEN BY
PETER J. TOMASI

PENCILS BY
LEE GARBETT
ADAM KUBERT
FERNANDO PASARIN
JEREMY HAUN

INKS BY
TREVOR SCOTT
JOHN DELL
SANDU FLOREA
PRENTIS ROLLINS
WAYNE FAUCHER
JEREMY HAUN
LIVESAY

COLORS BY
CHRIS CHUCKRY
BRIAN REBER
HI-FI
THOMAS CHU

LETTERED BY
STEVE WANDS
TRAVIS LANHAM
SAL CIPRIANO

ORIGINAL SERIES COVERS
LEE GARBETT AND **TREVOR SCOTT**
ADAM KUBERT AND **JOHN DELL**
ANDREW ROBINSON
J.G. JONES

BATMAN CREATED BY
BOB KANE

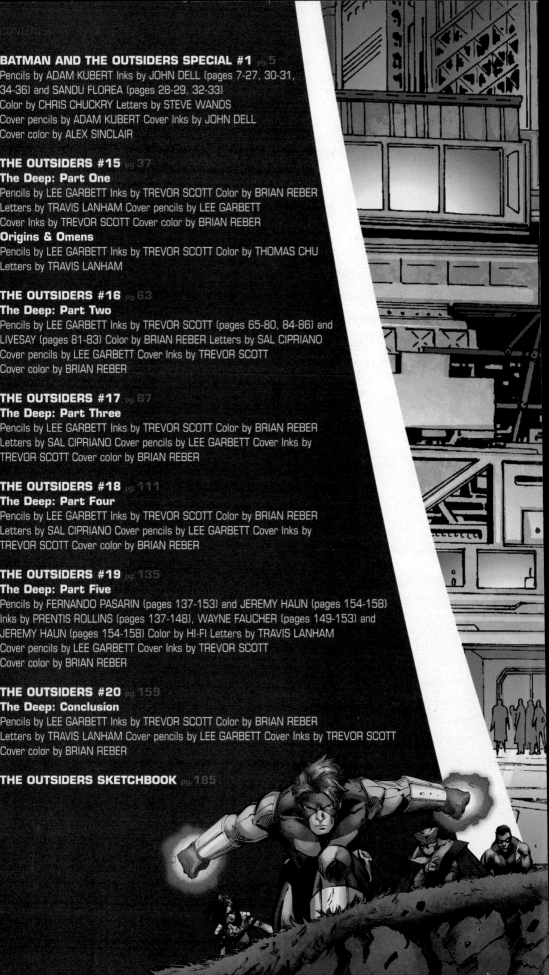

CONTENTS

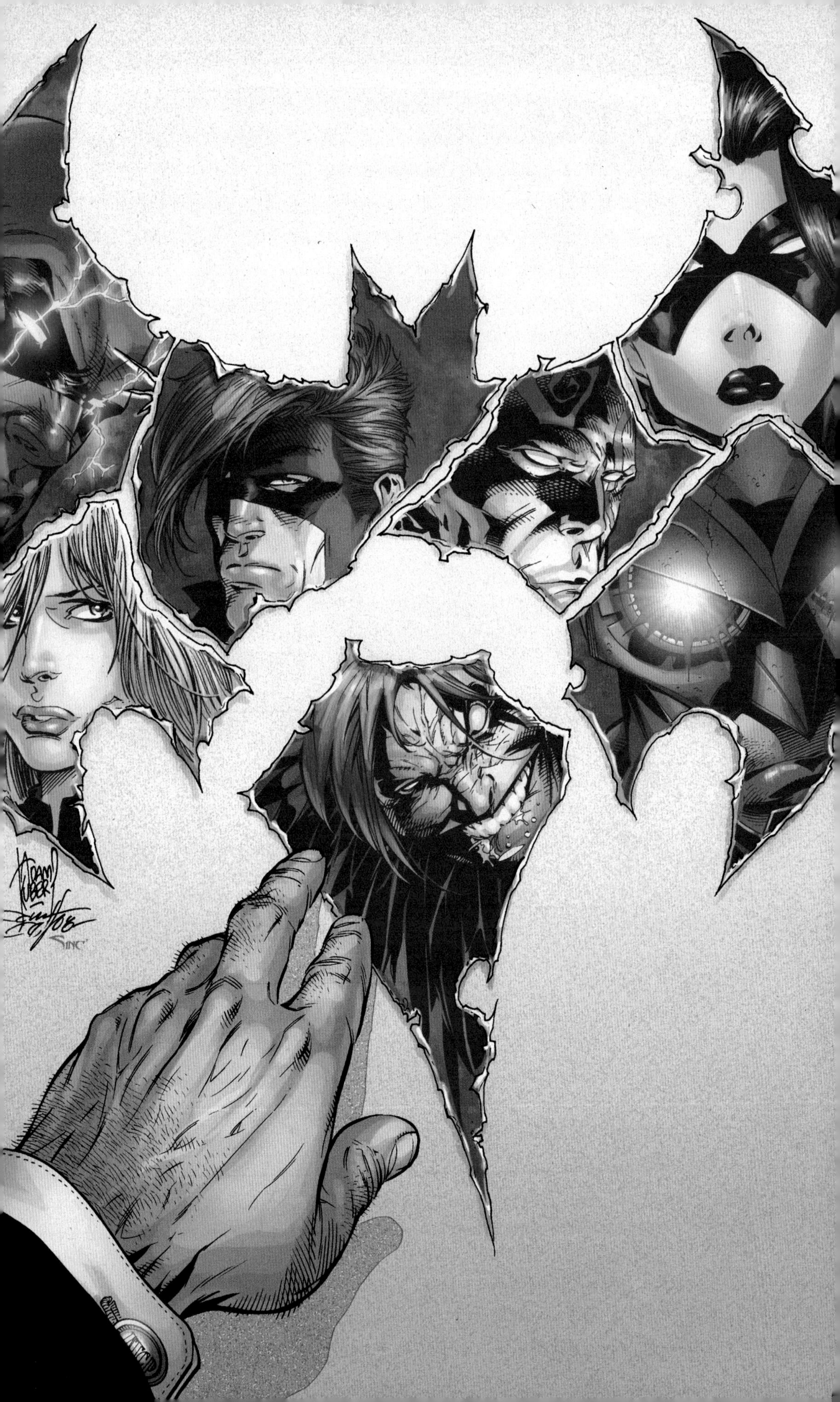

"Let me tell you why
I really started the Outsiders."

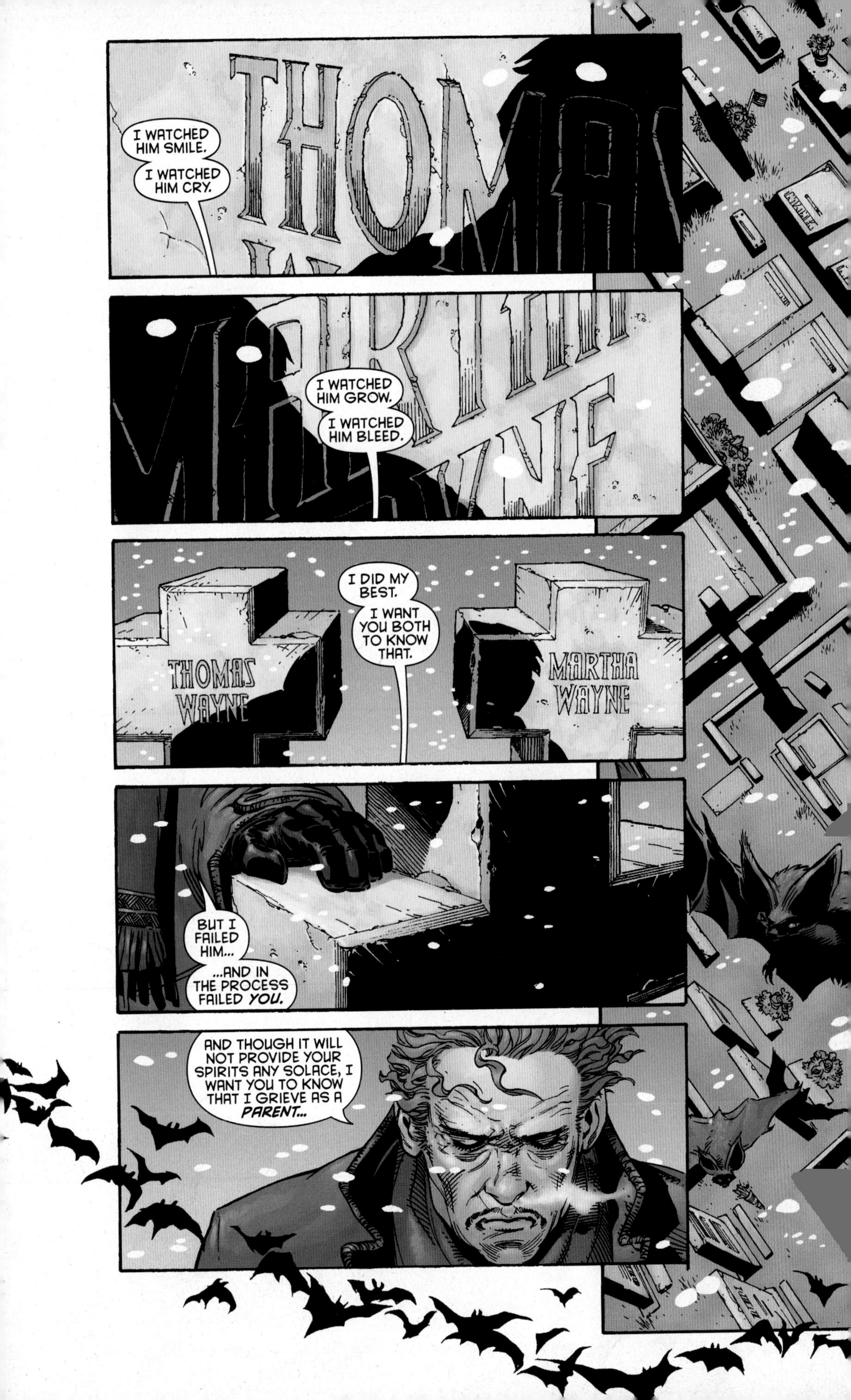
I WATCHED HIM SMILE.
I WATCHED HIM CRY.
I WATCHED HIM GROW.
I WATCHED HIM BLEED.
THOMAS WAYNE
I DID MY BEST.
I WANT YOU BOTH TO KNOW THAT.
MARTHA WAYNE
BUT I FAILED HIM...
...AND IN THE PROCESS FAILED *YOU.*
AND THOUGH IT WILL NOT PROVIDE YOUR SPIRITS ANY SOLACE, I WANT YOU TO KNOW THAT I GRIEVE AS A *PARENT...*

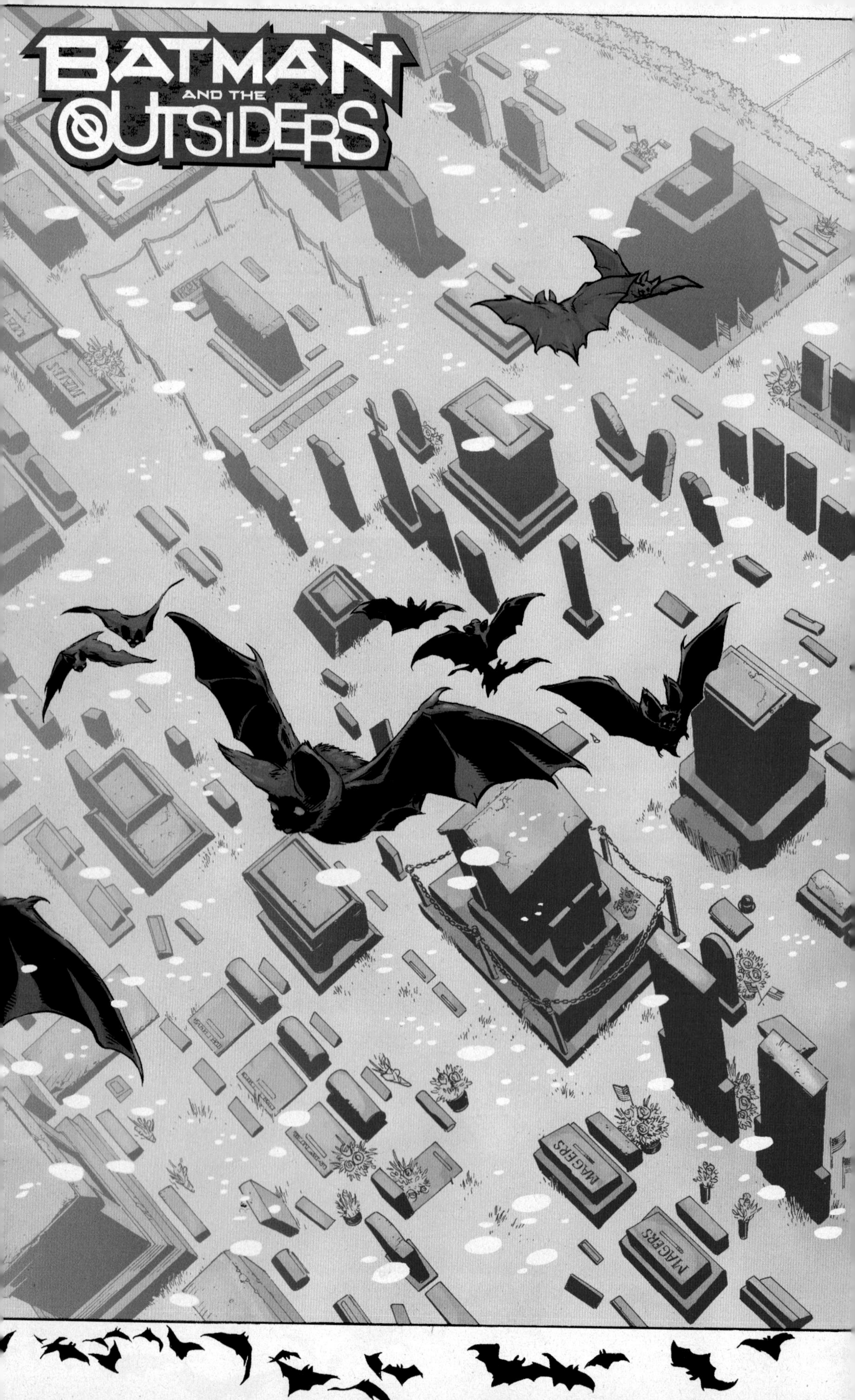
BATMAN
AND THE
OUTSIDERS
MAGERS
MAGERS

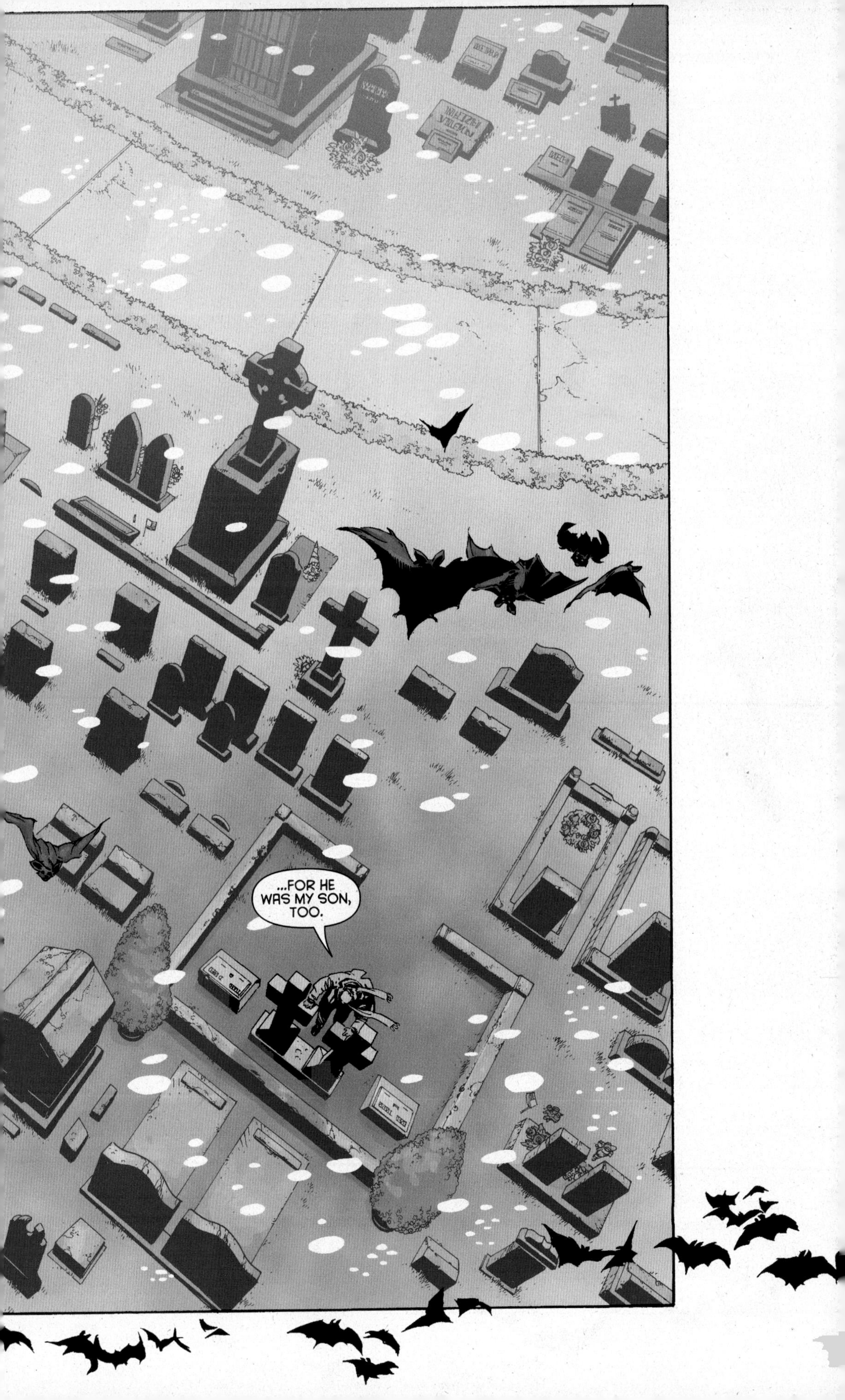
...FOR HE WAS MY SON, TOO.

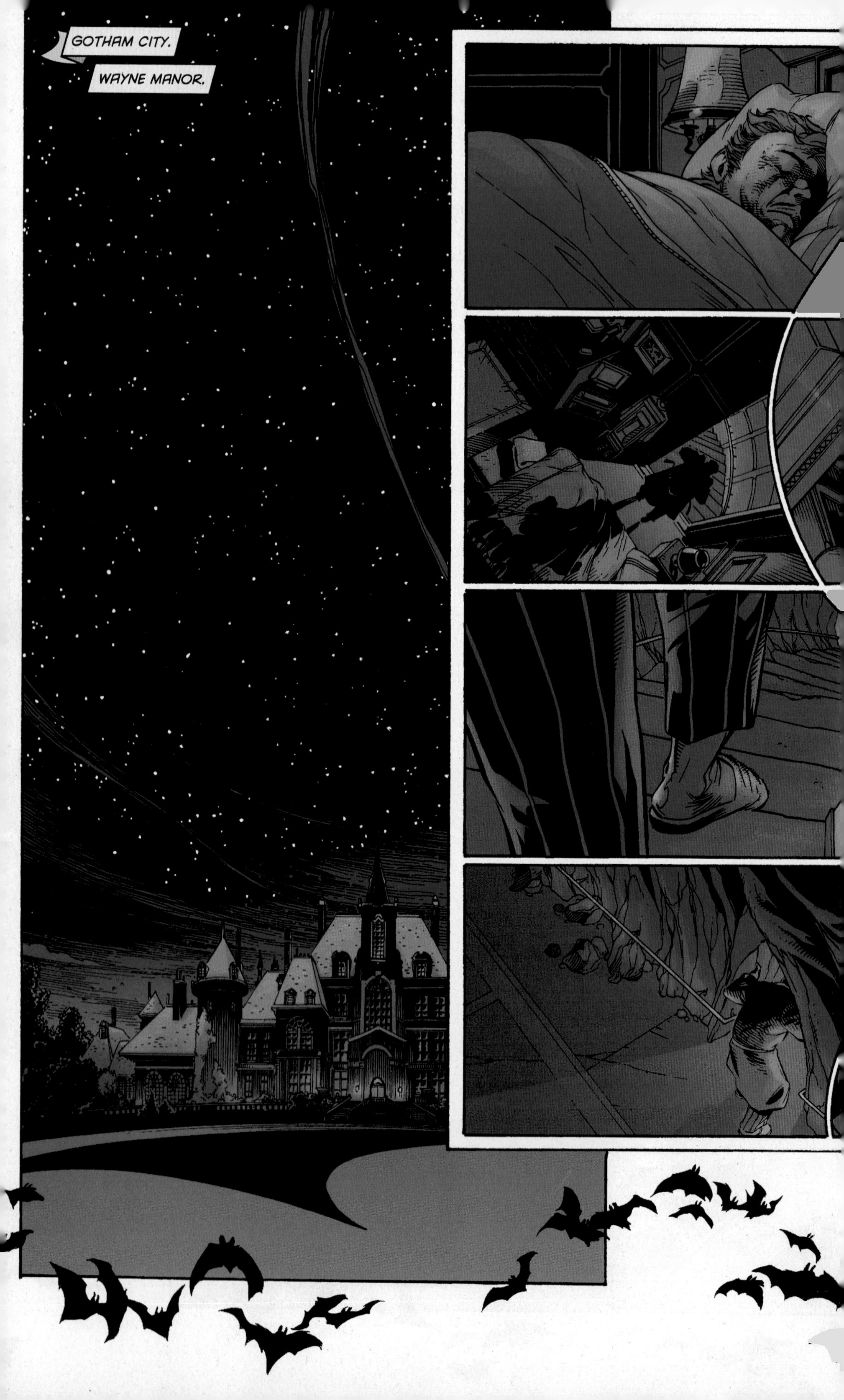
GOTHAM CITY.
WAYNE MANOR.

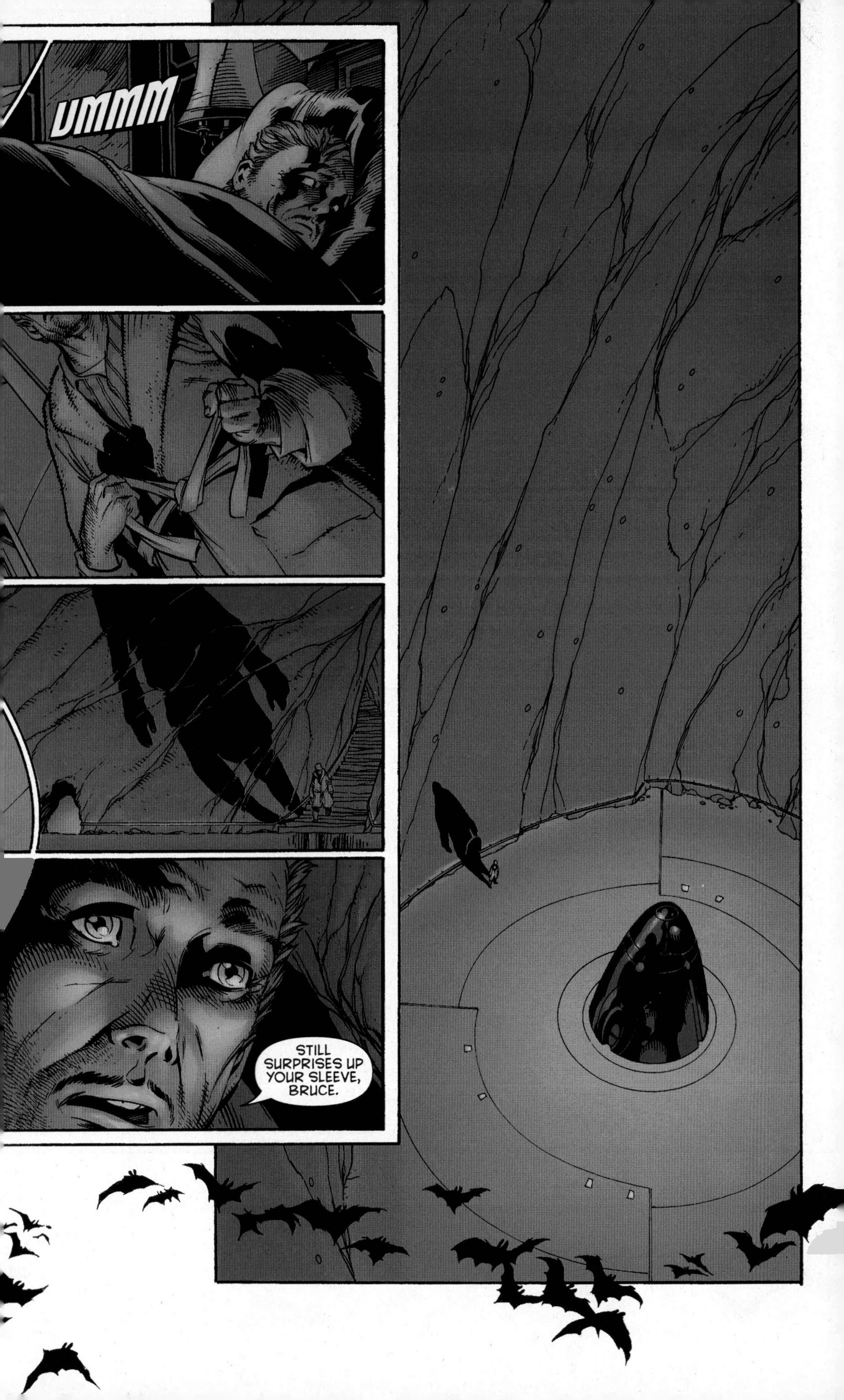
UMMM
STILL SURPRISES UP YOUR SLEEVE, BRUCE.

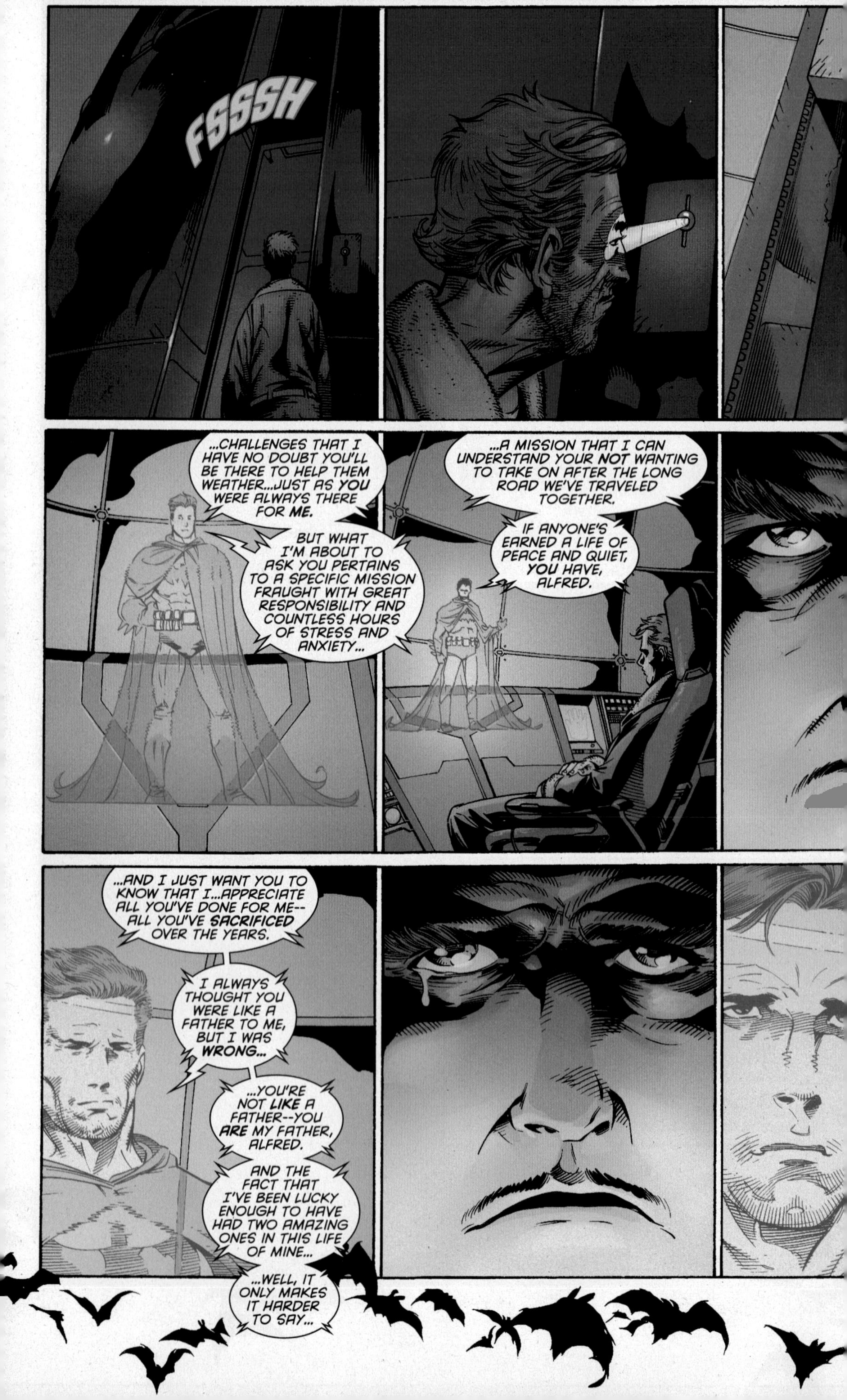
FSSSH
...CHALLENGES THAT I HAVE NO DOUBT YOU'LL BE THERE TO HELP THEM WEATHER...JUST AS YOU WERE ALWAYS THERE FOR ME.
BUT WHAT I'M ABOUT TO ASK YOU PERTAINS TO A SPECIFIC MISSION FRAUGHT WITH GREAT RESPONSIBILITY AND COUNTLESS HOURS OF STRESS AND ANXIETY...
...A MISSION THAT I CAN UNDERSTAND YOUR NOT WANTING TO TAKE ON AFTER THE LONG ROAD WE'VE TRAVELED TOGETHER.
IF ANYONE'S EARNED A LIFE OF PEACE AND QUIET, YOU HAVE, ALFRED.
...AND I JUST WANT YOU TO KNOW THAT I...APPRECIATE ALL YOU'VE DONE FOR ME-- ALL YOU'VE SACRIFICED OVER THE YEARS.
I ALWAYS THOUGHT YOU WERE LIKE A FATHER TO ME, BUT I WAS WRONG...
...YOU'RE NOT LIKE A FATHER--YOU ARE MY FATHER, ALFRED.
AND THE FACT THAT I'VE BEEN LUCKY ENOUGH TO HAVE HAD TWO AMAZING ONES IN THIS LIFE OF MINE...
...WELL, IT ONLY MAKES IT HARDER TO SAY...

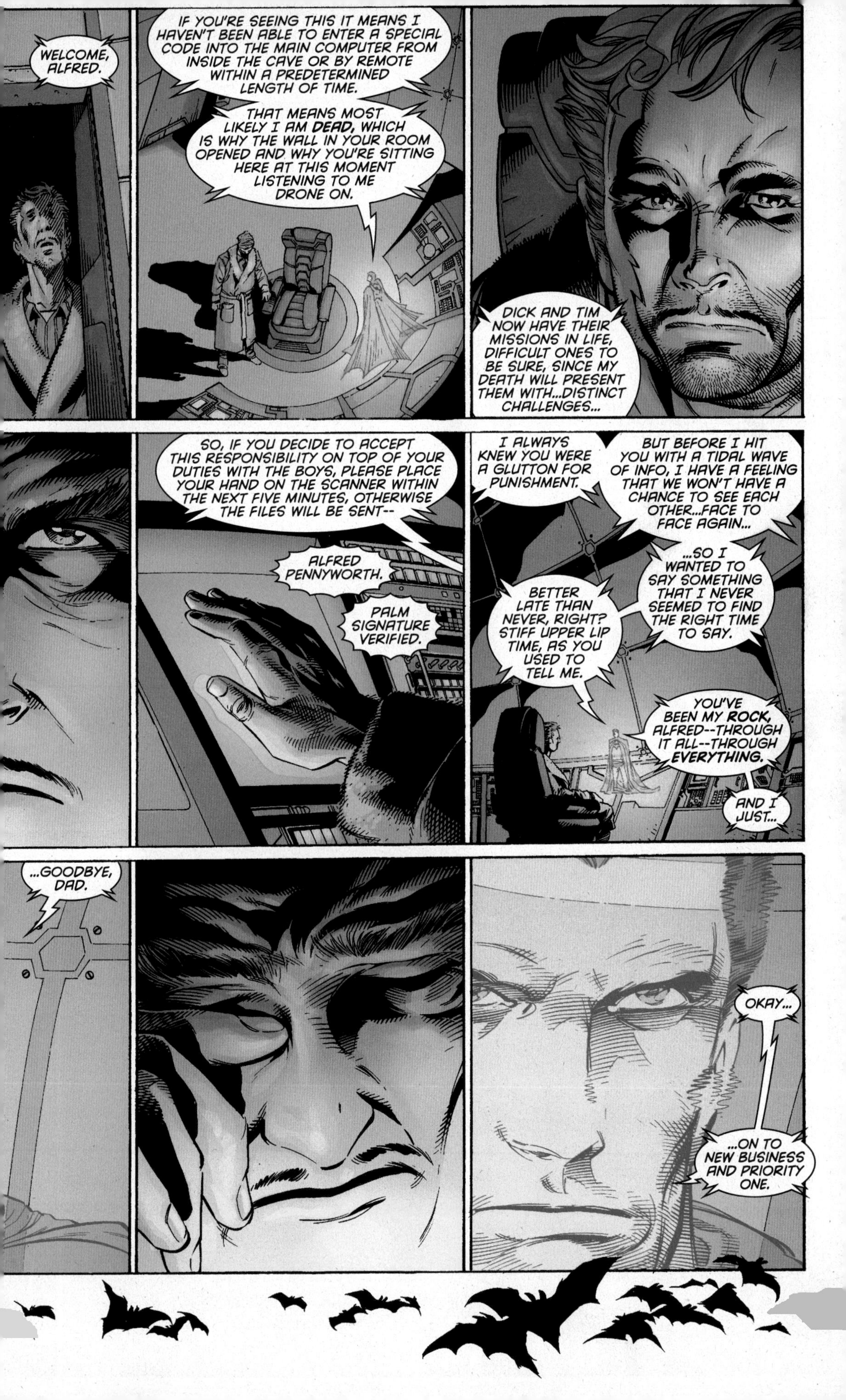
WELCOME, ALFRED.
IF YOU'RE SEEING THIS IT MEANS I HAVEN'T BEEN ABLE TO ENTER A SPECIAL CODE INTO THE MAIN COMPUTER FROM INSIDE THE CAVE OR BY REMOTE WITHIN A PREDETERMINED LENGTH OF TIME.
THAT MEANS MOST LIKELY I AM DEAD, WHICH IS WHY THE WALL IN YOUR ROOM OPENED AND WHY YOU'RE SITTING HERE AT THIS MOMENT LISTENING TO ME DRONE ON.
DICK AND TIM NOW HAVE THEIR MISSIONS IN LIFE, DIFFICULT ONES TO BE SURE, SINCE MY DEATH WILL PRESENT THEM WITH...DISTINCT CHALLENGES...
SO, IF YOU DECIDE TO ACCEPT THIS RESPONSIBILITY ON TOP OF YOUR DUTIES WITH THE BOYS, PLEASE PLACE YOUR HAND ON THE SCANNER WITHIN THE NEXT FIVE MINUTES, OTHERWISE THE FILES WILL BE SENT--
ALFRED PENNYWORTH.
PALM SIGNATURE VERIFIED.
I ALWAYS KNEW YOU WERE A GLUTTON FOR PUNISHMENT.
BUT BEFORE I HIT YOU WITH A TIDAL WAVE OF INFO, I HAVE A FEELING THAT WE WON'T HAVE A CHANCE TO SEE EACH OTHER...FACE TO FACE AGAIN...
...SO I WANTED TO SAY SOMETHING THAT I NEVER SEEMED TO FIND THE RIGHT TIME TO SAY.
BETTER LATE THAN NEVER, RIGHT? STIFF UPPER LIP TIME, AS YOU USED TO TELL ME.
YOU'VE BEEN MY ROCK, ALFRED--THROUGH IT ALL--THROUGH EVERYTHING.
AND I JUST...
...GOODBYE, DAD.
OKAY...
...ON TO NEW BUSINESS AND PRIORITY ONE.

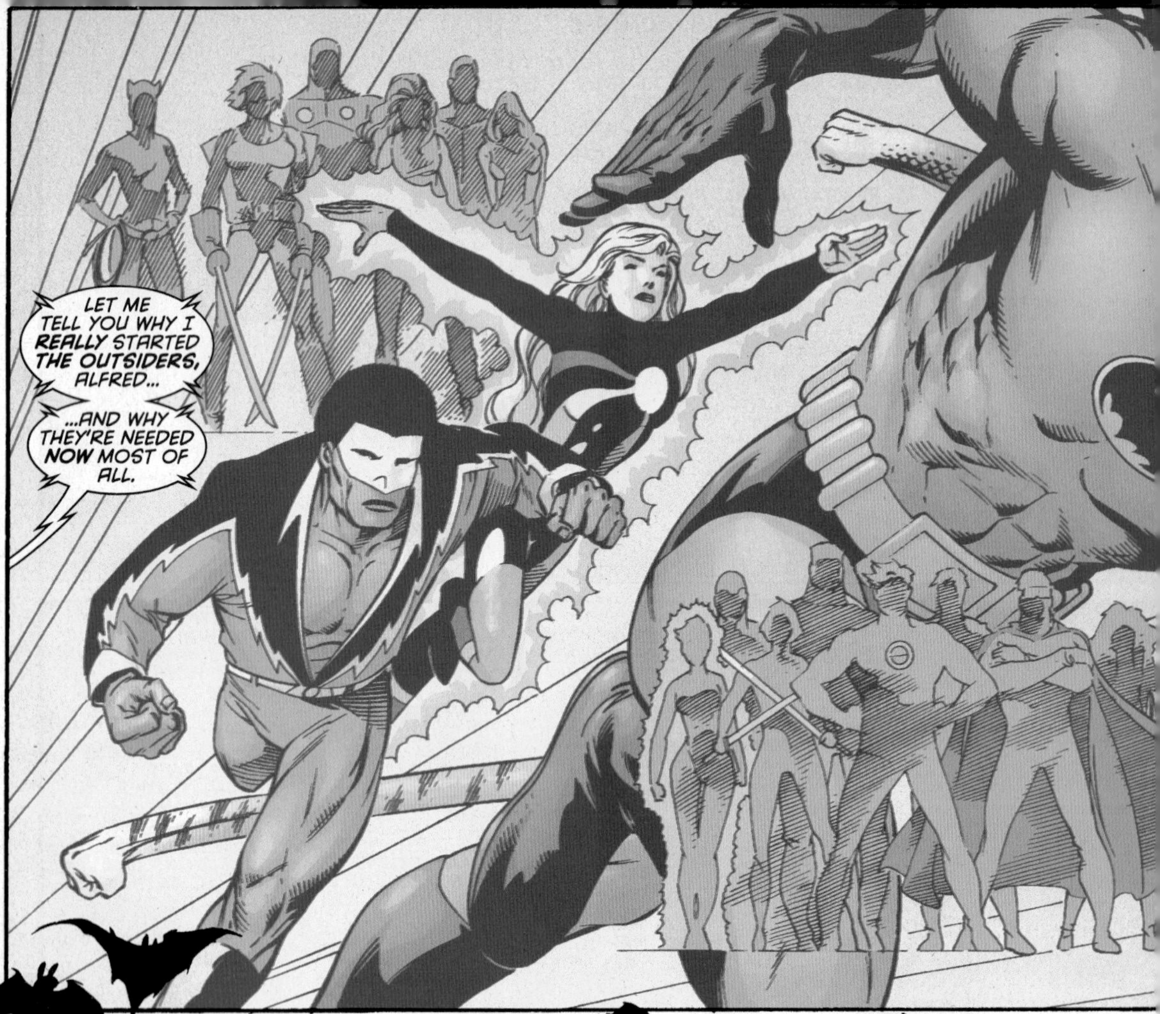
LET ME TELL YOU WHY I REALLY STARTED THE OUTSIDERS, ALFRED...
...AND WHY THEY'RE NEEDED NOW MOST OF ALL.

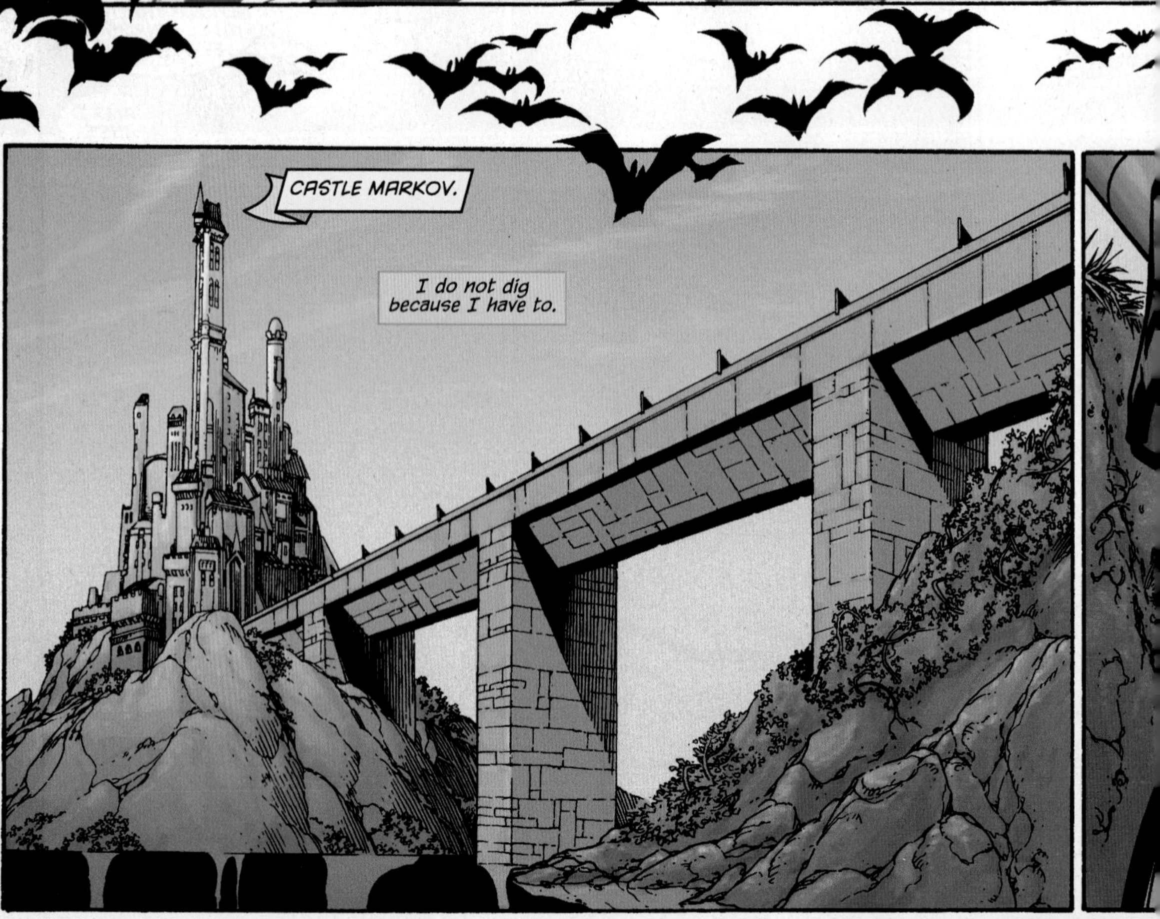
CASTLE MARKOV.
I do not dig because I have to.

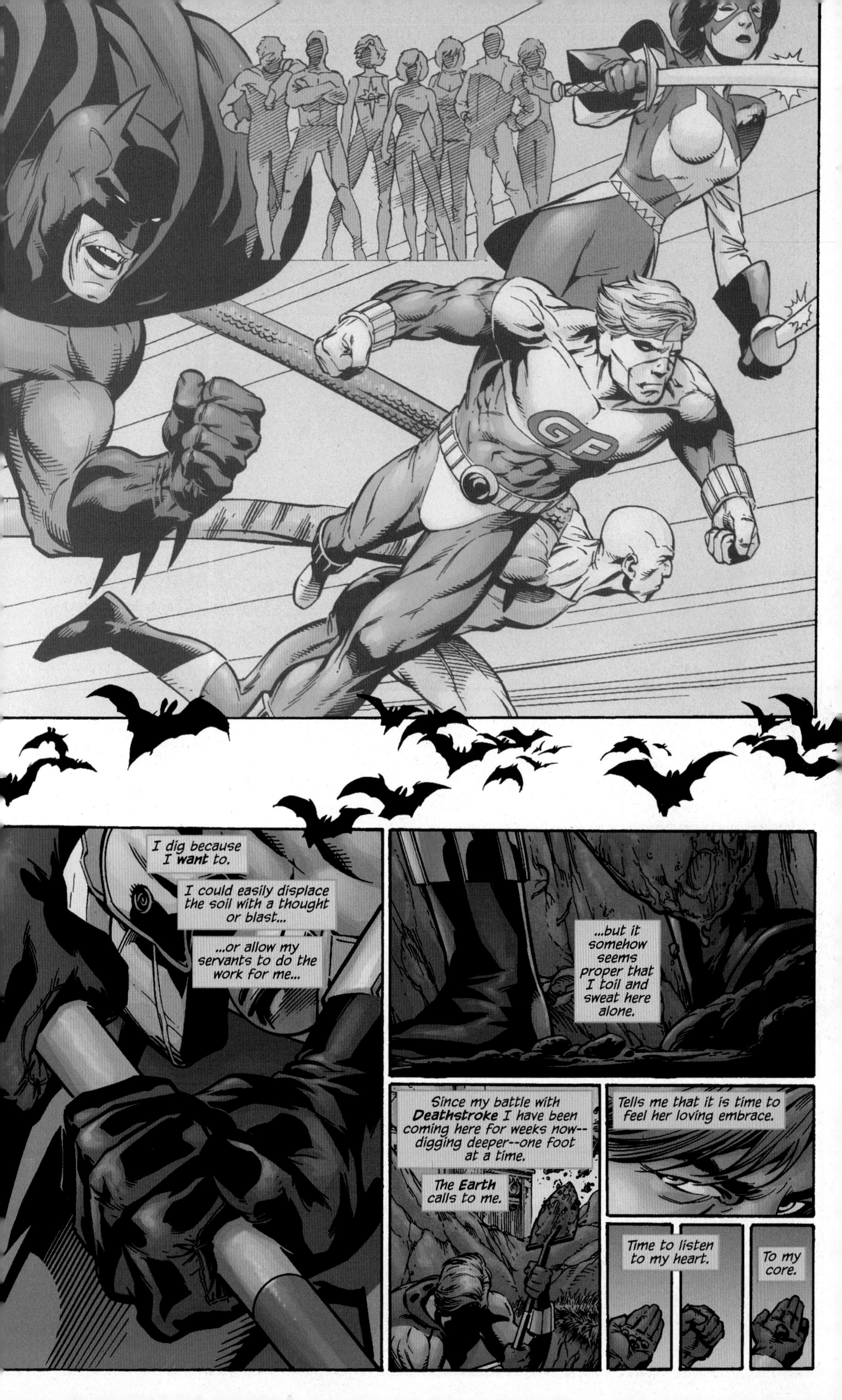
I dig because I *want* to.
I could easily displace the soil with a thought or blast...
...or allow my servants to do the work for me...
...but it somehow seems proper that I toil and sweat here alone.
Since my battle with **Deathstroke** I have been coming here for weeks now--digging deeper--one foot at a time.
The **Earth** calls to me.
Tells me that it is time to feel her loving embrace.
Time to listen to my heart.
To my core.

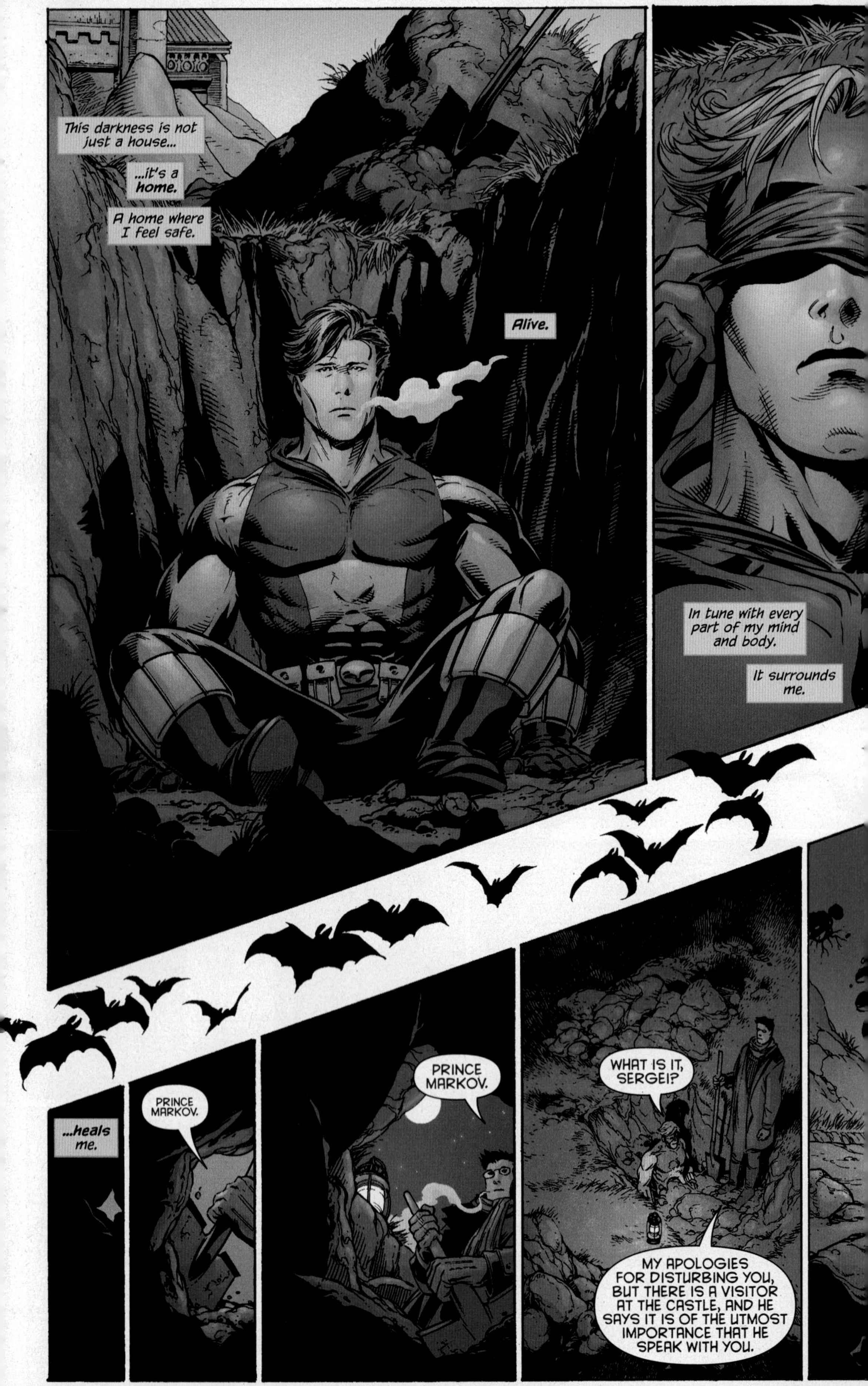

This darkness is not just a house...
...it's a home.
A home where I feel safe.
Alive.
In tune with every part of my mind and body.
It surrounds me.
...heals me.
PRINCE MARKOV.
PRINCE MARKOV.
WHAT IS IT, SERGEI?
MY APOLOGIES FOR DISTURBING YOU, BUT THERE IS A VISITOR AT THE CASTLE, AND HE SAYS IT IS OF THE UTMOST IMPORTANCE THAT HE SPEAK WITH YOU.

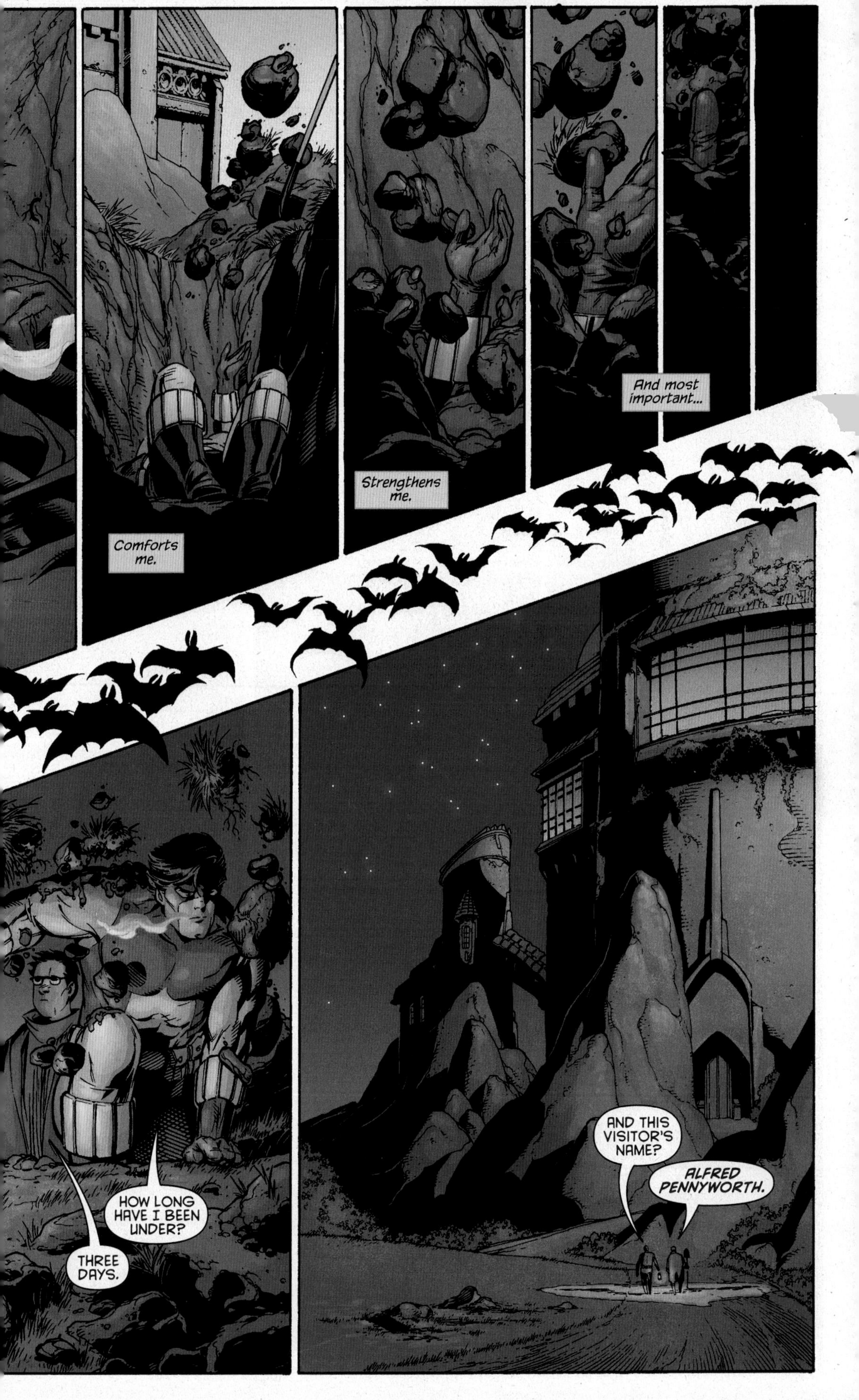
Comforts me.
Strengthens me.
And most important...
HOW LONG HAVE I BEEN UNDER?
THREE DAYS.
AND THIS VISITOR'S NAME?
ALFRED PENNYWORTH.

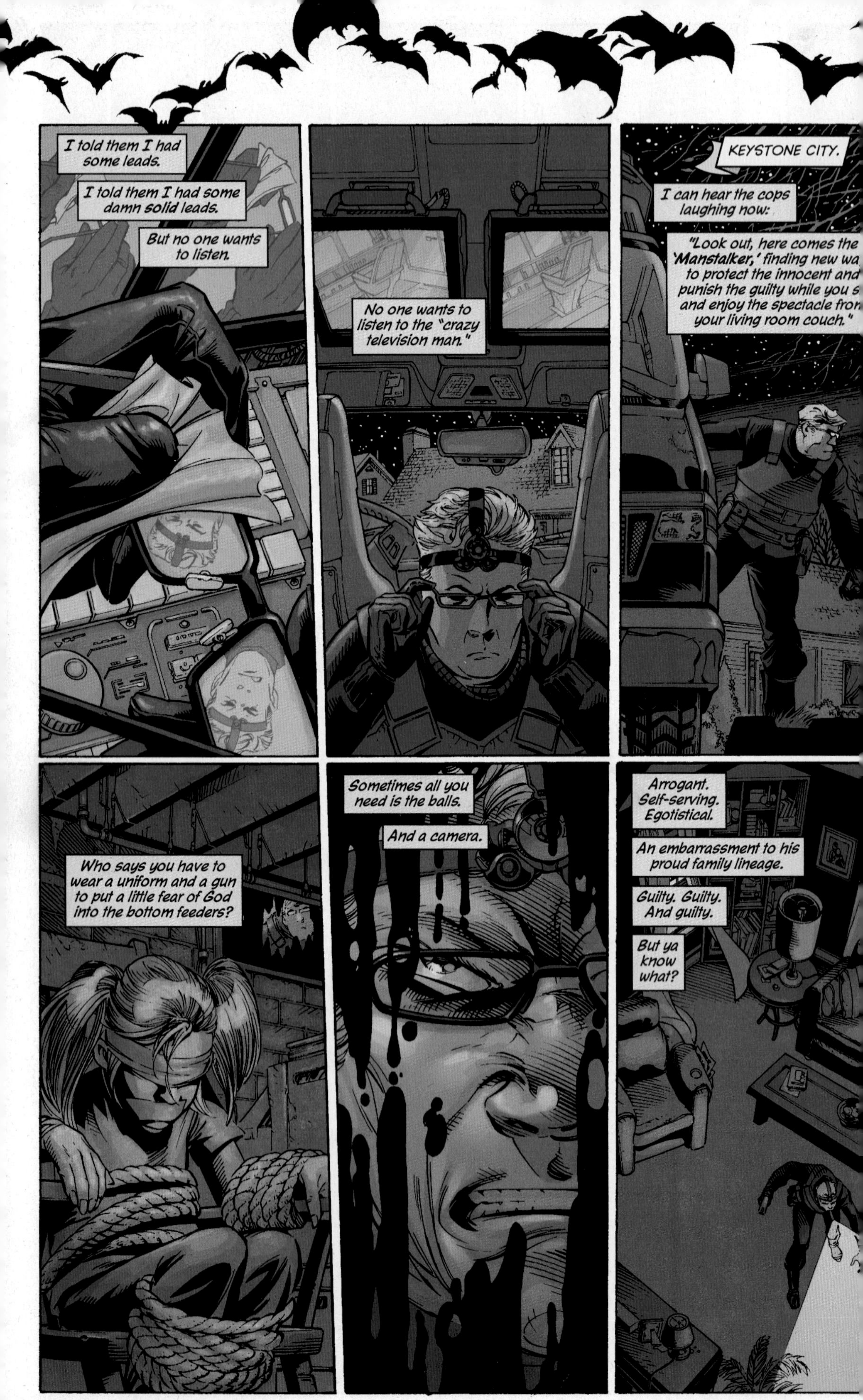

I told them I had some leads.
I told them I had some damn solid leads.
But no one wants to listen.
No one wants to listen to the "crazy television man."
KEYSTONE CITY.
I can hear the cops laughing now:
"Look out, here comes the 'Manstalker,' finding new wa to protect the innocent and punish the guilty while you s and enjoy the spectacle fron your living room couch."
Who says you have to wear a uniform and a gun to put a little fear of God into the bottom feeders?
Sometimes all you need is the balls.
And a camera.
Arrogant. Self-serving. Egotistical.
An embarrassment to his proud family lineage.
Guilty. Guilty. And guilty.
But ya know what?

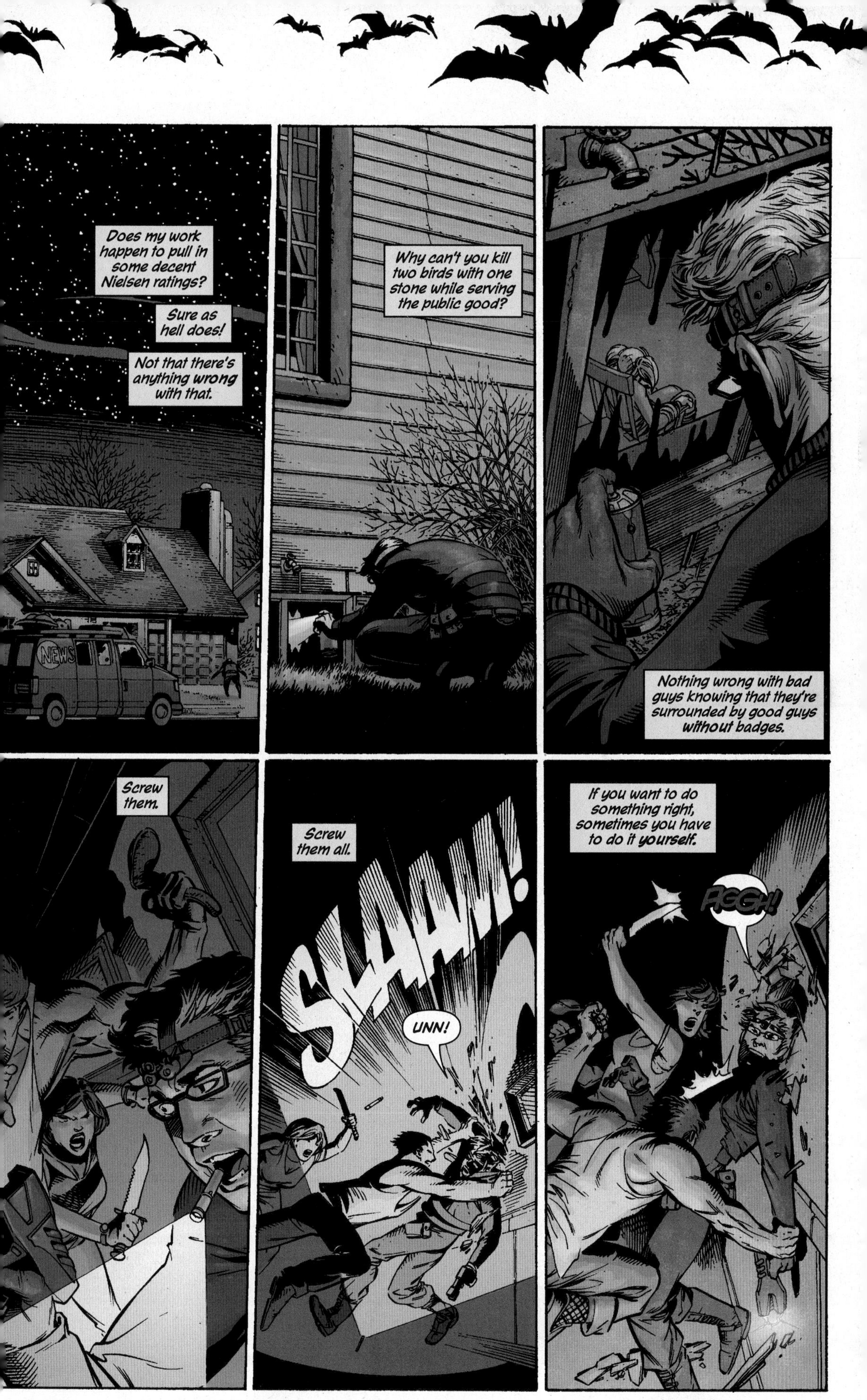
Does my work happen to pull in some decent Nielsen ratings?
Sure as hell does!
Not that there's anything wrong with that.
NEWS
Why can't you kill two birds with one stone while serving the public good?
Nothing wrong with bad guys knowing that they're surrounded by good guys without badges.
Screw them.
Screw them all.
SLAM!
UNN!
If you want to do something right, sometimes you have to do it yourself.
AGGH!

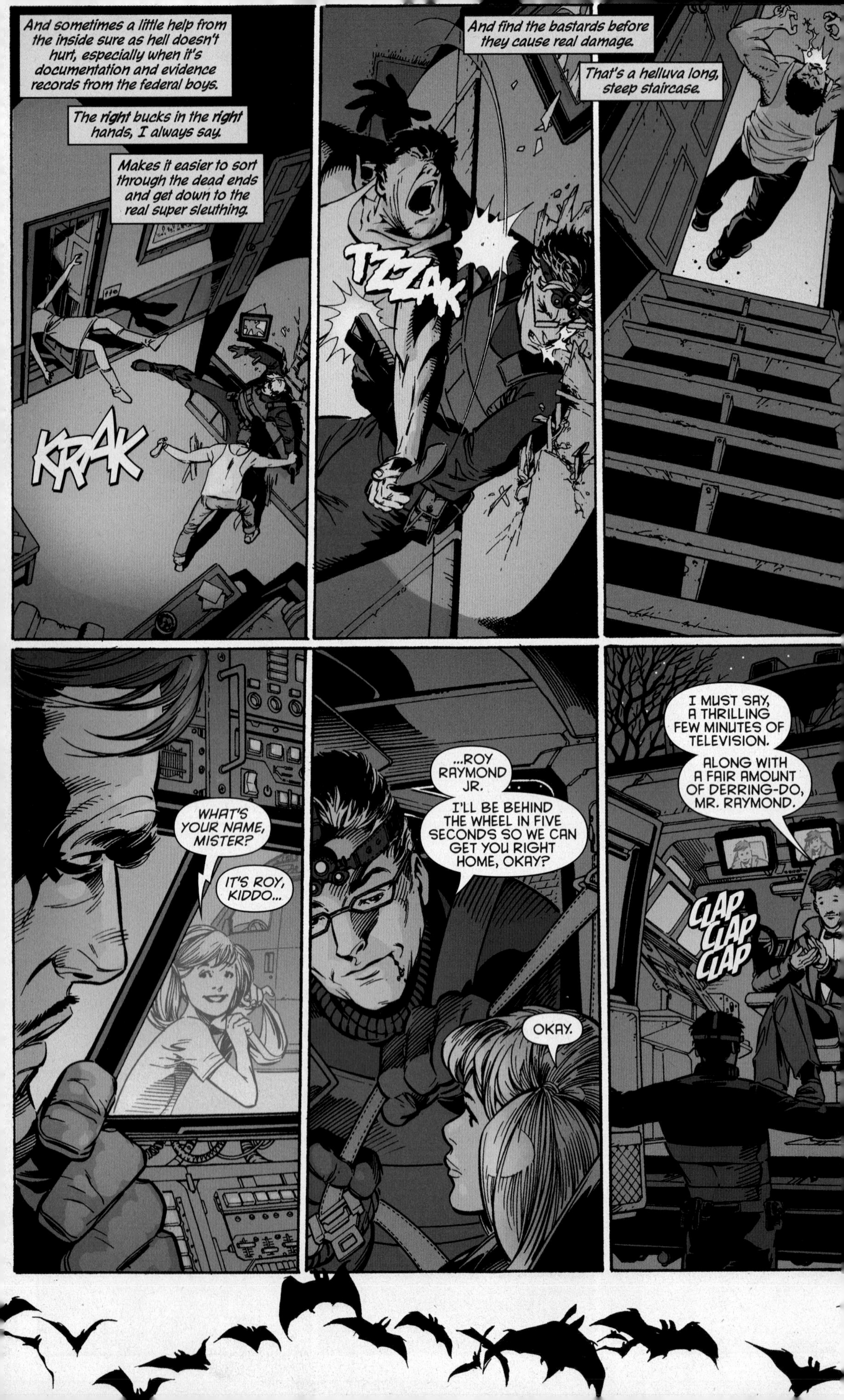
And sometimes a little help from the inside sure as hell doesn't hurt, especially when it's documentation and evidence records from the federal boys.
The right bucks in the right hands, I always say.
Makes it easier to sort through the dead ends and get down to the real super sleuthing.
KRAK
And find the bastards before they cause real damage.
TZZZAK
That's a helluva long, steep staircase.
WHAT'S YOUR NAME, MISTER?
IT'S ROY, KIDDO...
...ROY RAYMOND JR.
I'LL BE BEHIND THE WHEEL IN FIVE SECONDS SO WE CAN GET YOU RIGHT HOME, OKAY?
OKAY.
I MUST SAY, A THRILLING FEW MINUTES OF TELEVISION.
ALONG WITH A FAIR AMOUNT OF DERRING-DO, MR. RAYMOND.
CLAP CLAP CLAP

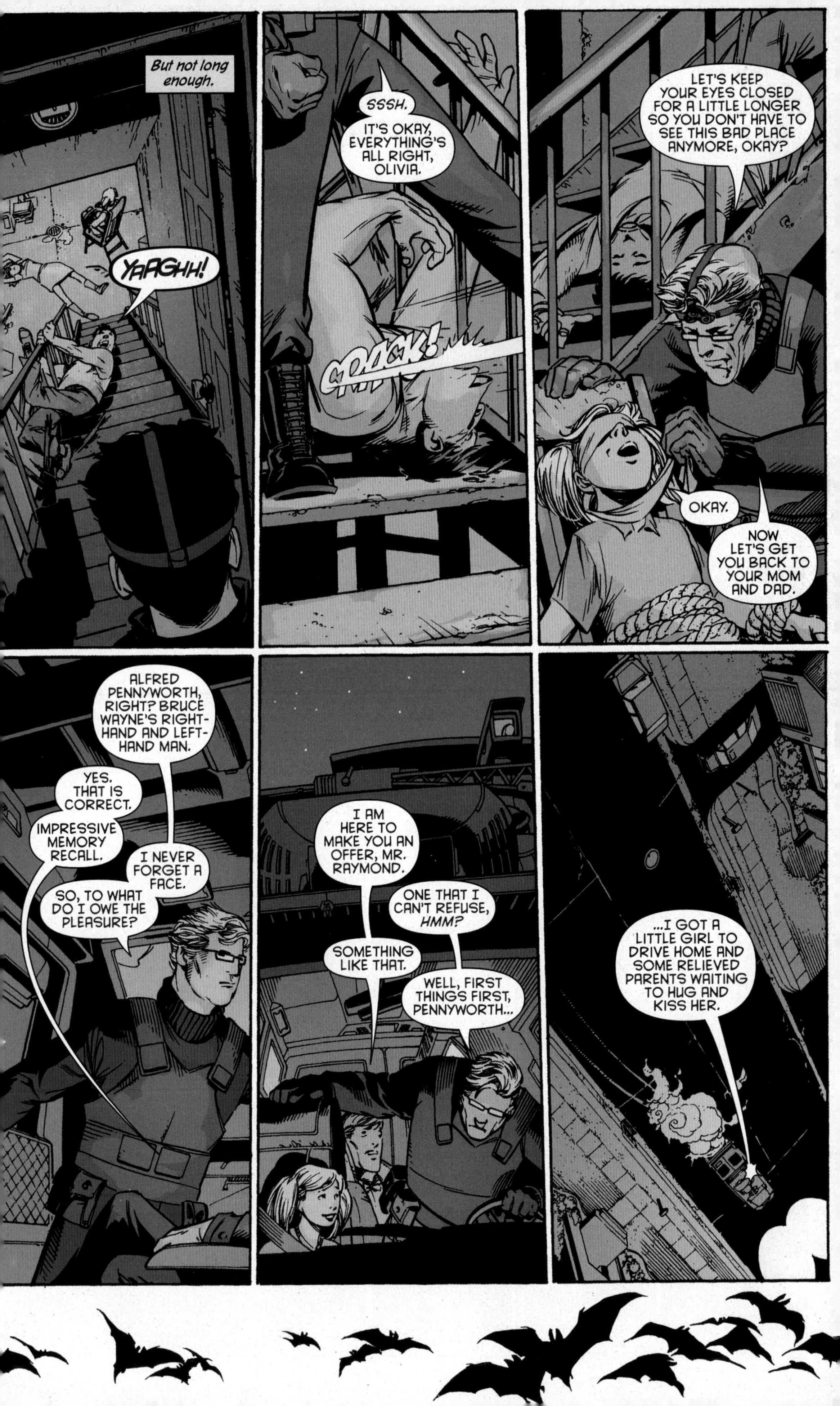

But not long enough.
YAAGHH!
SSSH.
IT'S OKAY, EVERYTHING'S ALL RIGHT, OLIVIA.
CRACK!
LET'S KEEP YOUR EYES CLOSED FOR A LITTLE LONGER SO YOU DON'T HAVE TO SEE THIS BAD PLACE ANYMORE, OKAY?
OKAY.
NOW LET'S GET YOU BACK TO YOUR MOM AND DAD.
ALFRED PENNYWORTH, RIGHT? BRUCE WAYNE'S RIGHT-HAND AND LEFT-HAND MAN.
YES. THAT IS CORRECT.
IMPRESSIVE MEMORY RECALL.
I NEVER FORGET A FACE.
SO, TO WHAT DO I OWE THE PLEASURE?
I AM HERE TO MAKE YOU AN OFFER, MR. RAYMOND.
ONE THAT I CAN'T REFUSE, *HMM?*
SOMETHING LIKE THAT.
WELL, FIRST THINGS FIRST, PENNYWORTH...
...I GOT A LITTLE GIRL TO DRIVE HOME AND SOME RELIEVED PARENTS WAITING TO HUG AND KISS HER.

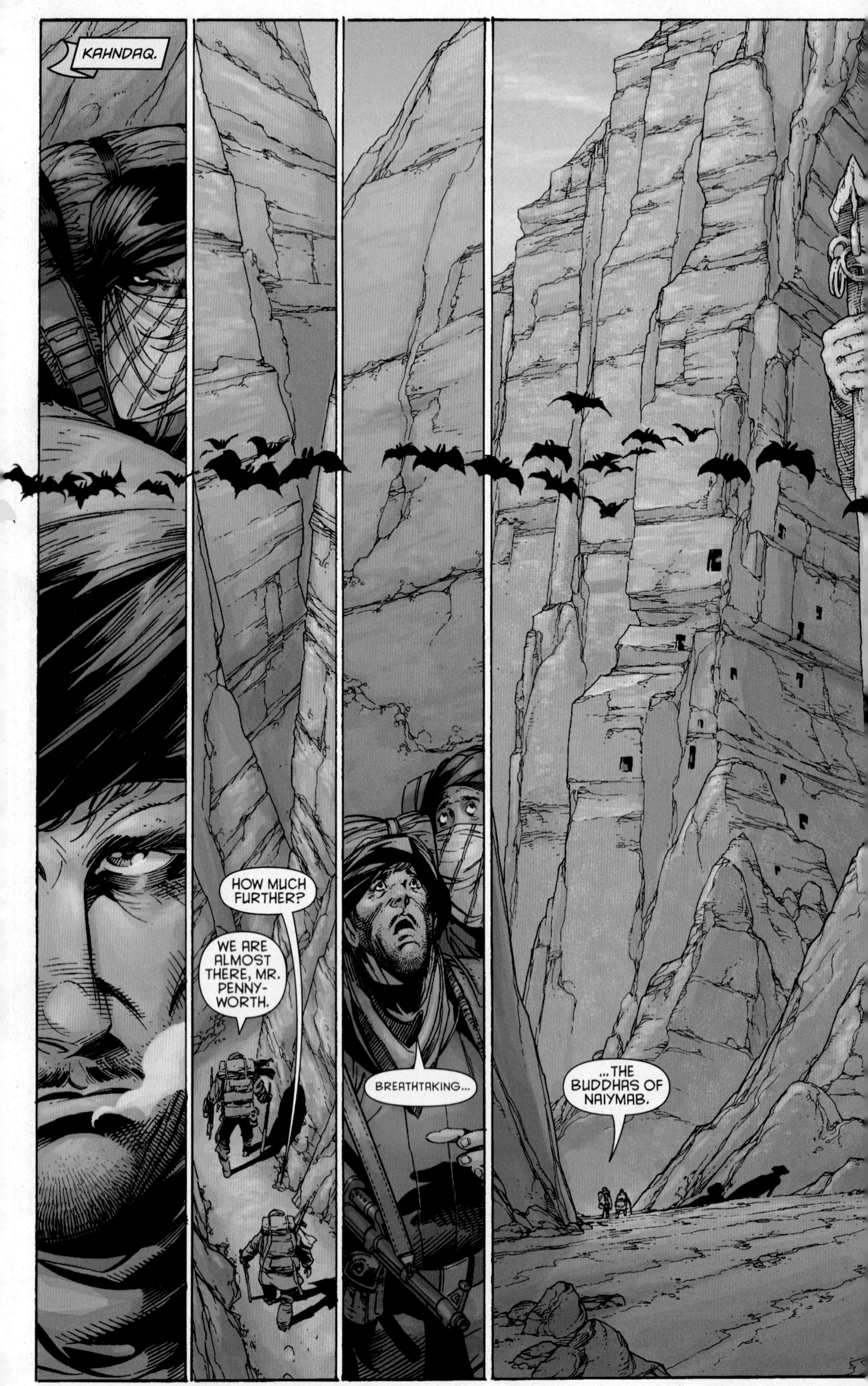
KAHNDAQ.
HOW MUCH FURTHER?
WE ARE ALMOST THERE, MR. PENNY-WORTH.
BREATHTAKING...
...THE BUDDHAS OF NAIYMAB.

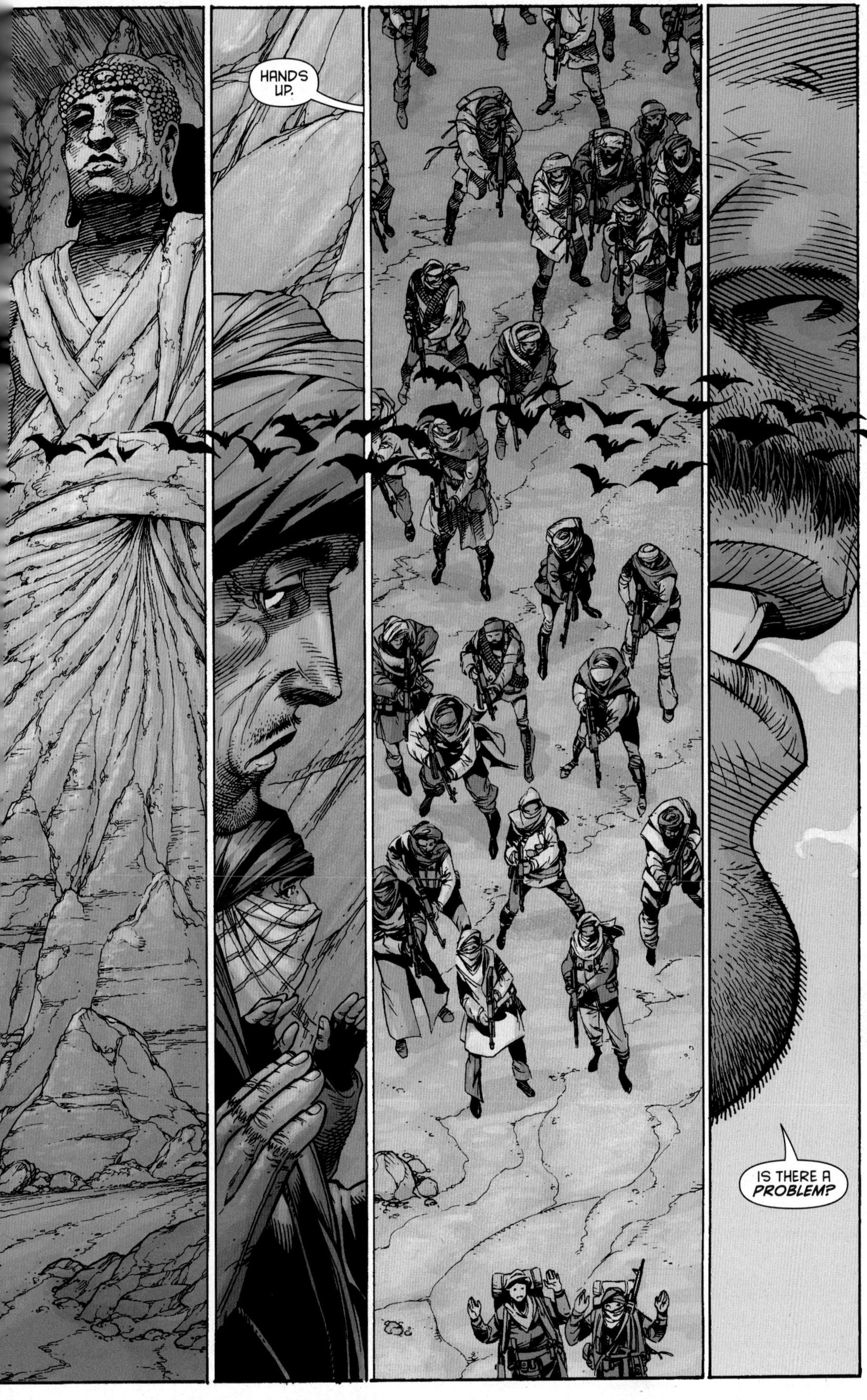
HANDS UP.
IS THERE A *PROBLEM?*

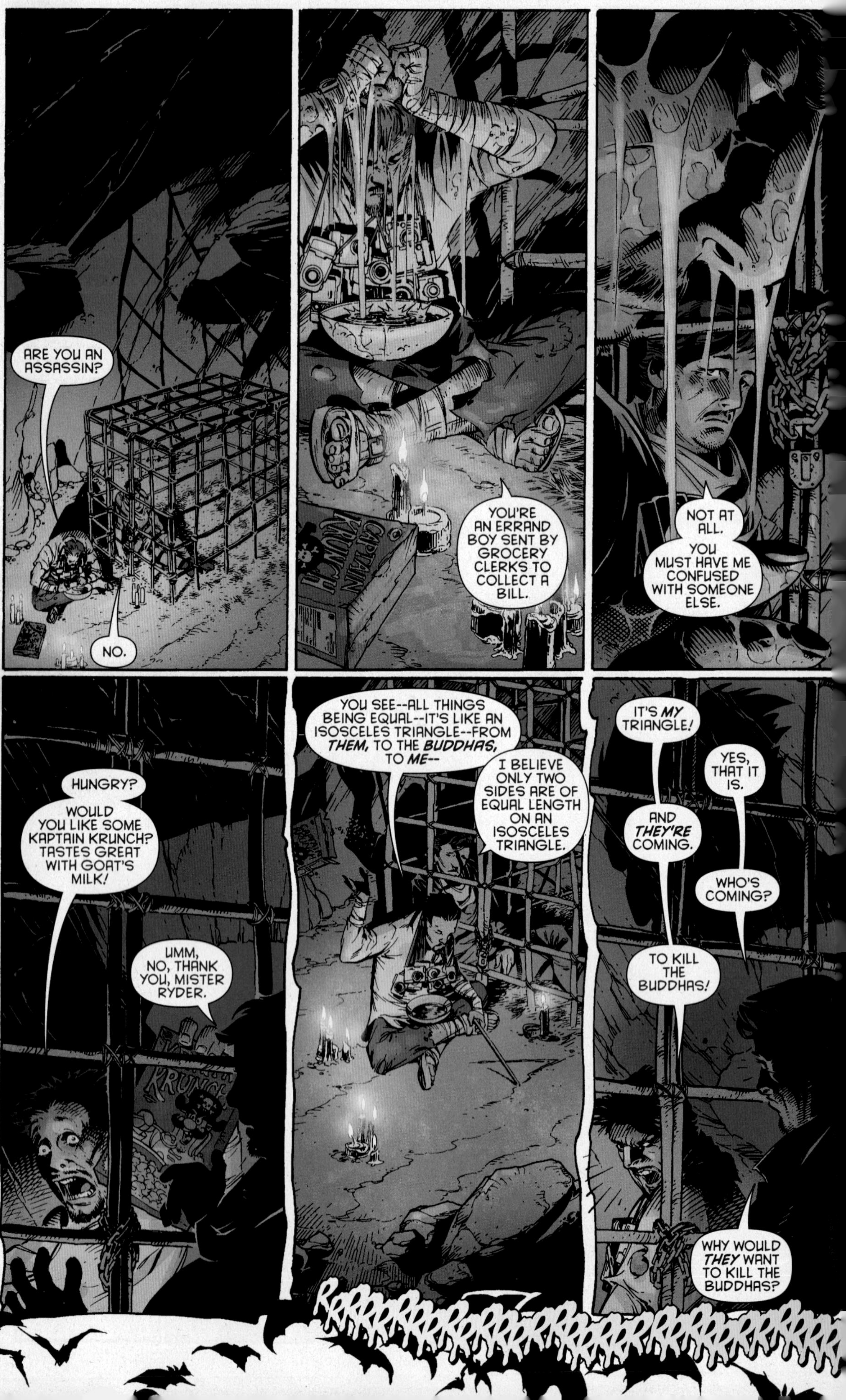

ARE YOU AN ASSASSIN?
NO.
YOU'RE AN ERRAND BOY SENT BY GROCERY CLERKS TO COLLECT A BILL.
NOT AT ALL.
YOU MUST HAVE ME CONFUSED WITH SOMEONE ELSE.
HUNGRY?
WOULD YOU LIKE SOME KAPTAIN KRUNCH? TASTES GREAT WITH GOAT'S MILK!
UMM, NO, THANK YOU, MISTER RYDER.
YOU SEE--ALL THINGS BEING EQUAL--IT'S LIKE AN ISOSCELES TRIANGLE--FROM THEM, TO THE BUDDHAS, TO ME--
I BELIEVE ONLY TWO SIDES ARE OF EQUAL LENGTH ON AN ISOSCELES TRIANGLE.
IT'S MY TRIANGLE!
YES, THAT IT IS.
AND THEY'RE COMING.
WHO'S COMING?
TO KILL THE BUDDHAS!
WHY WOULD THEY WANT TO KILL THE BUDDHAS?
RRRRRRRRRRRRRRRRRRRRRRRRRRRRRRRRRRRR

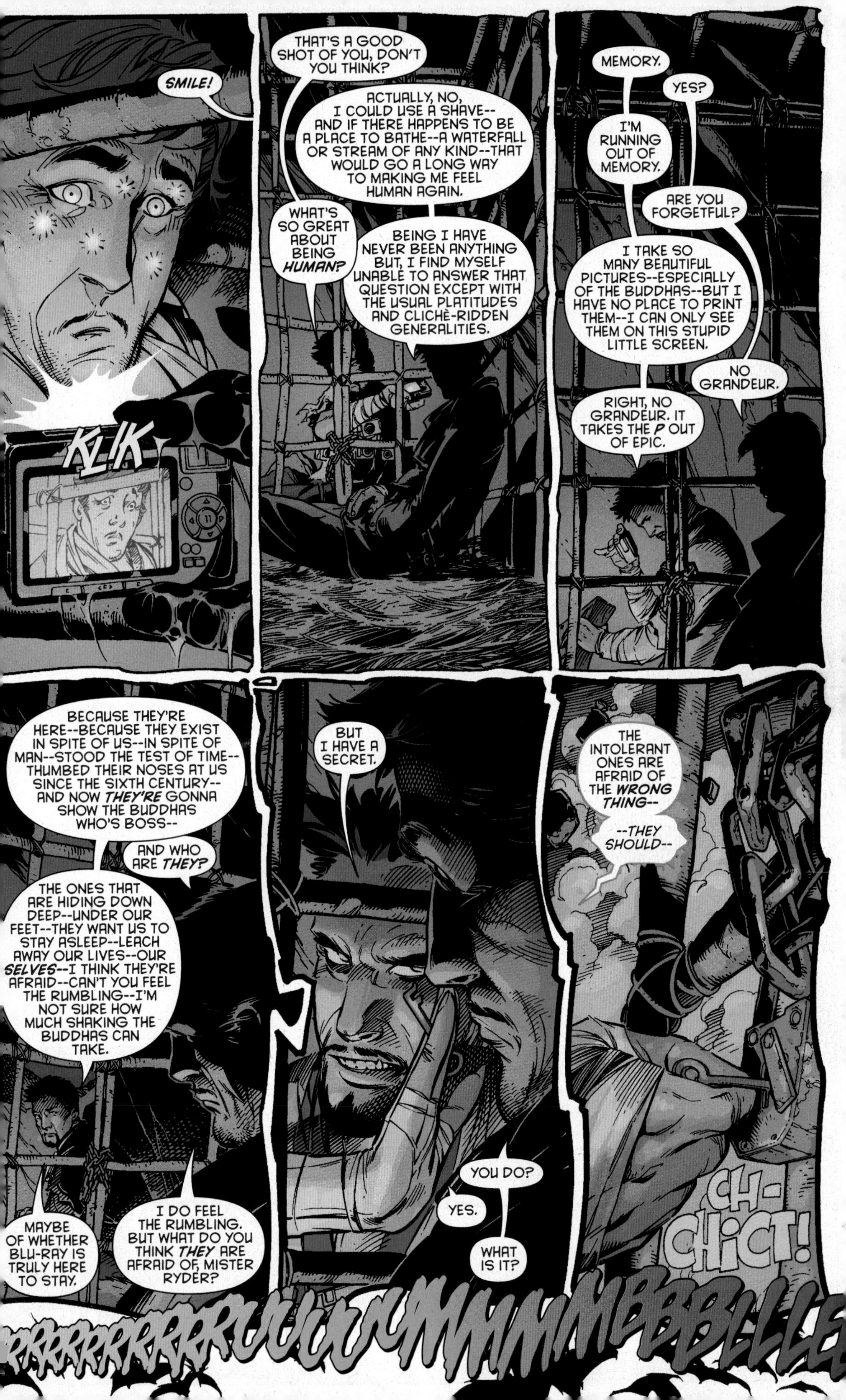
SMILE!
KLIK
THAT'S A GOOD SHOT OF YOU, DON'T YOU THINK?
ACTUALLY, NO, I COULD USE A SHAVE--AND IF THERE HAPPENS TO BE A PLACE TO BATHE--A WATERFALL OR STREAM OF ANY KIND--THAT WOULD GO A LONG WAY TO MAKING ME FEEL HUMAN AGAIN.
WHAT'S SO GREAT ABOUT BEING HUMAN?
BEING I HAVE NEVER BEEN ANYTHING BUT, I FIND MYSELF UNABLE TO ANSWER THAT QUESTION EXCEPT WITH THE USUAL PLATITUDES AND CLICHÈ-RIDDEN GENERALITIES.
MEMORY.
YES?
I'M RUNNING OUT OF MEMORY.
ARE YOU FORGETFUL?
I TAKE SO MANY BEAUTIFUL PICTURES--ESPECIALLY OF THE BUDDHAS--BUT I HAVE NO PLACE TO PRINT THEM--I CAN ONLY SEE THEM ON THIS STUPID LITTLE SCREEN.
NO GRANDEUR.
RIGHT, NO GRANDEUR. IT TAKES THE P OUT OF EPIC.
BECAUSE THEY'RE HERE--BECAUSE THEY EXIST IN SPITE OF US--IN SPITE OF MAN--STOOD THE TEST OF TIME--THUMBED THEIR NOSES AT US SINCE THE SIXTH CENTURY--AND NOW THEY'RE GONNA SHOW THE BUDDHAS WHO'S BOSS--
AND WHO ARE THEY?
THE ONES THAT ARE HIDING DOWN DEEP--UNDER OUR FEET--THEY WANT US TO STAY ASLEEP--LEACH AWAY OUR LIVES--OUR SELVES--I THINK THEY'RE AFRAID--CAN'T YOU FEEL THE RUMBLING--I'M NOT SURE HOW MUCH SHAKING THE BUDDHAS CAN TAKE.
I DO FEEL THE RUMBLING. BUT WHAT DO YOU THINK THEY ARE AFRAID OF, MISTER RYDER?
MAYBE OF WHETHER BLU-RAY IS TRULY HERE TO STAY.
BUT I HAVE A SECRET.
YOU DO?
YES.
WHAT IS IT?
THE INTOLERANT ONES ARE AFRAID OF THE WRONG THING--
--THEY SHOULD--
CH-CHICT!
RRRRRRRRRRRUUUUUMMMMMBBBLLLE

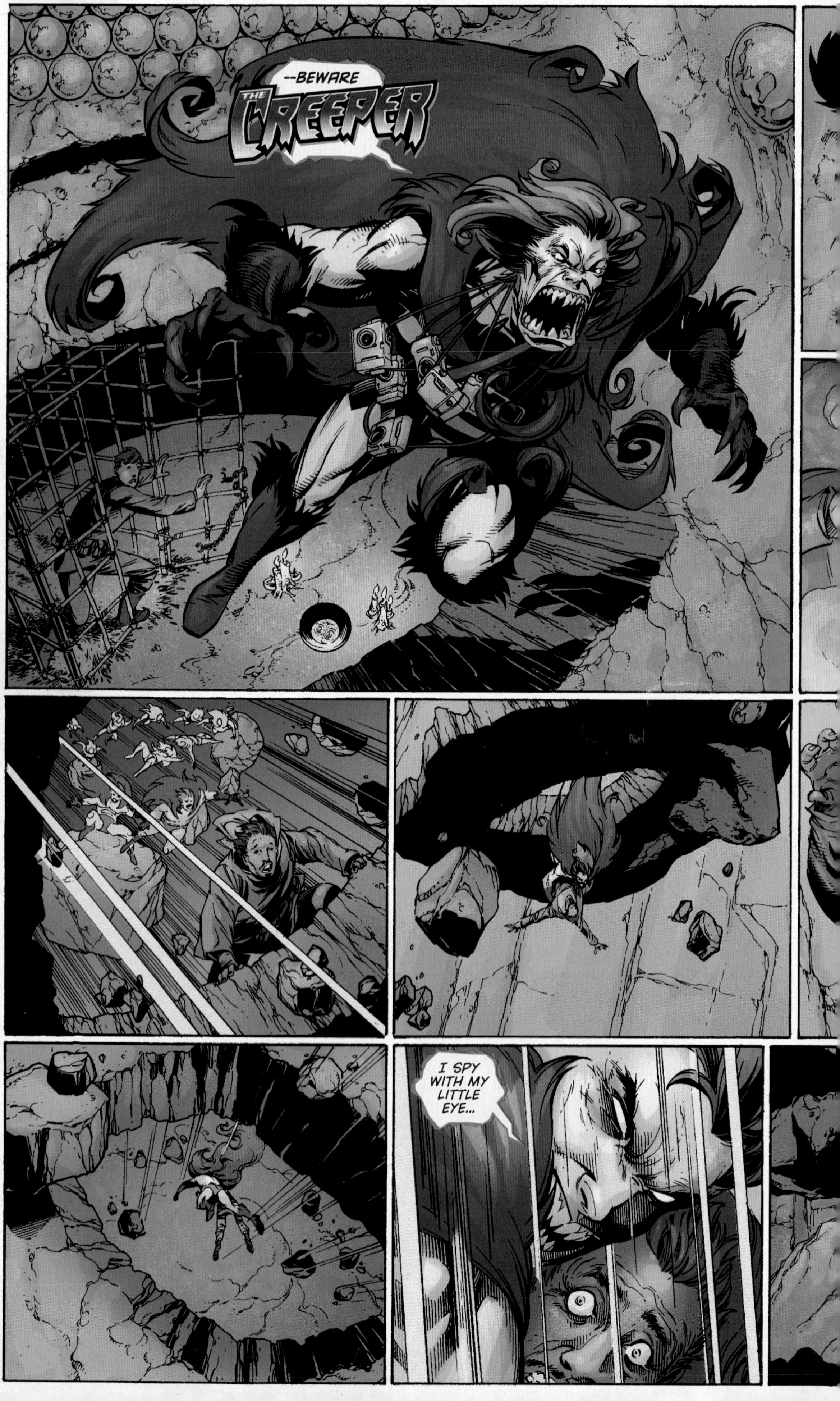
--BEWARE
THE CREEPER
I SPY WITH MY LITTLE EYE...

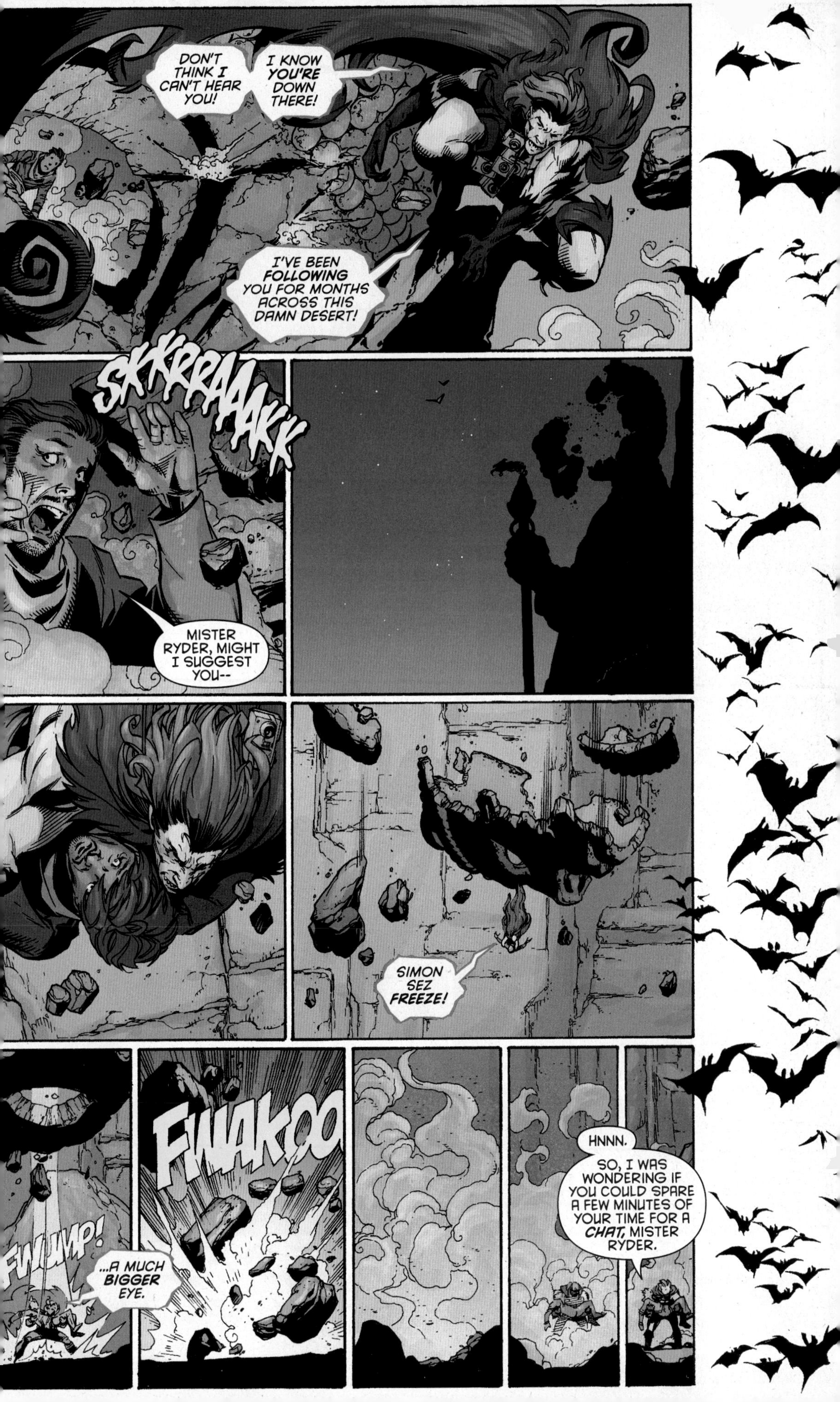
DON'T THINK I CAN'T HEAR YOU!
I KNOW YOU'RE DOWN THERE!
I'VE BEEN FOLLOWING YOU FOR MONTHS ACROSS THIS DAMN DESERT!
SKKRRAAAAKK
MISTER RYDER, MIGHT I SUGGEST YOU--
SIMON SEZ FREEZE!
FWUMP!
...A MUCH BIGGER EYE.
FWAKOO
HNNN.
SO, I WAS WONDERING IF YOU COULD SPARE A FEW MINUTES OF YOUR TIME FOR A CHAT, MISTER RYDER.

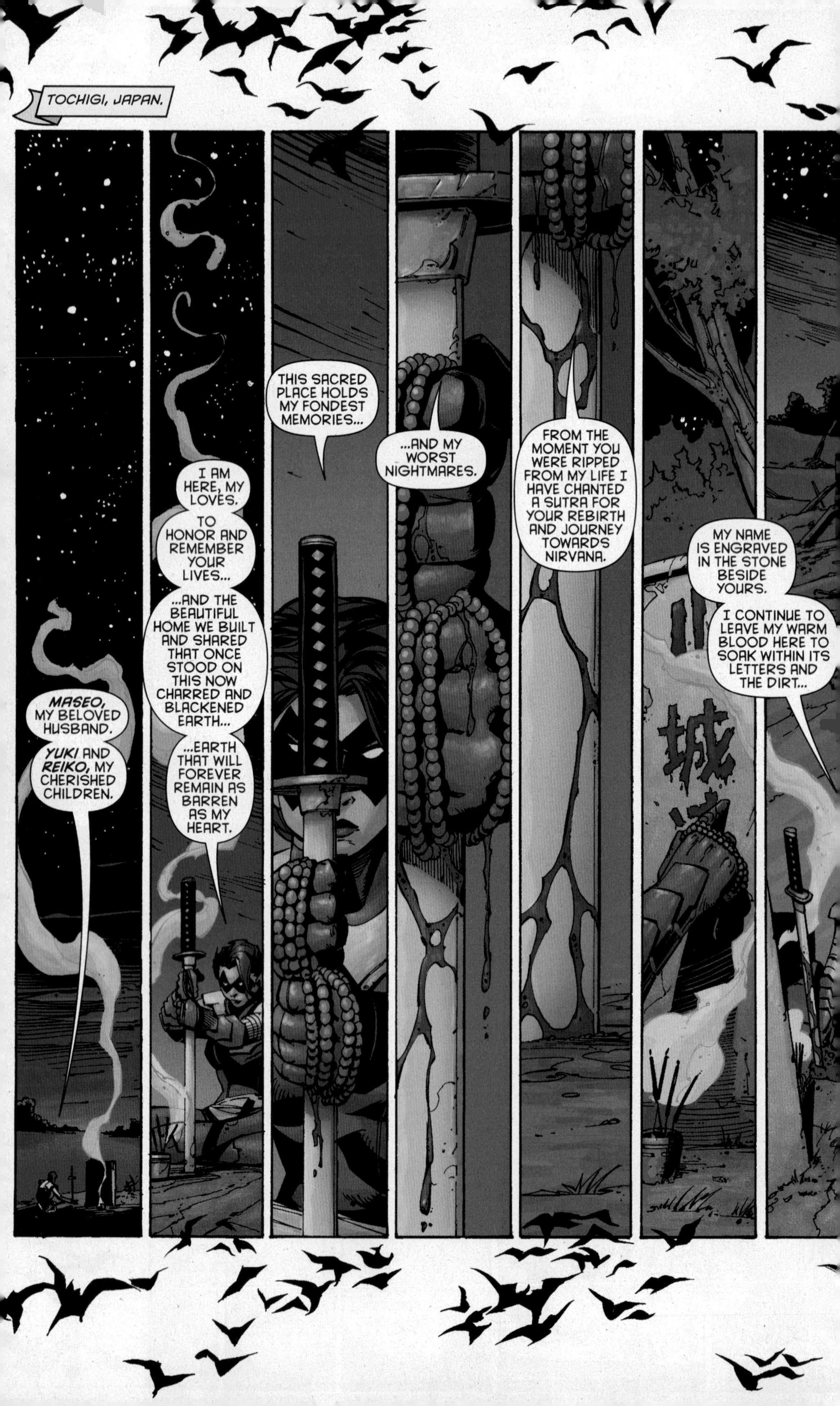

TOCHIGI, JAPAN.
MASEO, MY BELOVED HUSBAND.
YUKI AND REIKO, MY CHERISHED CHILDREN.
I AM HERE, MY LOVES.
TO HONOR AND REMEMBER YOUR LIVES...
...AND THE BEAUTIFUL HOME WE BUILT AND SHARED THAT ONCE STOOD ON THIS NOW CHARRED AND BLACKENED EARTH...
...EARTH THAT WILL FOREVER REMAIN AS BARREN AS MY HEART.
THIS SACRED PLACE HOLDS MY FONDEST MEMORIES...
...AND MY WORST NIGHTMARES.
FROM THE MOMENT YOU WERE RIPPED FROM MY LIFE I HAVE CHANTED A SUTRA FOR YOUR REBIRTH AND JOURNEY TOWARDS NIRVANA.
MY NAME IS ENGRAVED IN THE STONE BESIDE YOURS.
I CONTINUE TO LEAVE MY WARM BLOOD HERE TO SOAK WITHIN ITS LETTERS AND THE DIRT...

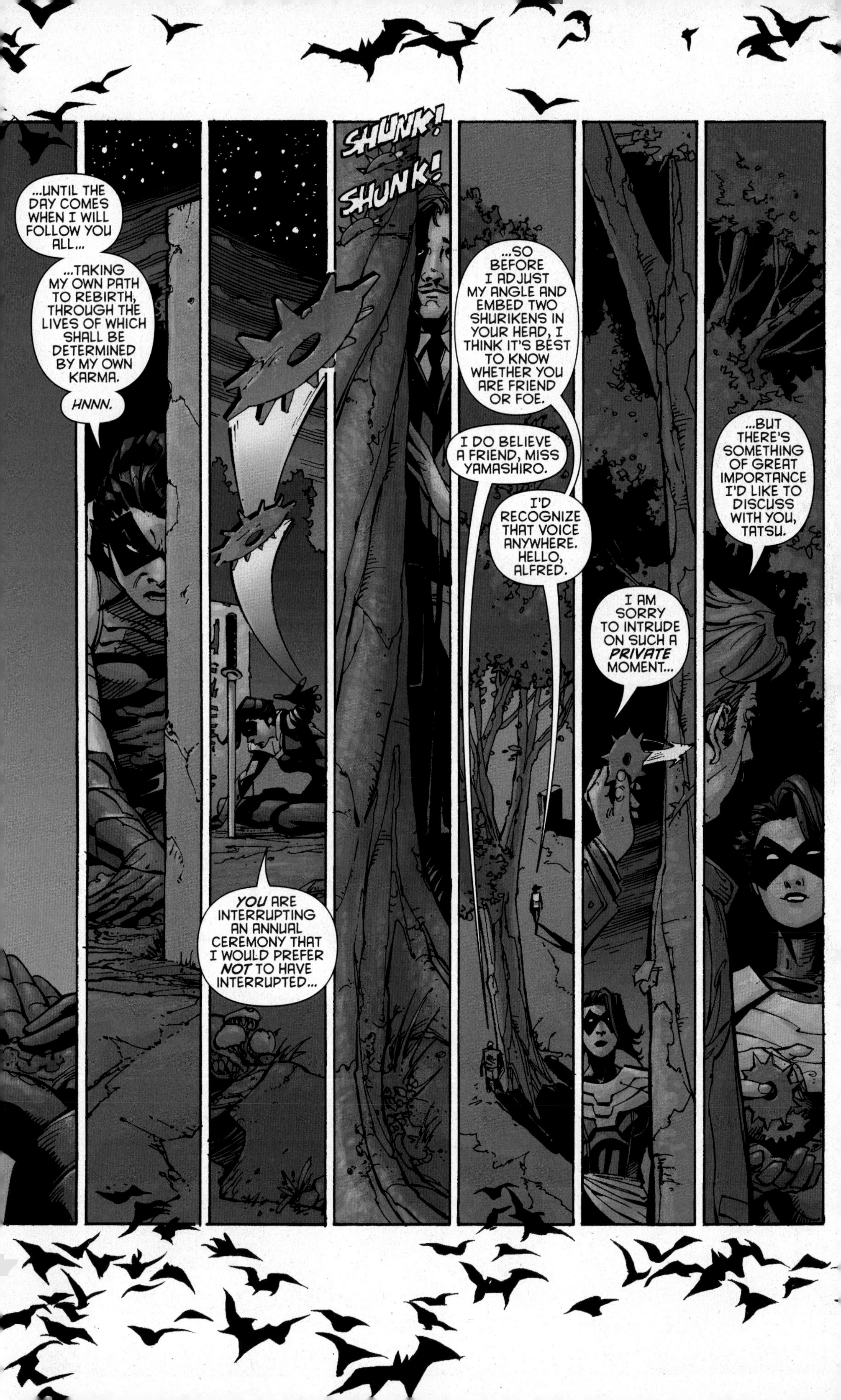

...UNTIL THE DAY COMES WHEN I WILL FOLLOW YOU ALL...
...TAKING MY OWN PATH TO REBIRTH, THROUGH THE LIVES OF WHICH SHALL BE DETERMINED BY MY OWN KARMA.
HNNN.
YOU ARE INTERRUPTING AN ANNUAL CEREMONY THAT I WOULD PREFER NOT TO HAVE INTERRUPTED...
SHUNK!
SHUNK!
...SO BEFORE I ADJUST MY ANGLE AND EMBED TWO SHURIKENS IN YOUR HEAD, I THINK IT'S BEST TO KNOW WHETHER YOU ARE FRIEND OR FOE.
I DO BELIEVE A FRIEND, MISS YAMASHIRO.
I'D RECOGNIZE THAT VOICE ANYWHERE. HELLO, ALFRED.
I AM SORRY TO INTRUDE ON SUCH A PRIVATE MOMENT...
...BUT THERE'S SOMETHING OF GREAT IMPORTANCE I'D LIKE TO DISCUSS WITH YOU, TATSU.

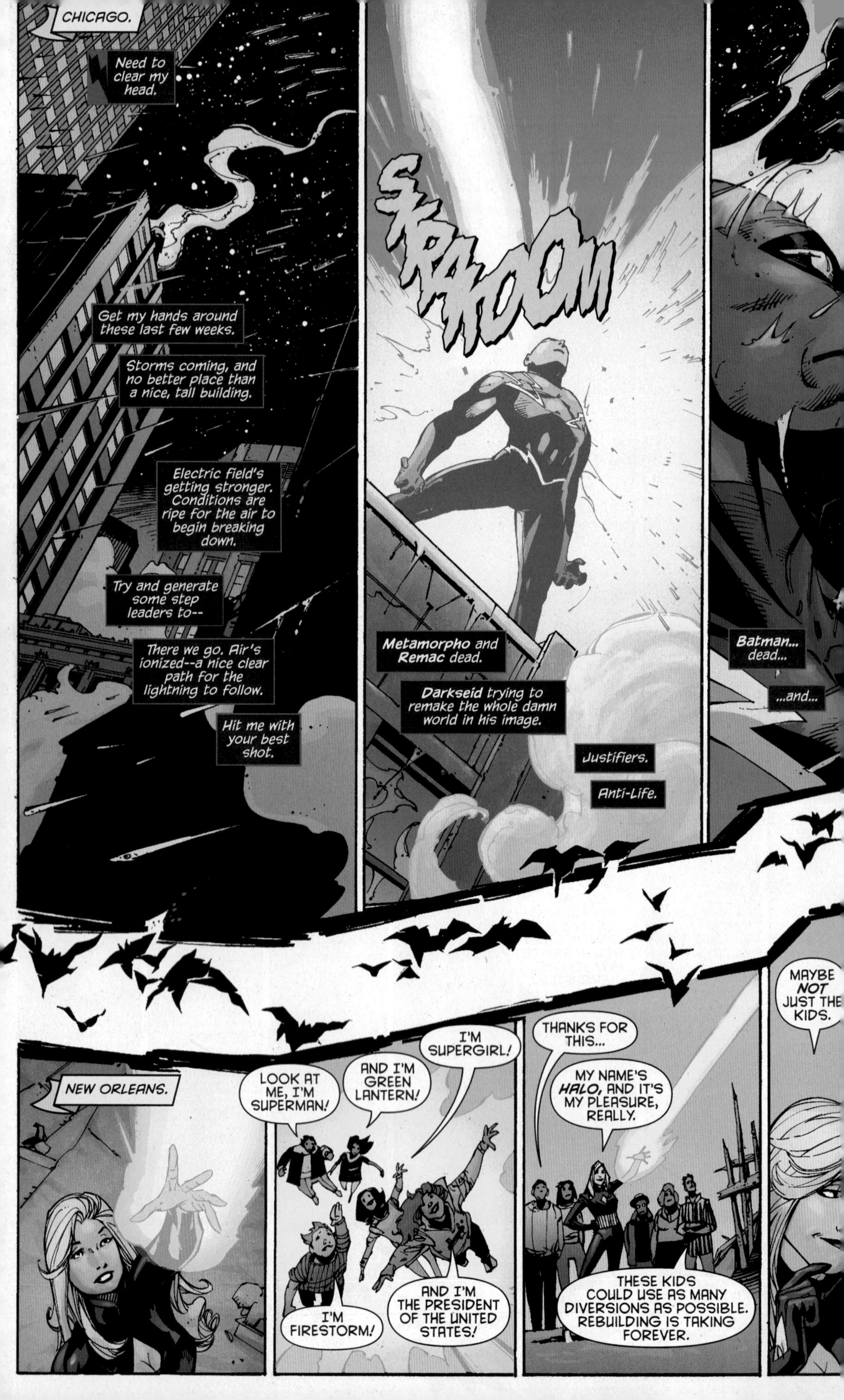

CHICAGO.
Need to clear my head.
Get my hands around these last few weeks.
Storms coming, and no better place than a nice, tall building.
Electric field's getting stronger. Conditions are ripe for the air to begin breaking down.
Try and generate some step leaders to--
There we go. Air's ionized--a nice clear path for the lightning to follow.
Hit me with your best shot.
SKRAKOOM
Metamorpho and Remac dead.
Darkseid trying to remake the whole damn world in his image.
Justifiers.
Anti-Life.
Batman... dead...
...and...
NEW ORLEANS.
LOOK AT ME, I'M SUPERMAN!
AND I'M GREEN LANTERN!
I'M SUPERGIRL!
I'M FIRESTORM!
AND I'M THE PRESIDENT OF THE UNITED STATES!
THANKS FOR THIS...
MY NAME'S HALO, AND IT'S MY PLEASURE, REALLY.
THESE KIDS COULD USE AS MANY DIVERSIONS AS POSSIBLE. REBUILDING IS TAKING FOREVER.
MAYBE NOT JUST THE KIDS.

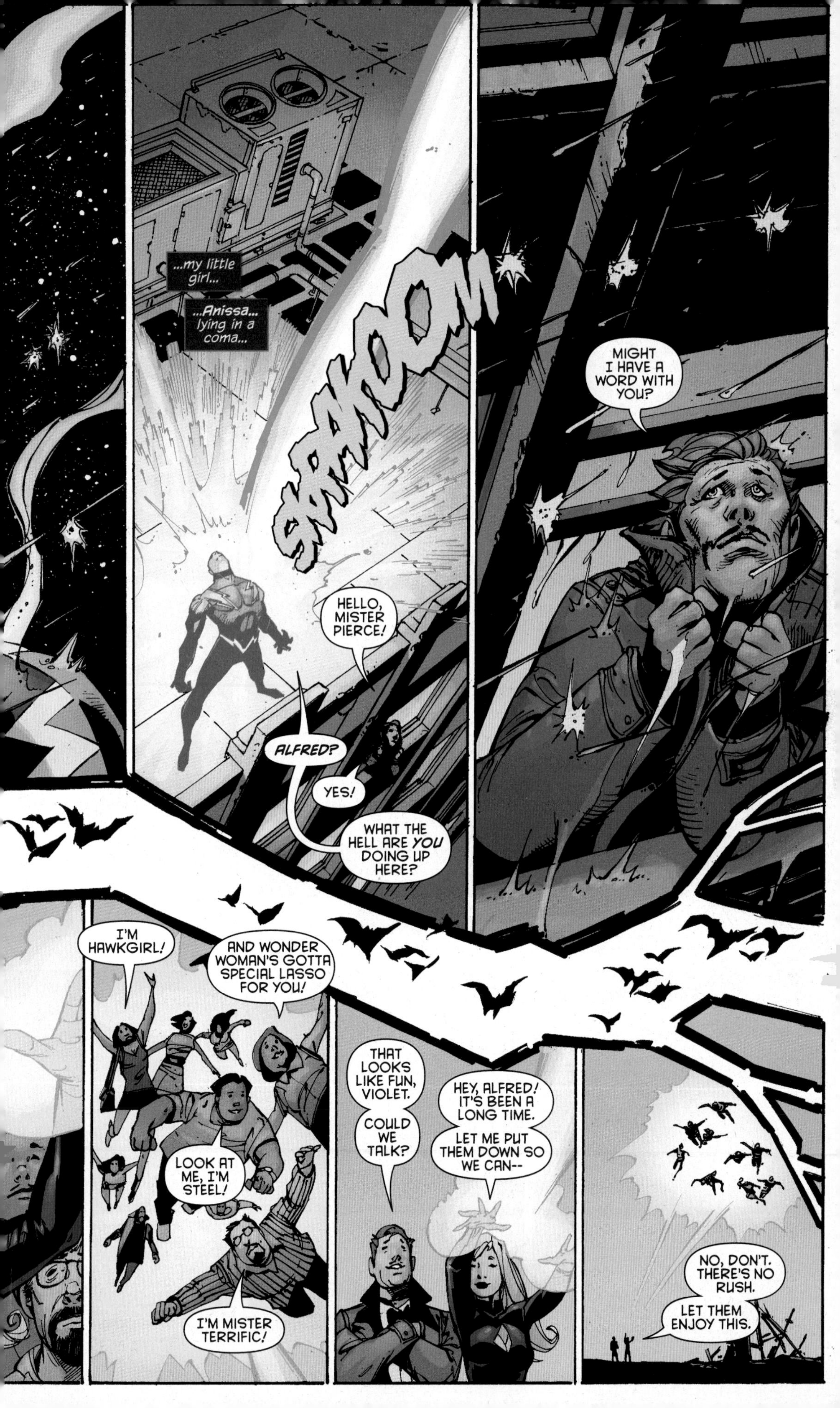
...my little girl...
...Anissa... lying in a coma...
SKRAKOOM
HELLO, MISTER PIERCE!
ALFRED?
YES!
WHAT THE HELL ARE YOU DOING UP HERE?
MIGHT I HAVE A WORD WITH YOU?
I'M HAWKGIRL!
AND WONDER WOMAN'S GOTTA SPECIAL LASSO FOR YOU!
LOOK AT ME, I'M STEEL!
I'M MISTER TERRIFIC!
THAT LOOKS LIKE FUN, VIOLET.
COULD WE TALK?
HEY, ALFRED! IT'S BEEN A LONG TIME.
LET ME PUT THEM DOWN SO WE CAN--
NO, DON'T. THERE'S NO RUSH.
LET THEM ENJOY THIS.

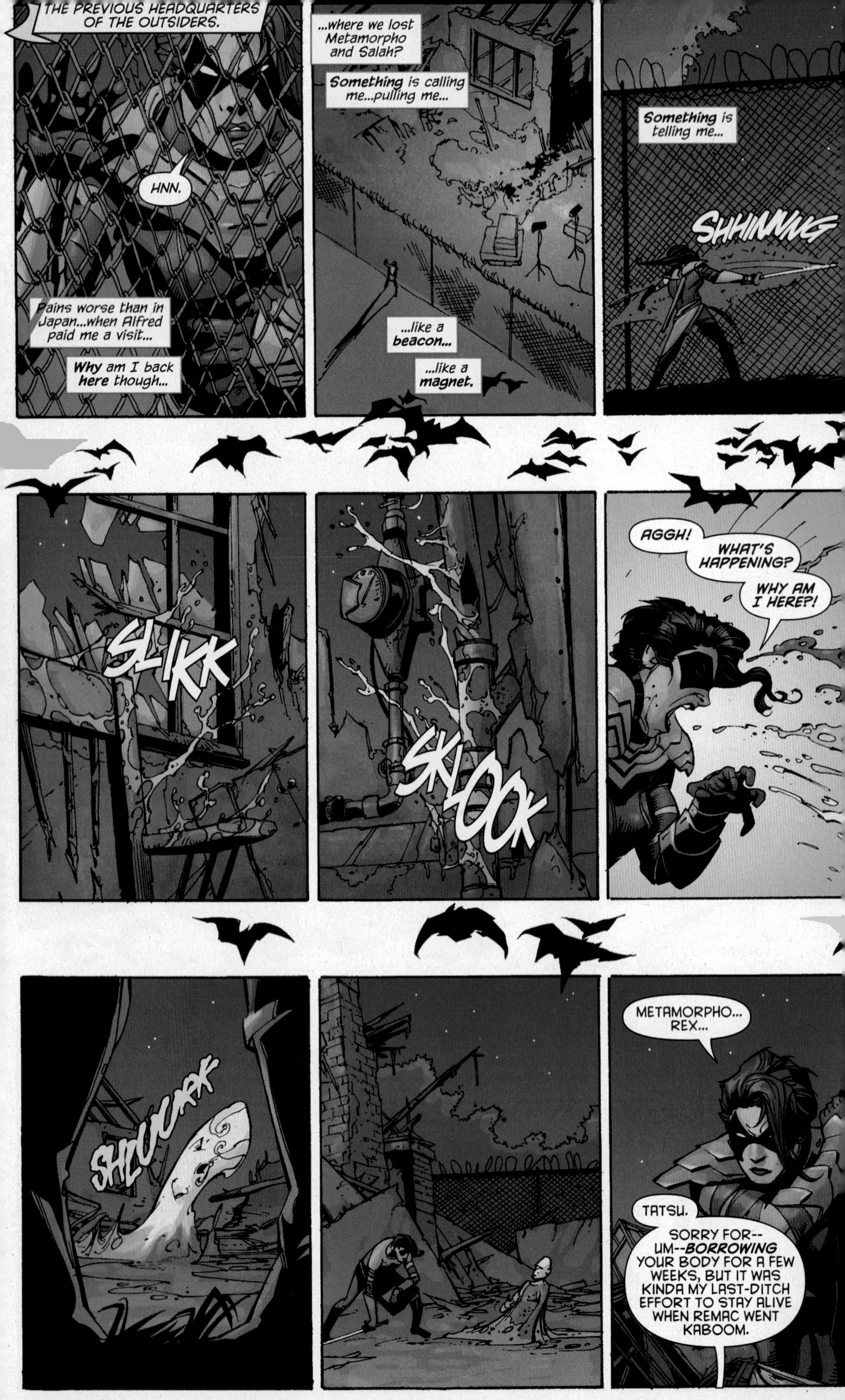
THE PREVIOUS HEADQUARTERS OF THE OUTSIDERS.
HNN.
Pains worse than in Japan...when Alfred paid me a visit...
Why am I back here though...
...where we lost Metamorpho and Salah?
Something is calling me...pulling me...
...like a beacon...
...like a magnet.
Something is telling me...
SHHINNNG
SLIKK
SKLOOK
AGGH!
WHAT'S HAPPENING?
WHY AM I HERE?!
SHLUCK
METAMORPHO... REX...
TATSU.
SORRY FOR-- UM--BORROWING YOUR BODY FOR A FEW WEEKS, BUT IT WAS KINDA MY LAST-DITCH EFFORT TO STAY ALIVE WHEN REMAC WENT KABOOM.

...I have to be here...now.

It doesn't make any sense that--

UNNN.

Stomach pains getting worse...

ARGHH!

NO!

WHATEVER YOU ARE--

--STAY AWAY FROM ME!

BLARRGGH

I GOT LUCKY, I WAS ABLE TO PERMEATE YOUR BODY WITH MY MAIN MASS BEFORE THE FORCE OF THE BLAST DISPELLED THE REST OF ME.

HOPE YOU DON'T MIND ME HITCHHIKING ON YA?

THAT'S WHAT FRIENDS ARE FOR, REX.

RETCHING ASIDE, I'M JUST GLAD YOU'RE ALIVE AND I WAS ABLE TO HELP.

BABY, YOU'RE THE GREATEST.

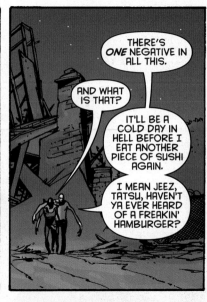

THERE'S ONE NEGATIVE IN ALL THIS.

AND WHAT IS THAT?

IT'LL BE A COLD DAY IN HELL BEFORE I EAT ANOTHER PIECE OF SUSHI AGAIN.

I MEAN JEEZ, TATSU, HAVEN'T YA EVER HEARD OF A FREAKIN' HAMBURGER?

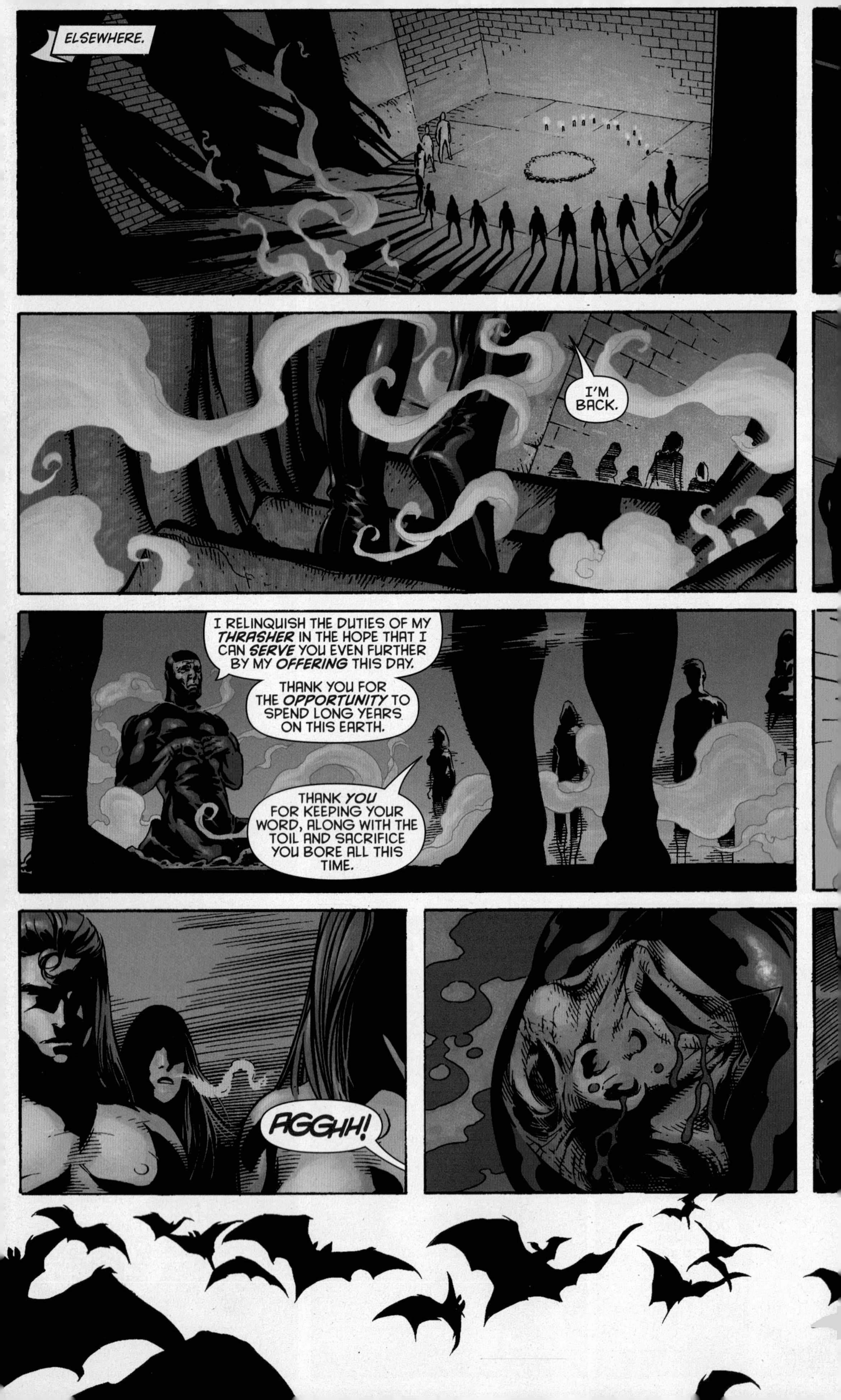
ELSEWHERE.
I'M BACK.
I RELINQUISH THE DUTIES OF MY THRASHER IN THE HOPE THAT I CAN SERVE YOU EVEN FURTHER BY MY OFFERING THIS DAY.
THANK YOU FOR THE OPPORTUNITY TO SPEND LONG YEARS ON THIS EARTH.
THANK YOU FOR KEEPING YOUR WORD, ALONG WITH THE TOIL AND SACRIFICE YOU BORE ALL THIS TIME.
AGGHH!

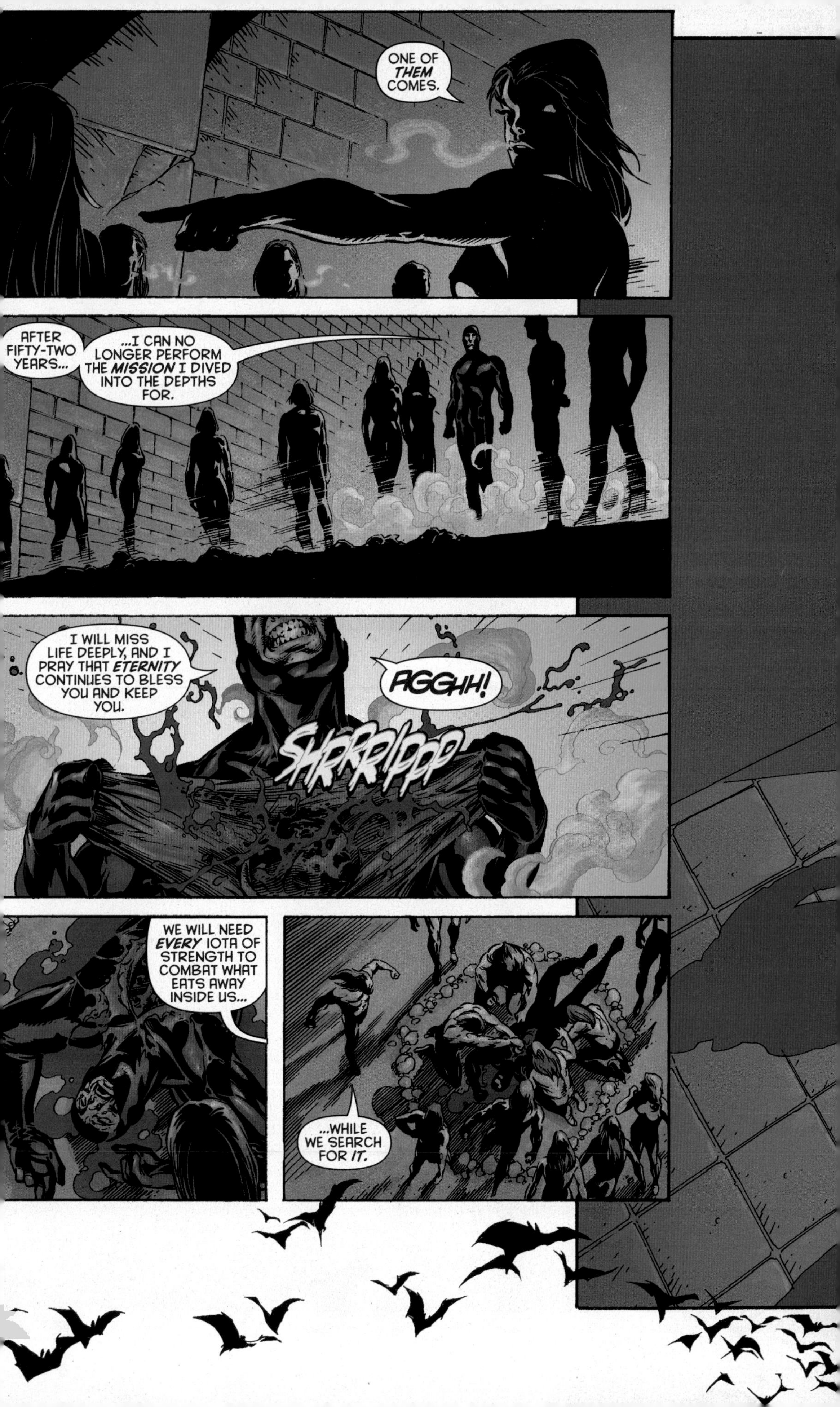
ONE OF THEM COMES.
AFTER FIFTY-TWO YEARS...
...I CAN NO LONGER PERFORM THE MISSION I DIVED INTO THE DEPTHS FOR.
I WILL MISS LIFE DEEPLY, AND I PRAY THAT ETERNITY CONTINUES TO BLESS YOU AND KEEP YOU.
AGGHH!
SHRRRIPPP
WE WILL NEED EVERY IOTA OF STRENGTH TO COMBAT WHAT EATS AWAY INSIDE US...
...WHILE WE SEARCH FOR IT.

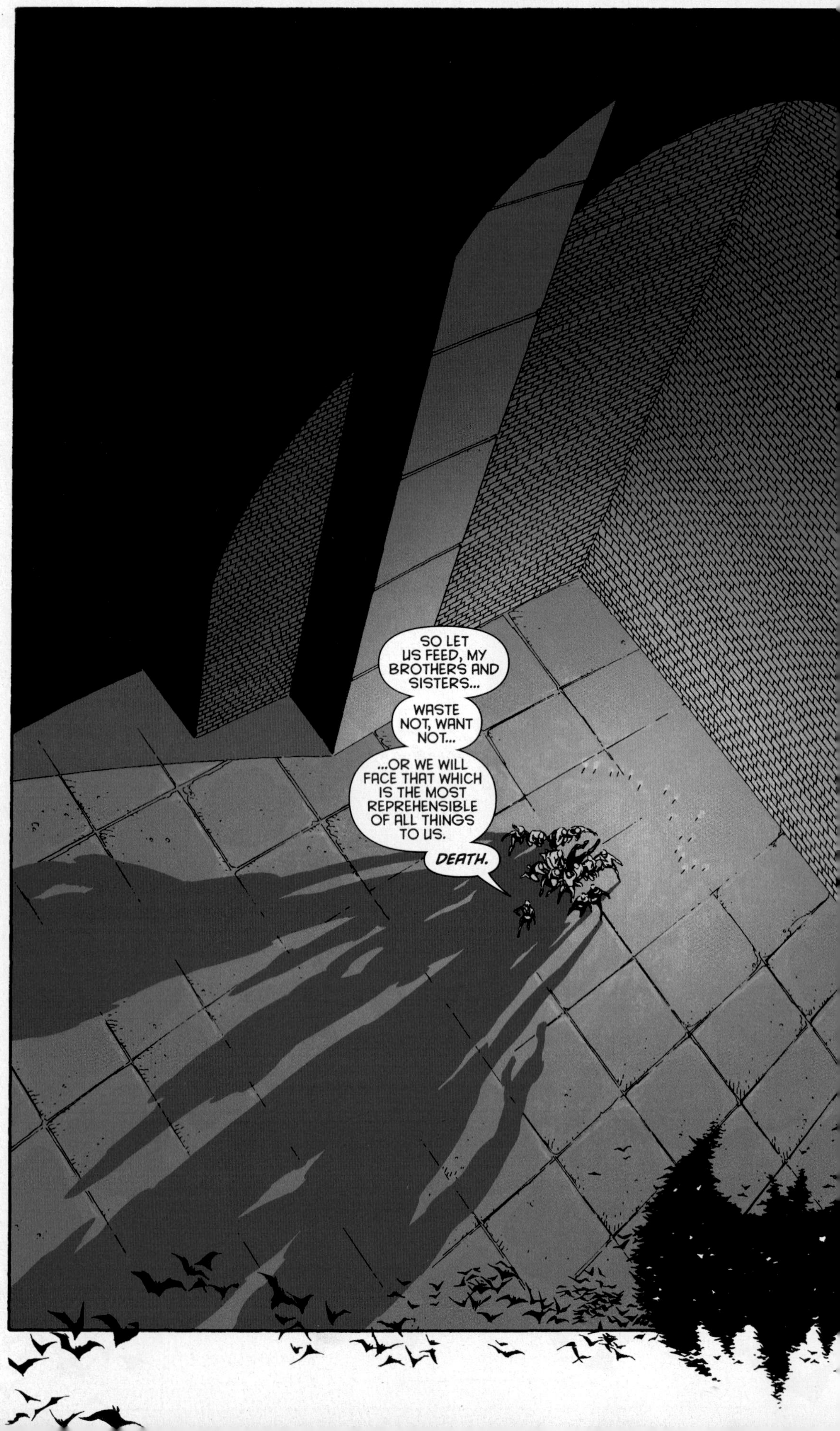
SO LET US FEED, MY BROTHERS AND SISTERS...
WASTE NOT, WANT NOT...
...OR WE WILL FACE THAT WHICH IS THE MOST REPREHENSIBLE OF ALL THINGS TO US.
DEATH.

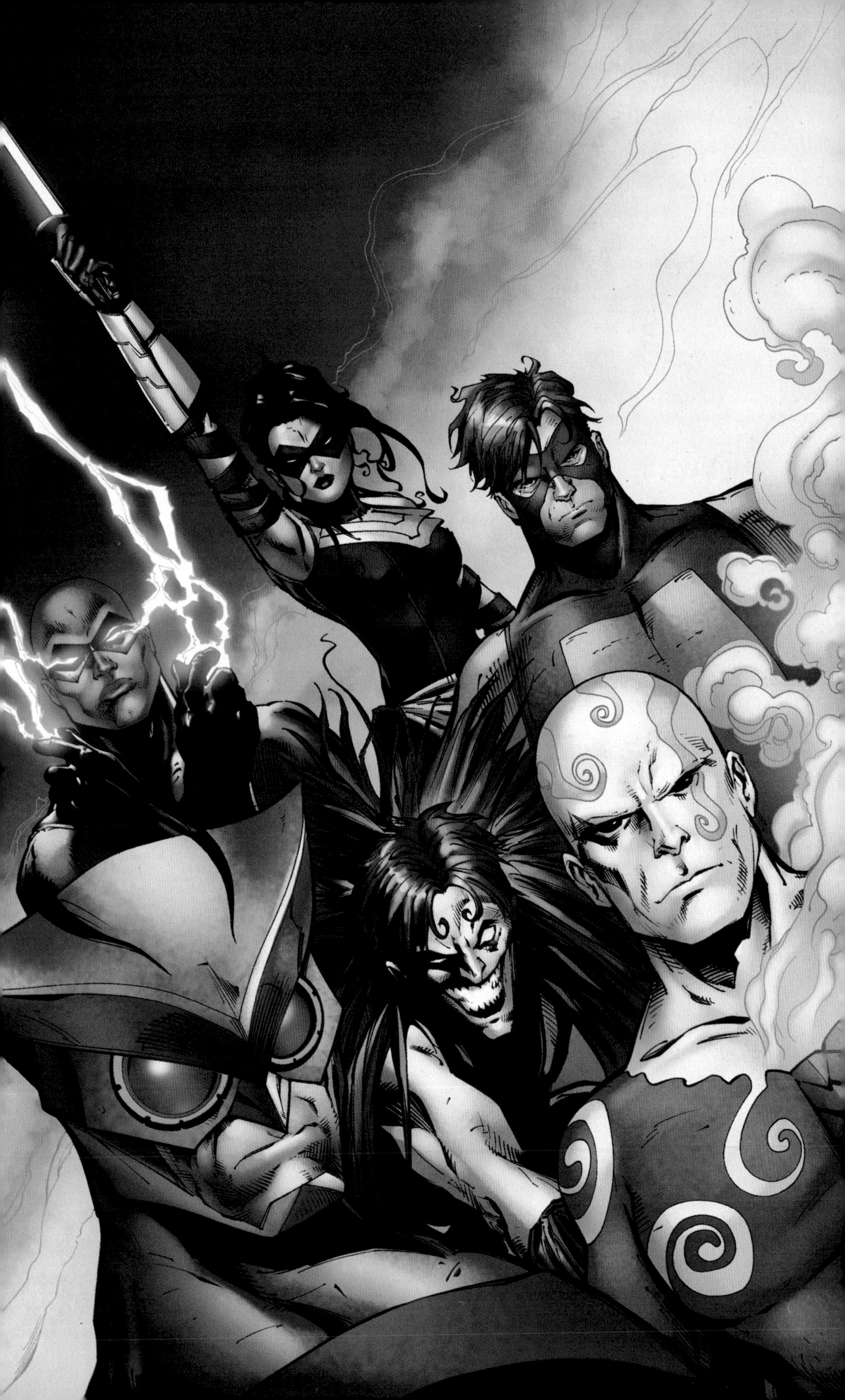

"There are to be no illusions here."

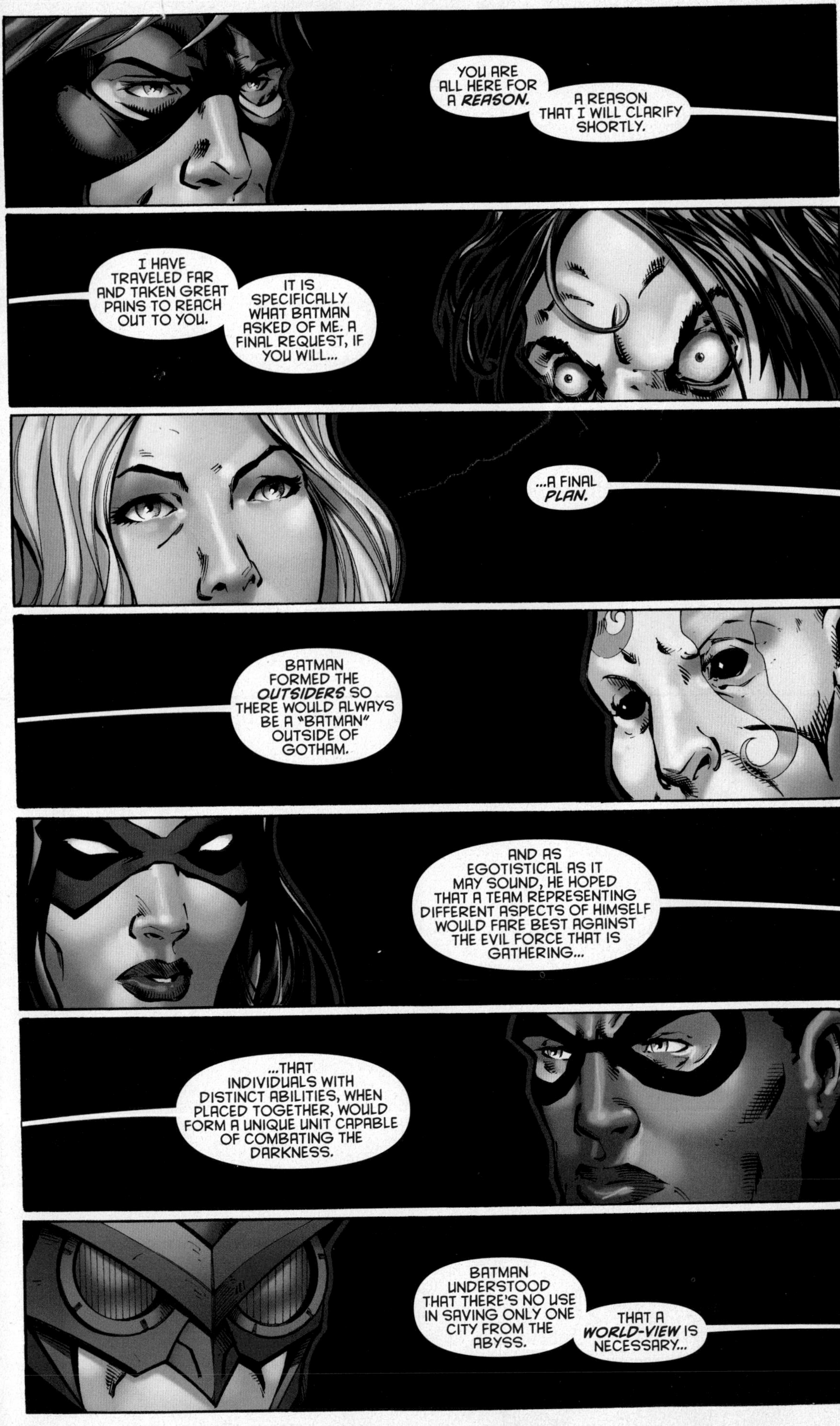
YOU ARE ALL HERE FOR A REASON.
A REASON THAT I WILL CLARIFY SHORTLY.
I HAVE TRAVELED FAR AND TAKEN GREAT PAINS TO REACH OUT TO YOU.
IT IS SPECIFICALLY WHAT BATMAN ASKED OF ME. A FINAL REQUEST, IF YOU WILL...
...A FINAL PLAN.
BATMAN FORMED THE OUTSIDERS SO THERE WOULD ALWAYS BE A "BATMAN" OUTSIDE OF GOTHAM.
AND AS EGOTISTICAL AS IT MAY SOUND, HE HOPED THAT A TEAM REPRESENTING DIFFERENT ASPECTS OF HIMSELF WOULD FARE BEST AGAINST THE EVIL FORCE THAT IS GATHERING...
...THAT INDIVIDUALS WITH DISTINCT ABILITIES, WHEN PLACED TOGETHER, WOULD FORM A UNIQUE UNIT CAPABLE OF COMBATING THE DARKNESS.
BATMAN UNDERSTOOD THAT THERE'S NO USE IN SAVING ONLY ONE CITY FROM THE ABYSS.
THAT A WORLD-VIEW IS NECESSARY...

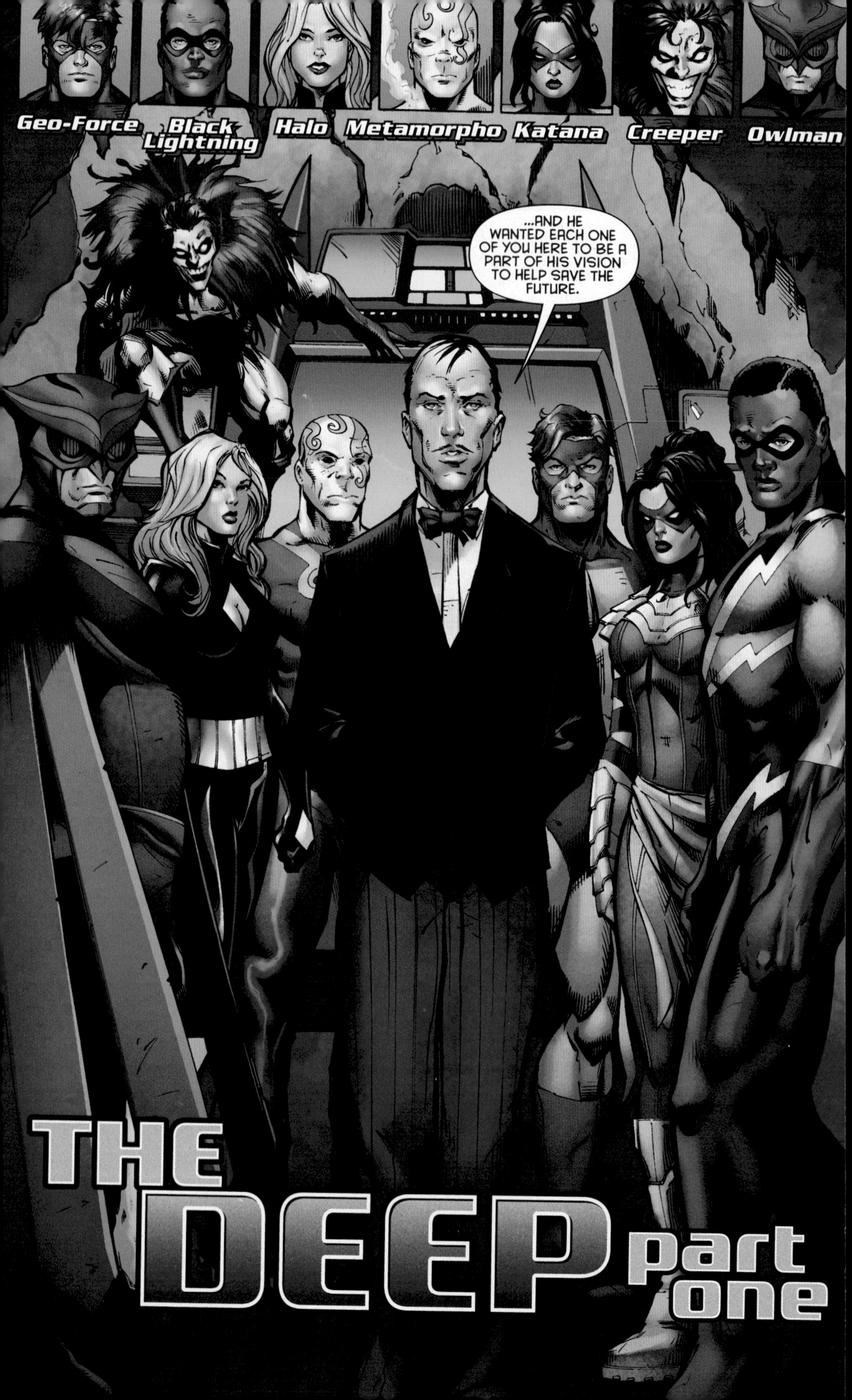
Geo-Force
Black Lightning
Halo
Metamorpho
Katana
Creeper
Owlman
...AND HE WANTED EACH ONE OF YOU HERE TO BE A PART OF HIS VISION TO HELP SAVE THE FUTURE.
THE DEEP part one

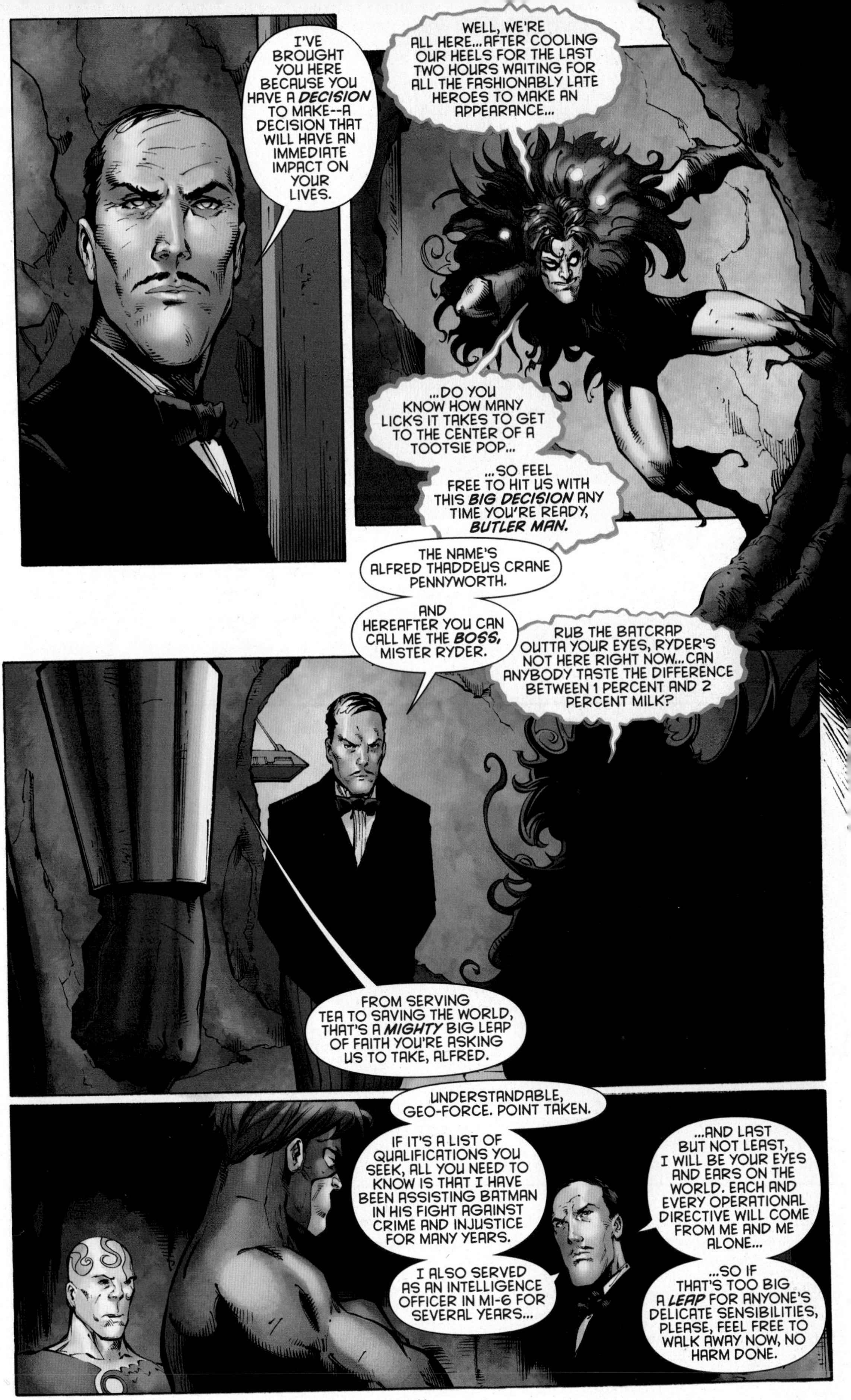

I'VE BROUGHT YOU HERE BECAUSE YOU HAVE A *DECISION* TO MAKE--A DECISION THAT WILL HAVE AN IMMEDIATE IMPACT ON YOUR LIVES.
WELL, WE'RE ALL HERE...AFTER COOLING OUR HEELS FOR THE LAST TWO HOURS WAITING FOR ALL THE FASHIONABLY LATE HEROES TO MAKE AN APPEARANCE...
...DO YOU KNOW HOW MANY LICKS IT TAKES TO GET TO THE CENTER OF A TOOTSIE POP...
...SO FEEL FREE TO HIT US WITH THIS ***BIG DECISION*** ANY TIME YOU'RE READY, ***BUTLER MAN.***
THE NAME'S ALFRED THADDEUS CRANE PENNYWORTH.
AND HEREAFTER YOU CAN CALL ME THE *BOSS,* MISTER RYDER.
RUB THE BATCRAP OUTTA YOUR EYES, RYDER'S NOT HERE RIGHT NOW...CAN ANYBODY TASTE THE DIFFERENCE BETWEEN 1 PERCENT AND 2 PERCENT MILK?
FROM SERVING TEA TO SAVING THE WORLD, THAT'S A *MIGHTY* BIG LEAP OF FAITH YOU'RE ASKING US TO TAKE, ALFRED.
UNDERSTANDABLE, GEO-FORCE. POINT TAKEN.
IF IT'S A LIST OF QUALIFICATIONS YOU SEEK, ALL YOU NEED TO KNOW IS THAT I HAVE BEEN ASSISTING BATMAN IN HIS FIGHT AGAINST CRIME AND INJUSTICE FOR MANY YEARS.
I ALSO SERVED AS AN INTELLIGENCE OFFICER IN MI-6 FOR SEVERAL YEARS...
...AND LAST BUT NOT LEAST, I WILL BE YOUR EYES AND EARS ON THE WORLD. EACH AND EVERY OPERATIONAL DIRECTIVE WILL COME FROM ME AND ME ALONE...
...SO IF THAT'S TOO BIG A *LEAP* FOR ANYONE'S DELICATE SENSIBILITIES, PLEASE, FEEL FREE TO WALK AWAY NOW, NO HARM DONE.

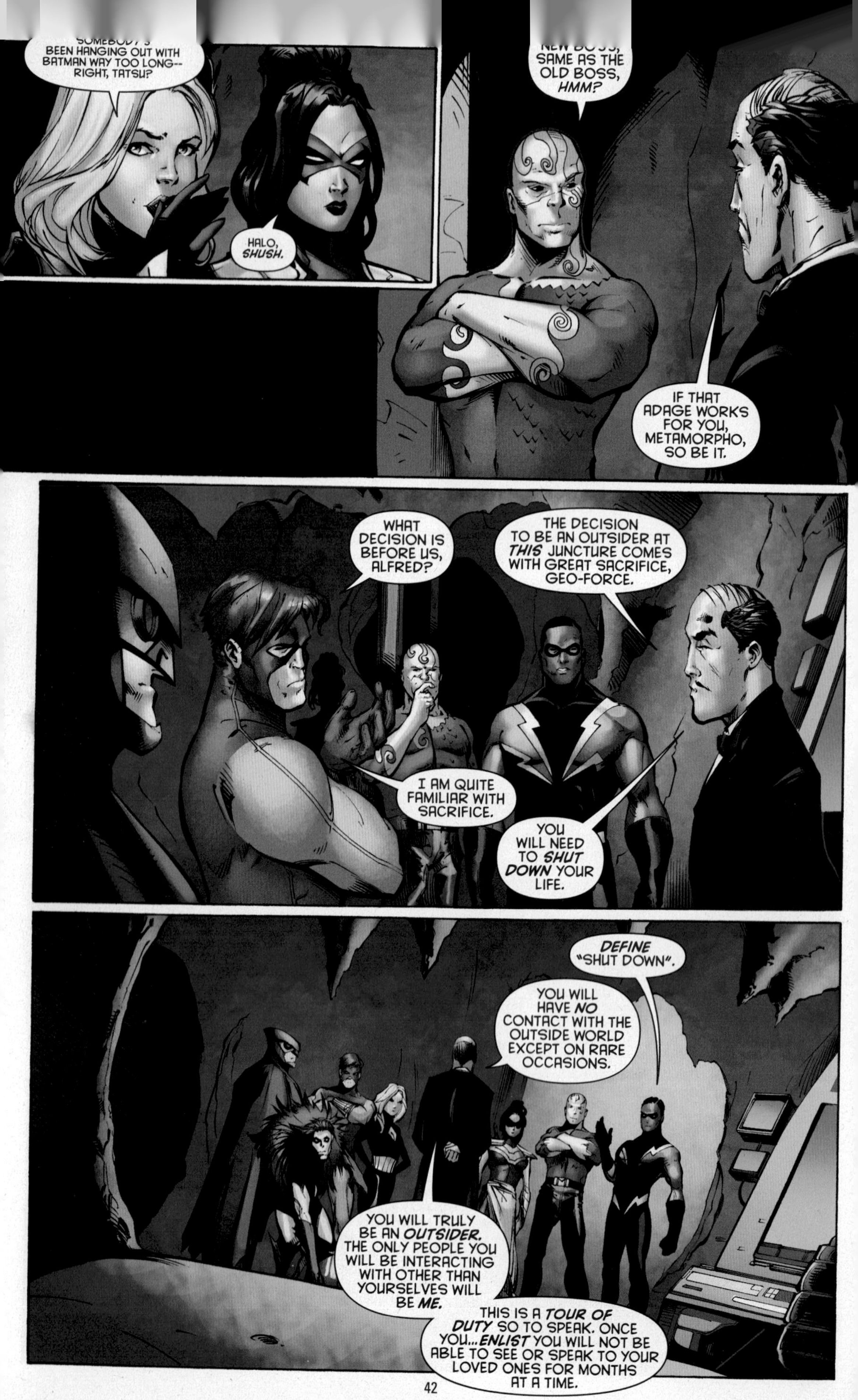

BEEN HANGING OUT WITH BATMAN WAY TOO LONG-- RIGHT, TATSU?
HALO, SHUSH.
SAME AS THE OLD BOSS, HMM?
IF THAT ADAGE WORKS FOR YOU, METAMORPHO, SO BE IT.
WHAT DECISION IS BEFORE US, ALFRED?
THE DECISION TO BE AN OUTSIDER AT THIS JUNCTURE COMES WITH GREAT SACRIFICE, GEO-FORCE.
I AM QUITE FAMILIAR WITH SACRIFICE.
YOU WILL NEED TO SHUT DOWN YOUR LIFE.
DEFINE "SHUT DOWN".
YOU WILL HAVE NO CONTACT WITH THE OUTSIDE WORLD EXCEPT ON RARE OCCASIONS.
YOU WILL TRULY BE AN OUTSIDER. THE ONLY PEOPLE YOU WILL BE INTERACTING WITH OTHER THAN YOURSELVES WILL BE ME.
THIS IS A TOUR OF DUTY SO TO SPEAK. ONCE YOU...ENLIST YOU WILL NOT BE ABLE TO SEE OR SPEAK TO YOUR LOVED ONES FOR MONTHS AT A TIME.

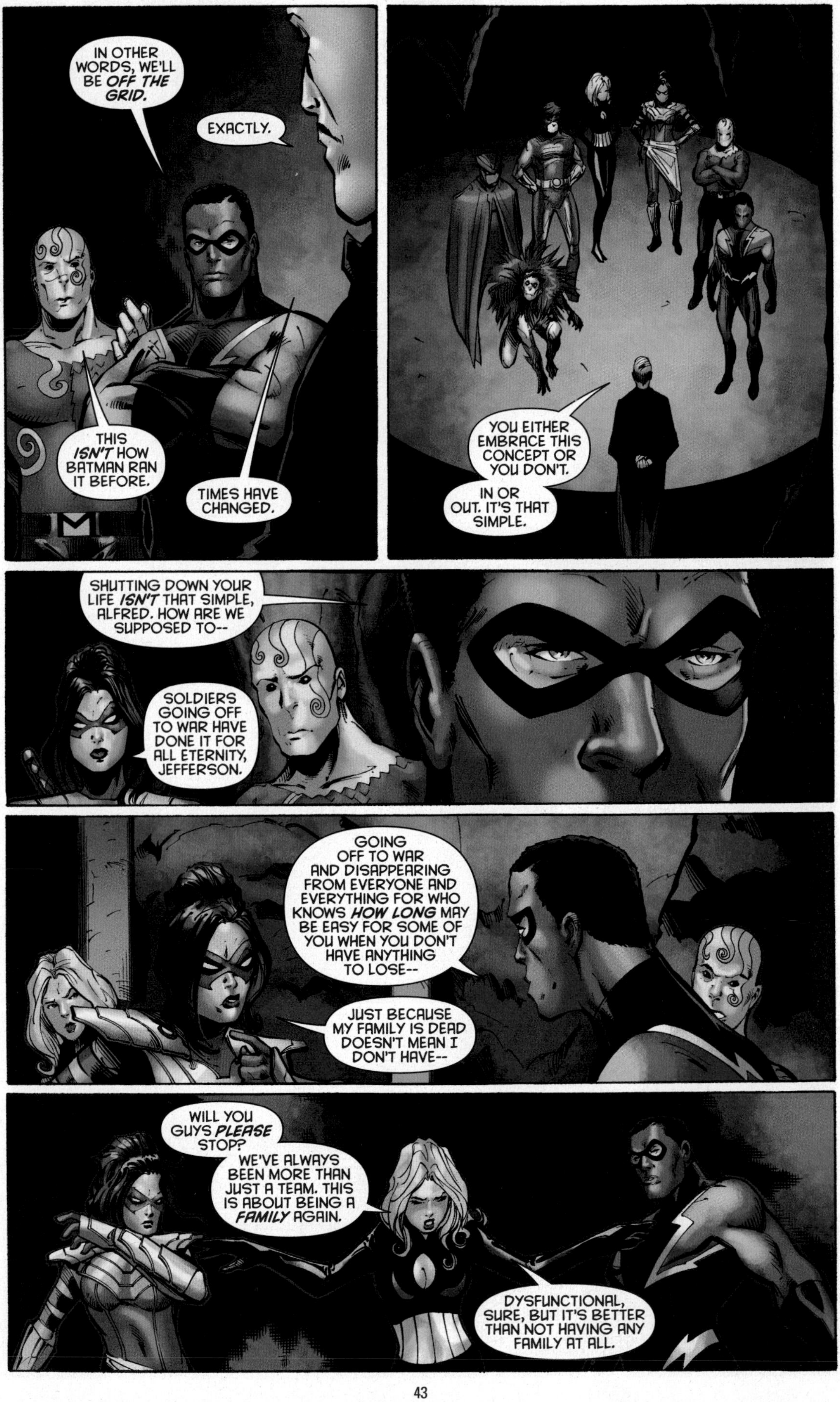
IN OTHER WORDS, WE'LL BE OFF THE GRID.
EXACTLY.
THIS ISN'T HOW BATMAN RAN IT BEFORE.
TIMES HAVE CHANGED.
YOU EITHER EMBRACE THIS CONCEPT OR YOU DON'T.
IN OR OUT. IT'S THAT SIMPLE.
SHUTTING DOWN YOUR LIFE ISN'T THAT SIMPLE, ALFRED. HOW ARE WE SUPPOSED TO--
SOLDIERS GOING OFF TO WAR HAVE DONE IT FOR ALL ETERNITY, JEFFERSON.
GOING OFF TO WAR AND DISAPPEARING FROM EVERYONE AND EVERYTHING FOR WHO KNOWS HOW LONG MAY BE EASY FOR SOME OF YOU WHEN YOU DON'T HAVE ANYTHING TO LOSE--
JUST BECAUSE MY FAMILY IS DEAD DOESN'T MEAN I DON'T HAVE--
WILL YOU GUYS PLEASE STOP?
WE'VE ALWAYS BEEN MORE THAN JUST A TEAM. THIS IS ABOUT BEING A FAMILY AGAIN.
DYSFUNCTIONAL, SURE, BUT IT'S BETTER THAN NOT HAVING ANY FAMILY AT ALL.

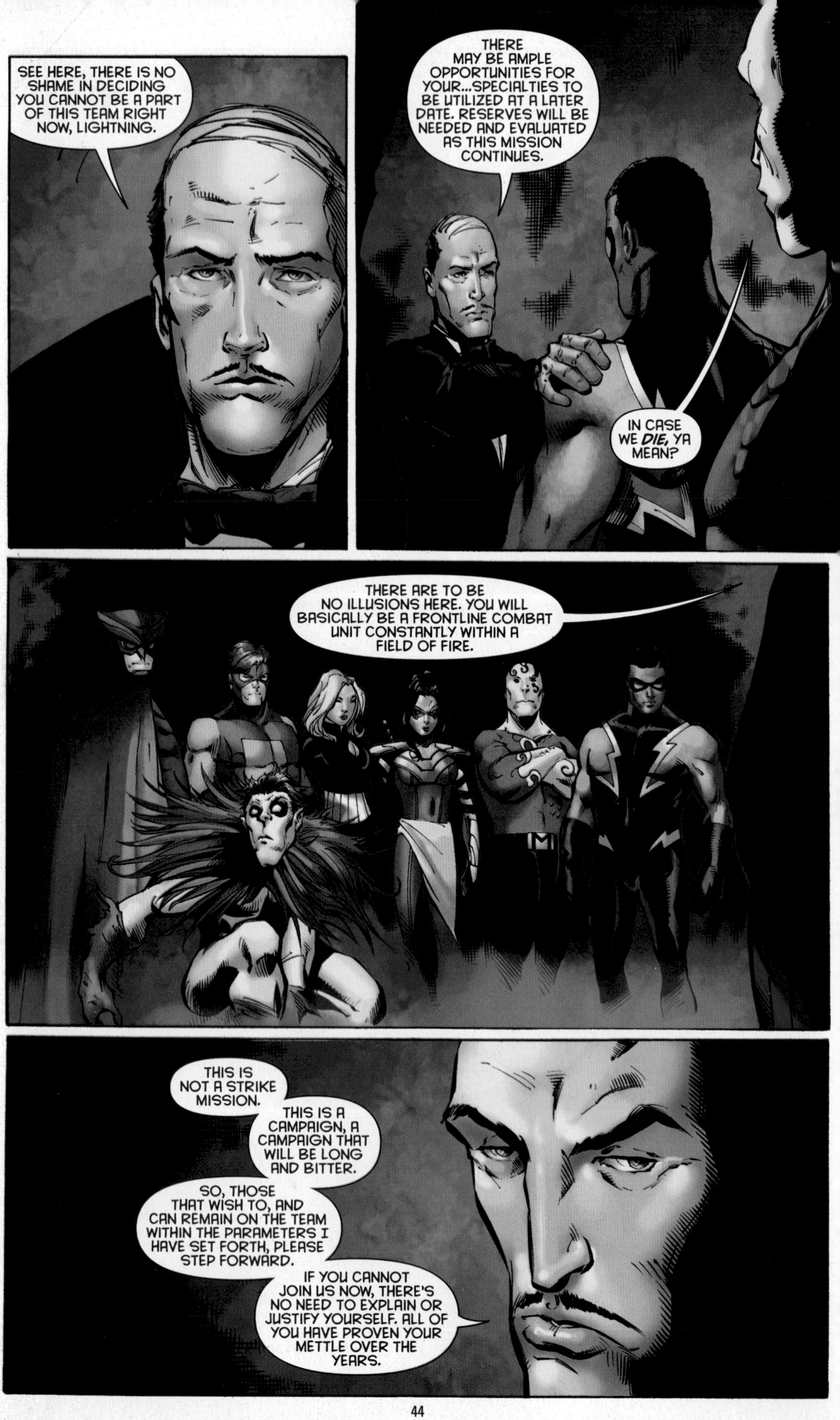
SEE HERE, THERE IS NO SHAME IN DECIDING YOU CANNOT BE A PART OF THIS TEAM RIGHT NOW, LIGHTNING.
THERE MAY BE AMPLE OPPORTUNITIES FOR YOUR...SPECIALTIES TO BE UTILIZED AT A LATER DATE. RESERVES WILL BE NEEDED AND EVALUATED AS THIS MISSION CONTINUES.
IN CASE WE DIE, YA MEAN?
THERE ARE TO BE NO ILLUSIONS HERE. YOU WILL BASICALLY BE A FRONTLINE COMBAT UNIT CONSTANTLY WITHIN A FIELD OF FIRE.
THIS IS NOT A STRIKE MISSION.
THIS IS A CAMPAIGN, A CAMPAIGN THAT WILL BE LONG AND BITTER.
SO, THOSE THAT WISH TO, AND CAN REMAIN ON THE TEAM WITHIN THE PARAMETERS I HAVE SET FORTH, PLEASE STEP FORWARD.
IF YOU CANNOT JOIN US NOW, THERE'S NO NEED TO EXPLAIN OR JUSTIFY YOURSELF. ALL OF YOU HAVE PROVEN YOUR METTLE OVER THE YEARS.

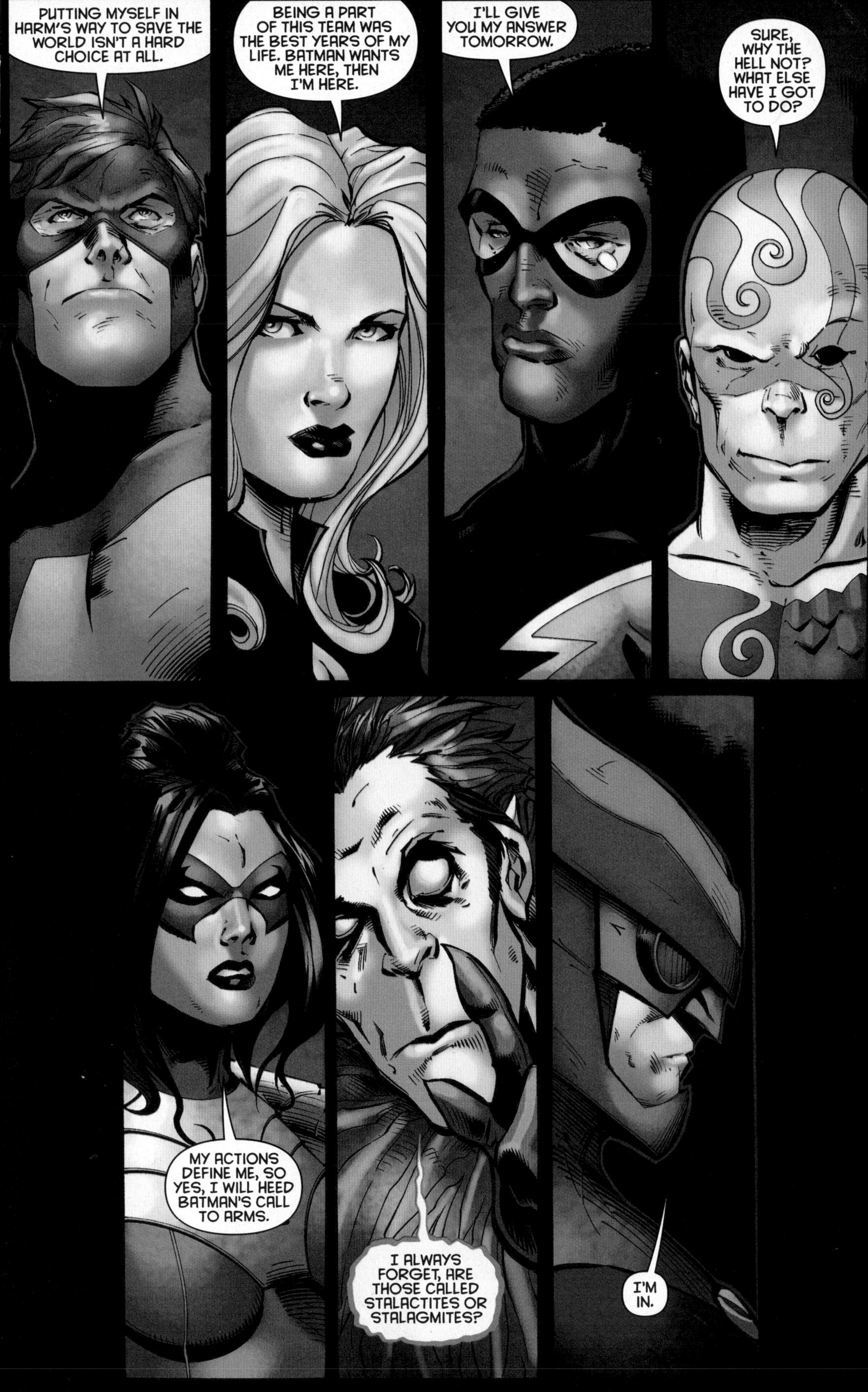
PUTTING MYSELF IN HARM'S WAY TO SAVE THE WORLD ISN'T A HARD CHOICE AT ALL.
BEING A PART OF THIS TEAM WAS THE BEST YEARS OF MY LIFE. BATMAN WANTS ME HERE, THEN I'M HERE.
I'LL GIVE YOU MY ANSWER TOMORROW.
SURE, WHY THE HELL NOT? WHAT ELSE HAVE I GOT TO DO?
MY ACTIONS DEFINE ME, SO YES, I WILL HEED BATMAN'S CALL TO ARMS.
I ALWAYS FORGET, ARE THOSE CALLED STALACTITES OR STALAGMITES?
I'M IN.

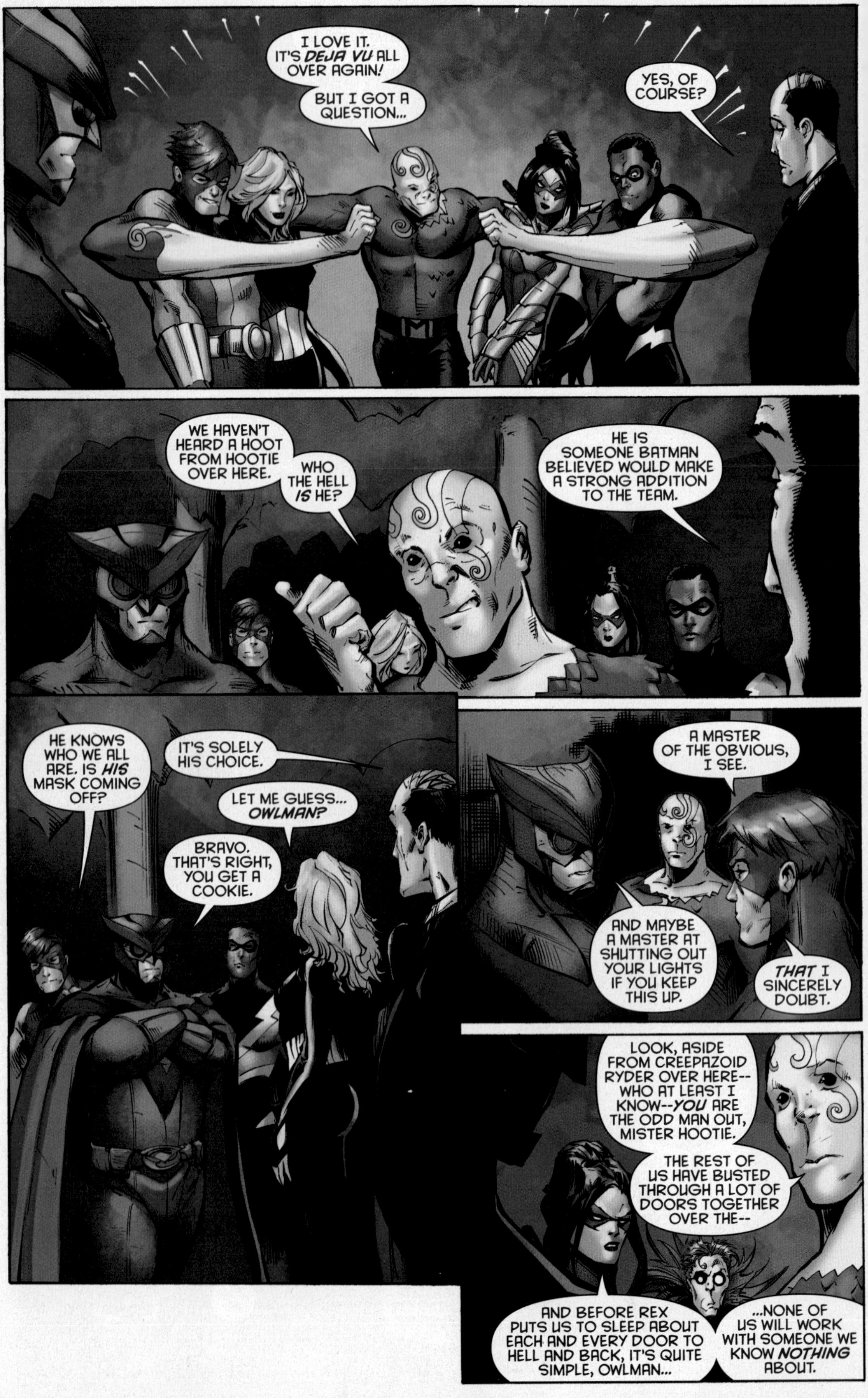
I LOVE IT. IT'S *DEJA VU* ALL OVER AGAIN!
BUT I GOT A QUESTION...
YES, OF COURSE?
WE HAVEN'T HEARD A HOOT FROM HOOTIE OVER HERE.
WHO THE HELL *IS* HE?
HE IS SOMEONE BATMAN BELIEVED WOULD MAKE A STRONG ADDITION TO THE TEAM.
HE KNOWS WHO WE ALL ARE. IS *HIS* MASK COMING OFF?
IT'S SOLELY HIS CHOICE.
LET ME GUESS... *OWLMAN?*
BRAVO. THAT'S RIGHT, YOU GET A COOKIE.
A MASTER OF THE OBVIOUS, I SEE.
AND MAYBE A MASTER AT SHUTTING OUT YOUR LIGHTS IF YOU KEEP THIS UP.
THAT I SINCERELY DOUBT.
LOOK, ASIDE FROM CREEPAZOID RYDER OVER HERE--WHO AT LEAST I KNOW--*YOU* ARE THE ODD MAN OUT, MISTER HOOTIE.
THE REST OF US HAVE BUSTED THROUGH A LOT OF DOORS TOGETHER OVER THE--
AND BEFORE REX PUTS US TO SLEEP ABOUT EACH AND EVERY DOOR TO HELL AND BACK, IT'S QUITE SIMPLE, OWLMAN...
...NONE OF US WILL WORK WITH SOMEONE WE KNOW *NOTHING* ABOUT.

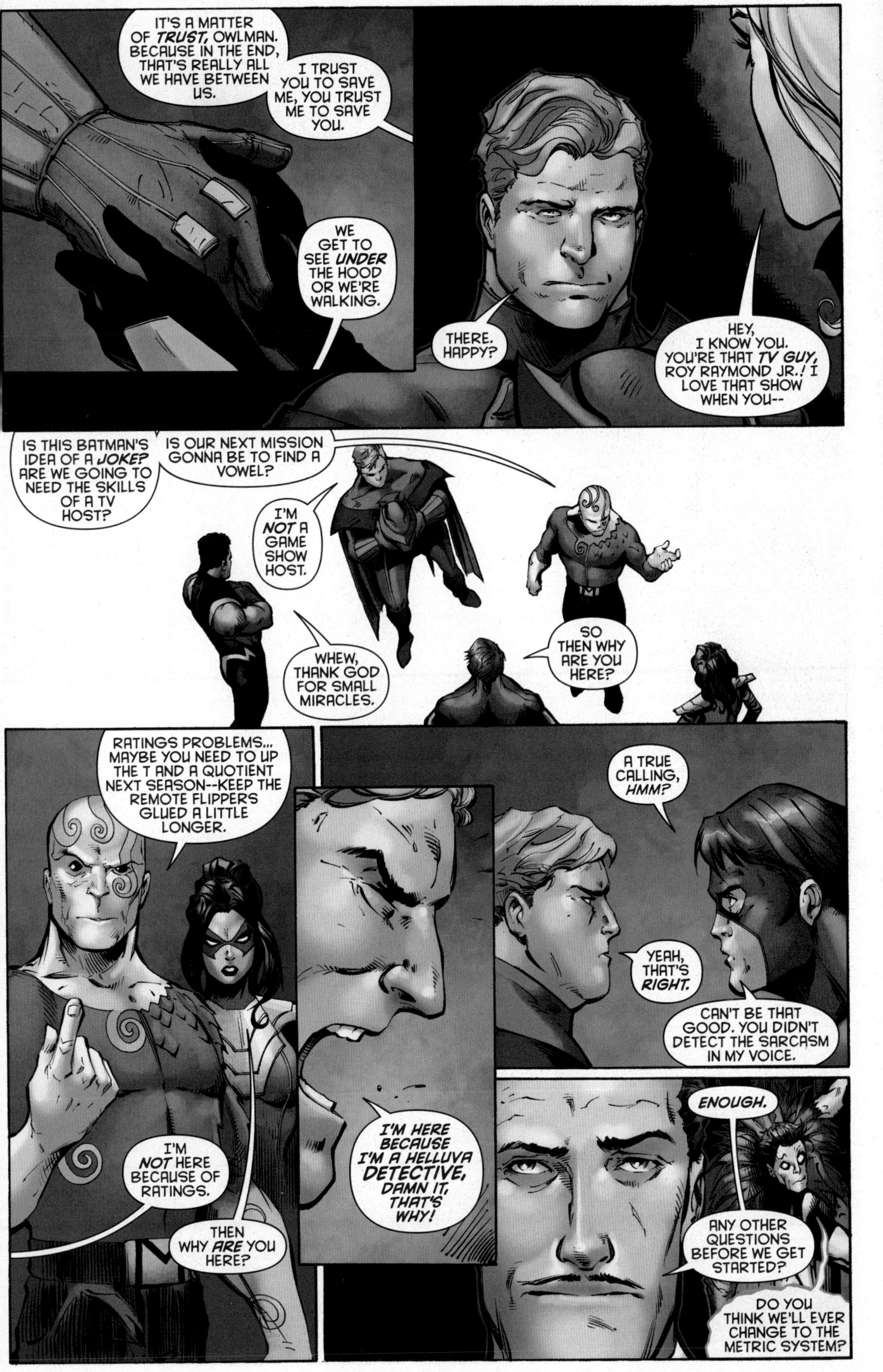
IT'S A MATTER OF TRUST, OWLMAN. BECAUSE IN THE END, THAT'S REALLY ALL WE HAVE BETWEEN US.
I TRUST YOU TO SAVE ME, YOU TRUST ME TO SAVE YOU.
WE GET TO SEE UNDER THE HOOD OR WE'RE WALKING.
THERE. HAPPY?
HEY, I KNOW YOU. YOU'RE THAT TV GUY, ROY RAYMOND JR.! I LOVE THAT SHOW WHEN YOU--
IS THIS BATMAN'S IDEA OF A JOKE? ARE WE GOING TO NEED THE SKILLS OF A TV HOST?
IS OUR NEXT MISSION GONNA BE TO FIND A VOWEL?
I'M NOT A GAME SHOW HOST.
WHEW, THANK GOD FOR SMALL MIRACLES.
SO THEN WHY ARE YOU HERE?
RATINGS PROBLEMS... MAYBE YOU NEED TO UP THE T AND A QUOTIENT NEXT SEASON--KEEP THE REMOTE FLIPPERS GLUED A LITTLE LONGER.
I'M NOT HERE BECAUSE OF RATINGS.
THEN WHY ARE YOU HERE?
I'M HERE BECAUSE I'M A HELLUVA DETECTIVE, DAMN IT, THAT'S WHY!
A TRUE CALLING, HMM?
YEAH, THAT'S RIGHT.
CAN'T BE THAT GOOD. YOU DIDN'T DETECT THE SARCASM IN MY VOICE.
ENOUGH.
ANY OTHER QUESTIONS BEFORE WE GET STARTED?
DO YOU THINK WE'LL EVER CHANGE TO THE METRIC SYSTEM?

I DON'T CARE WHAT THE DOCTORS SAY, I *KNOW* YOU CAN HEAR ME, ANISSA.

AND I KNOW THAT SOMETIME *SOON* YOU'RE GONNA WAKE UP AND GET OUT OF THAT HOSPITAL BED WHEN YOU'RE GOOD AND READY.

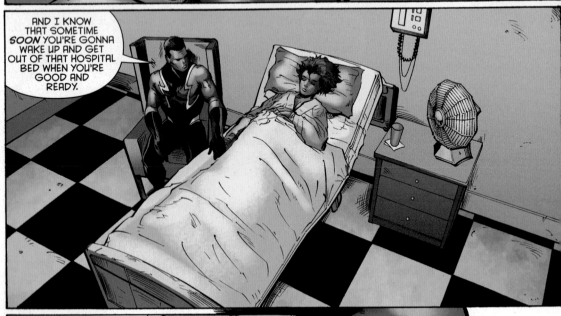

AND I WANT YOU TO KNOW THAT IF I'M NOT HERE WHEN YOU OPEN THOSE BIG, BEAUTIFUL BROWN EYES OF YOURS IT'S NOT BECAUSE I DON'T LOVE YOU...

...IT'S THE EXACT *OPPOSITE*, BABY.

I'M GOING AWAY FOR A WHILE *BECAUSE* OF HOW MUCH I LOVE YOU AND YOUR SISTER, JENNIFER-- THE TWO MOST IMPORTANT PEOPLE IN MY LIFE.

I'M GOING AWAY TO SAVE *YOUR* FUTURE.

SO FORGIVE YOUR OL' DAD FOR LEAVING YOU NOW WHILE YOU GO THROUGH THIS.

BUT JUST REMEMBER THAT I'LL ALWAYS BE IN YOUR HEART AND YOU'LL ALWAYS BE IN MINE NO *WHAT HAPPENS*, LITTLE GIRL, UNDERSTAND?

TAK TAK TAK

HEY, ALFRED.

I DIDN'T EXPECT ANYONE TO COME TO A DECISION SO SOON, HALO. YOU DON'T NEED TO BE HERE FOR ANOTHER TWO DAYS.

I'M SURE THERE'S SOMEONE YOU COULD BE SPENDING TIME WITH INSTEAD OF--

I FELT *YOU* COULD USE SOME COMPANY.

THAT IS MOST CONSIDERATE OF YOU, MS. HARPER, BUT--

VIOLET. CALL ME VIOLET.

I HAVE QUITE A LOT OF WORK TO GET TO, VIOLET, SO THANKS FOR THE VISIT.

I THINK YOU NEED A LITTLE MORE *LIGHT,* ALFRED.

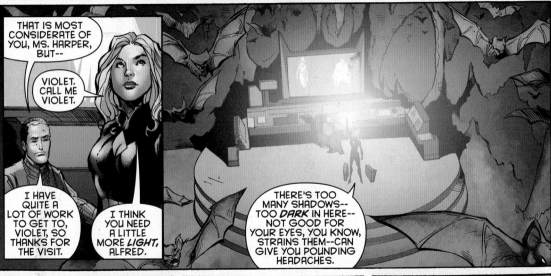

THERE'S TOO MANY SHADOWS-- TOO *DARK* IN HERE-- NOT GOOD FOR YOUR EYES, YOU KNOW, STRAINS THEM--CAN GIVE YOU POUNDING HEADACHES.

SORRY FOR SCARING THE BATS.

I'M SURE THEY WILL BE JUST FINE.

UM, WOULD IT BE OKAY IF I STAY HERE THE NEXT COUPLE OF DAYS?

WELL, IT MAY BE DIFFICULT TO FIND A SPARE ROOM FOR YOU HERE AT THE *MANOR.*

OH, THAT'S OKAY, I GUESS I SHOULDN'T HAVE--

THAT WAS A JOKE, VIOLET.

YOUR COMPANY... AND *DISTINCT* OUTLOOK AT THIS TIME WOULD BE MOST APPRECIATED.

YOU SURE, ALFRED?

QUITE.

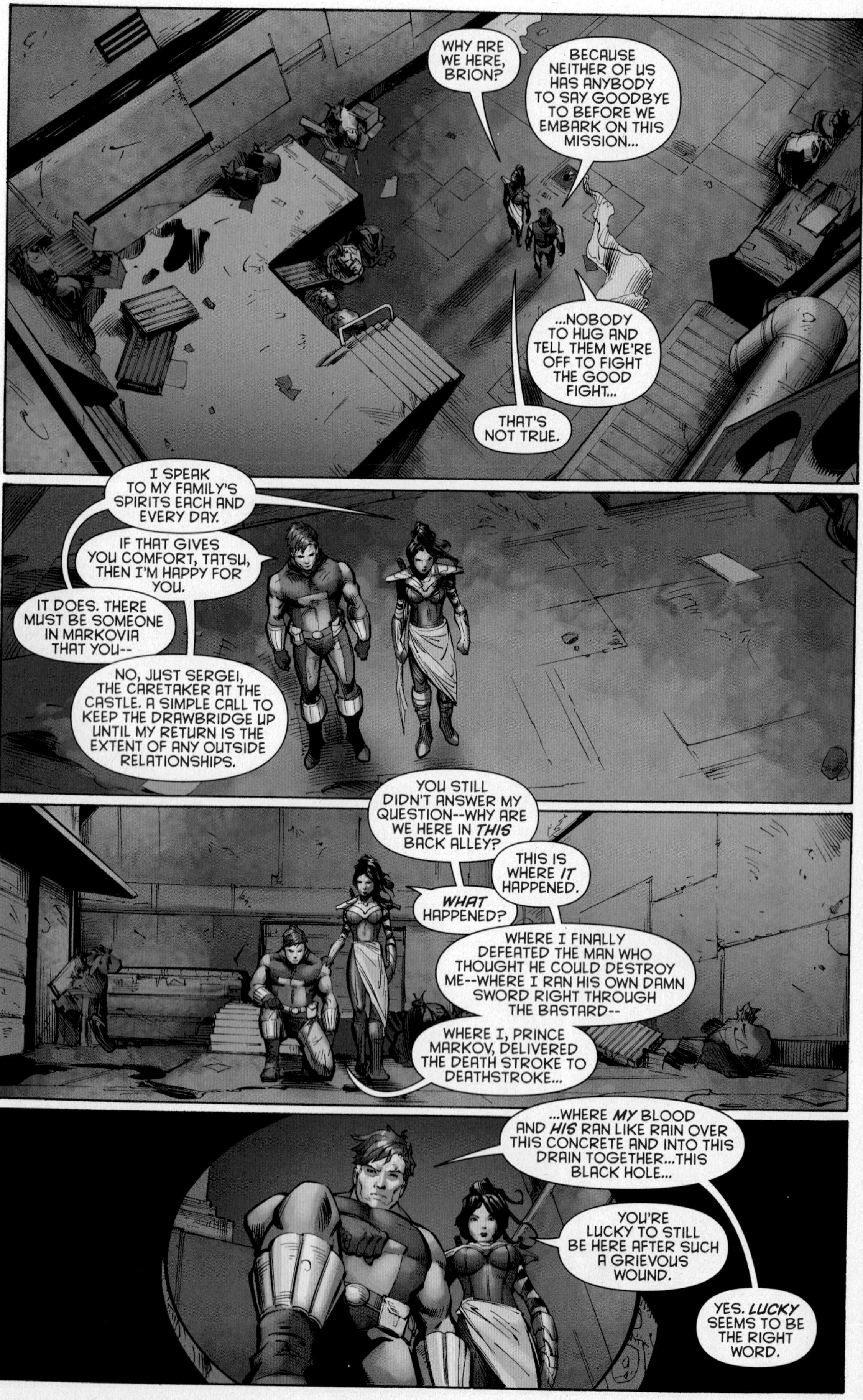
WHY ARE WE HERE, BRION?
BECAUSE NEITHER OF US HAS ANYBODY TO SAY GOODBYE TO BEFORE WE EMBARK ON THIS MISSION...
...NOBODY TO HUG AND TELL THEM WE'RE OFF TO FIGHT THE GOOD FIGHT...
THAT'S NOT TRUE.
I SPEAK TO MY FAMILY'S SPIRITS EACH AND EVERY DAY.
IF THAT GIVES YOU COMFORT, TATSU, THEN I'M HAPPY FOR YOU.
IT DOES. THERE MUST BE SOMEONE IN MARKOVIA THAT YOU--
NO, JUST SERGEI, THE CARETAKER AT THE CASTLE. A SIMPLE CALL TO KEEP THE DRAWBRIDGE UP UNTIL MY RETURN IS THE EXTENT OF ANY OUTSIDE RELATIONSHIPS.
YOU STILL DIDN'T ANSWER MY QUESTION--WHY ARE WE HERE IN *THIS* BACK ALLEY?
THIS IS WHERE *IT* HAPPENED.
WHAT HAPPENED?
WHERE I FINALLY DEFEATED THE MAN WHO THOUGHT HE COULD DESTROY ME--WHERE I RAN HIS OWN DAMN SWORD RIGHT THROUGH THE BASTARD--
WHERE I, PRINCE MARKOV, DELIVERED THE DEATH STROKE TO DEATHSTROKE...
...WHERE *MY* BLOOD AND *HIS* RAN LIKE RAIN OVER THIS CONCRETE AND INTO THIS DRAIN TOGETHER...THIS BLACK HOLE...
YOU'RE LUCKY TO STILL BE HERE AFTER SUCH A GRIEVOUS WOUND.
YES. *LUCKY* SEEMS TO BE THE RIGHT WORD.

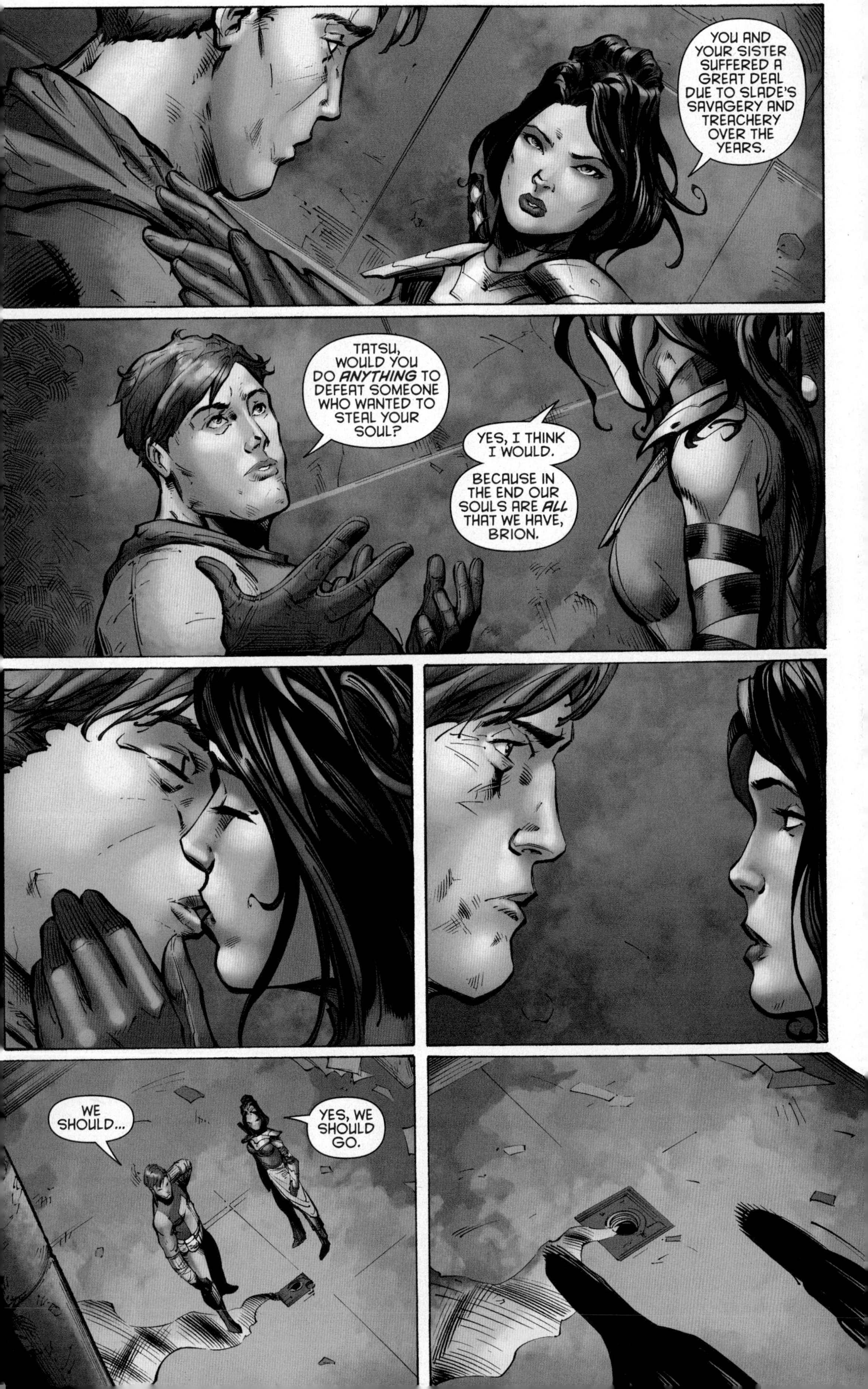
YOU AND YOUR SISTER SUFFERED A GREAT DEAL DUE TO SLADE'S SAVAGERY AND TREACHERY OVER THE YEARS.
TATSU, WOULD YOU DO ANYTHING TO DEFEAT SOMEONE WHO WANTED TO STEAL YOUR SOUL?
YES, I THINK I WOULD.
BECAUSE IN THE END OUR SOULS ARE ALL THAT WE HAVE, BRION.
WE SHOULD...
YES, WE SHOULD GO.

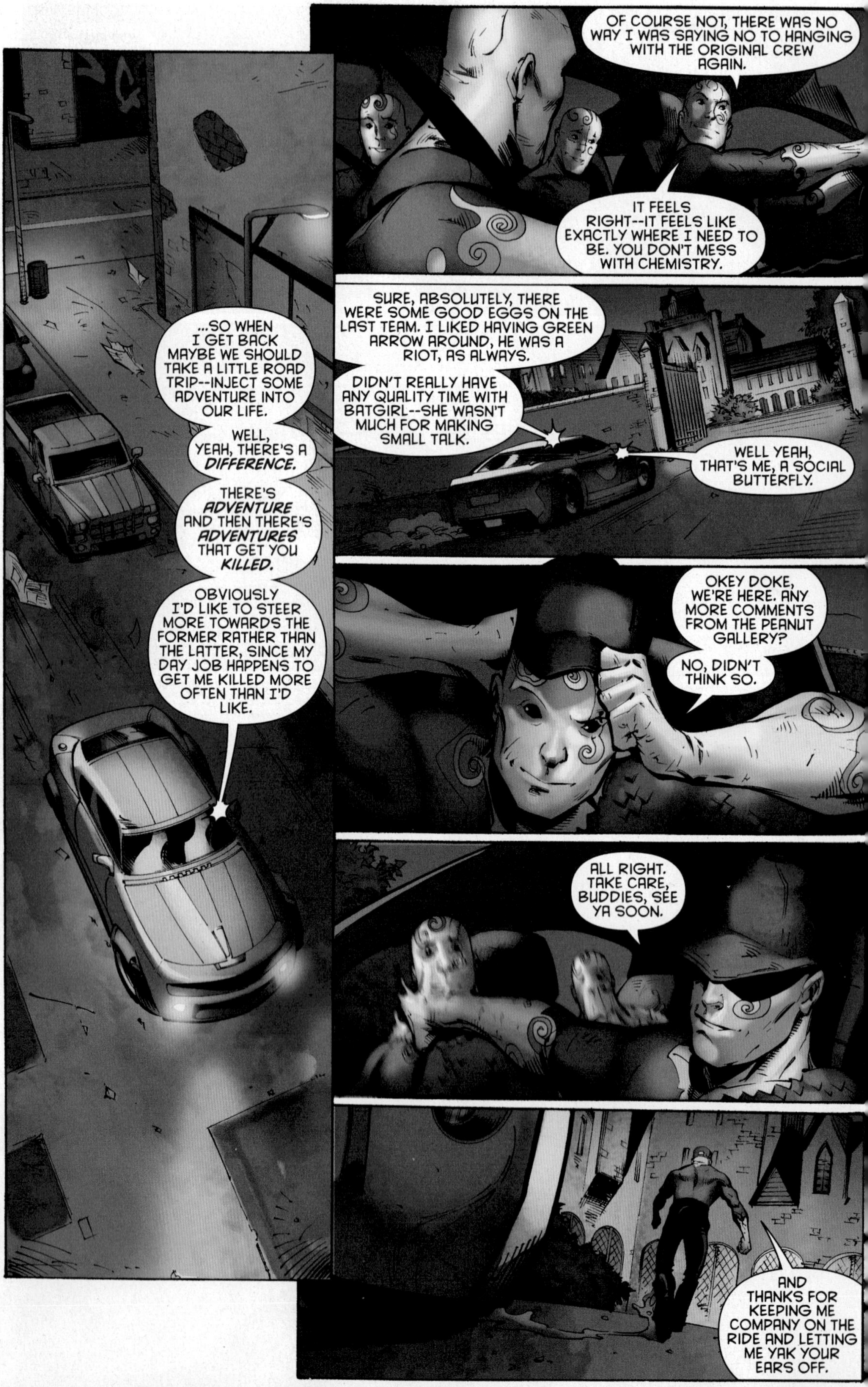
...SO WHEN I GET BACK MAYBE WE SHOULD TAKE A LITTLE ROAD TRIP--INJECT SOME ADVENTURE INTO OUR LIFE.
WELL, YEAH, THERE'S A *DIFFERENCE.*
THERE'S *ADVENTURE* AND THEN THERE'S *ADVENTURES* THAT GET YOU *KILLED.*
OBVIOUSLY I'D LIKE TO STEER MORE TOWARDS THE FORMER RATHER THAN THE LATTER, SINCE MY DAY JOB HAPPENS TO GET ME KILLED MORE OFTEN THAN I'D LIKE.
OF COURSE NOT, THERE WAS NO WAY I WAS SAYING NO TO HANGING WITH THE ORIGINAL CREW AGAIN.
IT FEELS RIGHT--IT FEELS LIKE EXACTLY WHERE I NEED TO BE. YOU DON'T MESS WITH CHEMISTRY.
SURE, ABSOLUTELY, THERE WERE SOME GOOD EGGS ON THE LAST TEAM. I LIKED HAVING GREEN ARROW AROUND, HE WAS A RIOT, AS ALWAYS.
DIDN'T REALLY HAVE ANY QUALITY TIME WITH BATGIRL--SHE WASN'T MUCH FOR MAKING SMALL TALK.
WELL YEAH, THAT'S ME, A SOCIAL BUTTERFLY.
OKEY DOKE, WE'RE HERE. ANY MORE COMMENTS FROM THE PEANUT GALLERY?
NO, DIDN'T THINK SO.
ALL RIGHT. TAKE CARE, BUDDIES, SEE YA SOON.
AND THANKS FOR KEEPING ME COMPANY ON THE RIDE AND LETTING ME YAK YOUR EARS OFF.

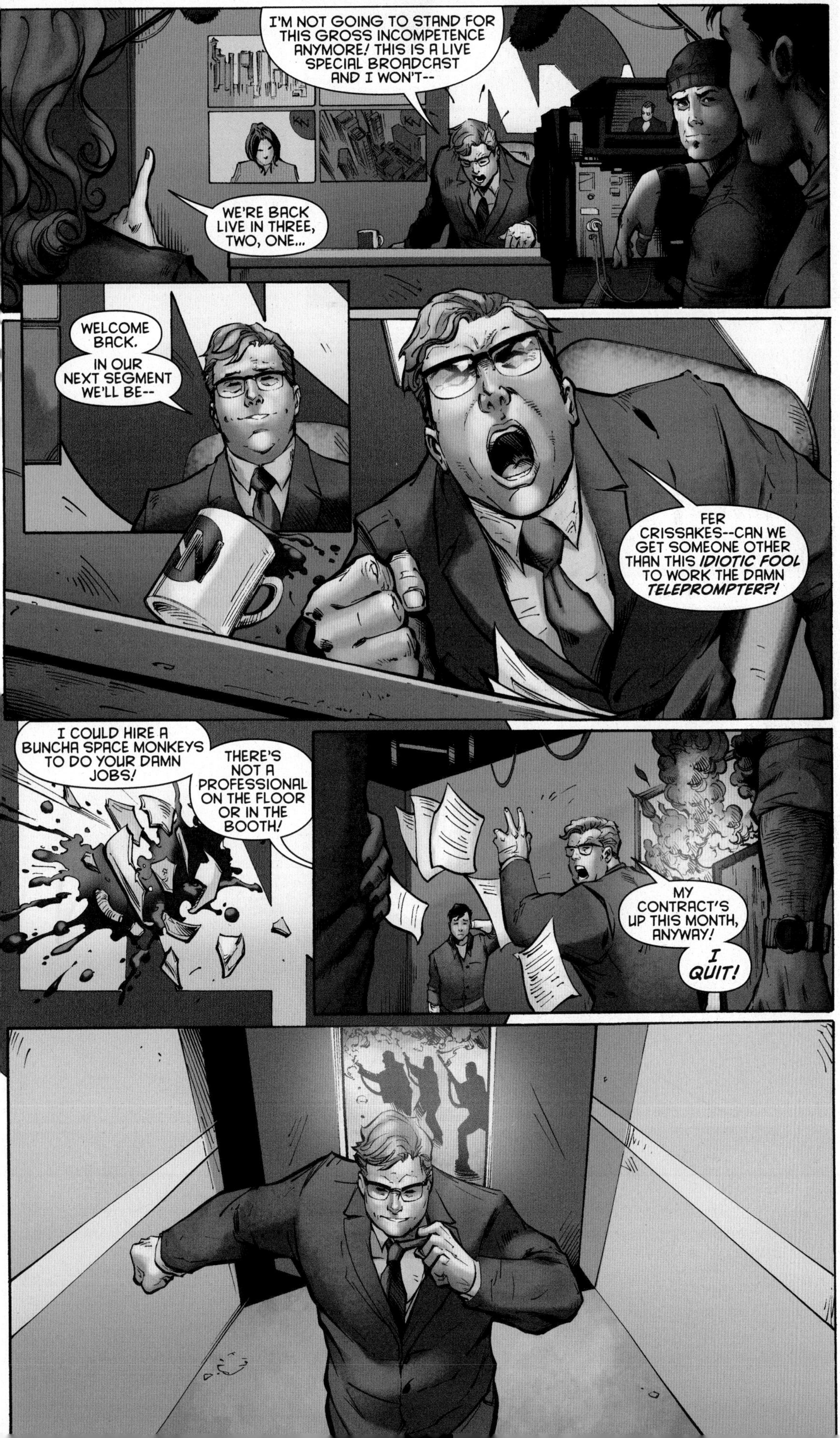
I'M NOT GOING TO STAND FOR THIS GROSS INCOMPETENCE ANYMORE! THIS IS A LIVE SPECIAL BROADCAST AND I WON'T--
WE'RE BACK LIVE IN THREE, TWO, ONE...
WELCOME BACK.
IN OUR NEXT SEGMENT WE'LL BE--
FER CRISSAKES--CAN WE GET SOMEONE OTHER THAN THIS *IDIOTIC FOOL* TO WORK THE DAMN *TELEPROMPTER?!*
I COULD HIRE A BUNCHA SPACE MONKEYS TO DO YOUR DAMN JOBS!
THERE'S NOT A PROFESSIONAL ON THE FLOOR OR IN THE BOOTH!
MY CONTRACT'S UP THIS MONTH, ANYWAY!
I QUIT!

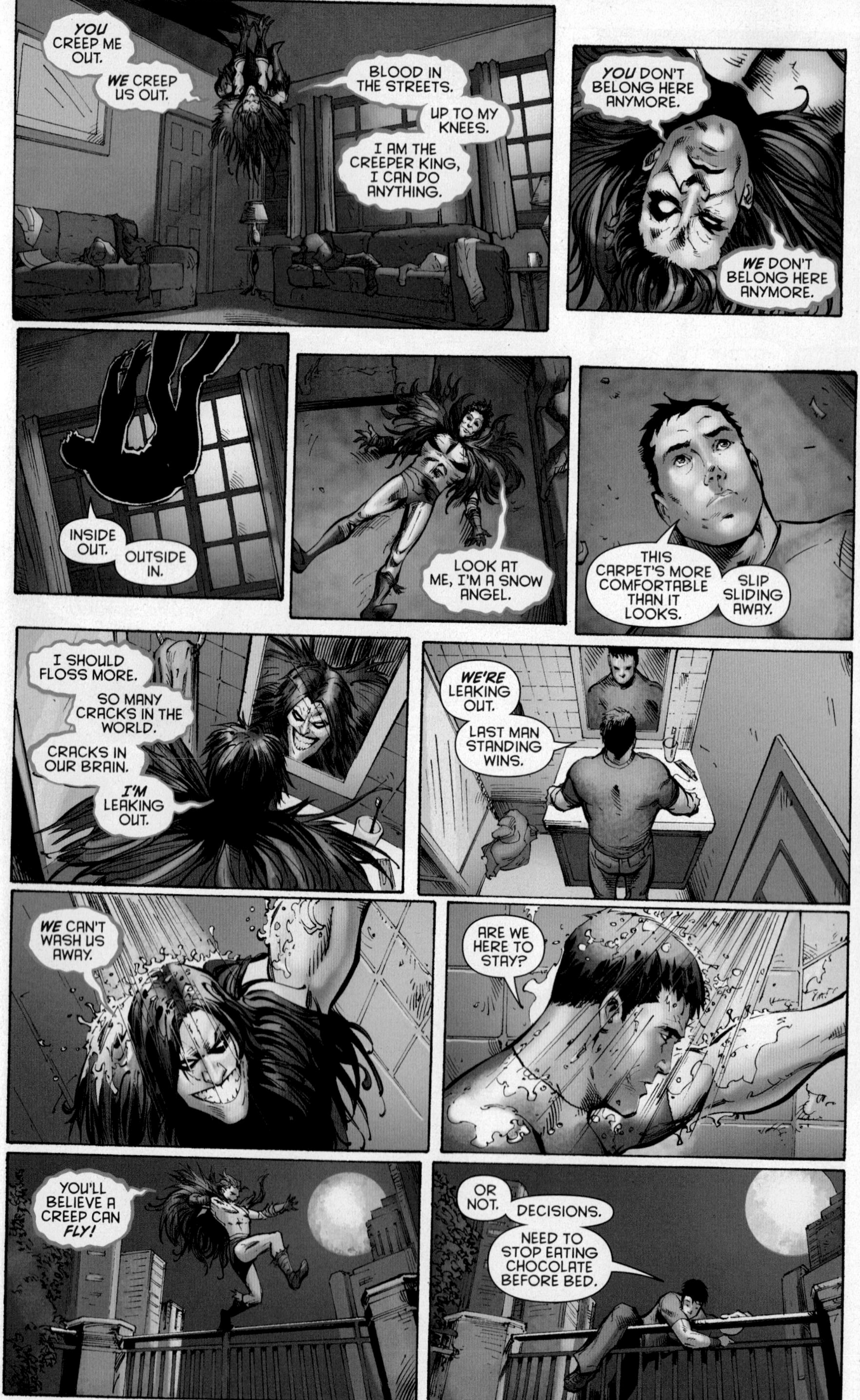

YOU CREEP ME OUT.
WE CREEP US OUT.
BLOOD IN THE STREETS.
UP TO MY KNEES.
I AM THE CREEPER KING, I CAN DO ANYTHING.
YOU DON'T BELONG HERE ANYMORE.
WE DON'T BELONG HERE ANYMORE.
INSIDE OUT.
OUTSIDE IN.
LOOK AT ME, I'M A SNOW ANGEL.
THIS CARPET'S MORE COMFORTABLE THAN IT LOOKS.
SLIP SLIDING AWAY.
I SHOULD FLOSS MORE.
SO MANY CRACKS IN THE WORLD.
CRACKS IN OUR BRAIN.
I'M LEAKING OUT.
WE'RE LEAKING OUT.
LAST MAN STANDING WINS.
WE CAN'T WASH US AWAY.
ARE WE HERE TO STAY?
YOU'LL BELIEVE A CREEP CAN FLY!
OR NOT.
DECISIONS.
NEED TO STOP EATING CHOCOLATE BEFORE BED.

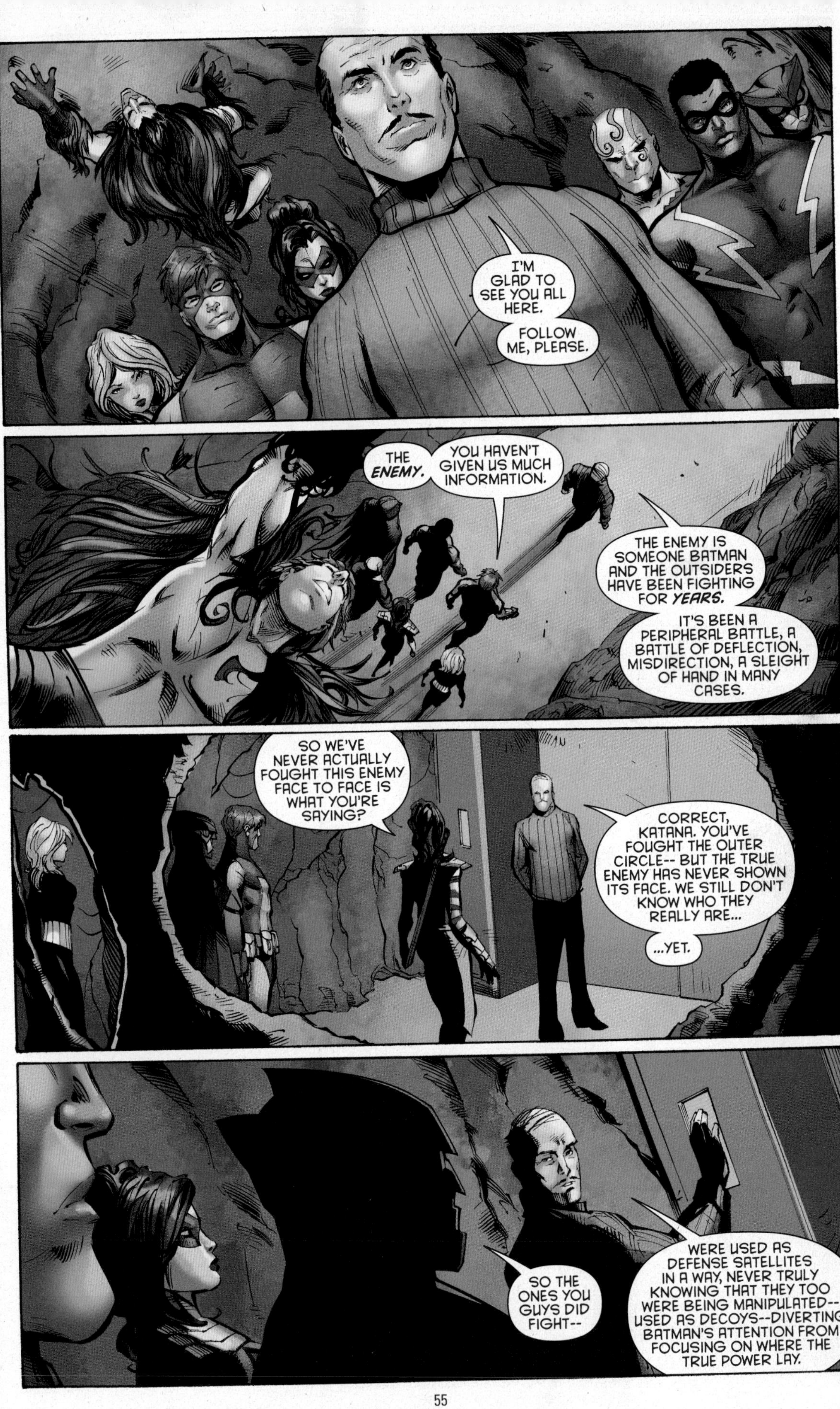

I'M GLAD TO SEE YOU ALL HERE.
FOLLOW ME, PLEASE.
THE *ENEMY.*
YOU HAVEN'T GIVEN US MUCH INFORMATION.
THE ENEMY IS SOMEONE BATMAN AND THE OUTSIDERS HAVE BEEN FIGHTING FOR *YEARS.*
IT'S BEEN A PERIPHERAL BATTLE, A BATTLE OF DEFLECTION, MISDIRECTION, A SLEIGHT OF HAND IN MANY CASES.
SO WE'VE NEVER ACTUALLY FOUGHT THIS ENEMY FACE TO FACE IS WHAT YOU'RE SAYING?
CORRECT, KATANA. YOU'VE FOUGHT THE OUTER CIRCLE-- BUT THE TRUE ENEMY HAS NEVER SHOWN ITS FACE. WE STILL DON'T KNOW WHO THEY REALLY ARE...
...YET.
SO THE ONES YOU GUYS DID FIGHT--
WERE USED AS DEFENSE SATELLITES IN A WAY, NEVER TRULY KNOWING THAT THEY TOO WERE BEING MANIPULATED-- USED AS DECOYS--DIVERTING BATMAN'S ATTENTION FROM FOCUSING ON WHERE THE TRUE POWER LAY.

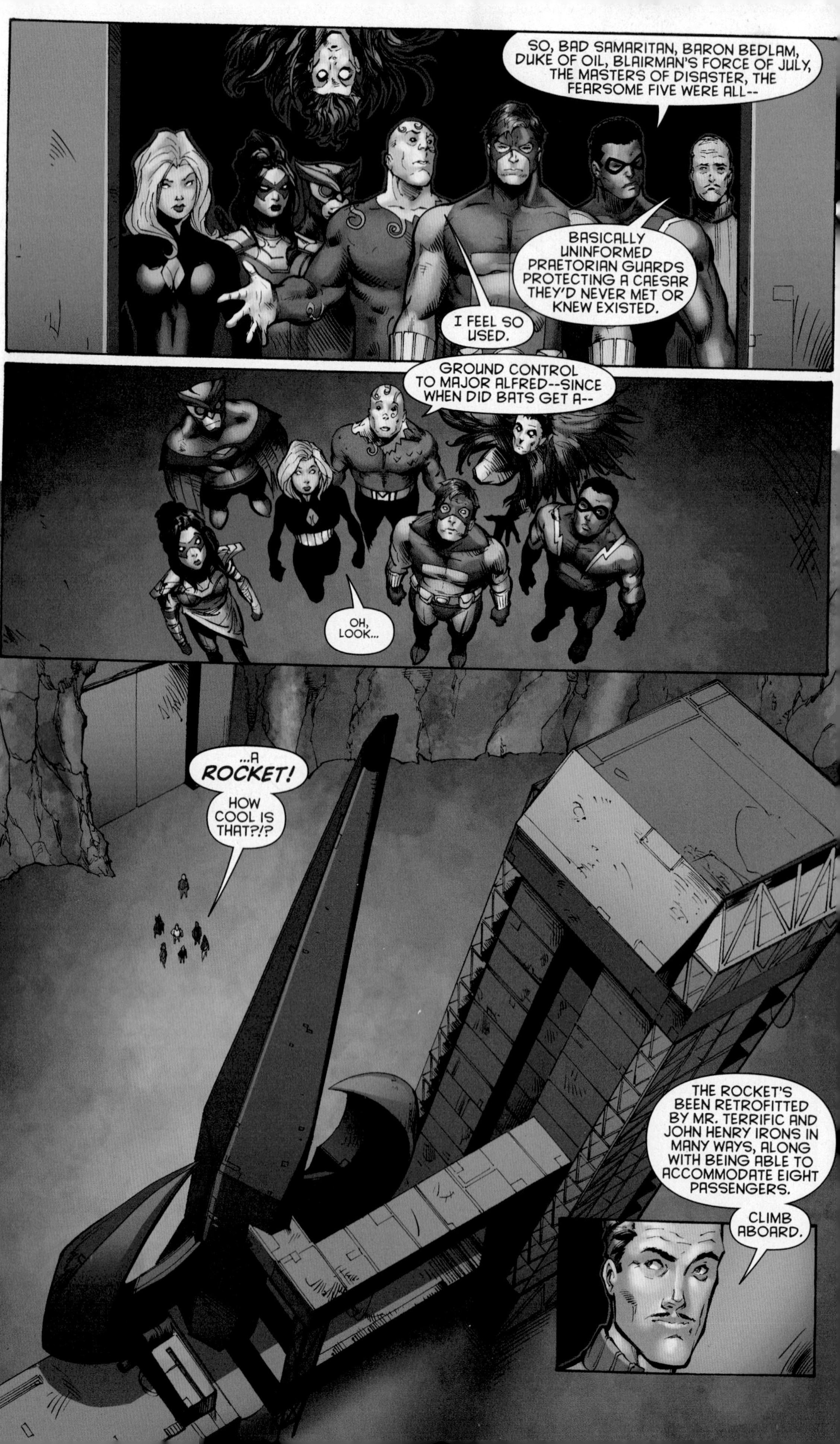
SO, BAD SAMARITAN, BARON BEDLAM, DUKE OF OIL, BLAIRMAN'S FORCE OF JULY, THE MASTERS OF DISASTER, THE FEARSOME FIVE WERE ALL--
BASICALLY UNINFORMED PRAETORIAN GUARDS PROTECTING A CAESAR THEY'D NEVER MET OR KNEW EXISTED.
I FEEL SO USED.
GROUND CONTROL TO MAJOR ALFRED--SINCE WHEN DID BATS GET A--
OH, LOOK...
...A ROCKET! HOW COOL IS THAT?!?
THE ROCKET'S BEEN RETROFITTED BY MR. TERRIFIC AND JOHN HENRY IRONS IN MANY WAYS, ALONG WITH BEING ABLE TO ACCOMMODATE EIGHT PASSENGERS.
CLIMB ABOARD.

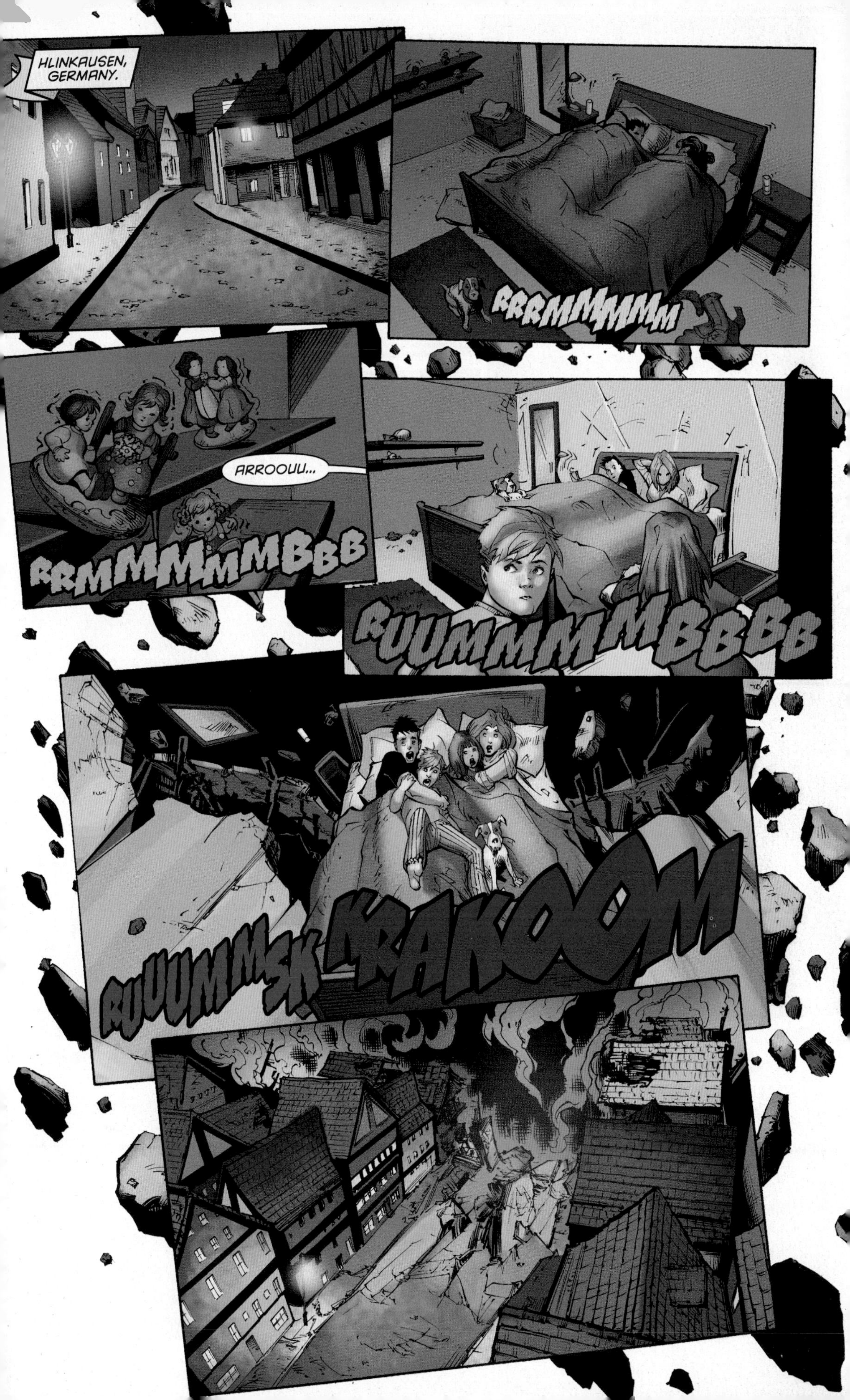
HLINKAUSEN, GERMANY.
RRRMMMMMM
ARROOUU...
RRMMMMMMBBB
RUUMMMMBBBB
RUUUMMSK KRAKOOM

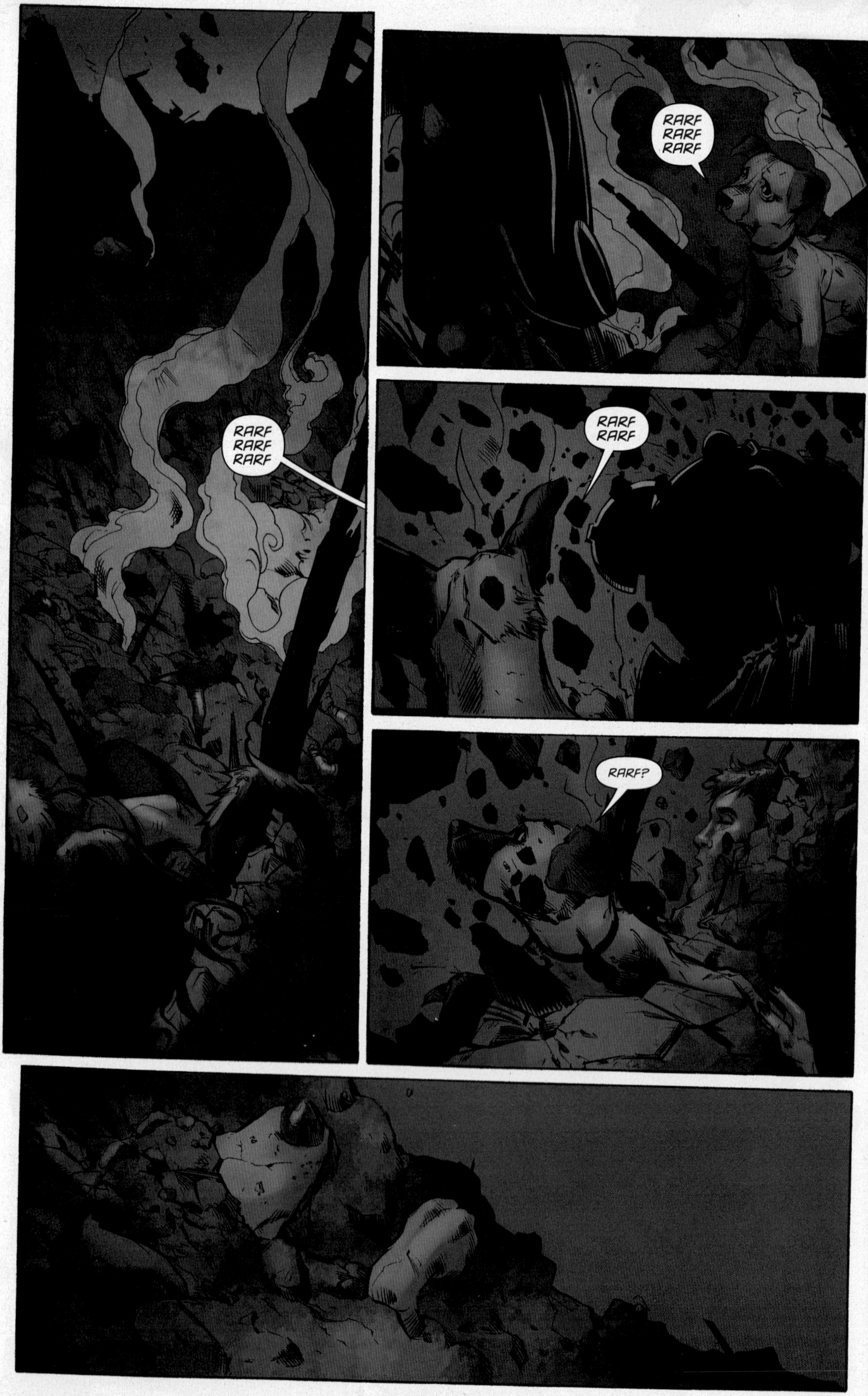
RARF RARF RARF
RARF RARF RARF
RARF RARF
RARF?

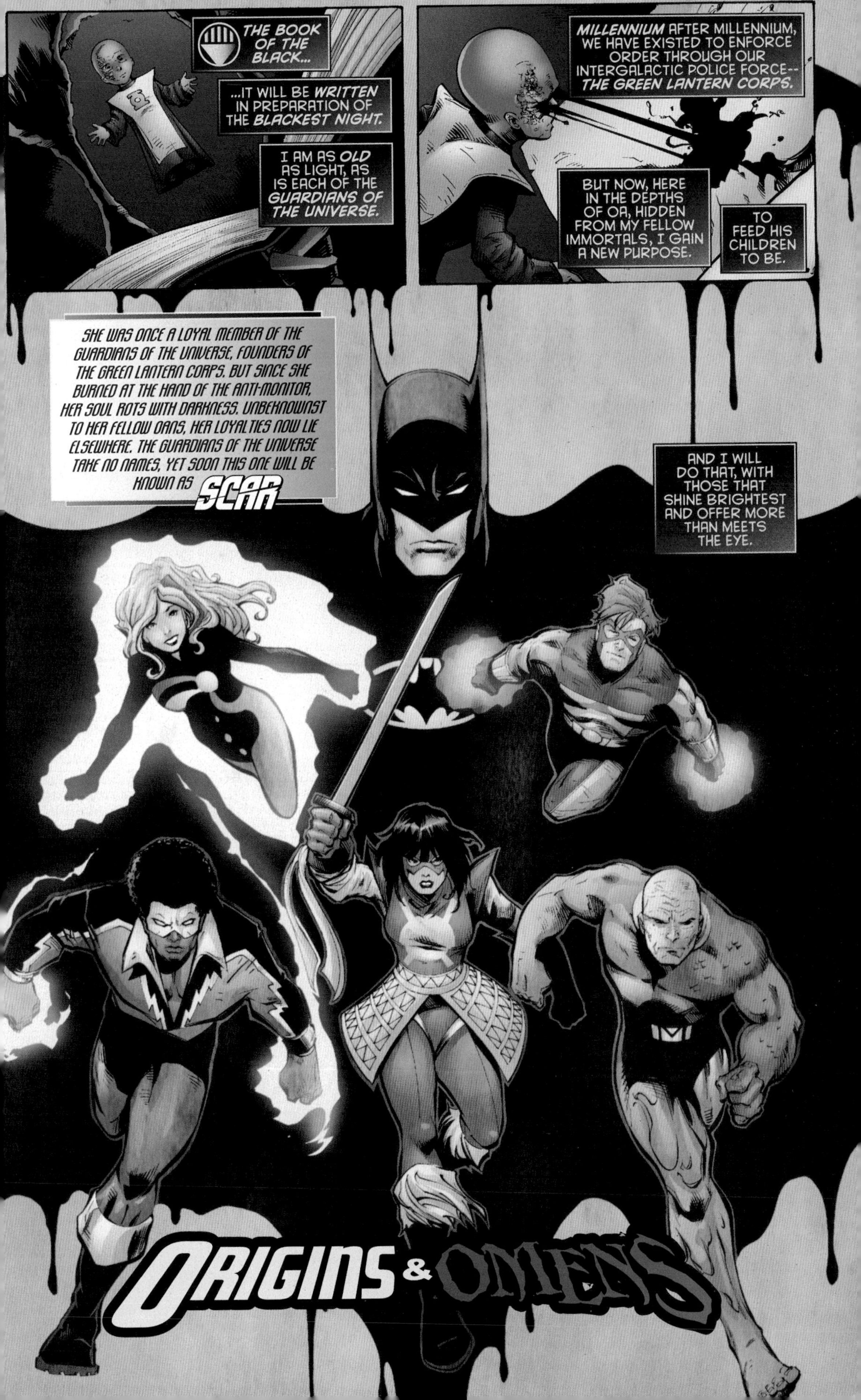
THE BOOK OF THE BLACK...
...IT WILL BE WRITTEN IN PREPARATION OF THE BLACKEST NIGHT.
I AM AS OLD AS LIGHT, AS IS EACH OF THE GUARDIANS OF THE UNIVERSE.
MILLENNIUM AFTER MILLENNIUM, WE HAVE EXISTED TO ENFORCE ORDER THROUGH OUR INTERGALACTIC POLICE FORCE-- THE GREEN LANTERN CORPS.
BUT NOW, HERE IN THE DEPTHS OF OA, HIDDEN FROM MY FELLOW IMMORTALS, I GAIN A NEW PURPOSE.
TO FEED HIS CHILDREN TO BE.
SHE WAS ONCE A LOYAL MEMBER OF THE GUARDIANS OF THE UNIVERSE, FOUNDERS OF THE GREEN LANTERN CORPS. BUT SINCE SHE BURNED AT THE HAND OF THE ANTI-MONITOR, HER SOUL ROTS WITH DARKNESS. UNBEKNOWNST TO HER FELLOW OANS, HER LOYALTIES NOW LIE ELSEWHERE. THE GUARDIANS OF THE UNIVERSE TAKE NO NAMES, YET SOON THIS ONE WILL BE KNOWN AS SCAR
AND I WILL DO THAT, WITH THOSE THAT SHINE BRIGHTEST AND OFFER MORE THAN MEETS THE EYE.
ORIGINS & OMENS

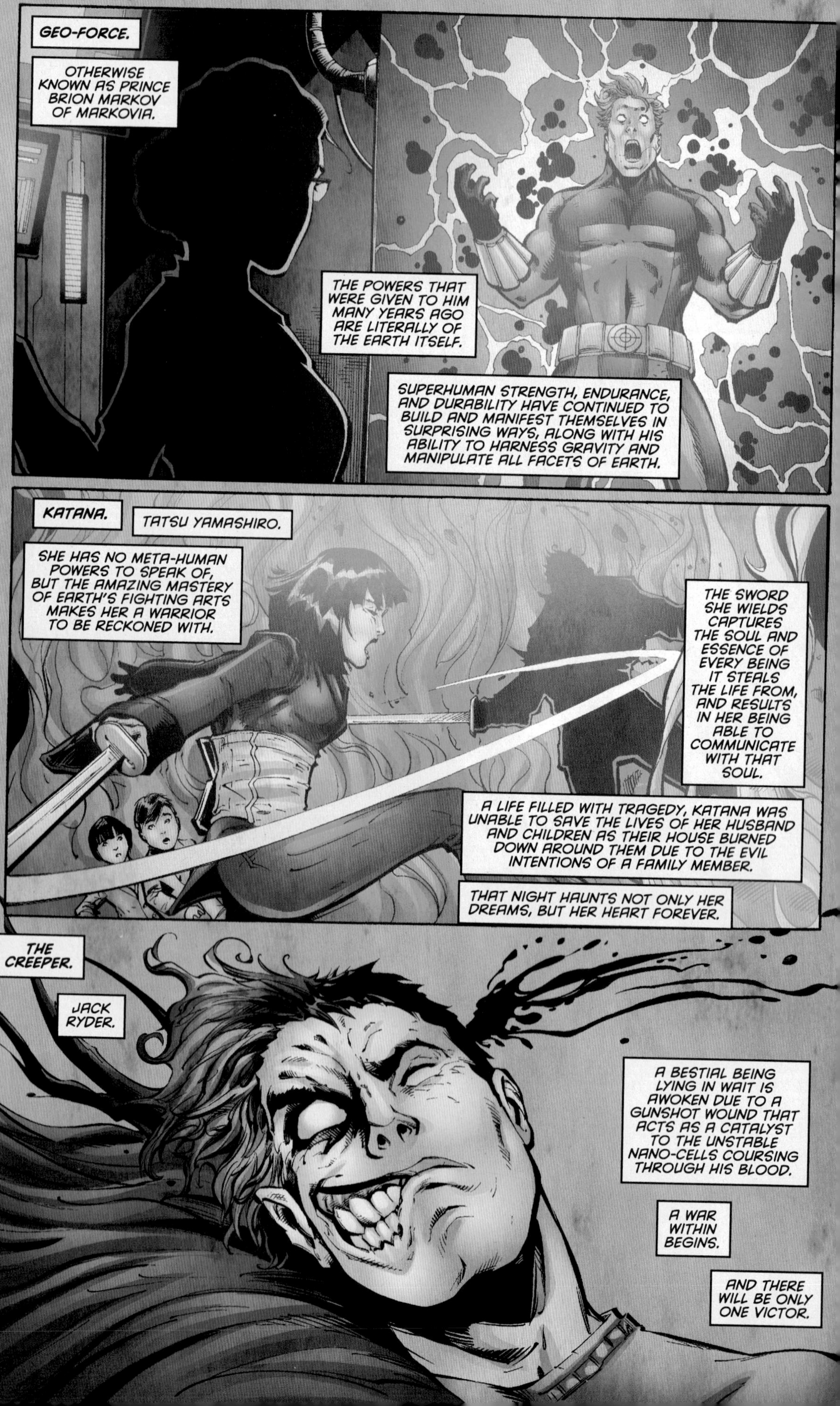
GEO-FORCE.
OTHERWISE KNOWN AS PRINCE BRION MARKOV OF MARKOVIA.
THE POWERS THAT WERE GIVEN TO HIM MANY YEARS AGO ARE LITERALLY OF THE EARTH ITSELF.
SUPERHUMAN STRENGTH, ENDURANCE, AND DURABILITY HAVE CONTINUED TO BUILD AND MANIFEST THEMSELVES IN SURPRISING WAYS, ALONG WITH HIS ABILITY TO HARNESS GRAVITY AND MANIPULATE ALL FACETS OF EARTH.
KATANA.
TATSU YAMASHIRO.
SHE HAS NO META-HUMAN POWERS TO SPEAK OF, BUT THE AMAZING MASTERY OF EARTH'S FIGHTING ARTS MAKES HER A WARRIOR TO BE RECKONED WITH.
THE SWORD SHE WIELDS CAPTURES THE SOUL AND ESSENCE OF EVERY BEING IT STEALS THE LIFE FROM, AND RESULTS IN HER BEING ABLE TO COMMUNICATE WITH THAT SOUL.
A LIFE FILLED WITH TRAGEDY, KATANA WAS UNABLE TO SAVE THE LIVES OF HER HUSBAND AND CHILDREN AS THEIR HOUSE BURNED DOWN AROUND THEM DUE TO THE EVIL INTENTIONS OF A FAMILY MEMBER.
THAT NIGHT HAUNTS NOT ONLY HER DREAMS, BUT HER HEART FOREVER.
THE CREEPER.
JACK RYDER.
A BESTIAL BEING LYING IN WAIT IS AWOKEN DUE TO A GUNSHOT WOUND THAT ACTS AS A CATALYST TO THE UNSTABLE NANO-CELLS COURSING THROUGH HIS BLOOD.
A WAR WITHIN BEGINS.
AND THERE WILL BE ONLY ONE VICTOR.

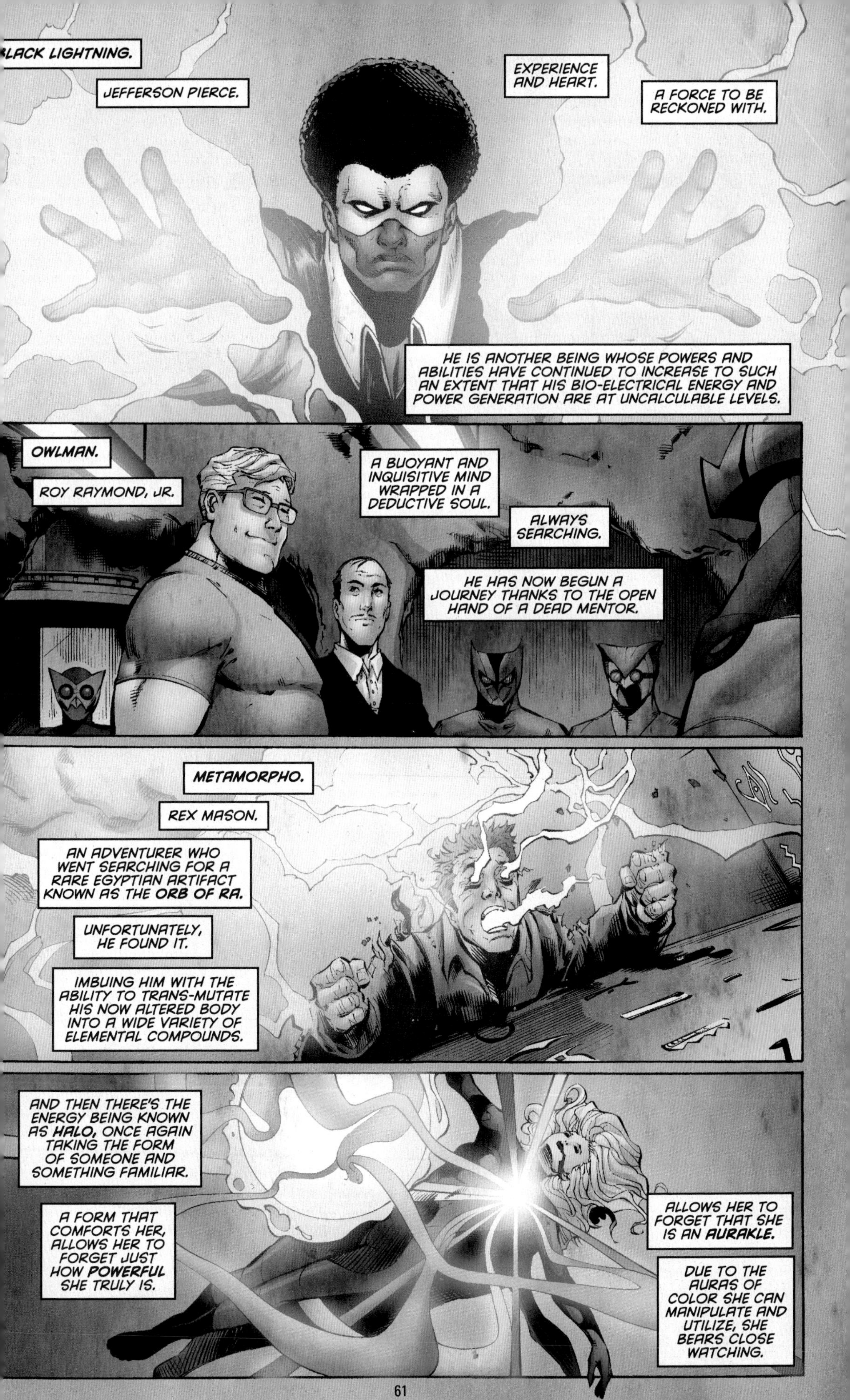
BLACK LIGHTNING.
JEFFERSON PIERCE.
EXPERIENCE AND HEART.
A FORCE TO BE RECKONED WITH.
HE IS ANOTHER BEING WHOSE POWERS AND ABILITIES HAVE CONTINUED TO INCREASE TO SUCH AN EXTENT THAT HIS BIO-ELECTRICAL ENERGY AND POWER GENERATION ARE AT UNCALCULABLE LEVELS.
OWLMAN.
ROY RAYMOND, JR.
A BUOYANT AND INQUISITIVE MIND WRAPPED IN A DEDUCTIVE SOUL.
ALWAYS SEARCHING.
HE HAS NOW BEGUN A JOURNEY THANKS TO THE OPEN HAND OF A DEAD MENTOR.
METAMORPHO.
REX MASON.
AN ADVENTURER WHO WENT SEARCHING FOR A RARE EGYPTIAN ARTIFACT KNOWN AS THE ORB OF RA.
UNFORTUNATELY, HE FOUND IT.
IMBUING HIM WITH THE ABILITY TO TRANS-MUTATE HIS NOW ALTERED BODY INTO A WIDE VARIETY OF ELEMENTAL COMPOUNDS.
AND THEN THERE'S THE ENERGY BEING KNOWN AS HALO, ONCE AGAIN TAKING THE FORM OF SOMEONE AND SOMETHING FAMILIAR.
A FORM THAT COMFORTS HER, ALLOWS HER TO FORGET JUST HOW POWERFUL SHE TRULY IS.
ALLOWS HER TO FORGET THAT SHE IS AN AURAKLE.
DUE TO THE AURAS OF COLOR SHE CAN MANIPULATE AND UTILIZE, SHE BEARS CLOSE WATCHING.

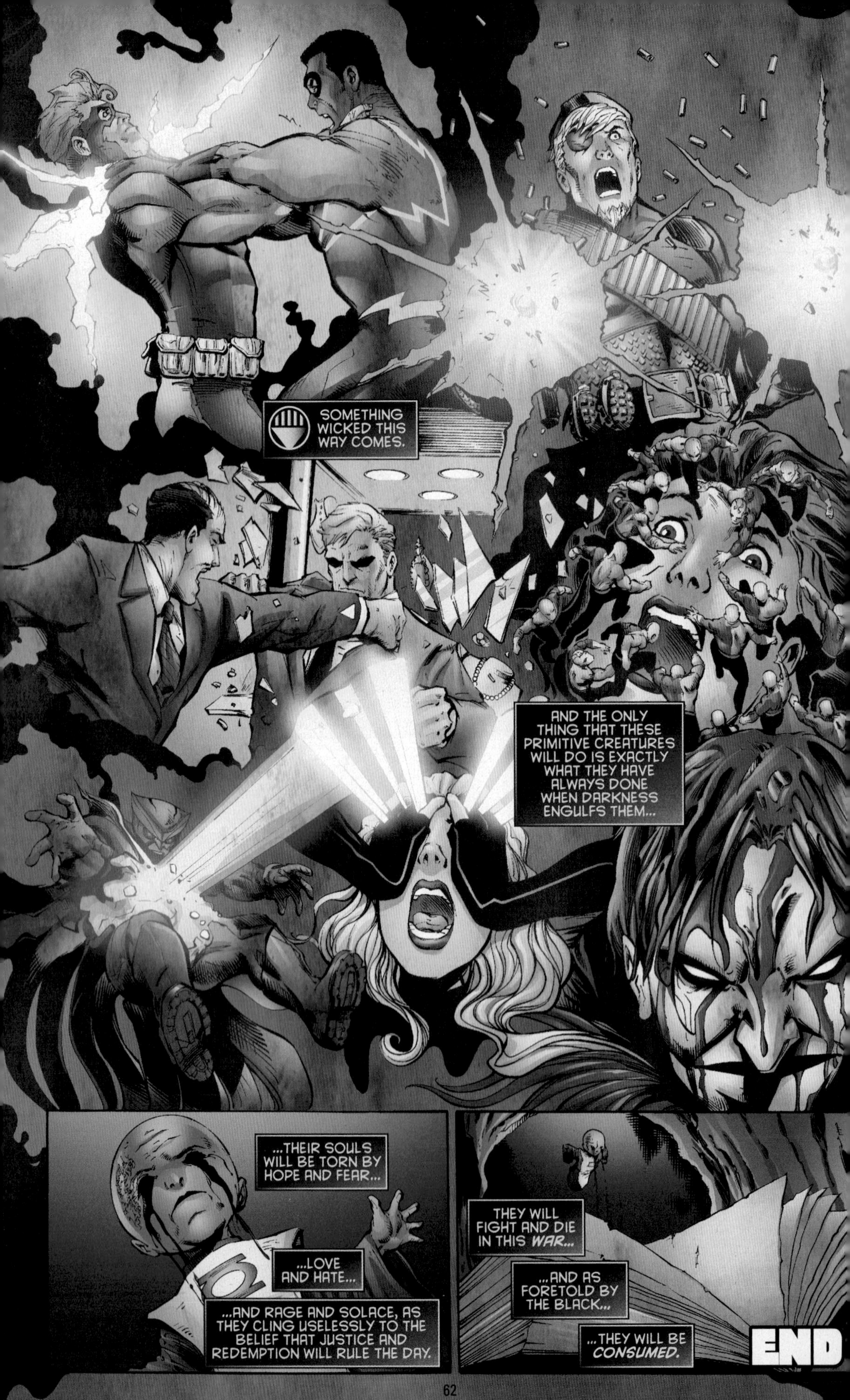
SOMETHING WICKED THIS WAY COMES.
AND THE ONLY THING THAT THESE PRIMITIVE CREATURES WILL DO IS EXACTLY WHAT THEY HAVE ALWAYS DONE WHEN DARKNESS ENGULFS THEM...
...THEIR SOULS WILL BE TORN BY HOPE AND FEAR...
...LOVE AND HATE...
...AND RAGE AND SOLACE, AS THEY CLING USELESSLY TO THE BELIEF THAT JUSTICE AND REDEMPTION WILL RULE THE DAY.
THEY WILL FIGHT AND DIE IN THIS *WAR*...
...AND AS FORETOLD BY THE BLACK...
...THEY WILL BE *CONSUMED.*
END

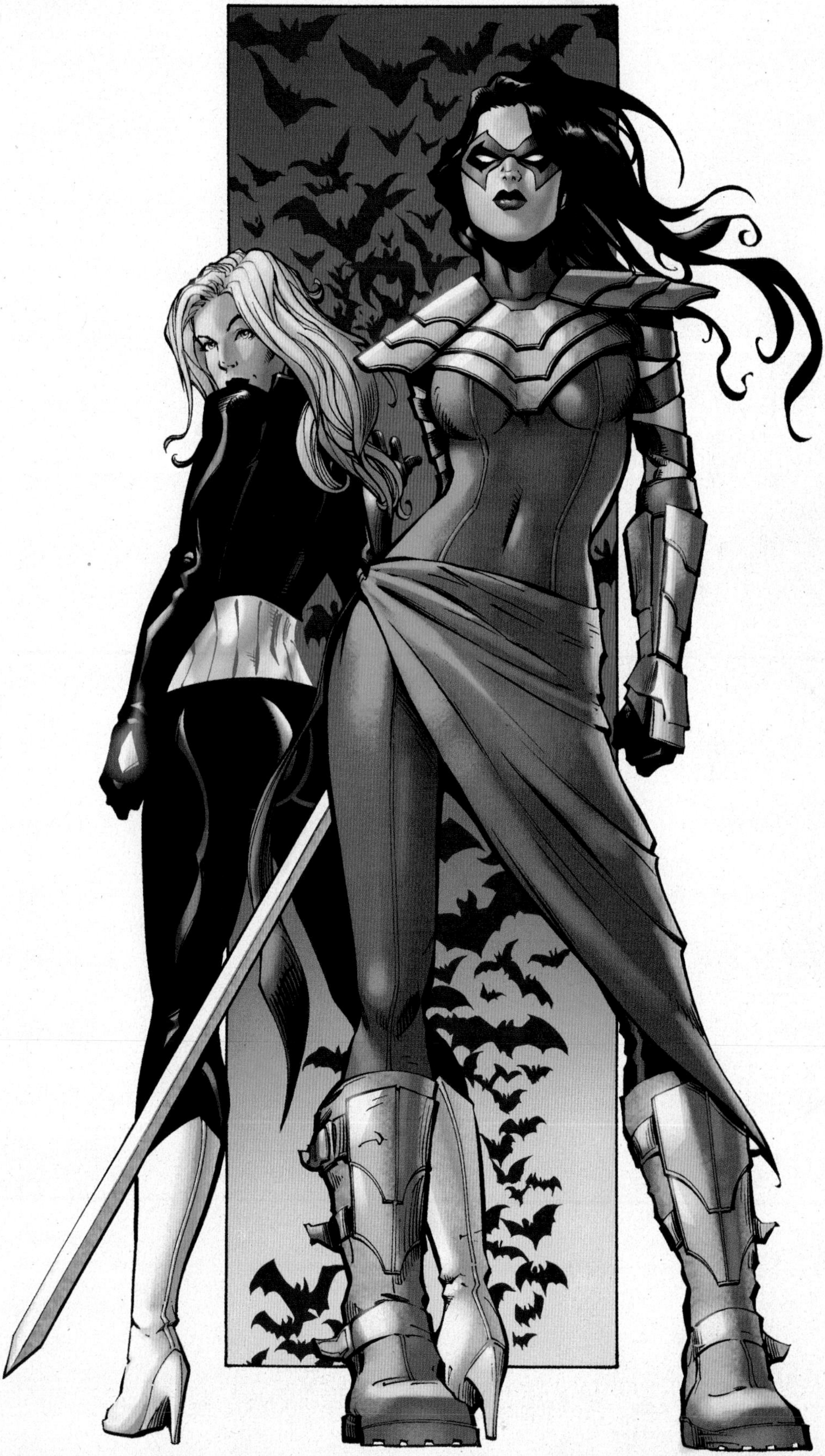

"Do not dwell on the past, my friends.
Do not dream of the future."

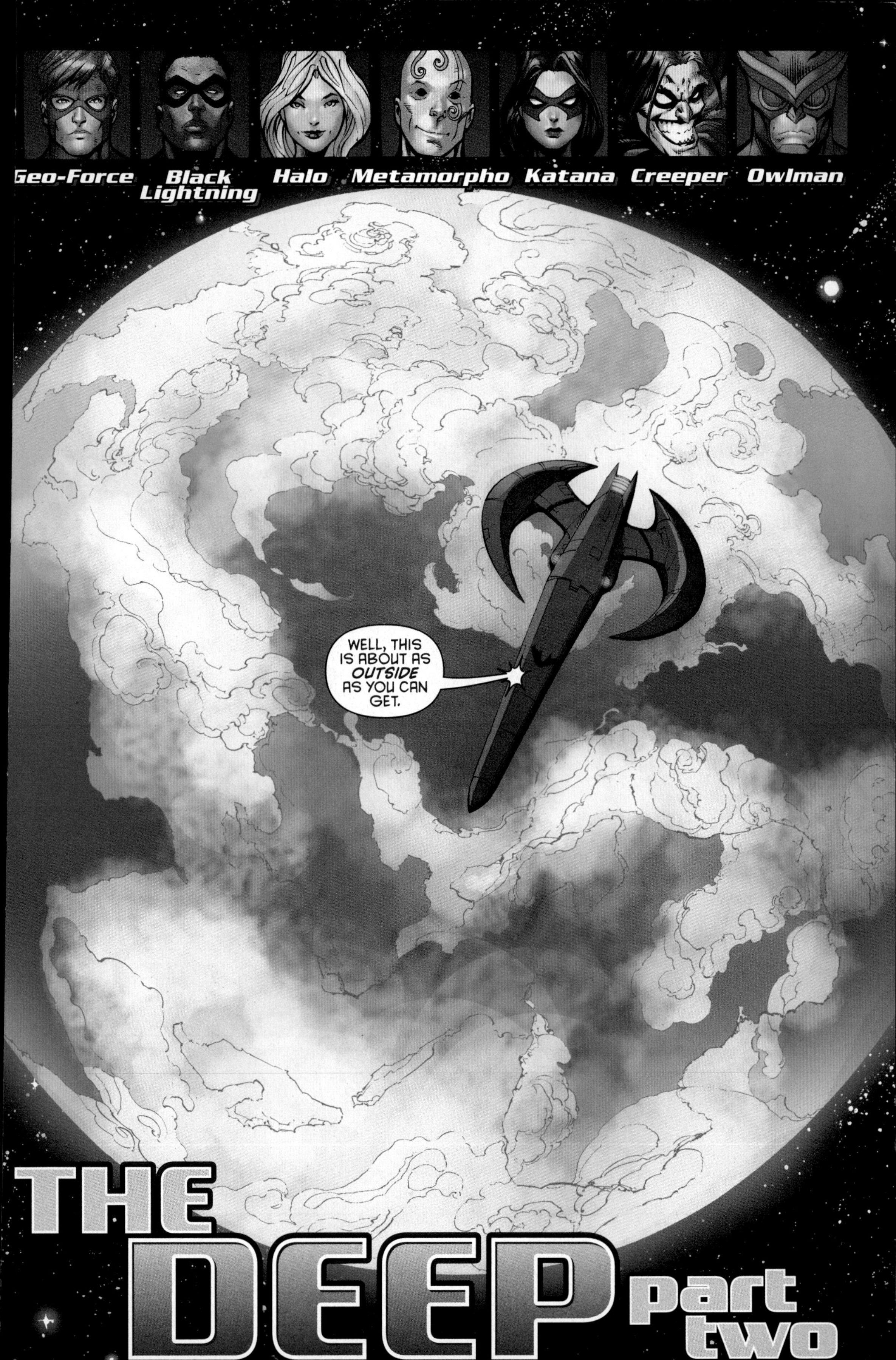
Geo-Force
Black Lightning
Halo
Metamorpho
Katana
Creeper
Owlman
WELL, THIS IS ABOUT AS OUTSIDE AS YOU CAN GET.
THE DEEP part two

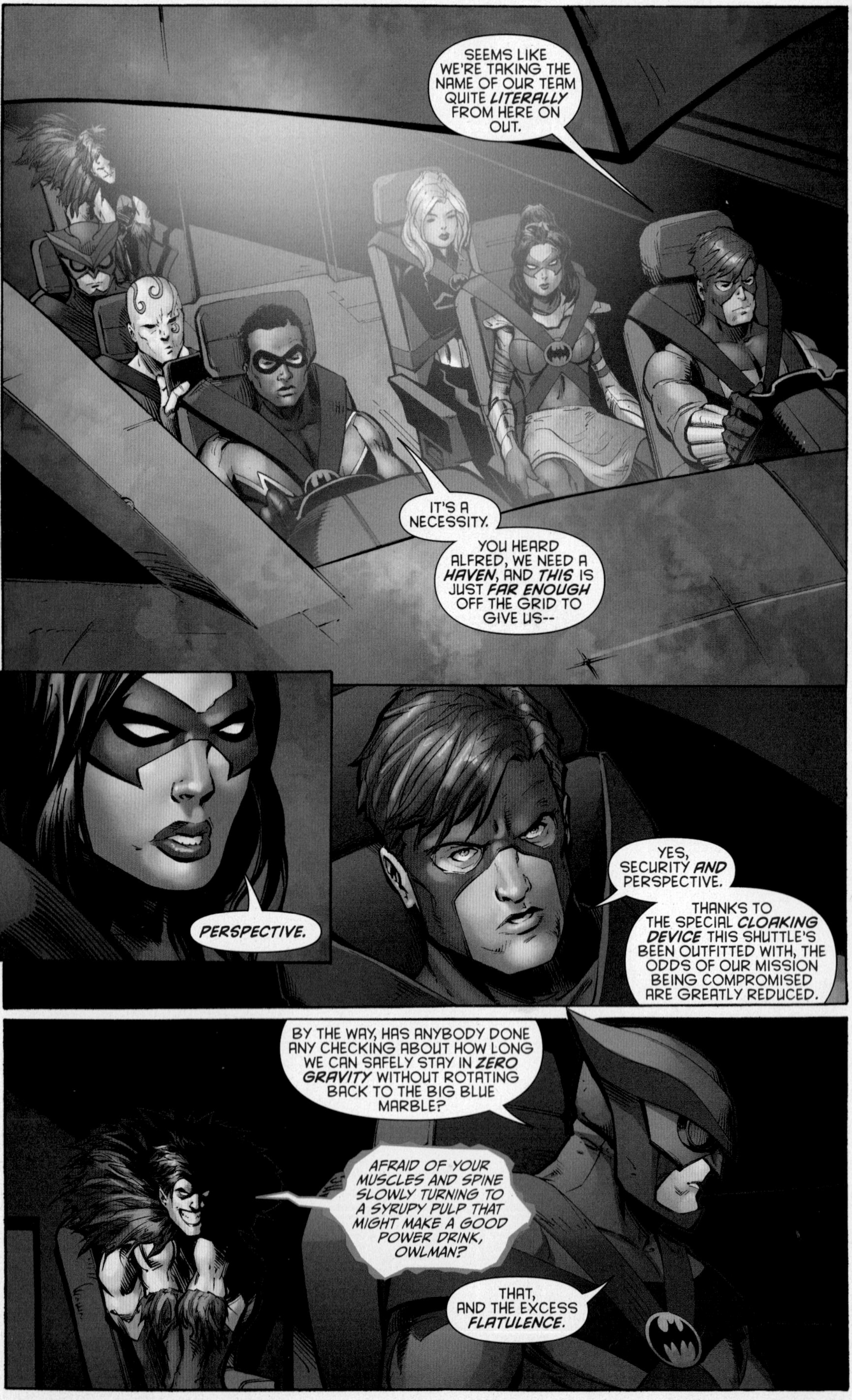
SEEMS LIKE WE'RE TAKING THE NAME OF OUR TEAM QUITE *LITERALLY* FROM HERE ON OUT.
IT'S A NECESSITY.
YOU HEARD ALFRED, WE NEED A *HAVEN*, AND *THIS* IS JUST *FAR ENOUGH* OFF THE GRID TO GIVE US--
PERSPECTIVE.
YES, SECURITY *AND* PERSPECTIVE.
THANKS TO THE SPECIAL *CLOAKING DEVICE* THIS SHUTTLE'S BEEN OUTFITTED WITH, THE ODDS OF OUR MISSION BEING COMPROMISED ARE GREATLY REDUCED.
BY THE WAY, HAS ANYBODY DONE ANY CHECKING ABOUT HOW LONG WE CAN SAFELY STAY IN *ZERO GRAVITY* WITHOUT ROTATING BACK TO THE BIG BLUE MARBLE?
AFRAID OF YOUR MUSCLES AND SPINE SLOWLY TURNING TO A SYRUPY PULP THAT MIGHT MAKE A GOOD POWER DRINK, OWLMAN?
THAT, AND THE EXCESS *FLATULENCE*.

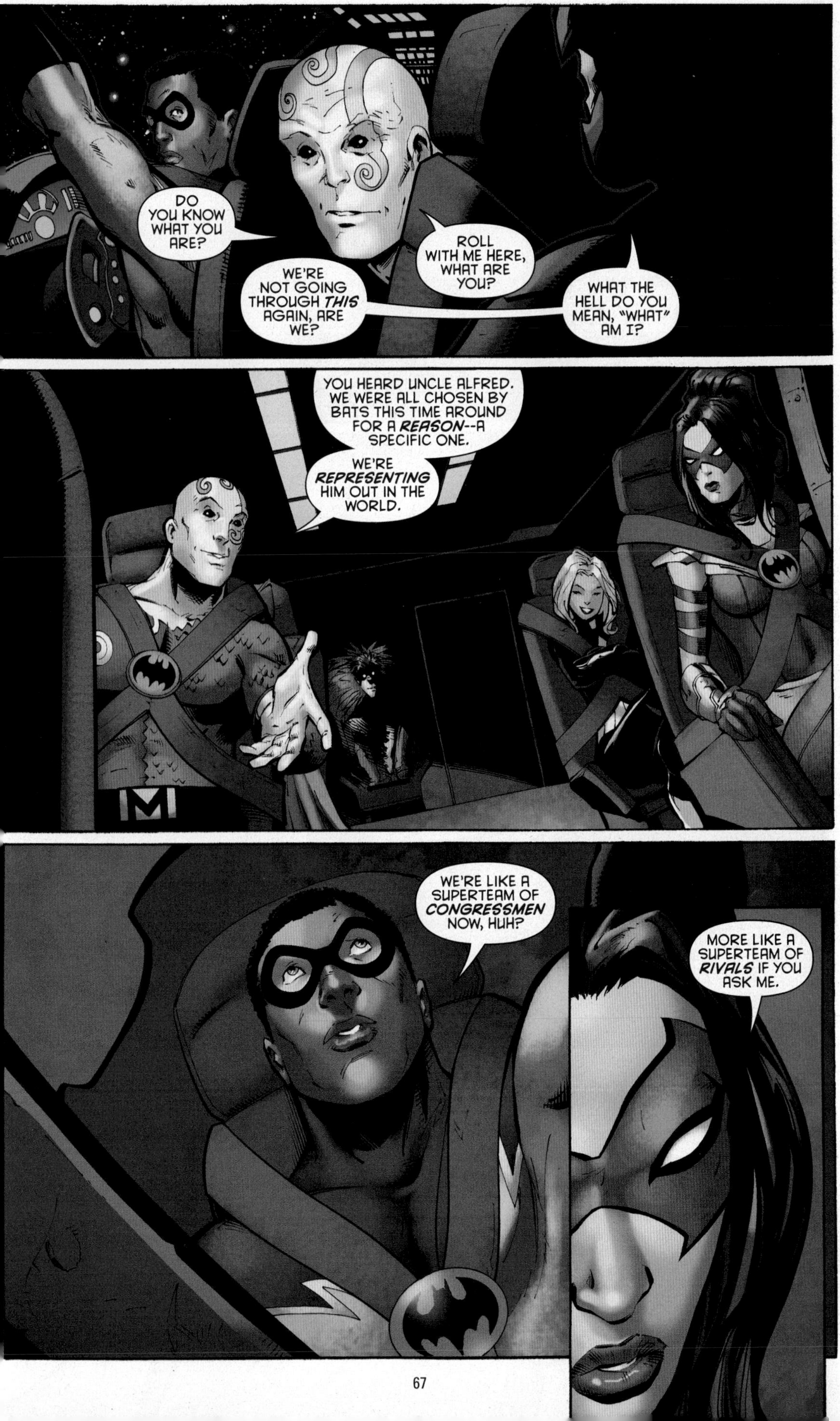
DO YOU KNOW WHAT YOU ARE?
WE'RE NOT GOING THROUGH *THIS* AGAIN, ARE WE?
ROLL WITH ME HERE, WHAT ARE YOU?
WHAT THE HELL DO YOU MEAN, "WHAT" AM I?
YOU HEARD UNCLE ALFRED. WE WERE ALL CHOSEN BY BATS THIS TIME AROUND FOR A *REASON*--A SPECIFIC ONE.
WE'RE *REPRESENTING* HIM OUT IN THE WORLD.
WE'RE LIKE A SUPERTEAM OF *CONGRESSMEN* NOW, HUH?
MORE LIKE A SUPERTEAM OF *RIVALS* IF YOU ASK ME.

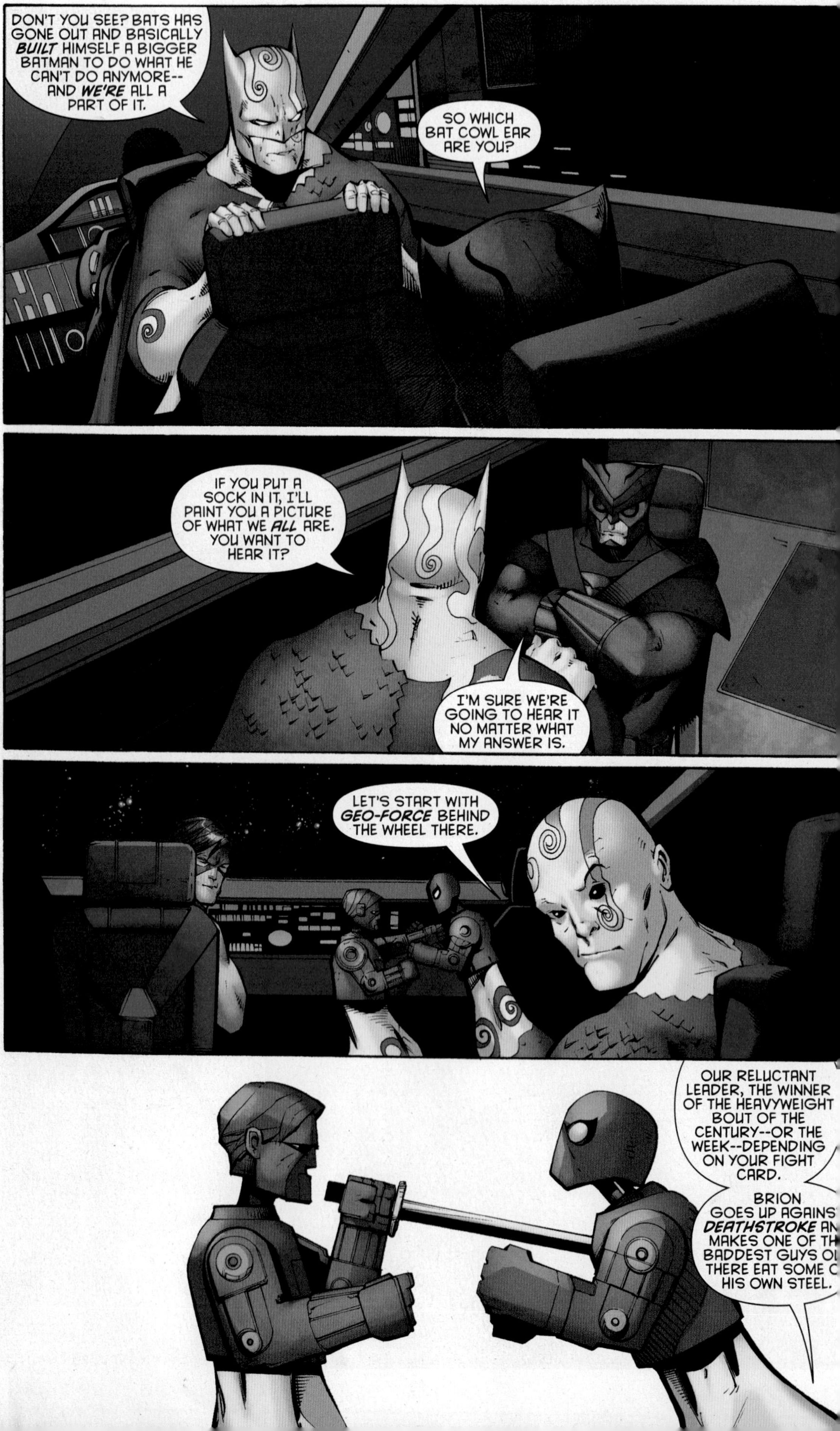
DON'T YOU SEE? BATS HAS GONE OUT AND BASICALLY *BUILT* HIMSELF A BIGGER BATMAN TO DO WHAT HE CAN'T DO ANYMORE-- AND *WE'RE* ALL A PART OF IT.
SO WHICH BAT COWL EAR ARE YOU?
IF YOU PUT A SOCK IN IT, I'LL PAINT YOU A PICTURE OF WHAT WE *ALL* ARE. YOU WANT TO HEAR IT?
I'M SURE WE'RE GOING TO HEAR IT NO MATTER WHAT MY ANSWER IS.
LET'S START WITH *GEO-FORCE* BEHIND THE WHEEL THERE.
OUR RELUCTANT LEADER, THE WINNER OF THE HEAVYWEIGHT BOUT OF THE CENTURY--OR THE WEEK--DEPENDING ON YOUR FIGHT CARD.
BRION GOES UP AGAINS *DEATHSTROKE* AN MAKES ONE OF TH BADDEST GUYS O THERE EAT SOME C HIS OWN STEEL.

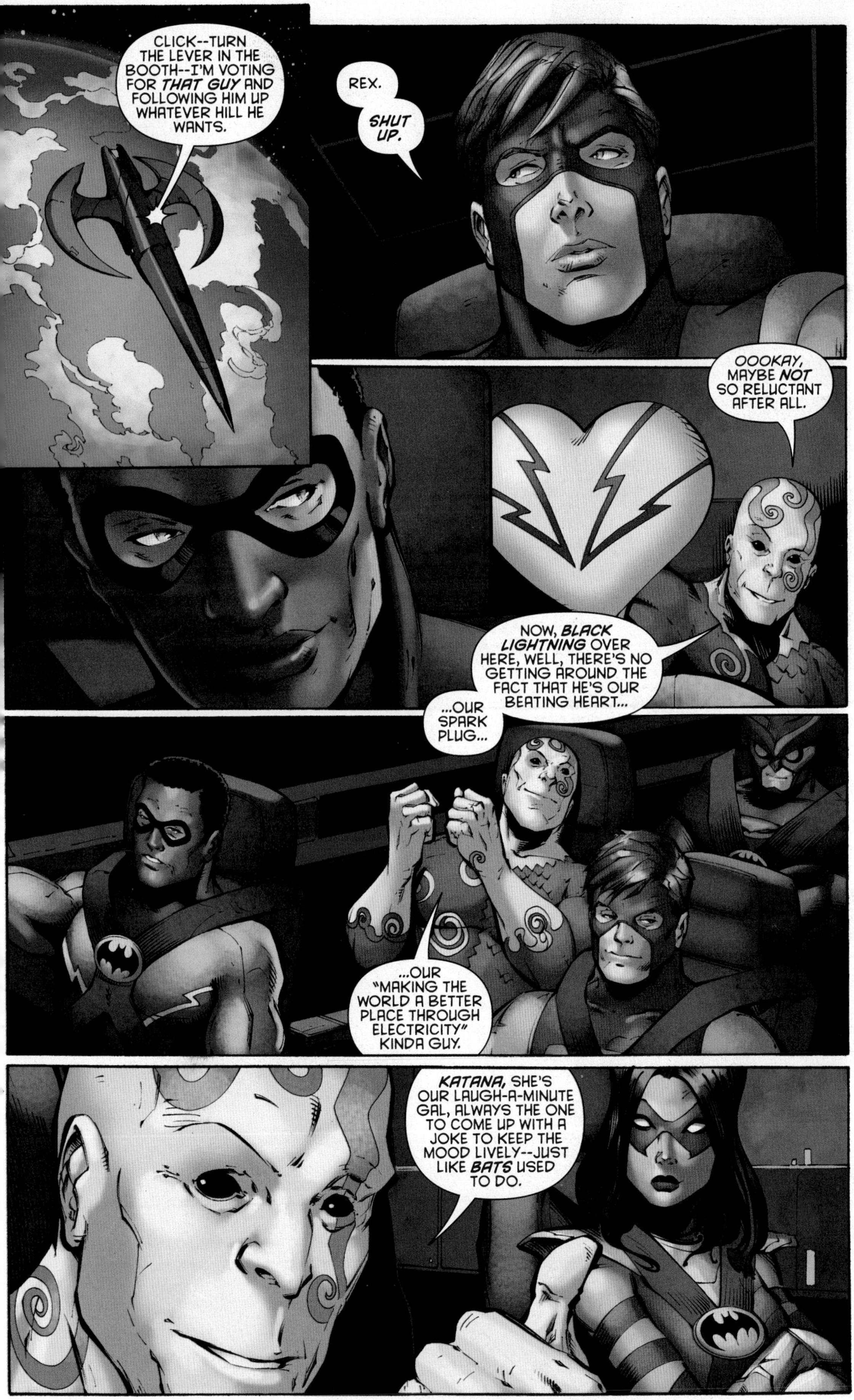
CLICK--TURN THE LEVER IN THE BOOTH--I'M VOTING FOR *THAT GUY* AND FOLLOWING HIM UP WHATEVER HILL HE WANTS.
REX.
SHUT UP.
OOOKAY, MAYBE *NOT* SO RELUCTANT AFTER ALL.
NOW, *BLACK LIGHTNING* OVER HERE, WELL, THERE'S NO GETTING AROUND THE FACT THAT HE'S OUR BEATING HEART...
...OUR SPARK PLUG...
...OUR "MAKING THE WORLD A BETTER PLACE THROUGH ELECTRICITY" KINDA GUY.
KATANA, SHE'S OUR LAUGH-A-MINUTE GAL, ALWAYS THE ONE TO COME UP WITH A JOKE TO KEEP THE MOOD LIVELY--JUST LIKE *BATS* USED TO DO.

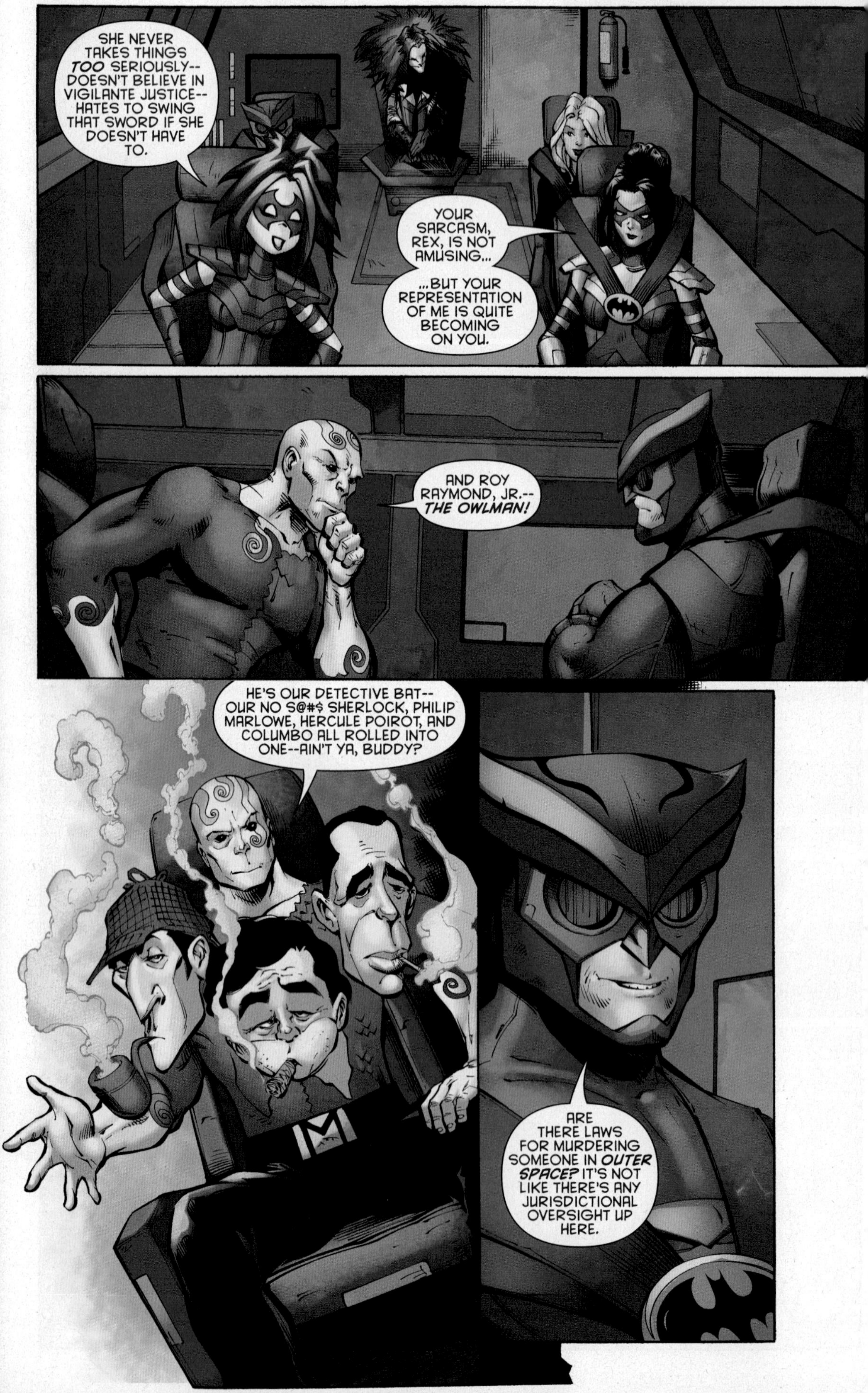
SHE NEVER TAKES THINGS TOO SERIOUSLY-- DOESN'T BELIEVE IN VIGILANTE JUSTICE-- HATES TO SWING THAT SWORD IF SHE DOESN'T HAVE TO.
YOUR SARCASM, REX, IS NOT AMUSING...
...BUT YOUR REPRESENTATION OF ME IS QUITE BECOMING ON YOU.
AND ROY RAYMOND, JR.-- THE OWLMAN!
HE'S OUR DETECTIVE BAT-- OUR NO S@#$ SHERLOCK, PHILIP MARLOWE, HERCULE POIROT, AND COLUMBO ALL ROLLED INTO ONE--AIN'T YA, BUDDY?
ARE THERE LAWS FOR MURDERING SOMEONE IN OUTER SPACE? IT'S NOT LIKE THERE'S ANY JURISDICTIONAL OVERSIGHT UP HERE.

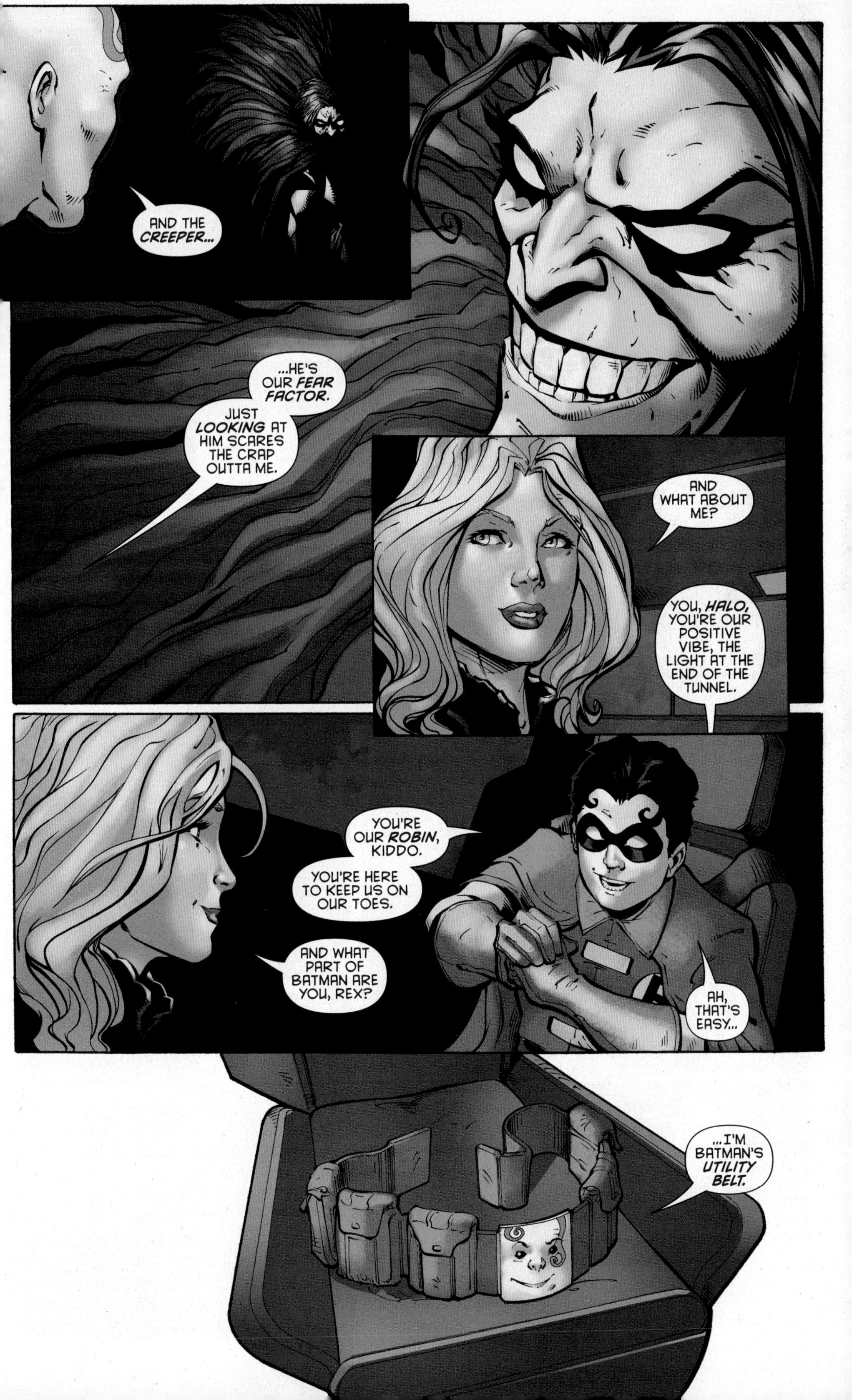

AND THE *CREEPER*...
...HE'S OUR *FEAR FACTOR*.
JUST *LOOKING* AT HIM SCARES THE CRAP OUTTA ME.
AND WHAT ABOUT ME?
YOU, *HALO*, YOU'RE OUR POSITIVE VIBE, THE LIGHT AT THE END OF THE TUNNEL.
YOU'RE OUR *ROBIN*, KIDDO.
YOU'RE HERE TO KEEP US ON OUR TOES.
AND WHAT PART OF BATMAN ARE YOU, REX?
AH, THAT'S EASY...
...I'M BATMAN'S *UTILITY BELT*.

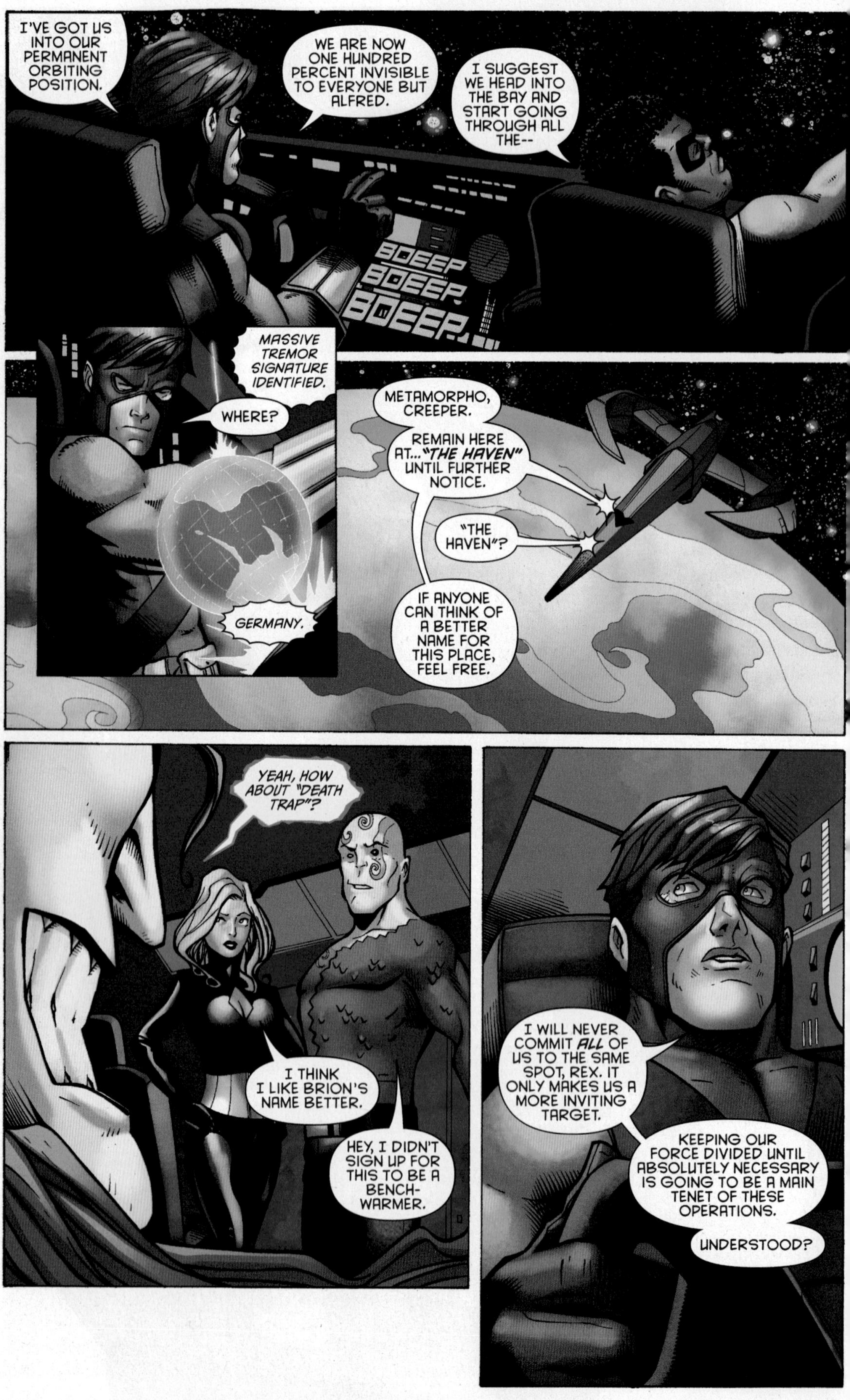
I'VE GOT US INTO OUR PERMANENT ORBITING POSITION.
WE ARE NOW ONE HUNDRED PERCENT INVISIBLE TO EVERYONE BUT ALFRED.
I SUGGEST WE HEAD INTO THE BAY AND START GOING THROUGH ALL THE--
BOEEP BOEEP BOEEP
MASSIVE TREMOR SIGNATURE IDENTIFIED.
WHERE?
GERMANY.
METAMORPHO, CREEPER.
REMAIN HERE AT..."THE HAVEN" UNTIL FURTHER NOTICE.
"THE HAVEN"?
IF ANYONE CAN THINK OF A BETTER NAME FOR THIS PLACE, FEEL FREE.
YEAH, HOW ABOUT "DEATH TRAP"?
I THINK I LIKE BRION'S NAME BETTER.
HEY, I DIDN'T SIGN UP FOR THIS TO BE A BENCH-WARMER.
I WILL NEVER COMMIT ALL OF US TO THE SAME SPOT, REX. IT ONLY MAKES US A MORE INVITING TARGET.
KEEPING OUR FORCE DIVIDED UNTIL ABSOLUTELY NECESSARY IS GOING TO BE A MAIN TENET OF THESE OPERATIONS.
UNDERSTOOD?

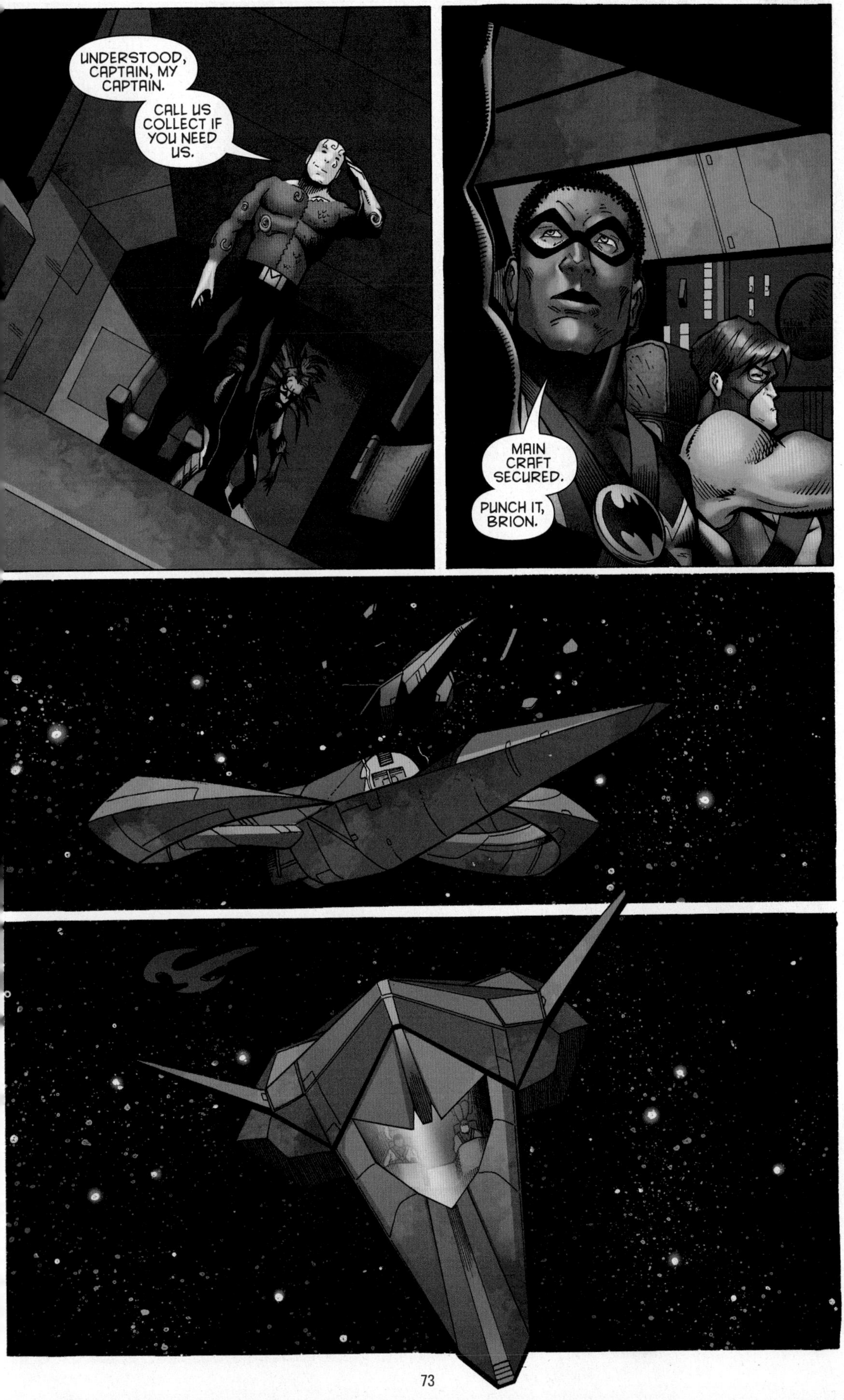
UNDERSTOOD, CAPTAIN, MY CAPTAIN.
CALL US COLLECT IF YOU NEED US.
MAIN CRAFT SECURED.
PUNCH IT, BRION.

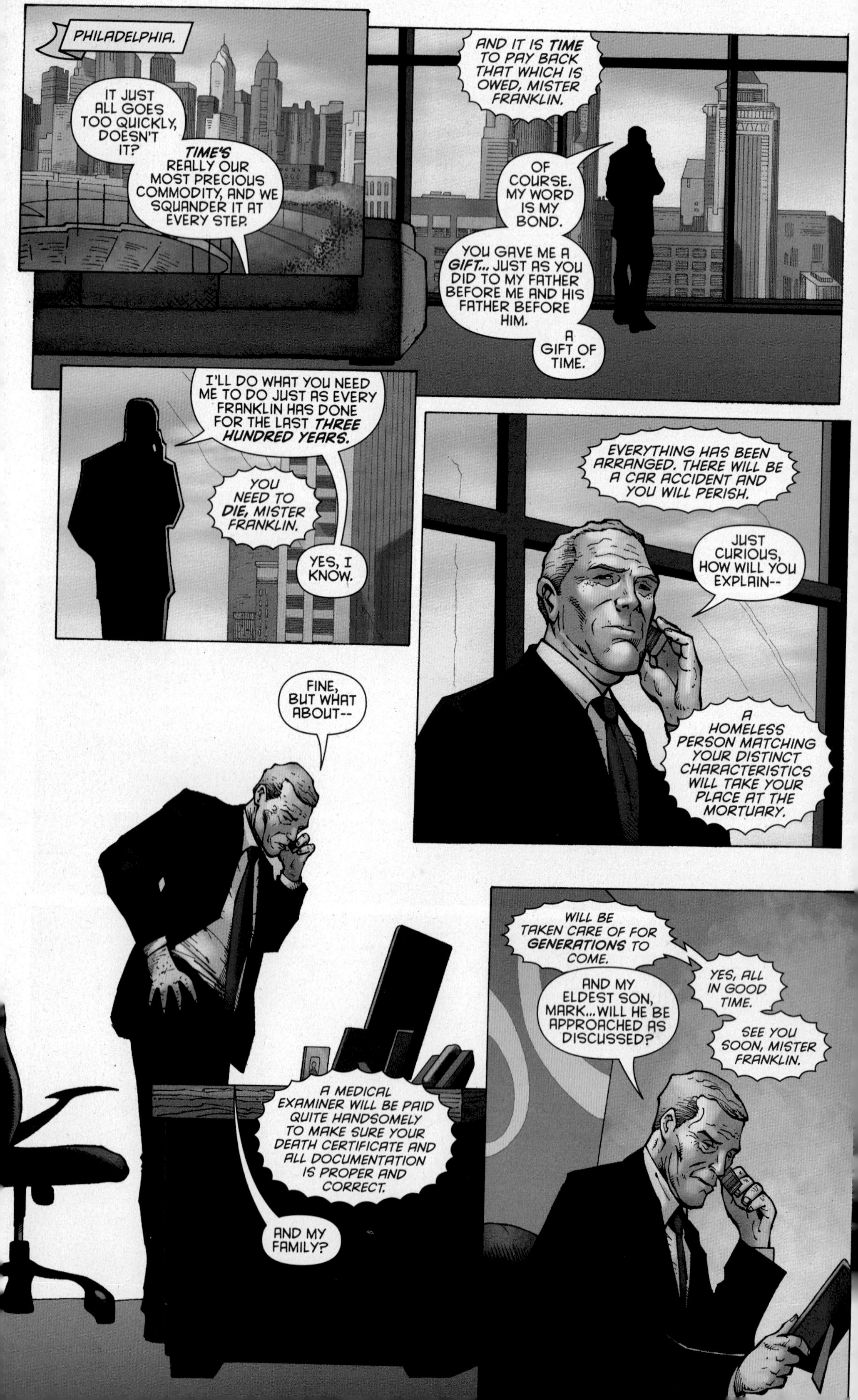
PHILADELPHIA.
IT JUST ALL GOES TOO QUICKLY, DOESN'T IT?
TIME'S REALLY OUR MOST PRECIOUS COMMODITY, AND WE SQUANDER IT AT EVERY STEP.
AND IT IS TIME TO PAY BACK THAT WHICH IS OWED, MISTER FRANKLIN.
OF COURSE. MY WORD IS MY BOND.
YOU GAVE ME A GIFT... JUST AS YOU DID TO MY FATHER BEFORE ME AND HIS FATHER BEFORE HIM.
A GIFT OF TIME.
I'LL DO WHAT YOU NEED ME TO DO JUST AS EVERY FRANKLIN HAS DONE FOR THE LAST THREE HUNDRED YEARS.
YOU NEED TO DIE, MISTER FRANKLIN.
YES, I KNOW.
EVERYTHING HAS BEEN ARRANGED. THERE WILL BE A CAR ACCIDENT AND YOU WILL PERISH.
JUST CURIOUS, HOW WILL YOU EXPLAIN--
A HOMELESS PERSON MATCHING YOUR DISTINCT CHARACTERISTICS WILL TAKE YOUR PLACE AT THE MORTUARY.
FINE, BUT WHAT ABOUT--
A MEDICAL EXAMINER WILL BE PAID QUITE HANDSOMELY TO MAKE SURE YOUR DEATH CERTIFICATE AND ALL DOCUMENTATION IS PROPER AND CORRECT.
AND MY FAMILY?
WILL BE TAKEN CARE OF FOR GENERATIONS TO COME.
AND MY ELDEST SON, MARK...WILL HE BE APPROACHED AS DISCUSSED?
YES, ALL IN GOOD TIME.
SEE YOU SOON, MISTER FRANKLIN.

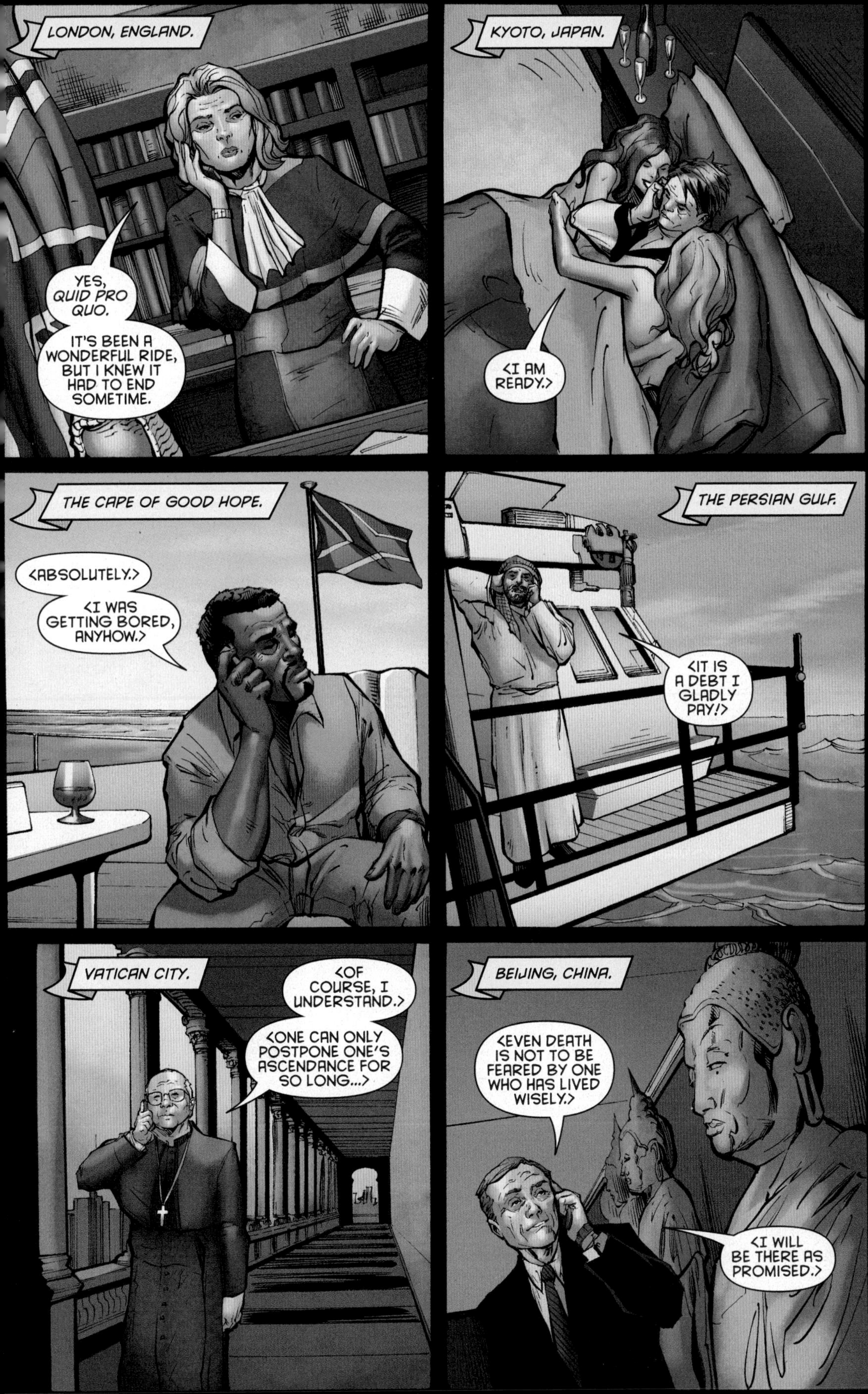
LONDON, ENGLAND.
YES, QUID PRO QUO.
IT'S BEEN A WONDERFUL RIDE, BUT I KNEW IT HAD TO END SOMETIME.
KYOTO, JAPAN.
<I AM READY.>
THE CAPE OF GOOD HOPE.
<ABSOLUTELY.>
<I WAS GETTING BORED, ANYHOW.>
THE PERSIAN GULF.
<IT IS A DEBT I GLADLY PAY!>
VATICAN CITY.
<OF COURSE, I UNDERSTAND.>
<ONE CAN ONLY POSTPONE ONE'S ASCENDANCE FOR SO LONG...>
BEIJING, CHINA.
<EVEN DEATH IS NOT TO BE FEARED BY ONE WHO HAS LIVED WISELY.>
<I WILL BE THERE AS PROMISED.>

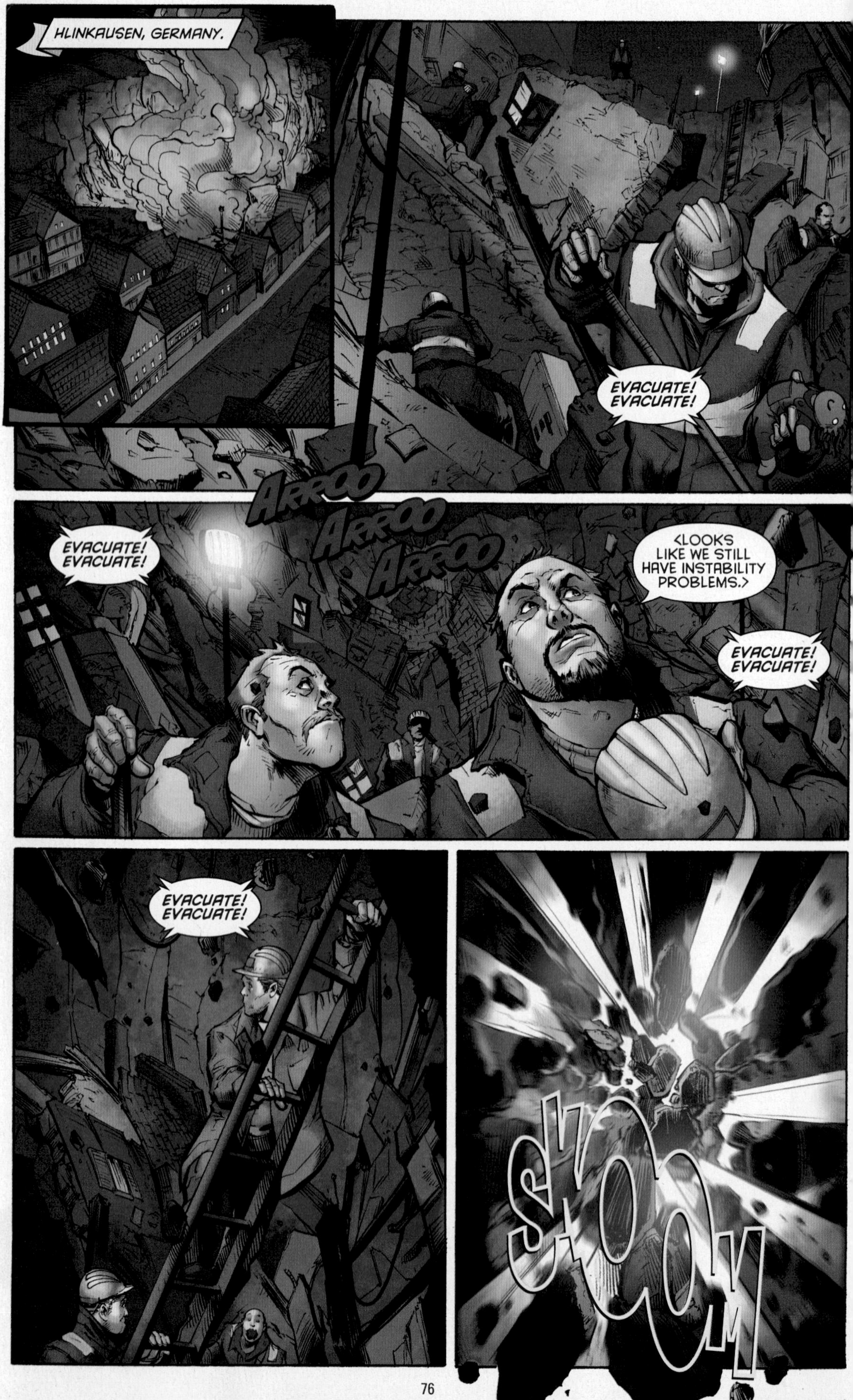

HLINKAUSEN, GERMANY.
EVACUATE! EVACUATE!
ARROO ARROO ARROO
EVACUATE! EVACUATE!
<LOOKS LIKE WE STILL HAVE INSTABILITY PROBLEMS.>
EVACUATE! EVACUATE!
EVACUATE! EVACUATE!
SHOOM

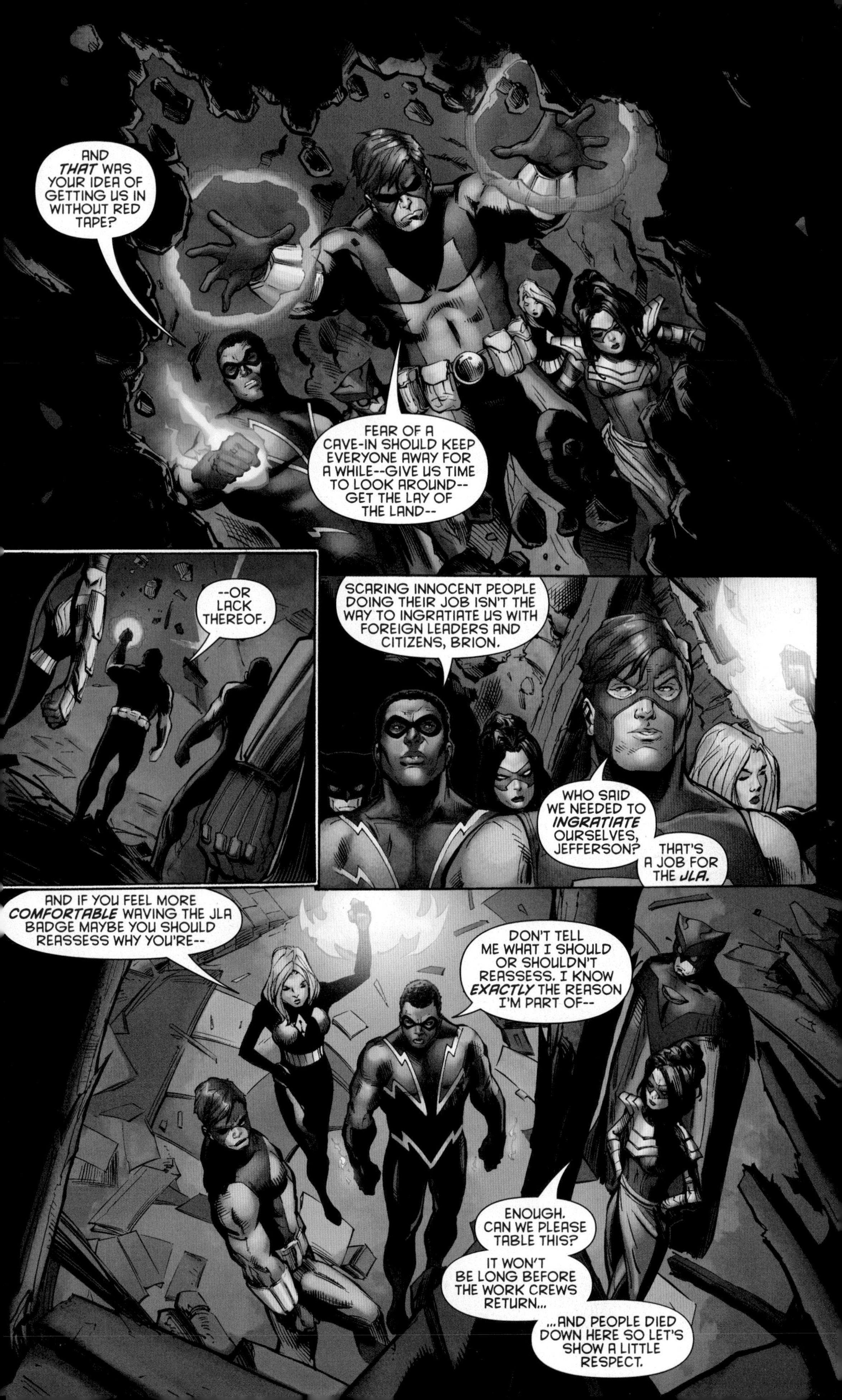
AND THAT WAS YOUR IDEA OF GETTING US IN WITHOUT RED TAPE?
FEAR OF A CAVE-IN SHOULD KEEP EVERYONE AWAY FOR A WHILE--GIVE US TIME TO LOOK AROUND--GET THE LAY OF THE LAND--
--OR LACK THEREOF.
SCARING INNOCENT PEOPLE DOING THEIR JOB ISN'T THE WAY TO INGRATIATE US WITH FOREIGN LEADERS AND CITIZENS, BRION.
WHO SAID WE NEEDED TO INGRATIATE OURSELVES, JEFFERSON?
THAT'S A JOB FOR THE JLA.
AND IF YOU FEEL MORE COMFORTABLE WAVING THE JLA BADGE MAYBE YOU SHOULD REASSESS WHY YOU'RE--
DON'T TELL ME WHAT I SHOULD OR SHOULDN'T REASSESS. I KNOW EXACTLY THE REASON I'M PART OF--
ENOUGH. CAN WE PLEASE TABLE THIS?
IT WON'T BE LONG BEFORE THE WORK CREWS RETURN...
...AND PEOPLE DIED DOWN HERE SO LET'S SHOW A LITTLE RESPECT.

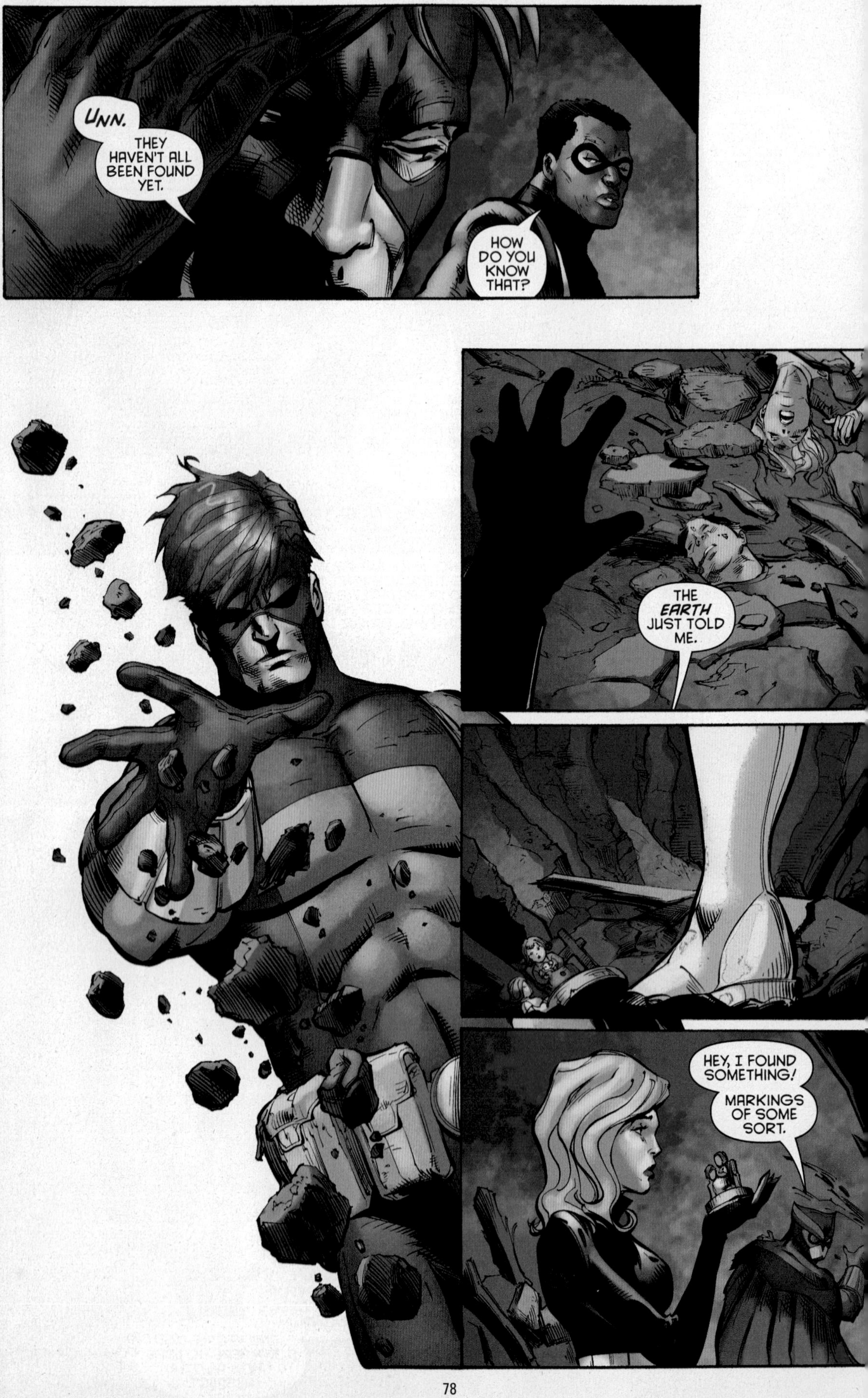
UNN.
THEY HAVEN'T ALL BEEN FOUND YET.
HOW DO YOU KNOW THAT?
THE EARTH JUST TOLD ME.
HEY, I FOUND SOMETHING!
MARKINGS OF SOME SORT.

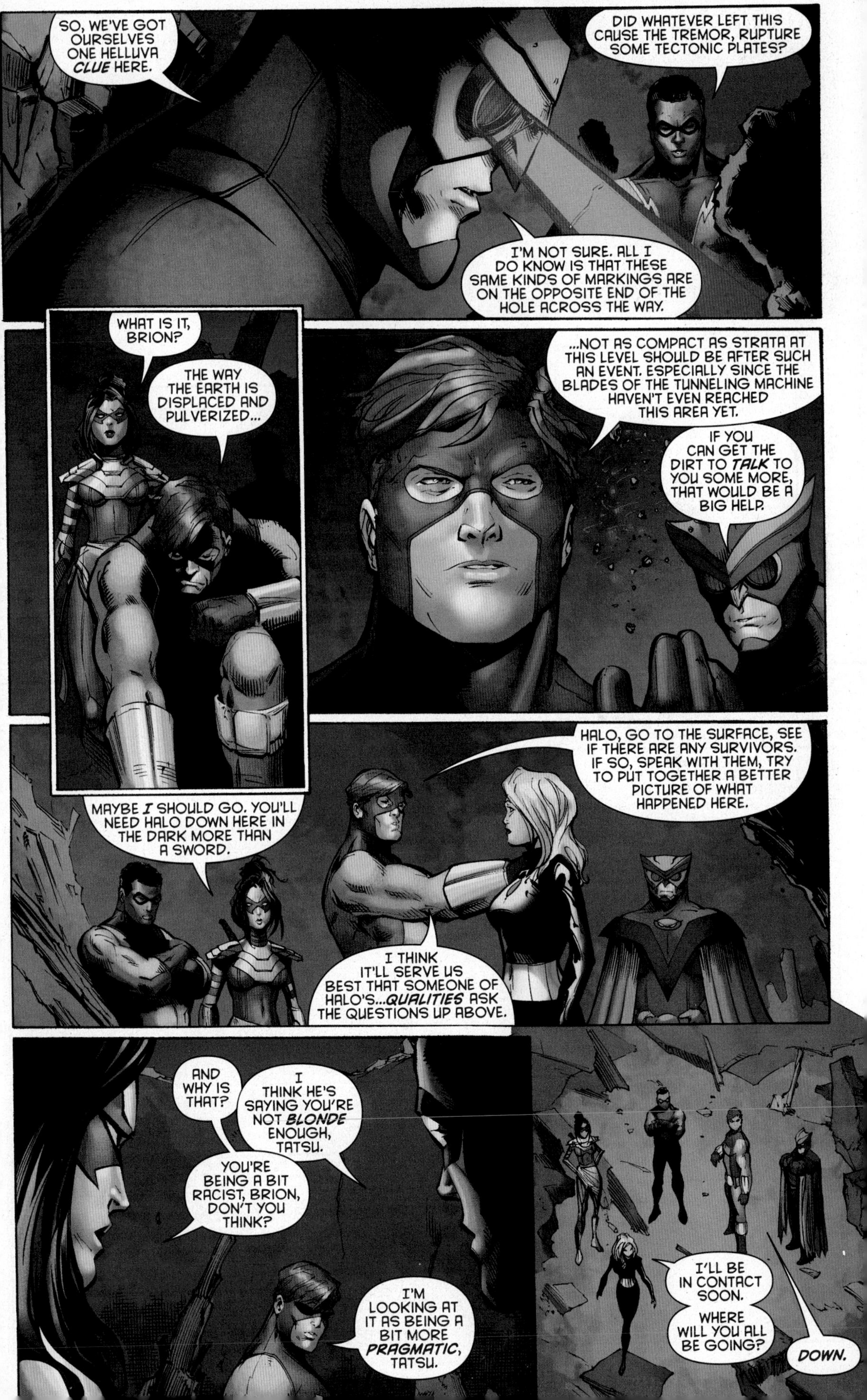
SO, WE'VE GOT OURSELVES ONE HELLUVA *CLUE* HERE.
DID WHATEVER LEFT THIS CAUSE THE TREMOR, RUPTURE SOME TECTONIC PLATES?
I'M NOT SURE. ALL I DO KNOW IS THAT THESE SAME KINDS OF MARKINGS ARE ON THE OPPOSITE END OF THE HOLE ACROSS THE WAY.
WHAT IS IT, BRION?
THE WAY THE EARTH IS DISPLACED AND PULVERIZED...
...NOT AS COMPACT AS STRATA AT THIS LEVEL SHOULD BE AFTER SUCH AN EVENT. ESPECIALLY SINCE THE BLADES OF THE TUNNELING MACHINE HAVEN'T EVEN REACHED THIS AREA YET.
IF YOU CAN GET THE DIRT TO *TALK* TO YOU SOME MORE, THAT WOULD BE A BIG HELP.
HALO, GO TO THE SURFACE, SEE IF THERE ARE ANY SURVIVORS. IF SO, SPEAK WITH THEM, TRY TO PUT TOGETHER A BETTER PICTURE OF WHAT HAPPENED HERE.
MAYBE *I* SHOULD GO. YOU'LL NEED HALO DOWN HERE IN THE DARK MORE THAN A SWORD.
I THINK IT'LL SERVE US BEST THAT SOMEONE OF HALO'S...*QUALITIES* ASK THE QUESTIONS UP ABOVE.
AND WHY IS THAT?
I THINK HE'S SAYING YOU'RE NOT *BLONDE* ENOUGH, TATSU.
YOU'RE BEING A BIT RACIST, BRION, DON'T YOU THINK?
I'M LOOKING AT IT AS BEING A BIT MORE *PRAGMATIC*, TATSU.
I'LL BE IN CONTACT SOON.
WHERE WILL YOU ALL BE GOING?
DOWN.

THANKS FOR LETTING ME SEE HER, DOCTOR.

KRANKENHAUS WESTLICHEINGANG

IT IS AGAINST PROTOCOL, BUT SINCE YOU COULD HAVE FOUND A WAY TO DO IT WITHOUT PERMISSION, I FELT I WAS BOUND TO HONOR YOUR HEARTFELT REQUEST.

AND SHE'S THE ONLY SURVIVOR?

YES, I'M AFRAID SO.

HER NAME IS EVA.

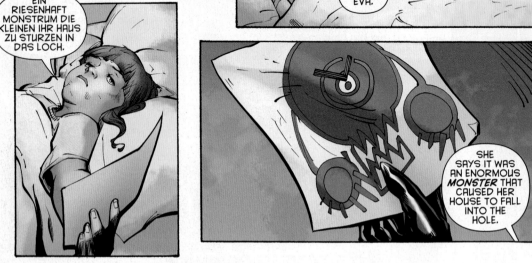

EIN RIESENHAFT MONSTRUM DIE KLEINEN IHR HAUS ZU STURZEN IN DAS LOCH.

SHE SAYS IT WAS AN ENORMOUS *MONSTER* THAT CAUSED HER HOUSE TO FALL INTO THE HOLE.

WERDEN SIE FANGEN DAS MONSTRUM DAS GETOTET MEINE FAMILIE?

YES, EVA, I WILL FIND THE MONSTER THAT KILLED YOUR FAMILY.

SHE--

I THINK I UNDERSTOOD HER.

JA, ICH WERDE FINDEN SIE DIE MONSTRUM.

DANKE SCHÖN.

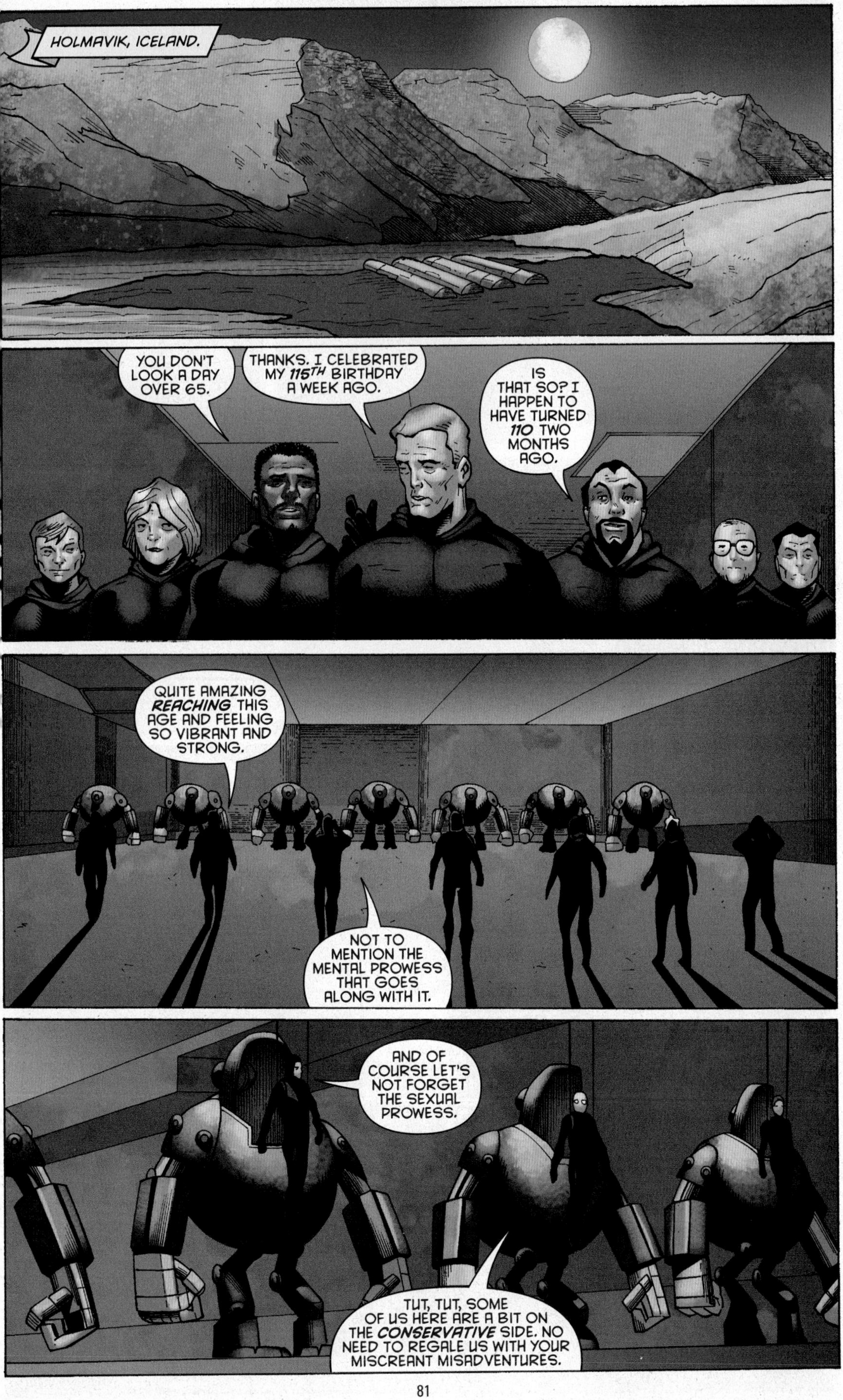

HOLMAVIK, ICELAND.
YOU DON'T LOOK A DAY OVER 65.
THANKS. I CELEBRATED MY 115TH BIRTHDAY A WEEK AGO.
IS THAT SO? I HAPPEN TO HAVE TURNED 110 TWO MONTHS AGO.
QUITE AMAZING REACHING THIS AGE AND FEELING SO VIBRANT AND STRONG.
NOT TO MENTION THE MENTAL PROWESS THAT GOES ALONG WITH IT.
AND OF COURSE LET'S NOT FORGET THE SEXUAL PROWESS.
TUT, TUT, SOME OF US HERE ARE A BIT ON THE CONSERVATIVE SIDE. NO NEED TO REGALE US WITH YOUR MISCREANT MISADVENTURES.

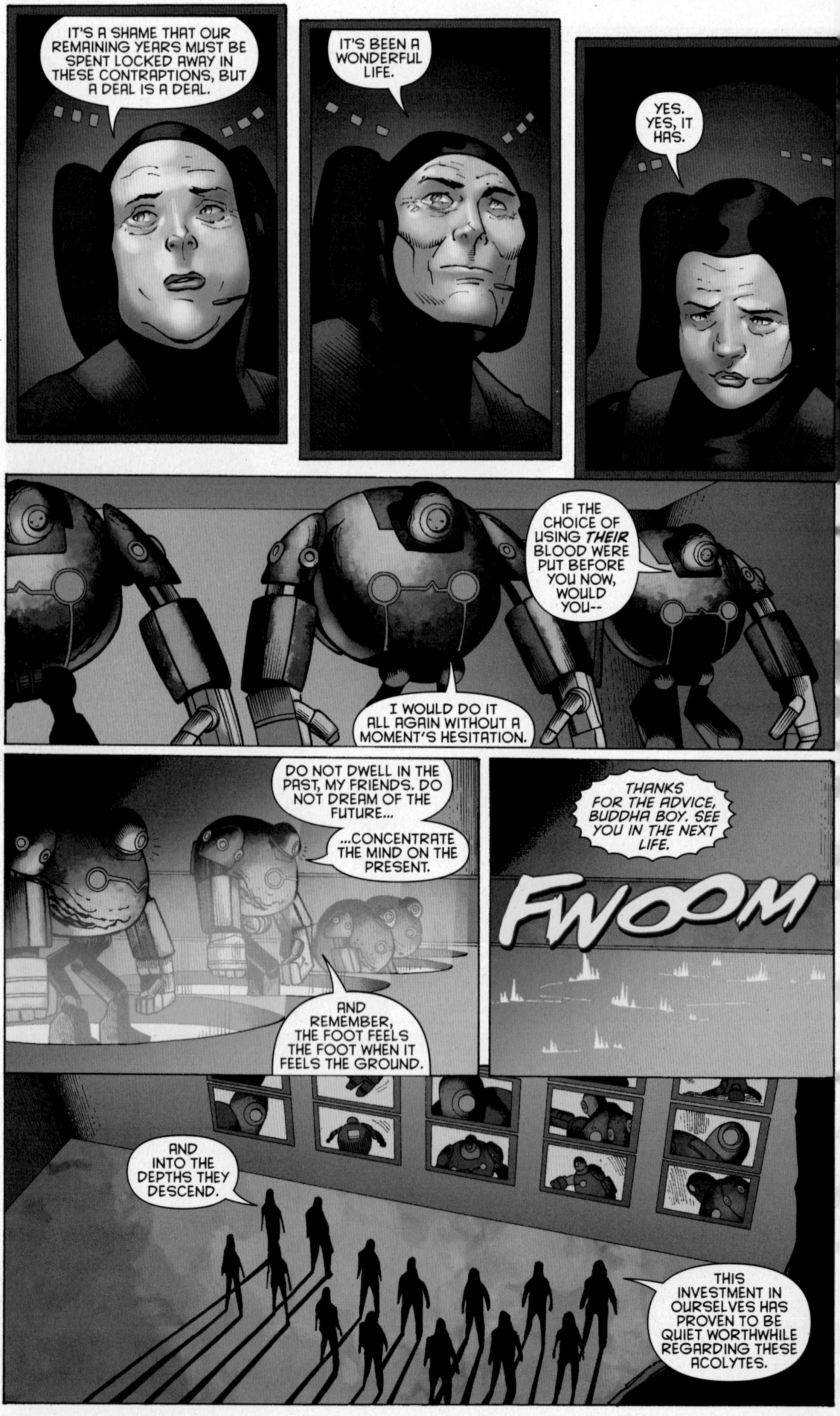
IT'S A SHAME THAT OUR REMAINING YEARS MUST BE SPENT LOCKED AWAY IN THESE CONTRAPTIONS, BUT A DEAL IS A DEAL.
IT'S BEEN A WONDERFUL LIFE.
YES. YES, IT HAS.
IF THE CHOICE OF USING THEIR BLOOD WERE PUT BEFORE YOU NOW, WOULD YOU--
I WOULD DO IT ALL AGAIN WITHOUT A MOMENT'S HESITATION.
DO NOT DWELL IN THE PAST, MY FRIENDS. DO NOT DREAM OF THE FUTURE...
...CONCENTRATE THE MIND ON THE PRESENT.
AND REMEMBER, THE FOOT FEELS THE FOOT WHEN IT FEELS THE GROUND.
THANKS FOR THE ADVICE, BUDDHA BOY. SEE YOU IN THE NEXT LIFE.
FWOOM
AND INTO THE DEPTHS THEY DESCEND.
THIS INVESTMENT IN OURSELVES HAS PROVEN TO BE QUIET WORTHWHILE REGARDING THESE ACOLYTES.

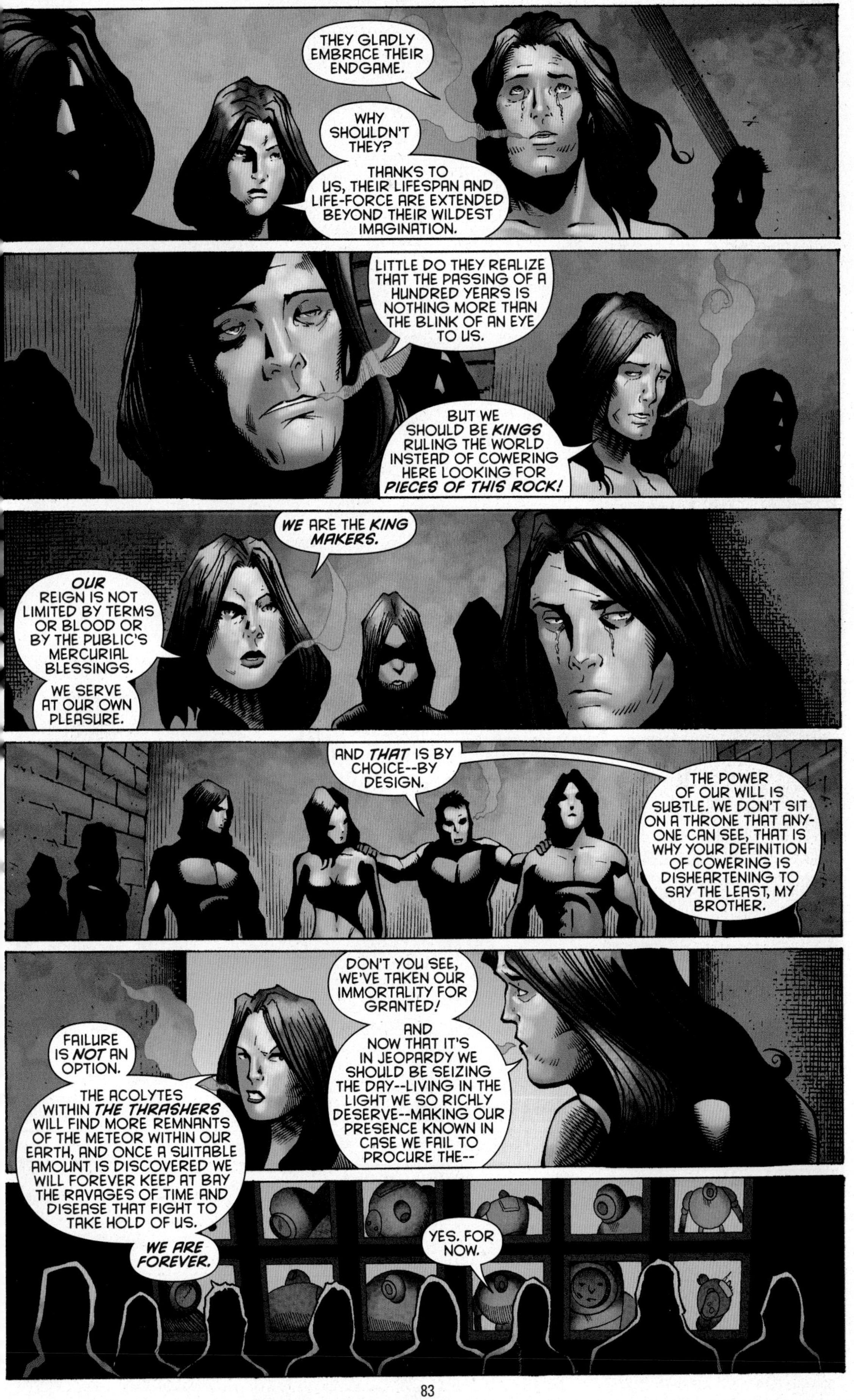
THEY GLADLY EMBRACE THEIR ENDGAME.
WHY SHOULDN'T THEY?
THANKS TO US, THEIR LIFESPAN AND LIFE-FORCE ARE EXTENDED BEYOND THEIR WILDEST IMAGINATION.
LITTLE DO THEY REALIZE THAT THE PASSING OF A HUNDRED YEARS IS NOTHING MORE THAN THE BLINK OF AN EYE TO US.
BUT WE SHOULD BE KINGS RULING THE WORLD INSTEAD OF COWERING HERE LOOKING FOR PIECES OF THIS ROCK!
WE ARE THE KING MAKERS.
OUR REIGN IS NOT LIMITED BY TERMS OR BLOOD OR BY THE PUBLIC'S MERCURIAL BLESSINGS.
WE SERVE AT OUR OWN PLEASURE.
AND THAT IS BY CHOICE--BY DESIGN.
THE POWER OF OUR WILL IS SUBTLE. WE DON'T SIT ON A THRONE THAT ANY-ONE CAN SEE, THAT IS WHY YOUR DEFINITION OF COWERING IS DISHEARTENING TO SAY THE LEAST, MY BROTHER.
DON'T YOU SEE, WE'VE TAKEN OUR IMMORTALITY FOR GRANTED!
AND NOW THAT IT'S IN JEOPARDY WE SHOULD BE SEIZING THE DAY--LIVING IN THE LIGHT WE SO RICHLY DESERVE--MAKING OUR PRESENCE KNOWN IN CASE WE FAIL TO PROCURE THE--
FAILURE IS NOT AN OPTION.
THE ACOLYTES WITHIN THE THRASHERS WILL FIND MORE REMNANTS OF THE METEOR WITHIN OUR EARTH, AND ONCE A SUITABLE AMOUNT IS DISCOVERED WE WILL FOREVER KEEP AT BAY THE RAVAGES OF TIME AND DISEASE THAT FIGHT TO TAKE HOLD OF US.
WE ARE FOREVER.
YES. FOR NOW.

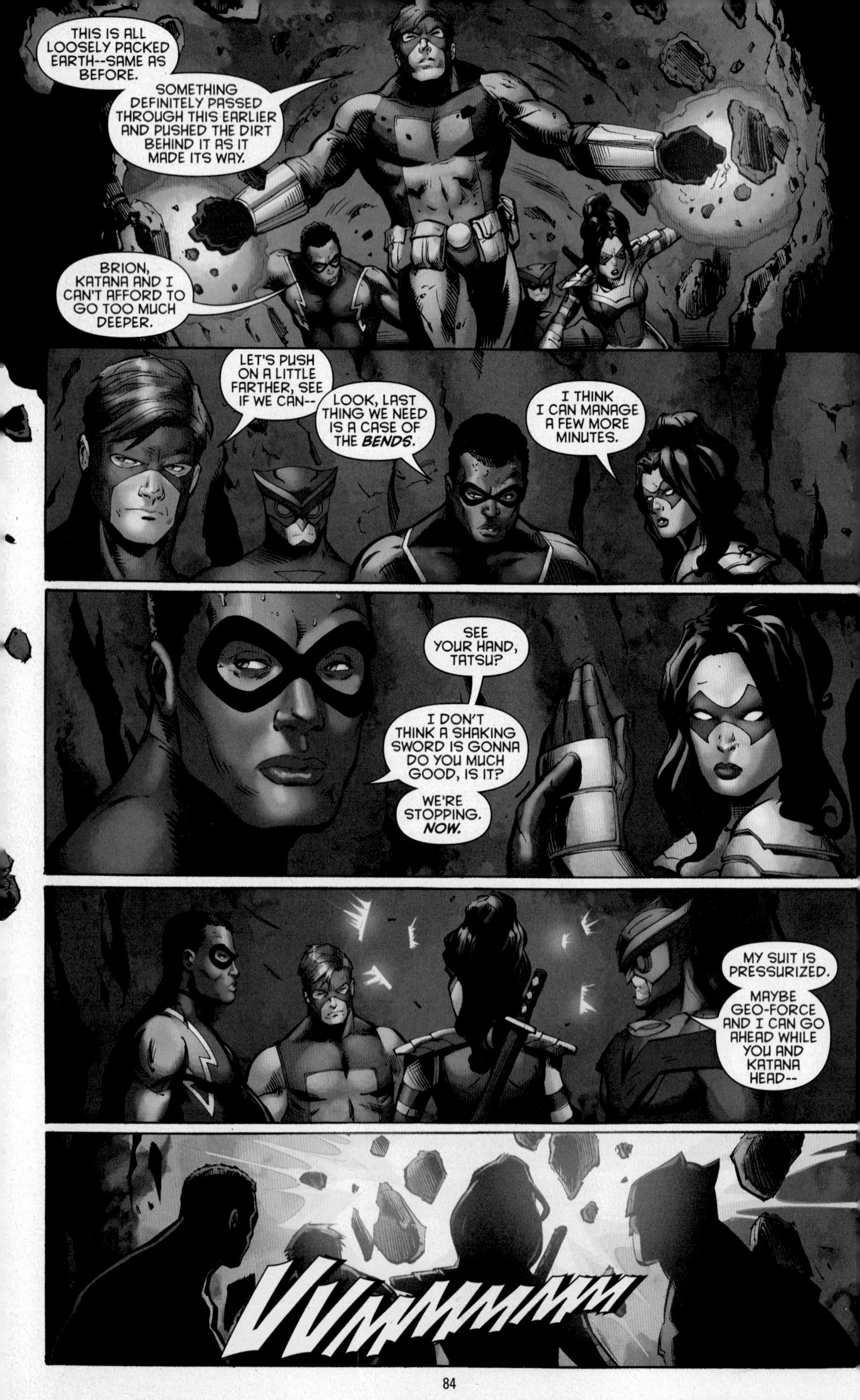

THIS IS ALL LOOSELY PACKED EARTH--SAME AS BEFORE.
SOMETHING DEFINITELY PASSED THROUGH THIS EARLIER AND PUSHED THE DIRT BEHIND IT AS IT MADE ITS WAY.
BRION, KATANA AND I CAN'T AFFORD TO GO TOO MUCH DEEPER.
LET'S PUSH ON A LITTLE FARTHER, SEE IF WE CAN--
LOOK, LAST THING WE NEED IS A CASE OF THE BENDS.
I THINK I CAN MANAGE A FEW MORE MINUTES.
SEE YOUR HAND, TATSU?
I DON'T THINK A SHAKING SWORD IS GONNA DO YOU MUCH GOOD, IS IT?
WE'RE STOPPING. NOW.
MY SUIT IS PRESSURIZED.
MAYBE GEO-FORCE AND I CAN GO AHEAD WHILE YOU AND KATANA HEAD--
VVMMMMMM

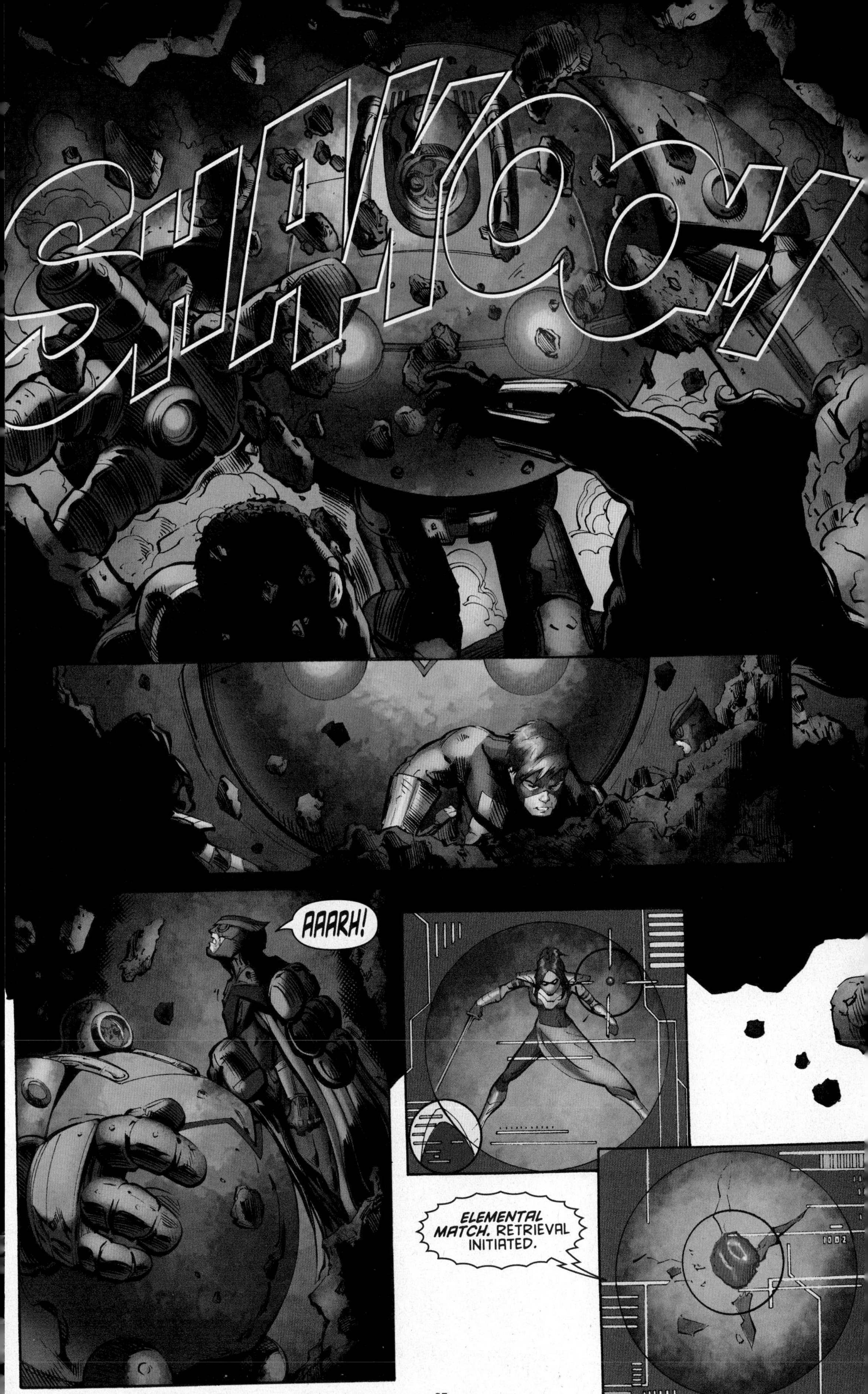
SHAKOOM
AAARH!
ELEMENTAL MATCH. RETRIEVAL INITIATED.

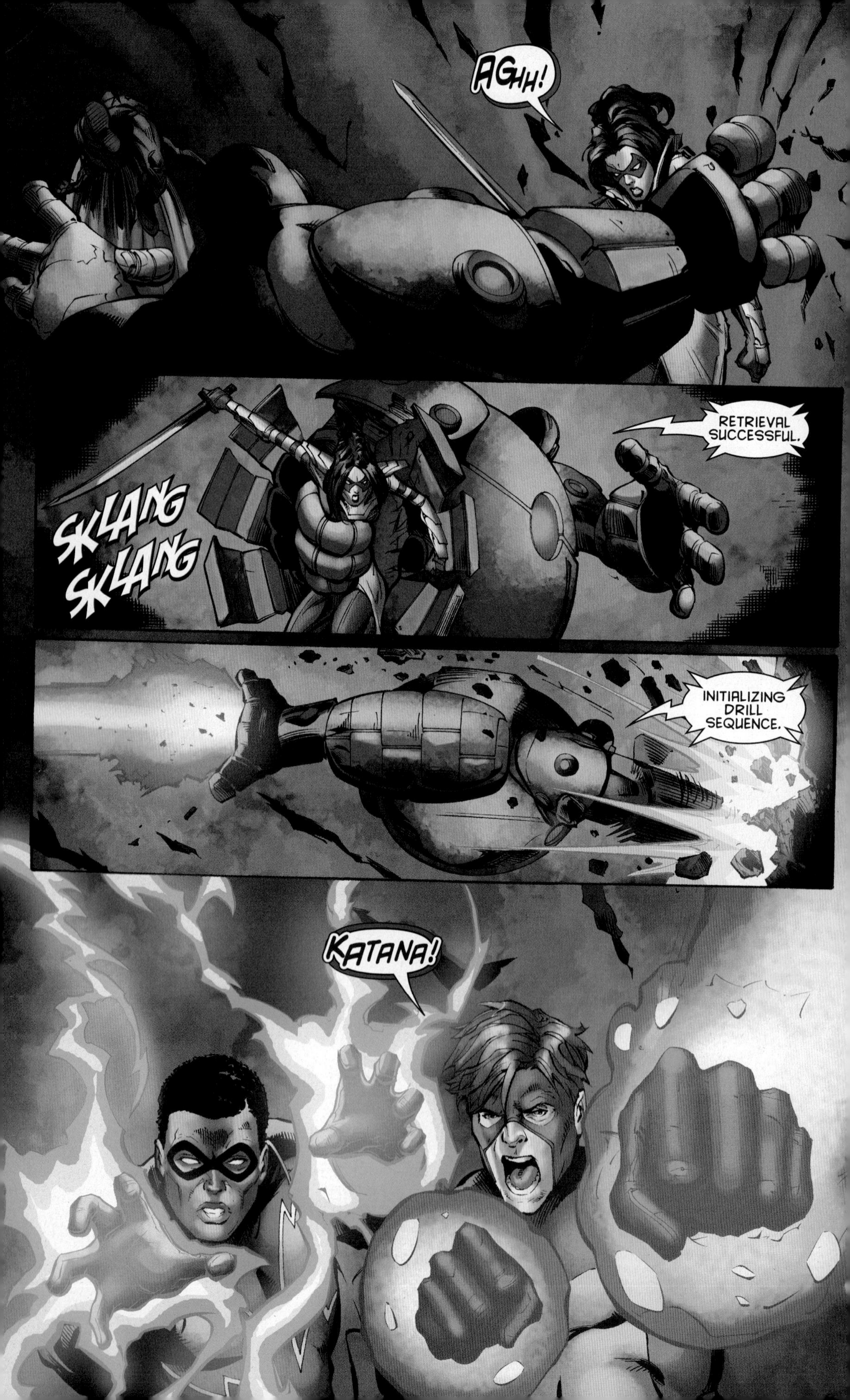
AGHH!
RETRIEVAL SUCCESSFUL.
SKLANG SKLANG
INITIALIZING DRILL SEQUENCE.
KATANA!

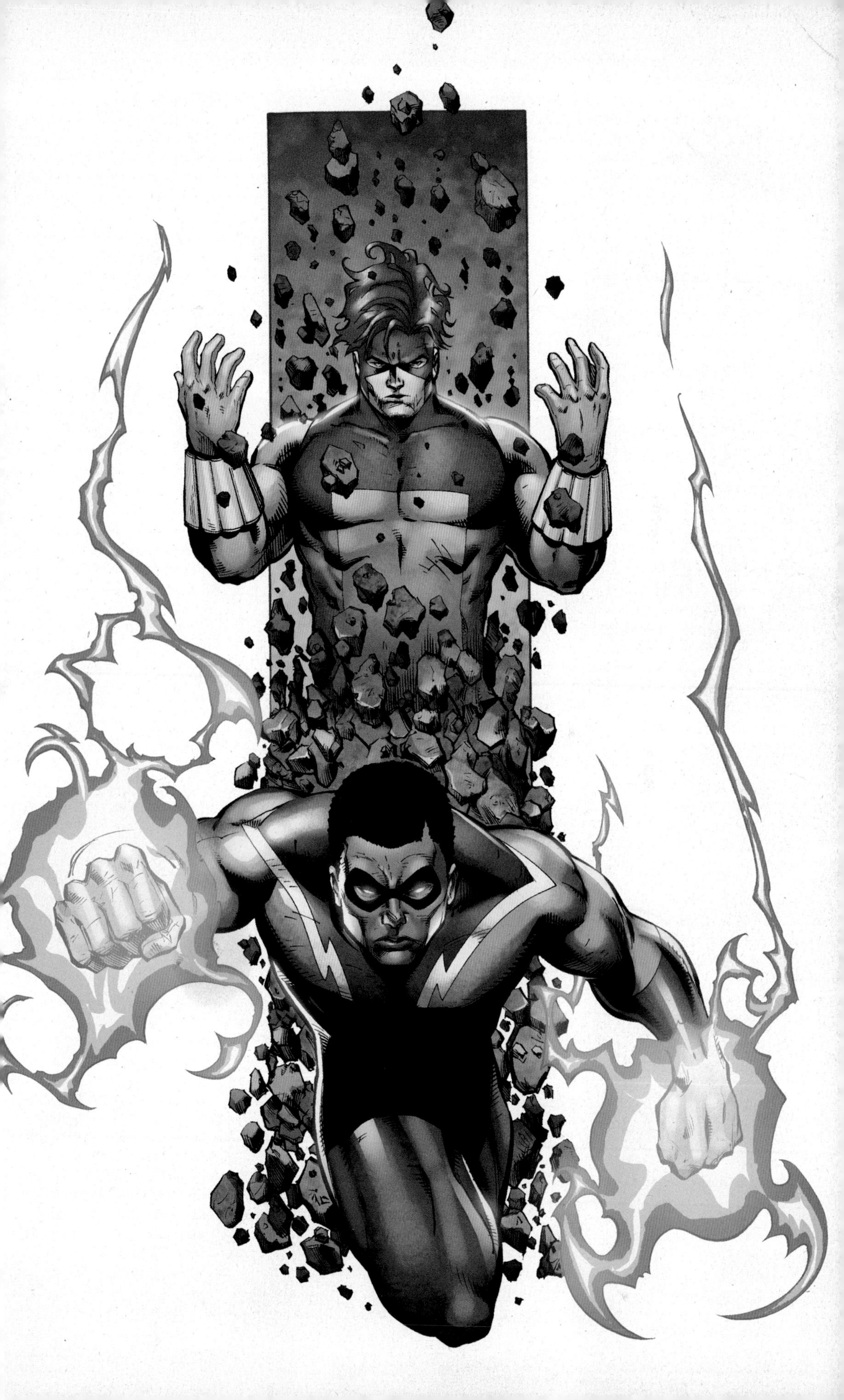

"I will not go softly
into the dark night."

I'll move heaven and Earth if I have to.

FRAAKKSSSH

This *thing's* got Katana.

VZZOOOM

Nobody puts the life of one of our team members in jeopardy and gets away with it.

VZZOOOM

Nobody.

IT'S CHANGED COURSE.

IT'S GOING STRAIGHT UP...

...AND SO ARE WE.

SKKRRKK

WHAT THE HELL ARE YOU DOING?

I'M FORMING--

KLAK KLAK KLAK KLAK

A ROCK MISSILE. TO KEEP OUR NOODLES INTACT AND GAIN US SOME TIME.

THEN LET'S ALL LIGHT THIS CANDLE AND GO GET KATANA.

KLAK KLAK KLAK

OWLMAN, JACK UP YOUR BOOT THRUSTERS AND I'LL GENERATE SOME EXTRA POWER TO GIVE US SOME VELOCITY...

...SO WE CAN CUT THIS THING OFF AT THE SURFACE.

FRHKOOM

BECAUSE AS THEY SAY...

SKRAKOOM

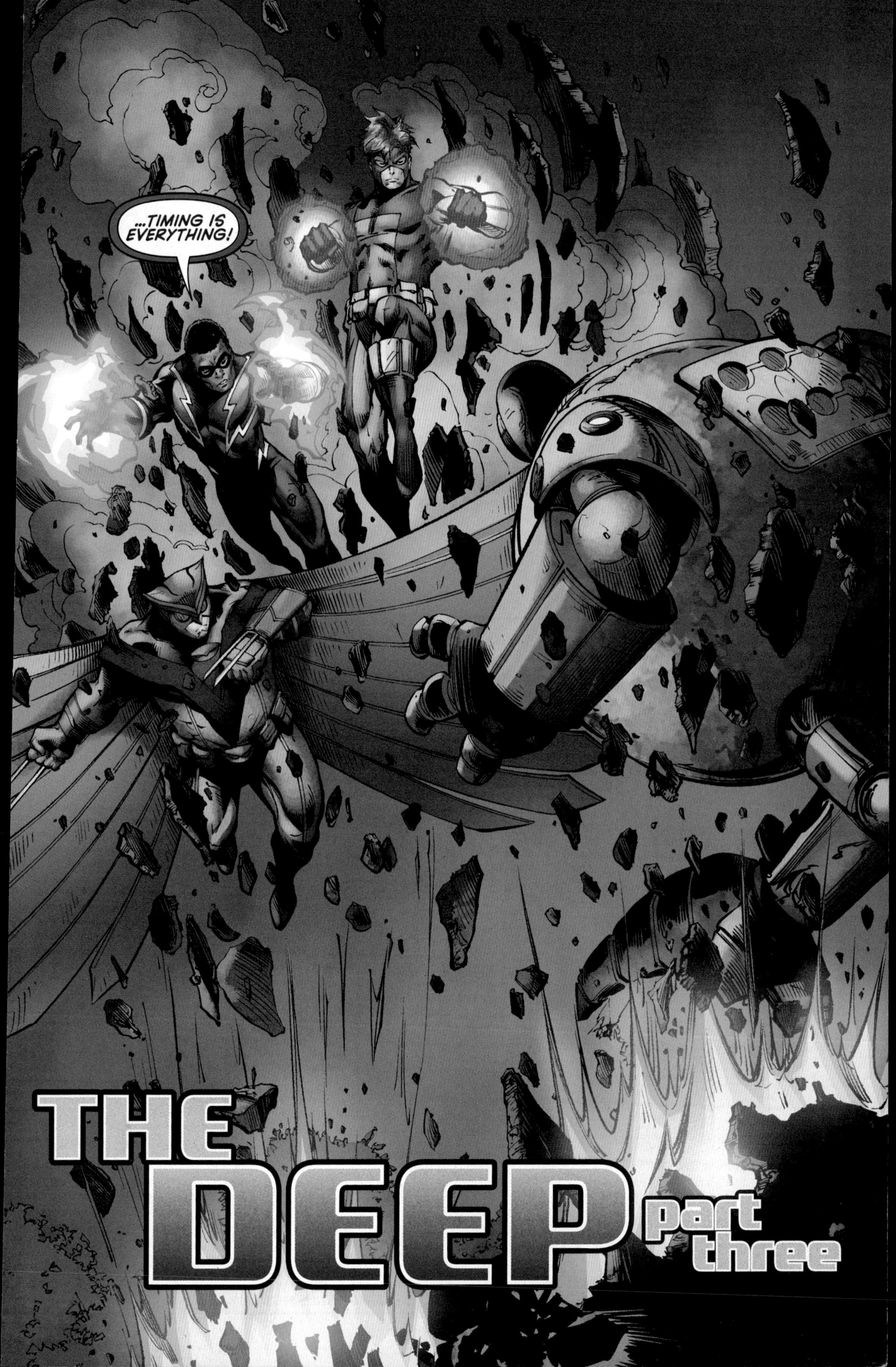
...TIMING IS EVERYTHING!
THE DEEP
part three

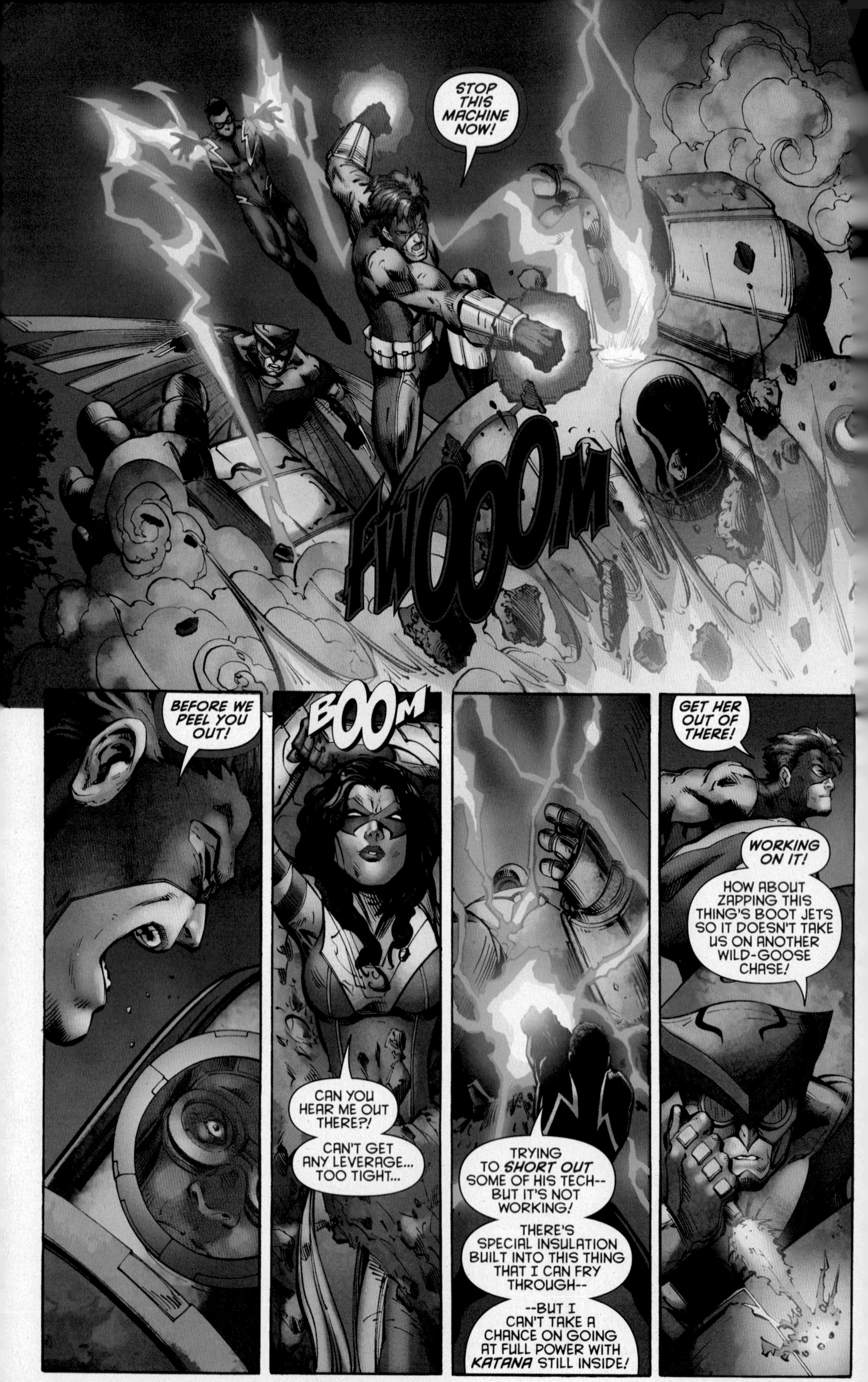

STOP THIS MACHINE NOW!
FWOOOM
BEFORE WE PEEL YOU OUT!
BOOM
CAN YOU HEAR ME OUT THERE?!
CAN'T GET ANY LEVERAGE... TOO TIGHT...
TRYING TO SHORT OUT SOME OF HIS TECH-- BUT IT'S NOT WORKING!
THERE'S SPECIAL INSULATION BUILT INTO THIS THING THAT I CAN FRY THROUGH--
--BUT I CAN'T TAKE A CHANCE ON GOING AT FULL POWER WITH KATANA STILL INSIDE!
GET HER OUT OF THERE!
WORKING ON IT!
HOW ABOUT ZAPPING THIS THING'S BOOT JETS SO IT DOESN'T TAKE US ON ANOTHER WILD-GOOSE CHASE!

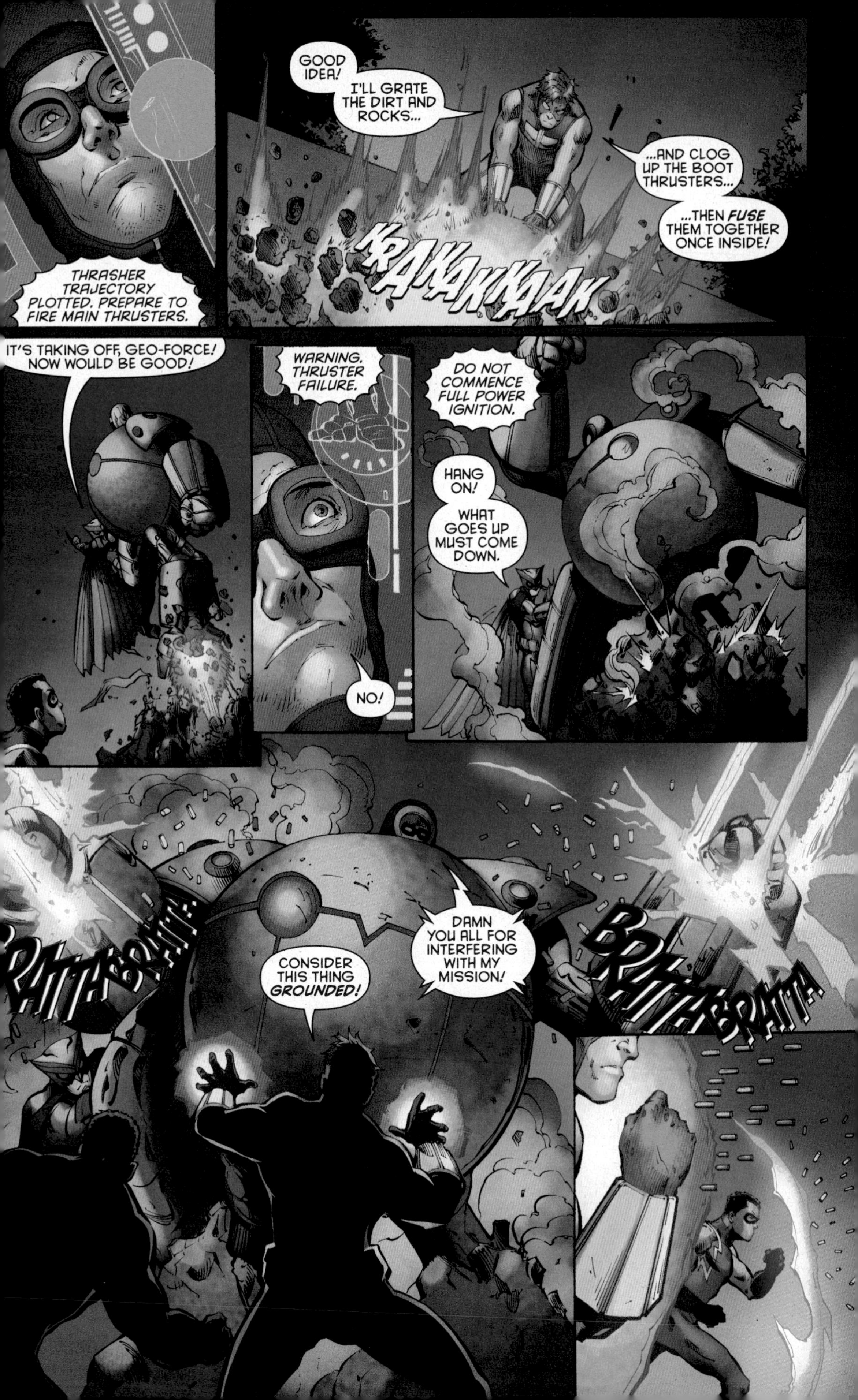
THRASHER TRAJECTORY PLOTTED. PREPARE TO FIRE MAIN THRUSTERS.
GOOD IDEA!
I'LL GRATE THE DIRT AND ROCKS...
...AND CLOG UP THE BOOT THRUSTERS...
...THEN FUSE THEM TOGETHER ONCE INSIDE!
KRAKAKKAAK
IT'S TAKING OFF, GEO-FORCE! NOW WOULD BE GOOD!
WARNING. THRUSTER FAILURE.
NO!
DO NOT COMMENCE FULL POWER IGNITION.
HANG ON!
WHAT GOES UP MUST COME DOWN.
BRATTATBRATTA
CONSIDER THIS THING GROUNDED!
DAMN YOU ALL FOR INTERFERING WITH MY MISSION!
BRATTATBRATTA

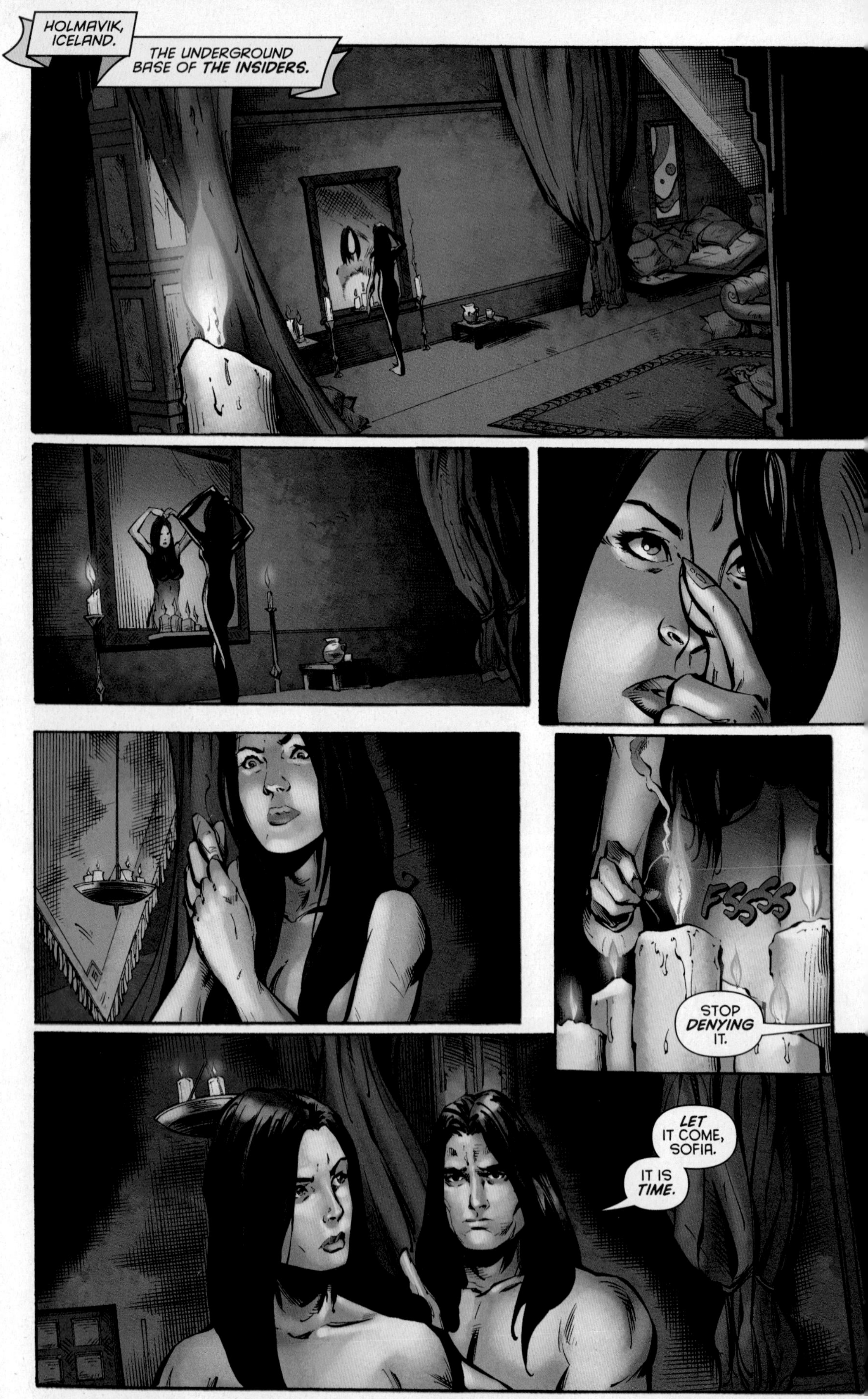
HOLMAVIK, ICELAND.
THE UNDERGROUND BASE OF THE INSIDERS.
FSSS
STOP DENYING IT.
LET IT COME, SOFIA.
IT IS TIME.

IT IS AN *ABERRATION!*

AND *I* WILL NOT GO SOFTLY INTO THE DARK NIGHT.

NOT WHEN THERE ARE *COUNTLESS DAWNS* LEFT FOR ME TO SEE.

SLAP

WHEN THE WORLD WAS YOUNG IT WAS EASY TO DO WHAT WE DO.

NOW, THE WORLD IS MUCH SMALLER THAN IT USED TO BE. *TOO* SMALL, ACTUALLY.

I WOULD RATHER HAVE OUR END DAYS *END* IN BLISS THAN IN THIS CONSTANT STATE OF TURMOIL AND FEAR, SOFIA.

THERE WILL BE *NO* ENDING, MICHAEL. *NOT FOR ME.*

ATTENTION, EVERYONE.

PLEASE COME TO THE VIEWING CENTER.

IT SEEMS WE HAVE A *SITUATION* IN GERMANY.

THE GOOD NEWS IS, THE ELEMENTAL SCANNER CONFIRMS A POSITIVE *ACQUISITION.*

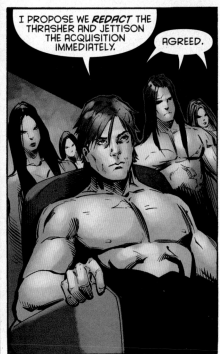

I PROPOSE WE *REDACT* THE THRASHER AND JETTISON THE ACQUISITION IMMEDIATELY.

AGREED.

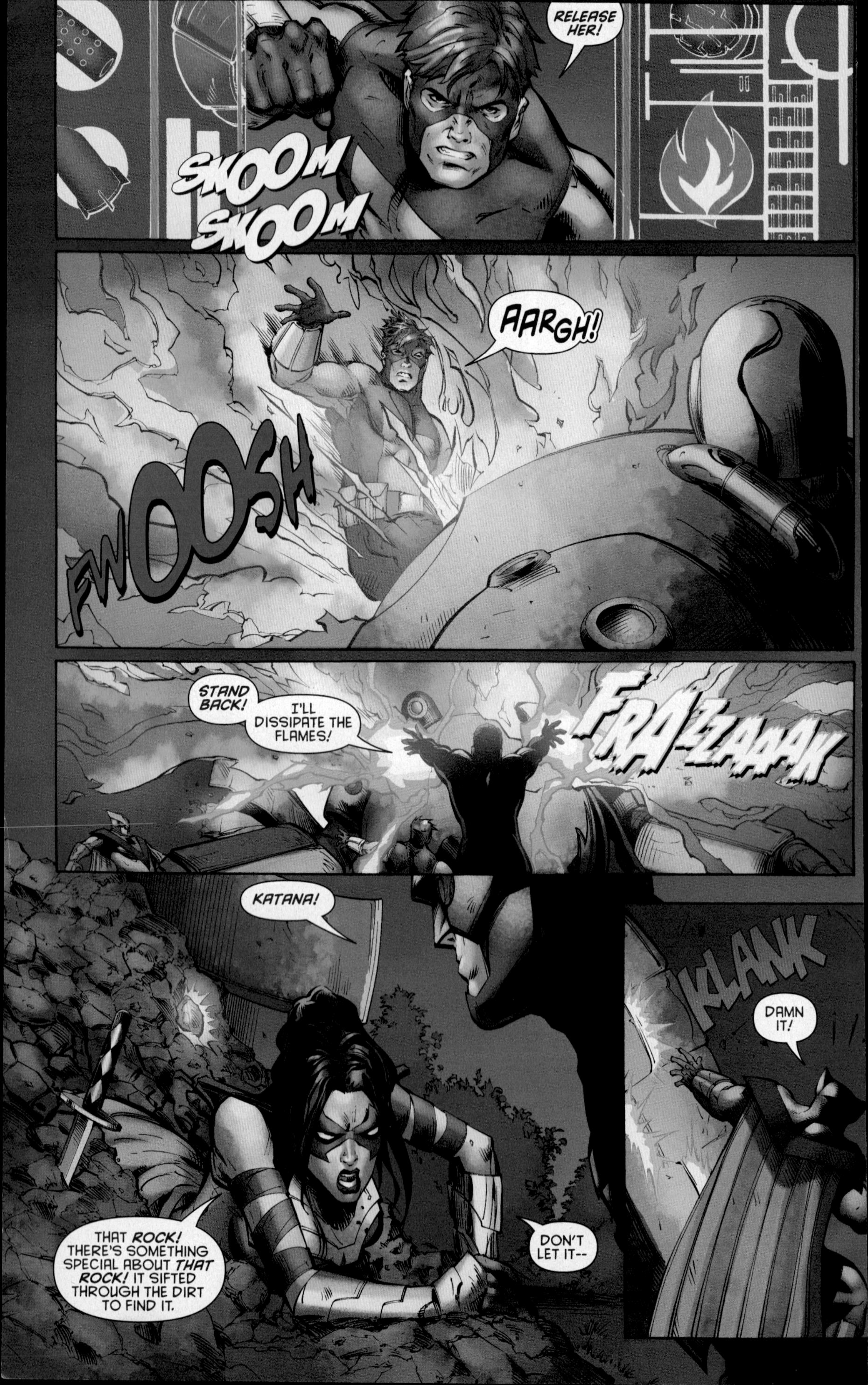
RELEASE HER!
SKOOM SKOOM
AARGH!
FWOOSH
STAND BACK!
I'LL DISSIPATE THE FLAMES!
FRA-ZAAAK
KATANA!
THAT ROCK! THERE'S SOMETHING SPECIAL ABOUT THAT ROCK! IT SIFTED THROUGH THE DIRT TO FIND IT.
DON'T LET IT--
KLANK
DAMN IT!

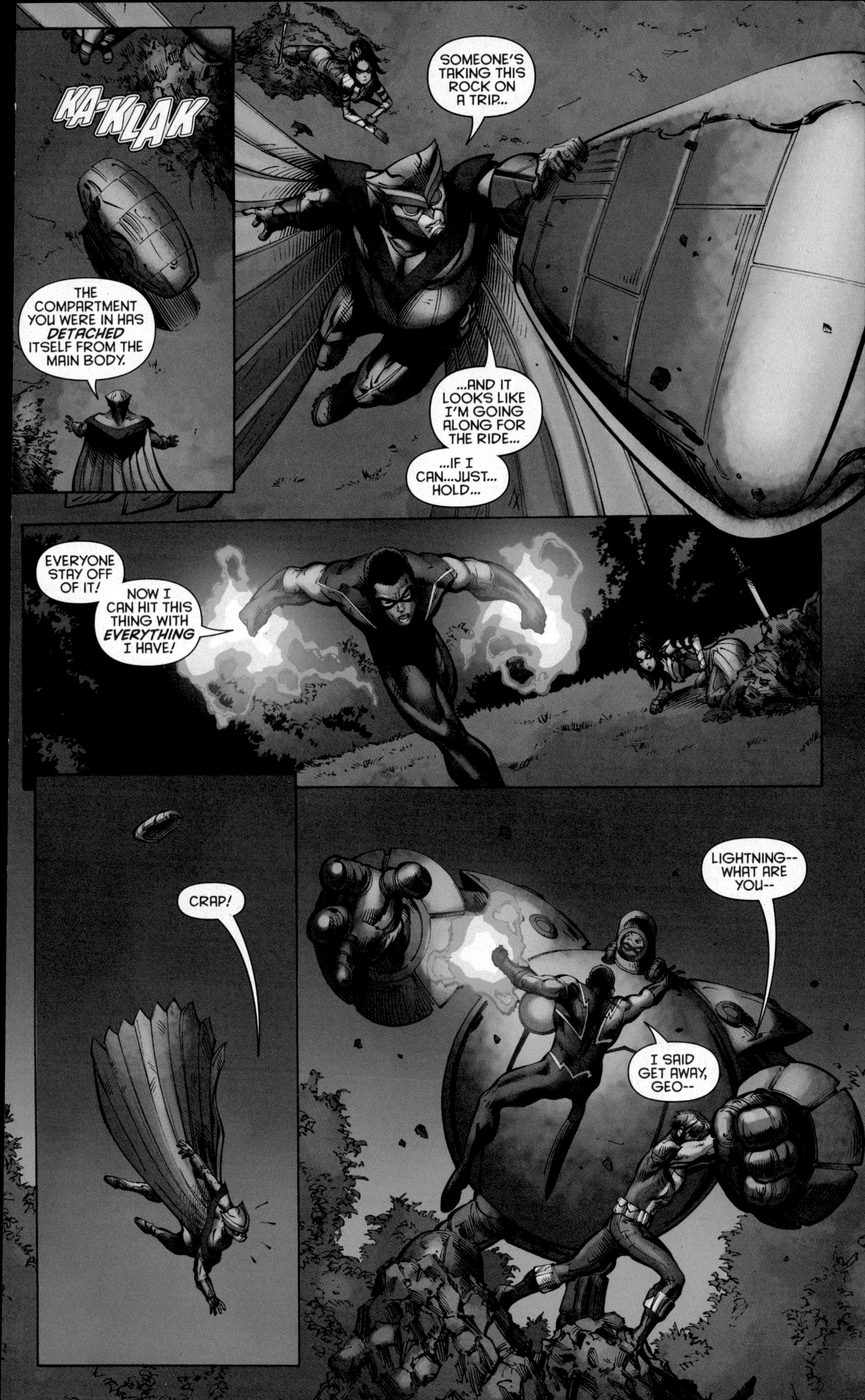
KA-KLAK
SOMEONE'S TAKING THIS ROCK ON A TRIP...
THE COMPARTMENT YOU WERE IN HAS *DETACHED* ITSELF FROM THE MAIN BODY.
...AND IT LOOKS LIKE I'M GOING ALONG FOR THE RIDE...
...IF I CAN...JUST... HOLD...
EVERYONE STAY OFF OF IT!
NOW I CAN HIT THIS THING WITH *EVERYTHING* I HAVE!
CRAP!
LIGHTNING-- WHAT ARE YOU--
I SAID GET AWAY, GEO--

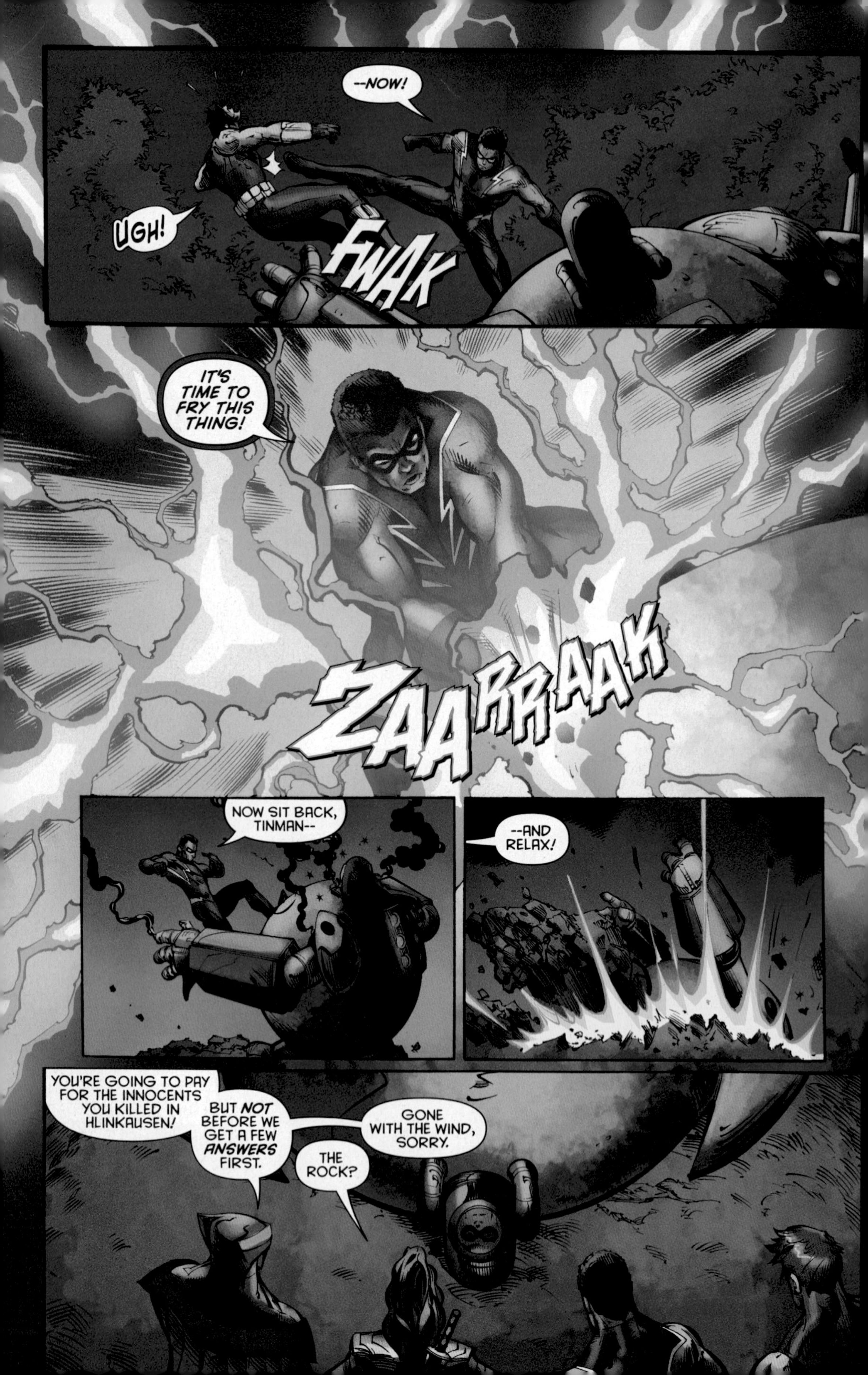
--NOW!
UGH!
FWAK
IT'S TIME TO FRY THIS THING!
ZAARRAAK
NOW SIT BACK, TINMAN--
--AND RELAX!
YOU'RE GOING TO PAY FOR THE INNOCENTS YOU KILLED IN HLINKAUSEN!
BUT NOT BEFORE WE GET A FEW ANSWERS FIRST.
THE ROCK?
GONE WITH THE WIND, SORRY.

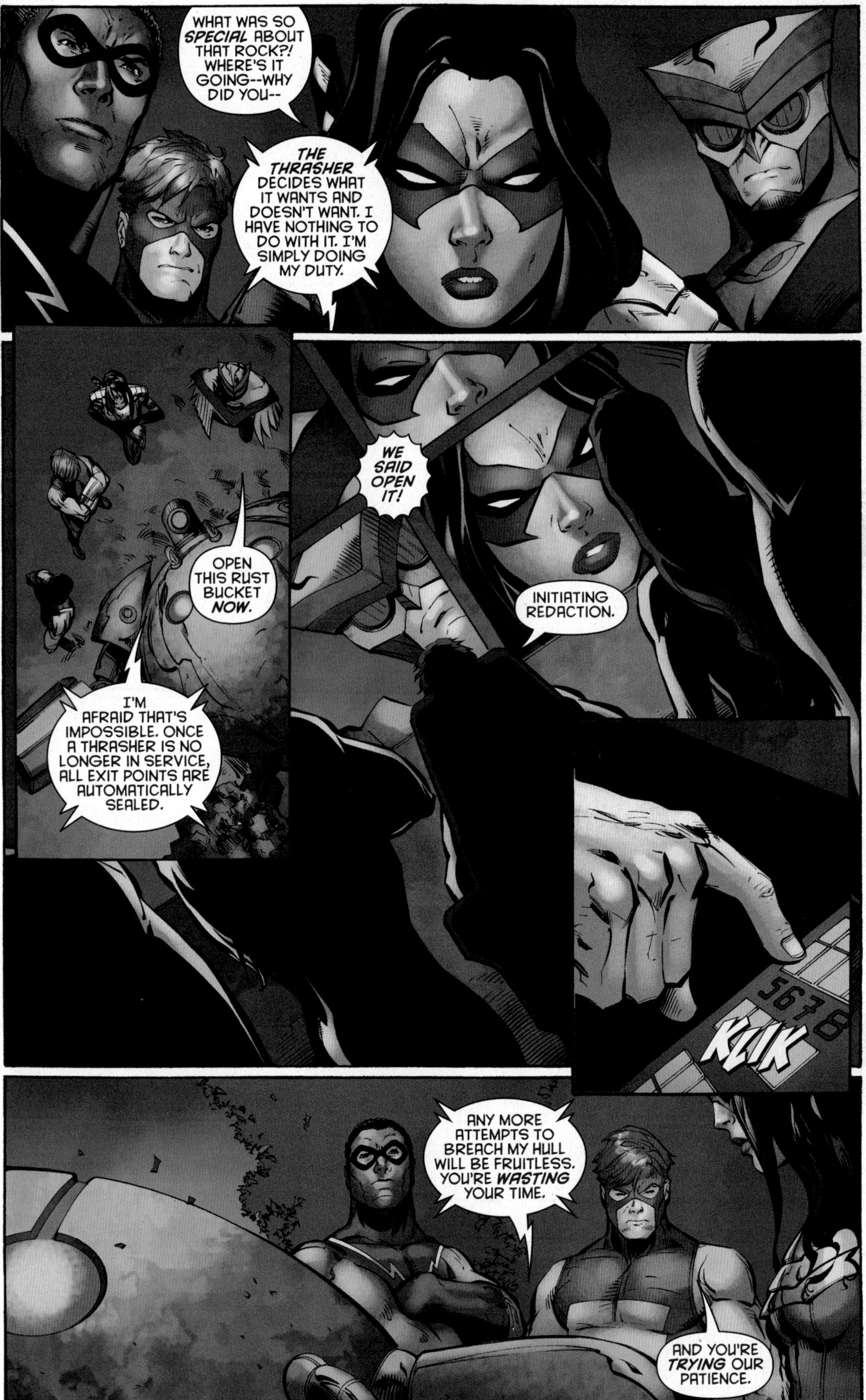
WHAT WAS SO SPECIAL ABOUT THAT ROCK?! WHERE'S IT GOING--WHY DID YOU--
THE THRASHER DECIDES WHAT IT WANTS AND DOESN'T WANT. I HAVE NOTHING TO DO WITH IT. I'M SIMPLY DOING MY DUTY.
OPEN THIS RUST BUCKET NOW.
I'M AFRAID THAT'S IMPOSSIBLE. ONCE A THRASHER IS NO LONGER IN SERVICE, ALL EXIT POINTS ARE AUTOMATICALLY SEALED.
WE SAID OPEN IT!
INITIATING REDACTION.
5678
KLIK
ANY MORE ATTEMPTS TO BREACH MY HULL WILL BE FRUITLESS. YOU'RE WASTING YOUR TIME.
AND YOU'RE TRYING OUR PATIENCE.

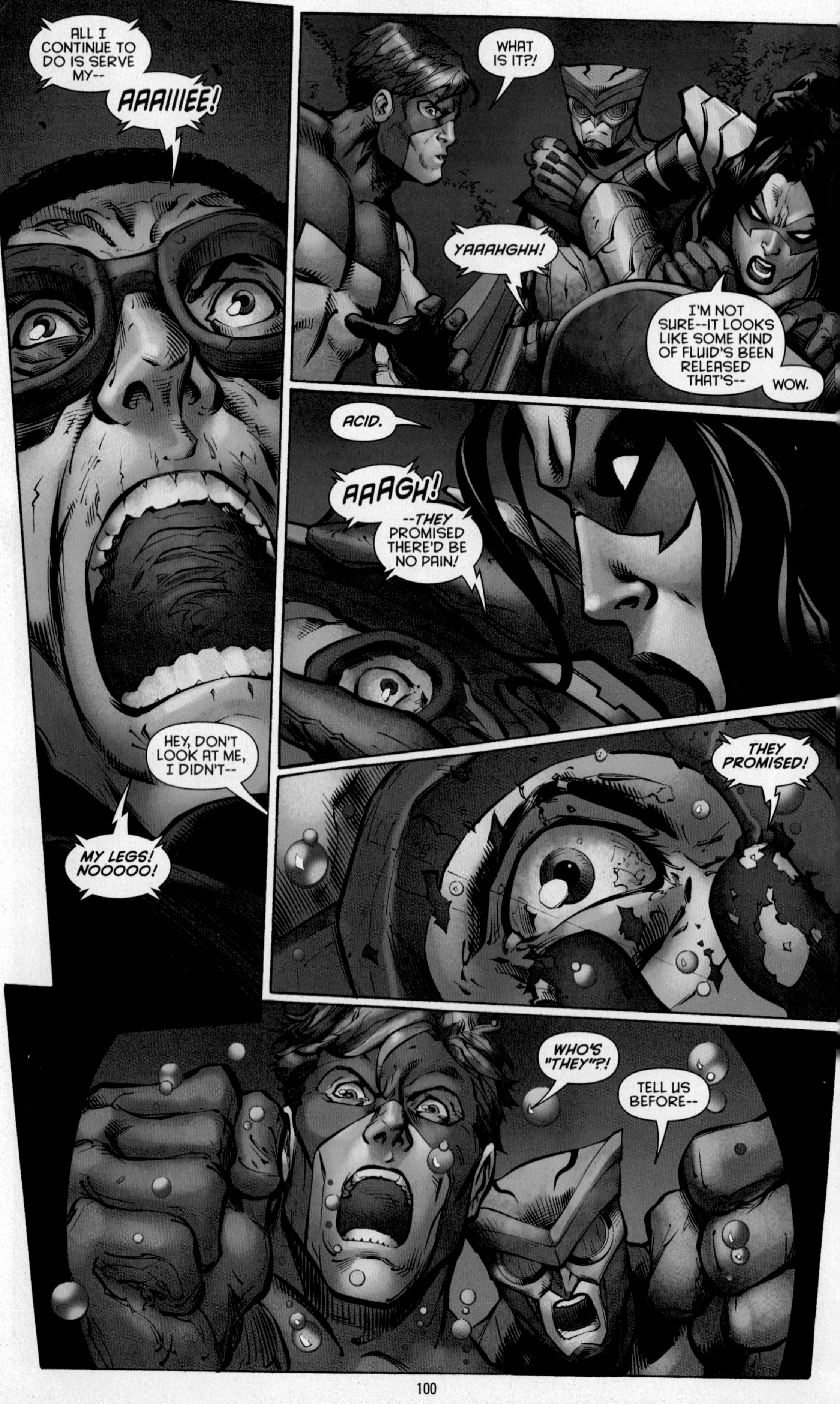
ALL I CONTINUE TO DO IS SERVE MY--
AAAIIIEE!
WHAT IS IT?!
YAAAHGHH!
I'M NOT SURE--IT LOOKS LIKE SOME KIND OF FLUID'S BEEN RELEASED THAT'S--
WOW.
ACID.
AAAGH!
--THEY PROMISED THERE'D BE NO PAIN!
HEY, DON'T LOOK AT ME, I DIDN'T--
MY LEGS! NOOOOO!
THEY PROMISED!
WHO'S "THEY"?!
TELL US BEFORE--

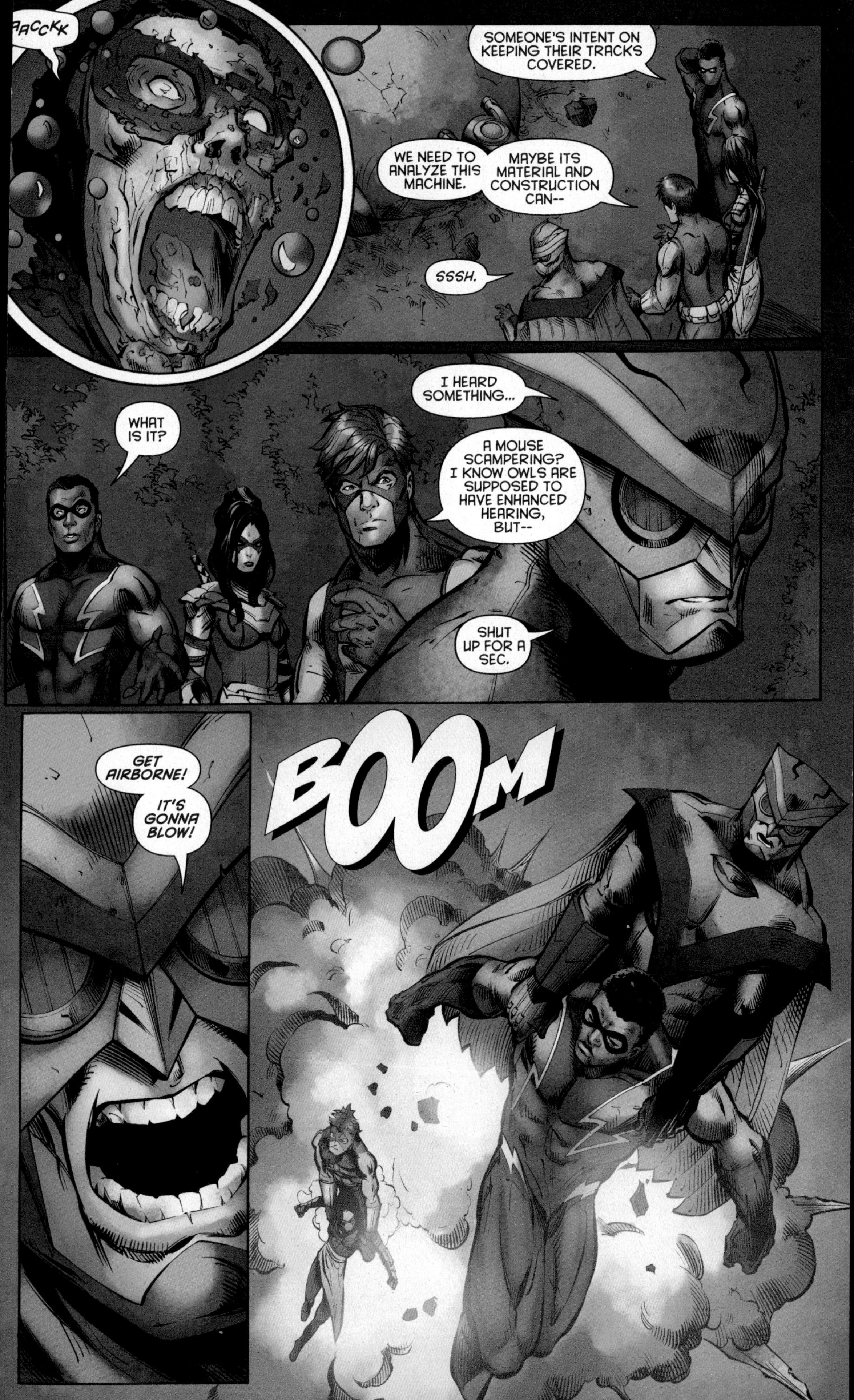
AACCKK
SOMEONE'S INTENT ON KEEPING THEIR TRACKS COVERED.
WE NEED TO ANALYZE THIS MACHINE.
MAYBE ITS MATERIAL AND CONSTRUCTION CAN--
SSSH.
I HEARD SOMETHING...
WHAT IS IT?
A MOUSE SCAMPERING? I KNOW OWLS ARE SUPPOSED TO HAVE ENHANCED HEARING, BUT--
SHUT UP FOR A SEC.
GET AIRBORNE!
IT'S GONNA BLOW!
BOOM

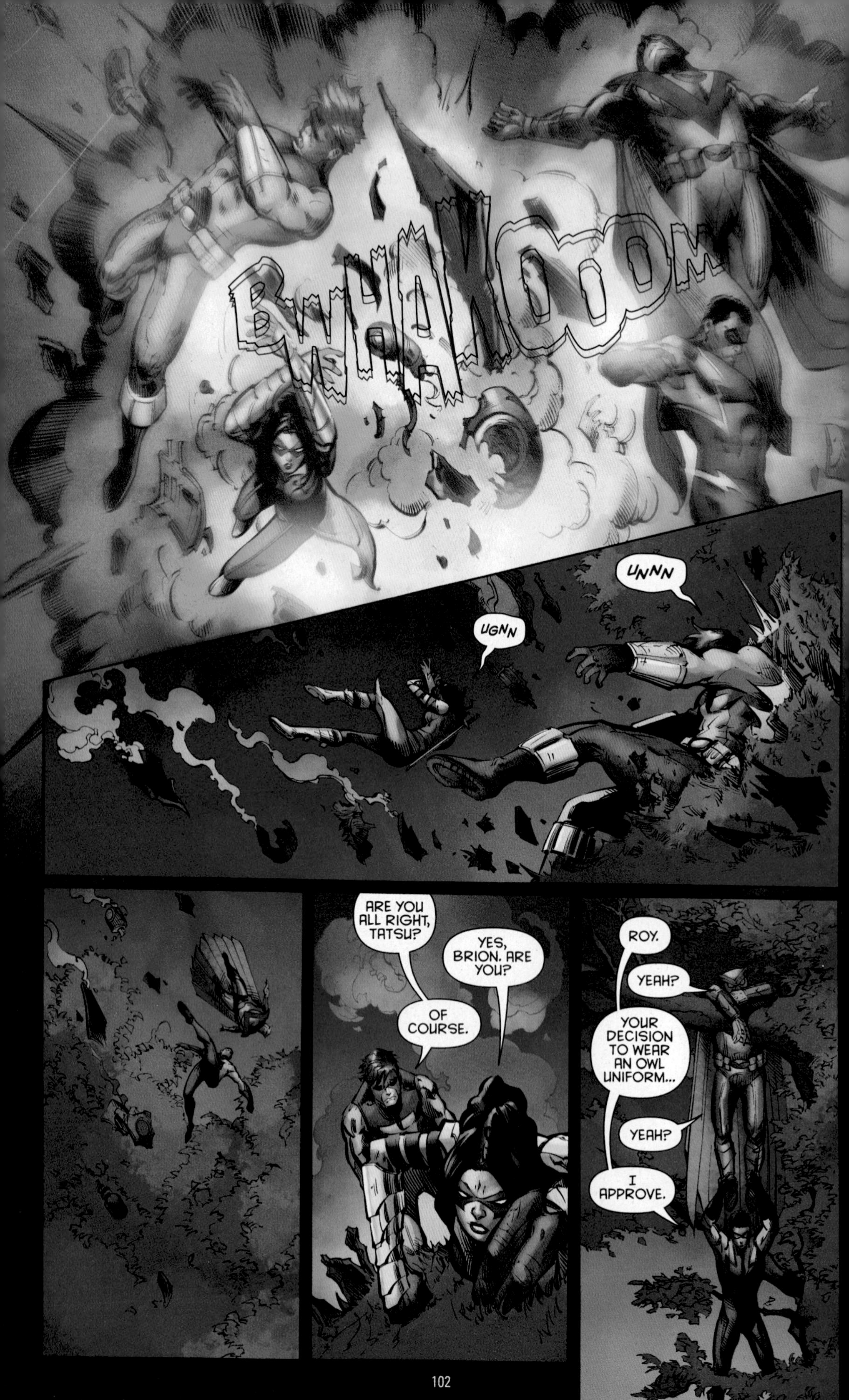
BWAKOOOM
UNNN
UGNN
ARE YOU ALL RIGHT, TATSU?
YES, BRION. ARE YOU?
OF COURSE.
ROY.
YEAH?
YOUR DECISION TO WEAR AN OWL UNIFORM...
YEAH?
I APPROVE.

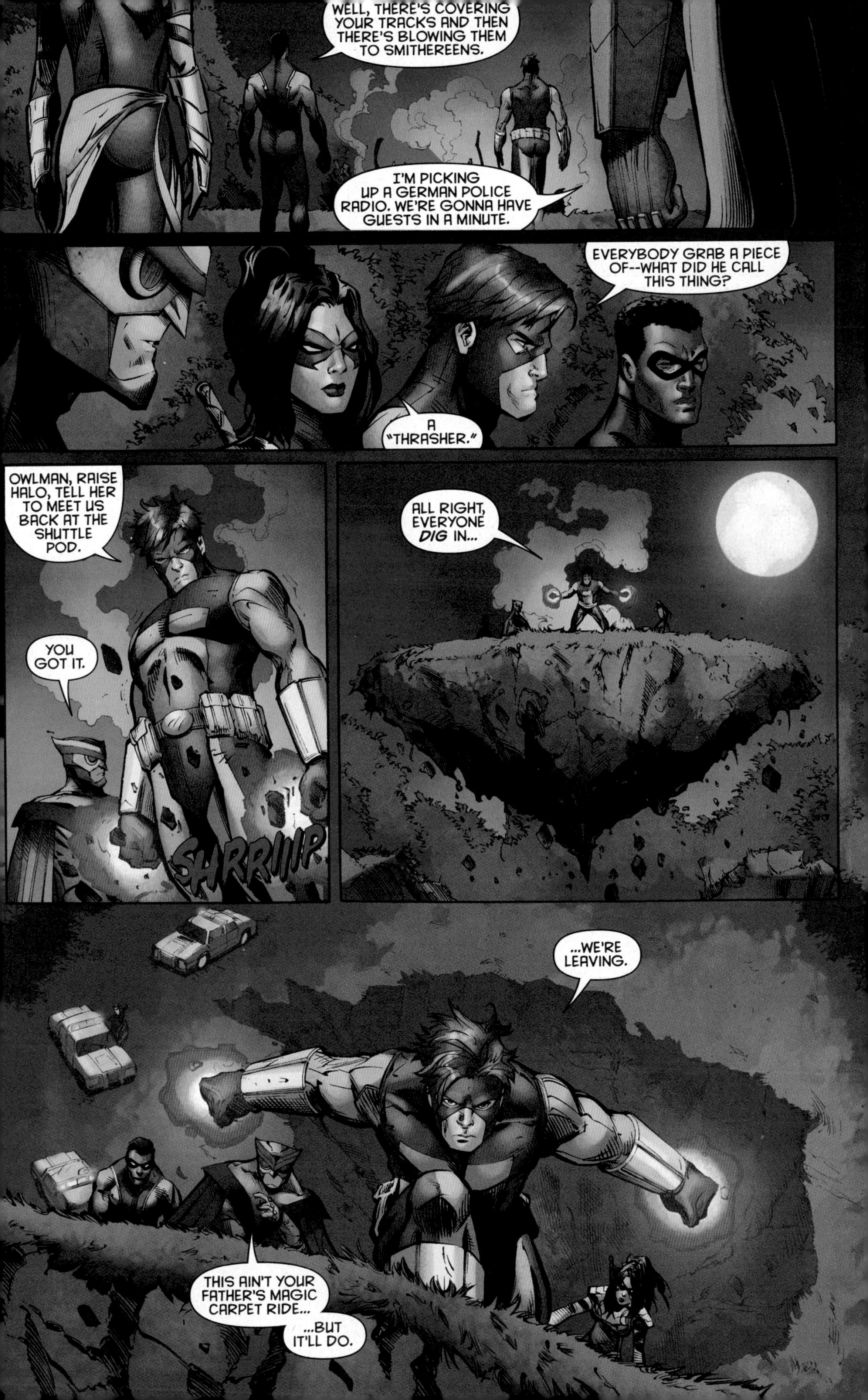

WELL, THERE'S COVERING YOUR TRACKS AND THEN THERE'S BLOWING THEM TO SMITHEREENS.
I'M PICKING UP A GERMAN POLICE RADIO. WE'RE GONNA HAVE GUESTS IN A MINUTE.
EVERYBODY GRAB A PIECE OF--WHAT DID HE CALL THIS THING?
A "THRASHER."
OWLMAN, RAISE HALO, TELL HER TO MEET US BACK AT THE SHUTTLE POD.
YOU GOT IT.
SHRRIIIP
ALL RIGHT, EVERYONE *DIG* IN...
...WE'RE LEAVING.
THIS AIN'T YOUR FATHER'S MAGIC CARPET RIDE...
...BUT IT'LL DO.

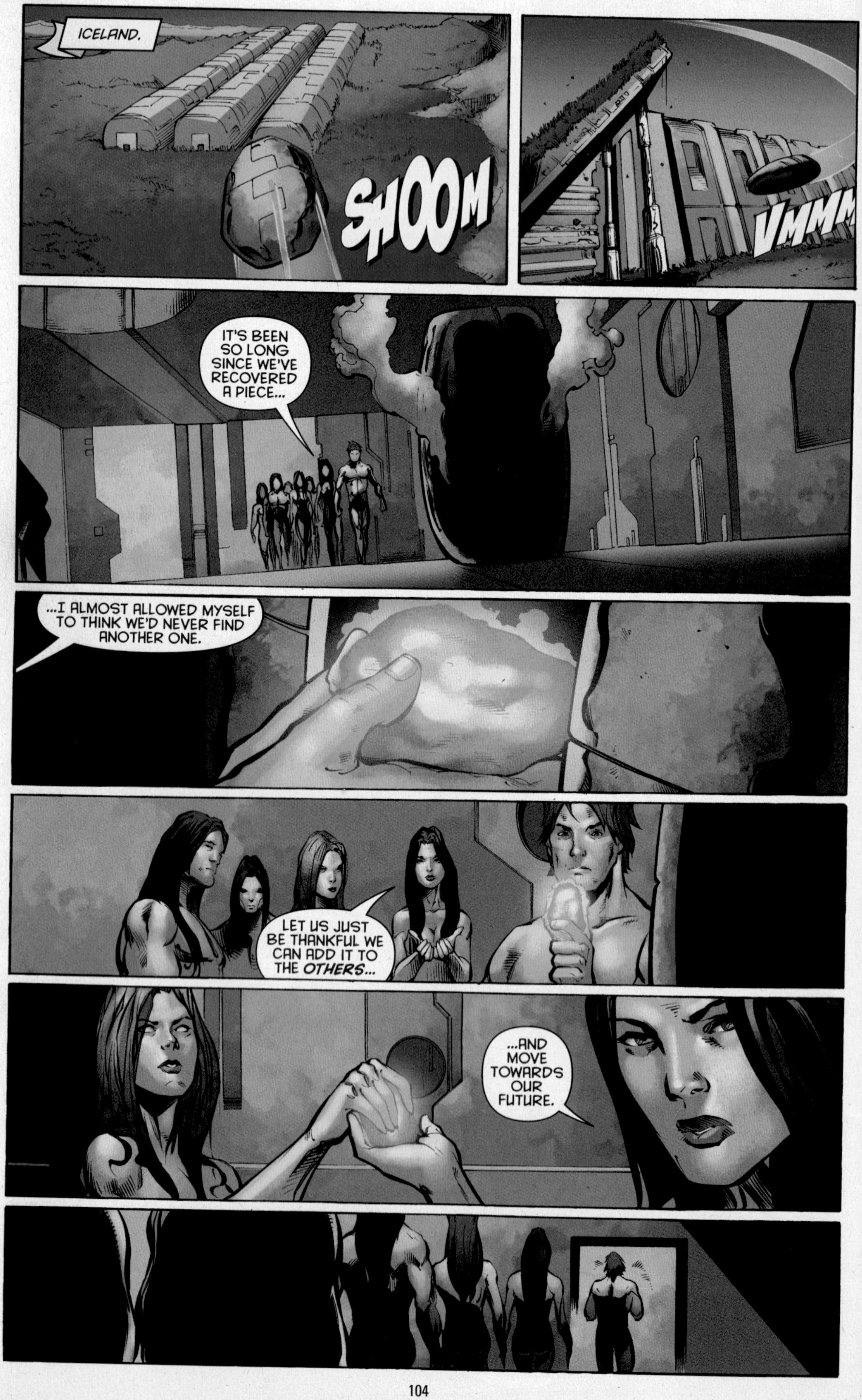
ICELAND.
SHOOM
VMMM
IT'S BEEN SO LONG SINCE WE'VE RECOVERED A PIECE...
...I ALMOST ALLOWED MYSELF TO THINK WE'D NEVER FIND ANOTHER ONE.
LET US JUST BE THANKFUL WE CAN ADD IT TO THE *OTHERS*...
...AND MOVE TOWARDS OUR FUTURE.

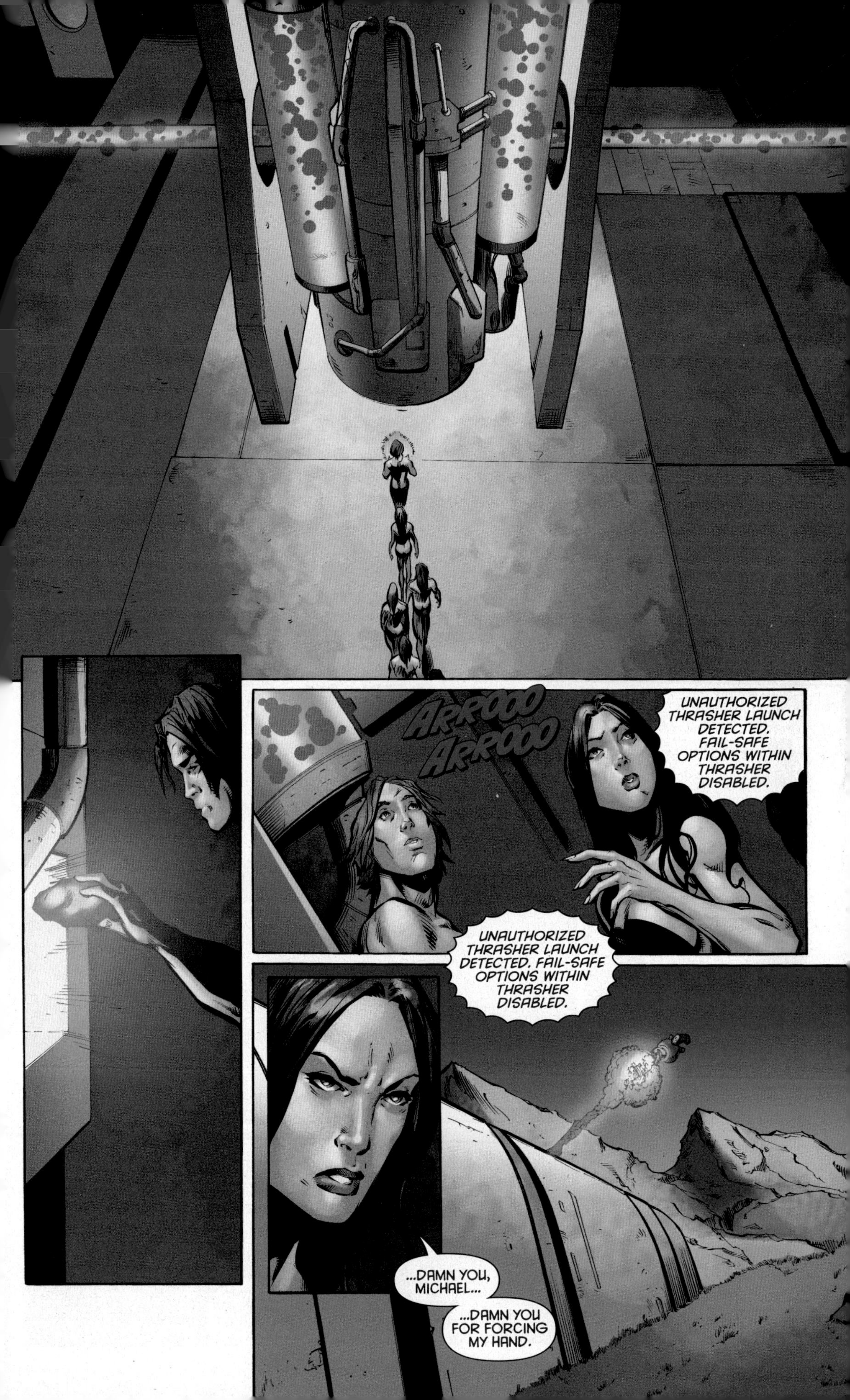
ARROOO ARROOO
UNAUTHORIZED THRASHER LAUNCH DETECTED. FAIL-SAFE OPTIONS WITHIN THRASHER DISABLED.
UNAUTHORIZED THRASHER LAUNCH DETECTED. FAIL-SAFE OPTIONS WITHIN THRASHER DISABLED.
...DAMN YOU, MICHAEL...
...DAMN YOU FOR FORCING MY HAND.

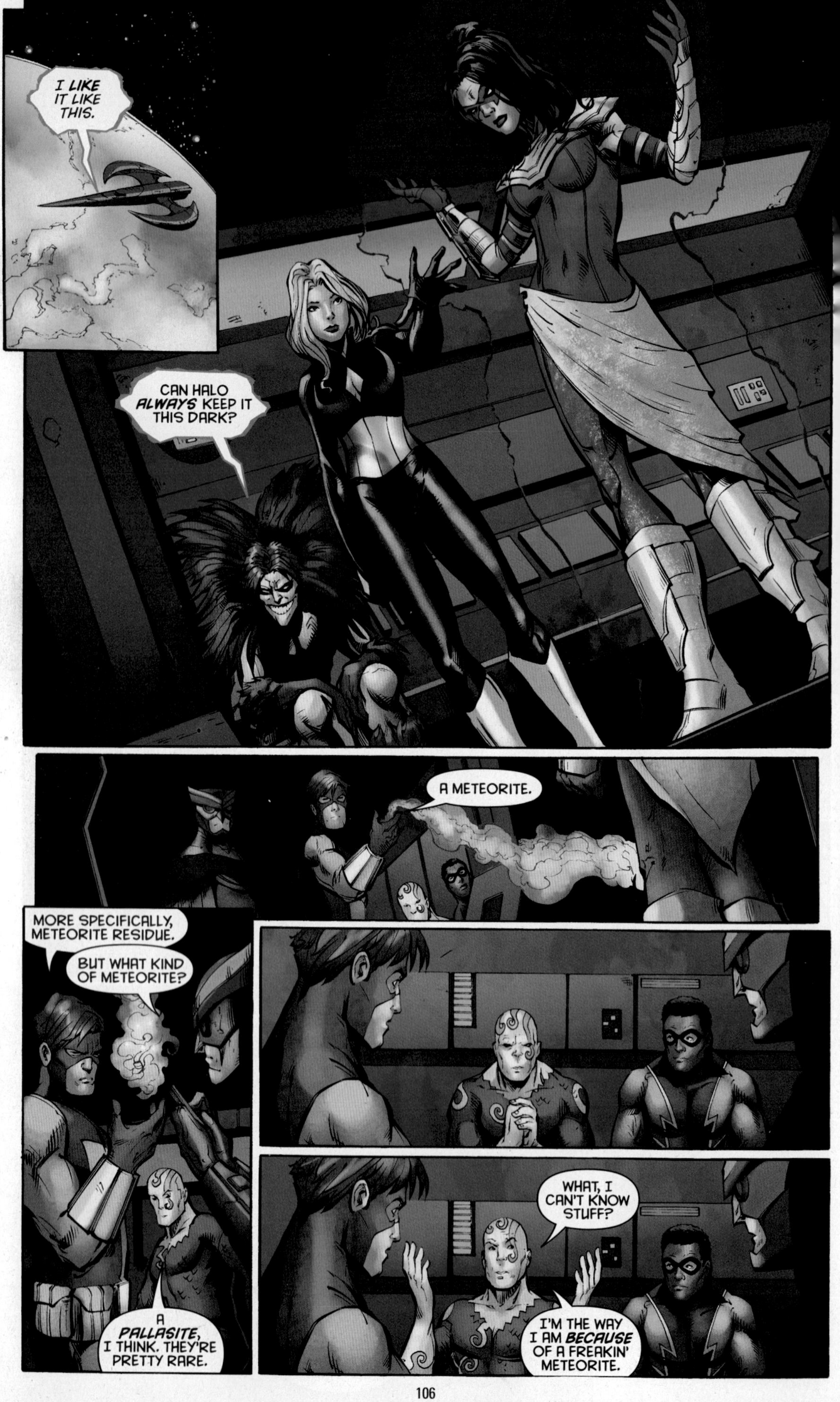

I LIKE IT LIKE THIS.
CAN HALO ALWAYS KEEP IT THIS DARK?
A METEORITE.
MORE SPECIFICALLY, METEORITE RESIDUE.
BUT WHAT KIND OF METEORITE?
A PALLASITE, I THINK. THEY'RE PRETTY RARE.
WHAT, I CAN'T KNOW STUFF?
I'M THE WAY I AM BECAUSE OF A FREAKIN' METEORITE.

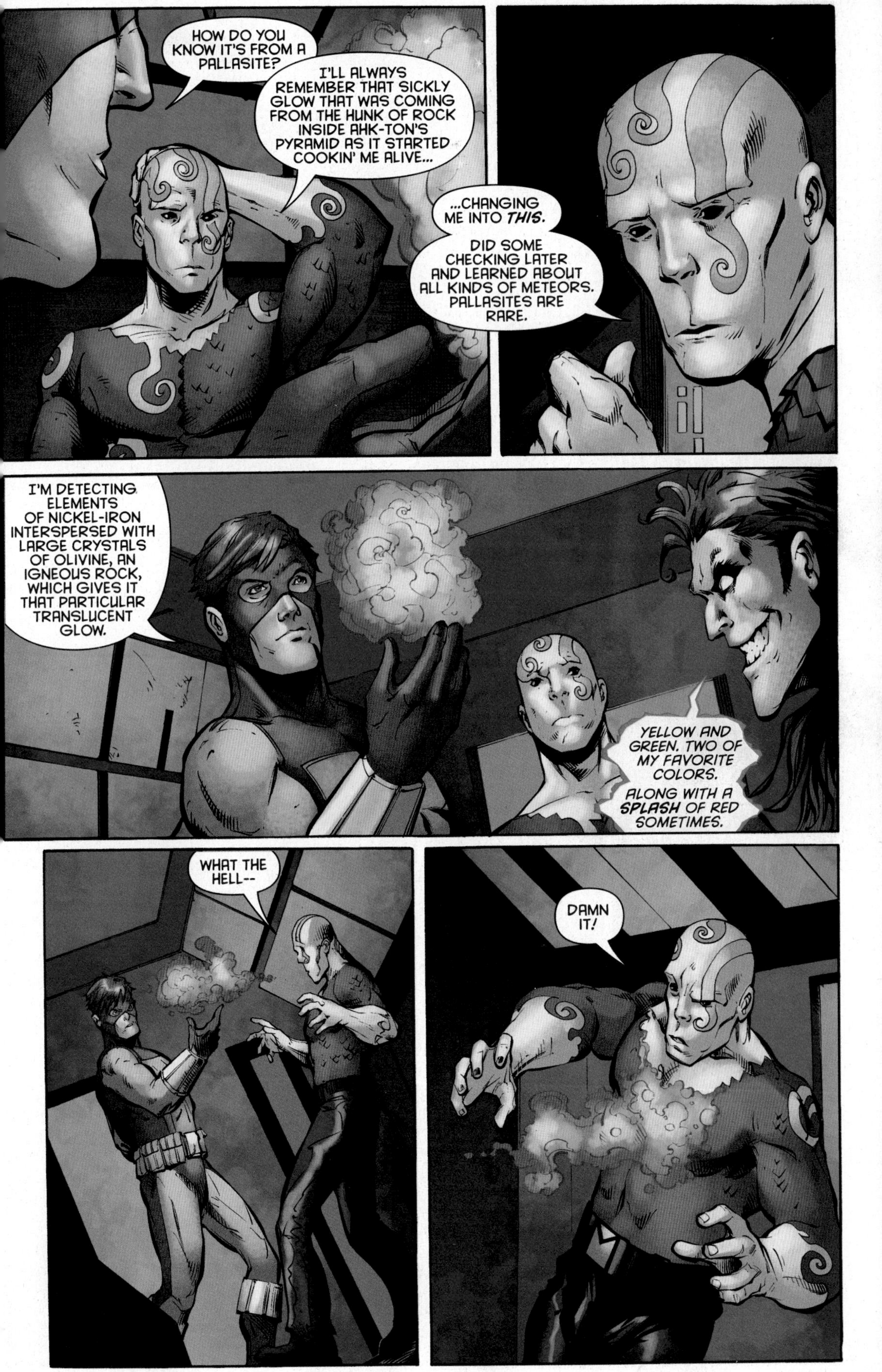

HOW DO YOU KNOW IT'S FROM A PALLASITE?
I'LL ALWAYS REMEMBER THAT SICKLY GLOW THAT WAS COMING FROM THE HUNK OF ROCK INSIDE AHK-TON'S PYRAMID AS IT STARTED COOKIN' ME ALIVE...
...CHANGING ME INTO THIS.
DID SOME CHECKING LATER AND LEARNED ABOUT ALL KINDS OF METEORS. PALLASITES ARE RARE.
I'M DETECTING ELEMENTS OF NICKEL-IRON INTERSPERSED WITH LARGE CRYSTALS OF OLIVINE, AN IGNEOUS ROCK, WHICH GIVES IT THAT PARTICULAR TRANSLUCENT GLOW.
YELLOW AND GREEN. TWO OF MY FAVORITE COLORS.
ALONG WITH A SPLASH OF RED SOMETIMES.
WHAT THE HELL--
DAMN IT!

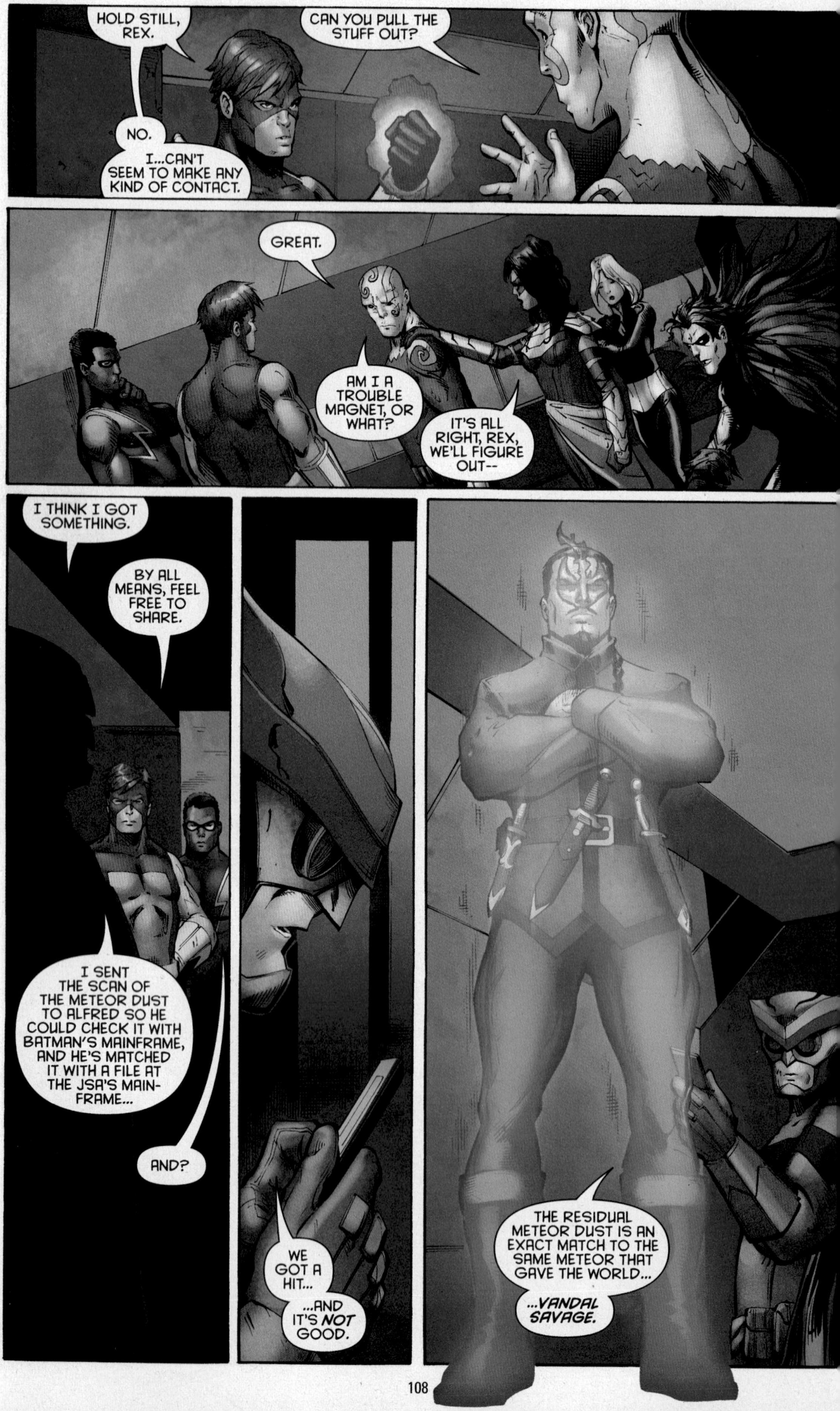

HOLD STILL, REX.
CAN YOU PULL THE STUFF OUT?
NO.
I...CAN'T SEEM TO MAKE ANY KIND OF CONTACT.
GREAT.
AM I A TROUBLE MAGNET, OR WHAT?
IT'S ALL RIGHT, REX, WE'LL FIGURE OUT--
I THINK I GOT SOMETHING.
BY ALL MEANS, FEEL FREE TO SHARE.
I SENT THE SCAN OF THE METEOR DUST TO ALFRED SO HE COULD CHECK IT WITH BATMAN'S MAINFRAME, AND HE'S MATCHED IT WITH A FILE AT THE JSA'S MAIN-FRAME...
AND?
WE GOT A HIT...
...AND IT'S *NOT* GOOD.
THE RESIDUAL METEOR DUST IS AN EXACT MATCH TO THE SAME METEOR THAT GAVE THE WORLD...
...*VANDAL SAVAGE.*

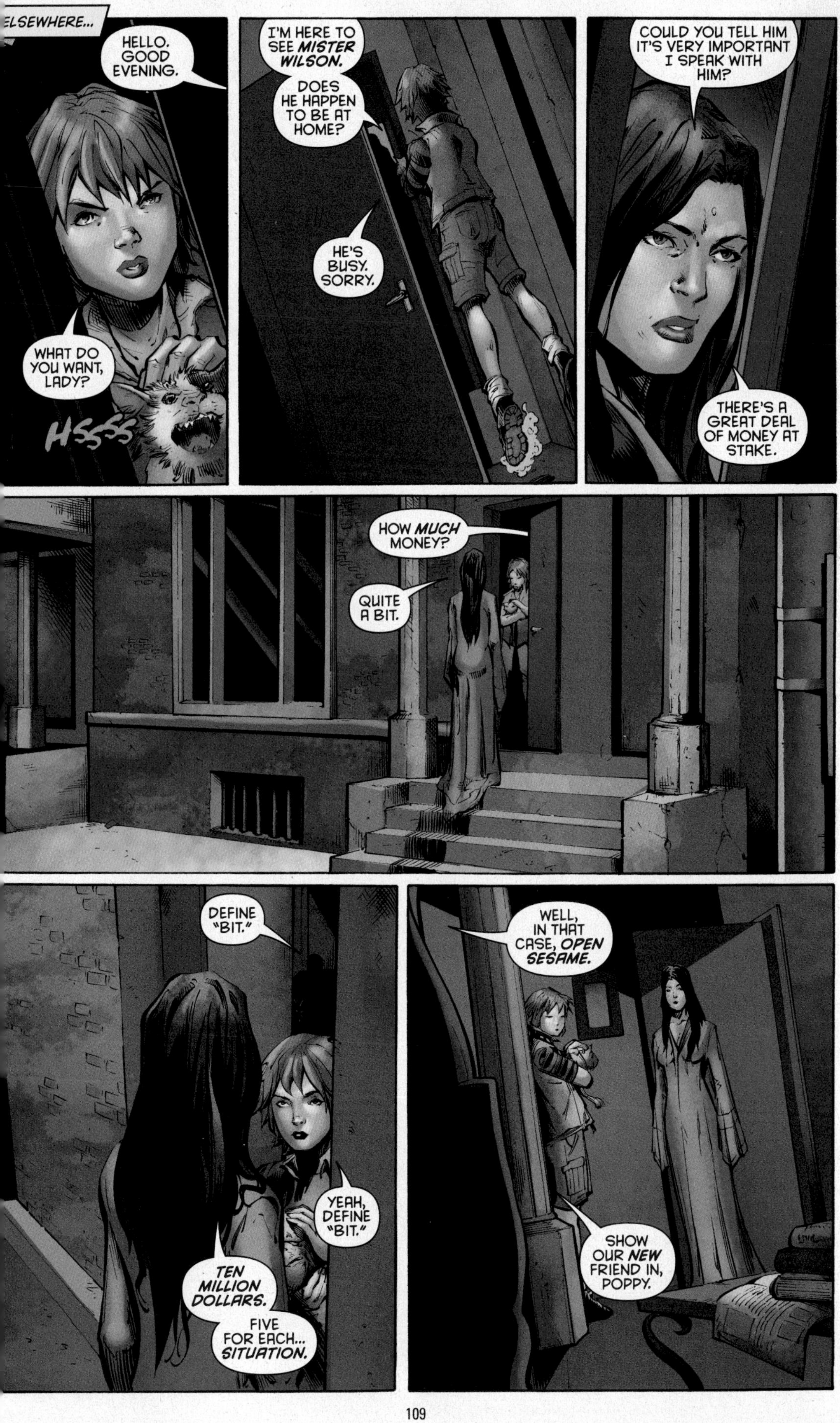

ELSEWHERE...
HELLO. GOOD EVENING.
WHAT DO YOU WANT, LADY?
HSSSS
I'M HERE TO SEE *MISTER WILSON.*
DOES HE HAPPEN TO BE AT HOME?
HE'S BUSY. SORRY.
COULD YOU TELL HIM IT'S VERY IMPORTANT I SPEAK WITH HIM?
THERE'S A GREAT DEAL OF MONEY AT STAKE.
HOW *MUCH* MONEY?
QUITE A BIT.
DEFINE "BIT."
YEAH, DEFINE "BIT."
TEN MILLION DOLLARS.
FIVE FOR EACH... *SITUATION.*
WELL, IN THAT CASE, *OPEN SESAME.*
SHOW OUR *NEW* FRIEND IN, POPPY.

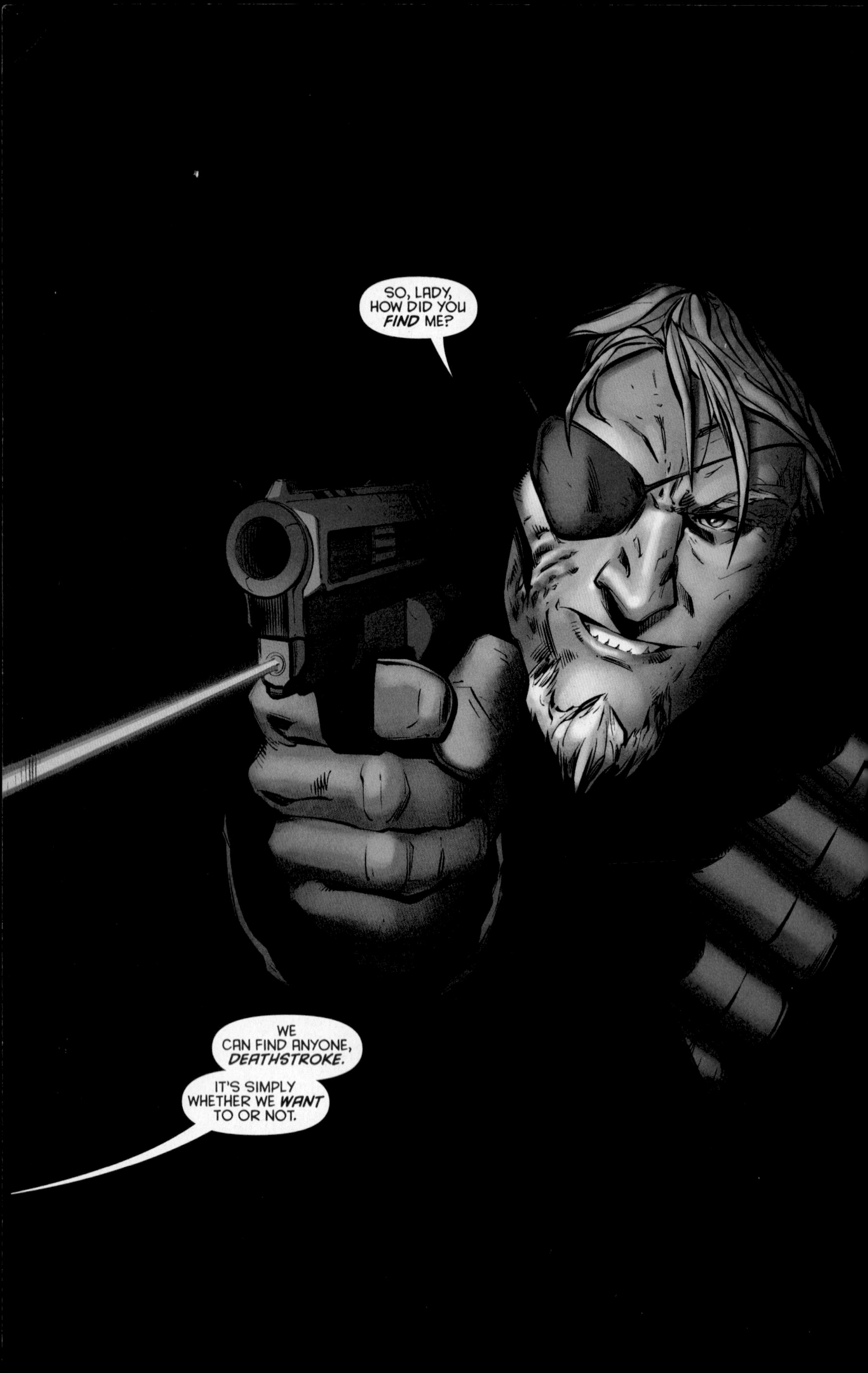
SO, LADY, HOW DID YOU *FIND* ME?
WE CAN FIND ANYONE, *DEATHSTROKE.*
IT'S SIMPLY WHETHER WE *WANT* TO OR NOT.

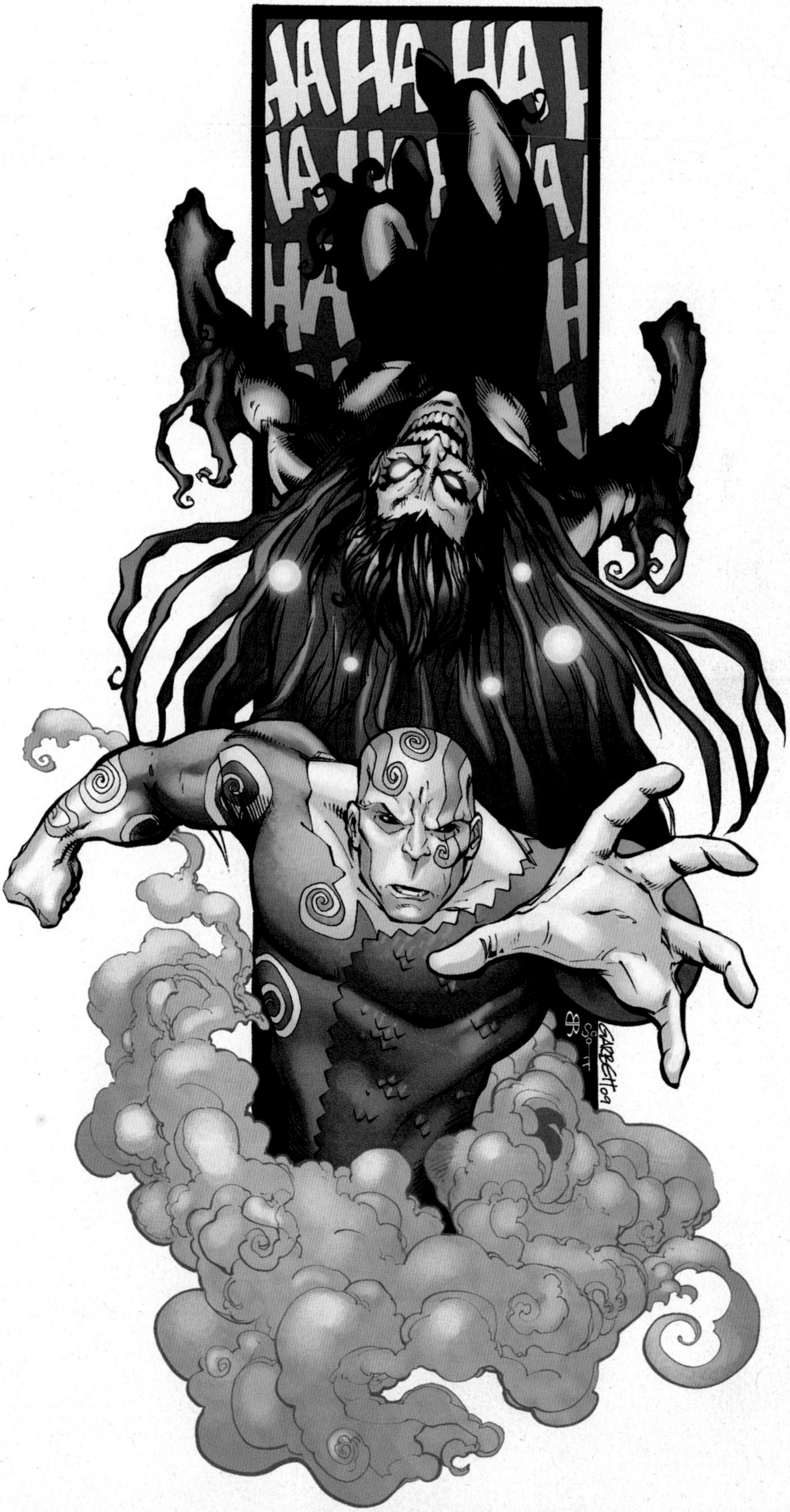
HA HA HA

"In this world we live in,
you're either a butcher or the animal."

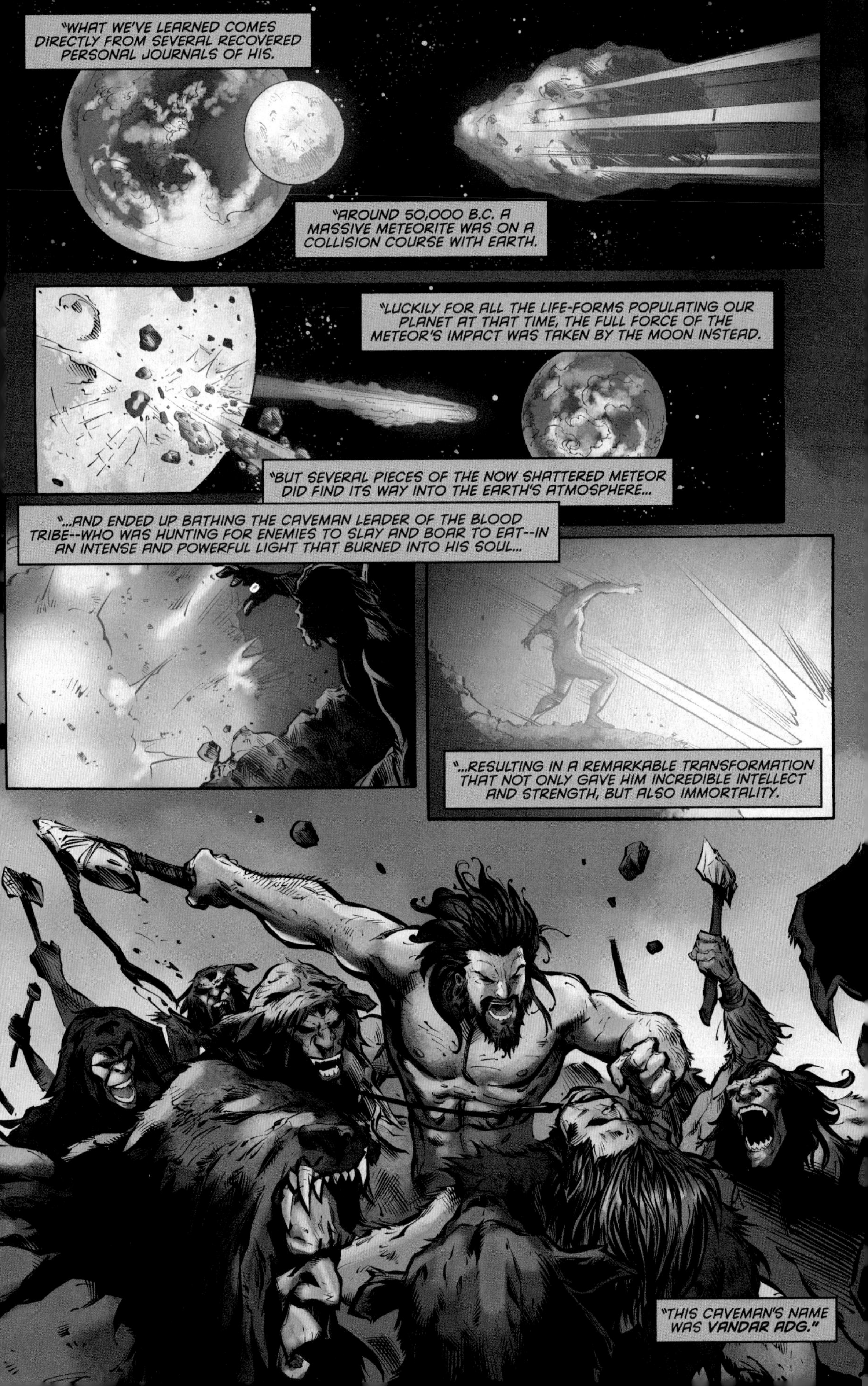
"WHAT WE'VE LEARNED COMES DIRECTLY FROM SEVERAL RECOVERED PERSONAL JOURNALS OF HIS.
"AROUND 50,000 B.C. A MASSIVE METEORITE WAS ON A COLLISION COURSE WITH EARTH.
"LUCKILY FOR ALL THE LIFE-FORMS POPULATING OUR PLANET AT THAT TIME, THE FULL FORCE OF THE METEOR'S IMPACT WAS TAKEN BY THE MOON INSTEAD.
"BUT SEVERAL PIECES OF THE NOW SHATTERED METEOR DID FIND ITS WAY INTO THE EARTH'S ATMOSPHERE...
"...AND ENDED UP BATHING THE CAVEMAN LEADER OF THE BLOOD TRIBE--WHO WAS HUNTING FOR ENEMIES TO SLAY AND BOAR TO EAT--IN AN INTENSE AND POWERFUL LIGHT THAT BURNED INTO HIS SOUL...
"...RESULTING IN A REMARKABLE TRANSFORMATION THAT NOT ONLY GAVE HIM INCREDIBLE INTELLECT AND STRENGTH, BUT ALSO IMMORTALITY.
"THIS CAVEMAN'S NAME WAS VANDAR ADG."

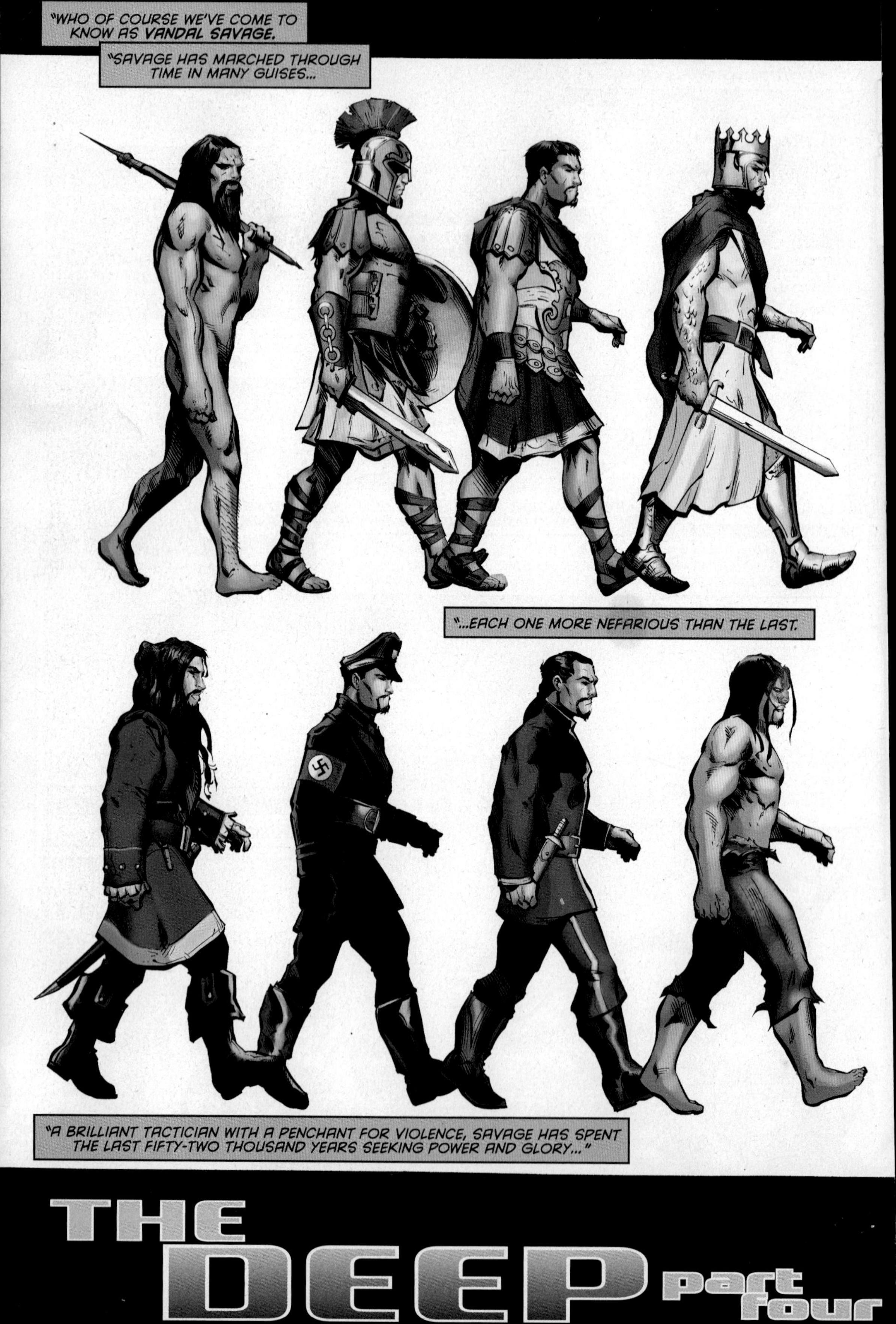
"WHO OF COURSE WE'VE COME TO KNOW AS VANDAL SAVAGE.
"SAVAGE HAS MARCHED THROUGH TIME IN MANY GUISES...
"...EACH ONE MORE NEFARIOUS THAN THE LAST.
"A BRILLIANT TACTICIAN WITH A PENCHANT FOR VIOLENCE, SAVAGE HAS SPENT THE LAST FIFTY-TWO THOUSAND YEARS SEEKING POWER AND GLORY..."
THE DEEP part four

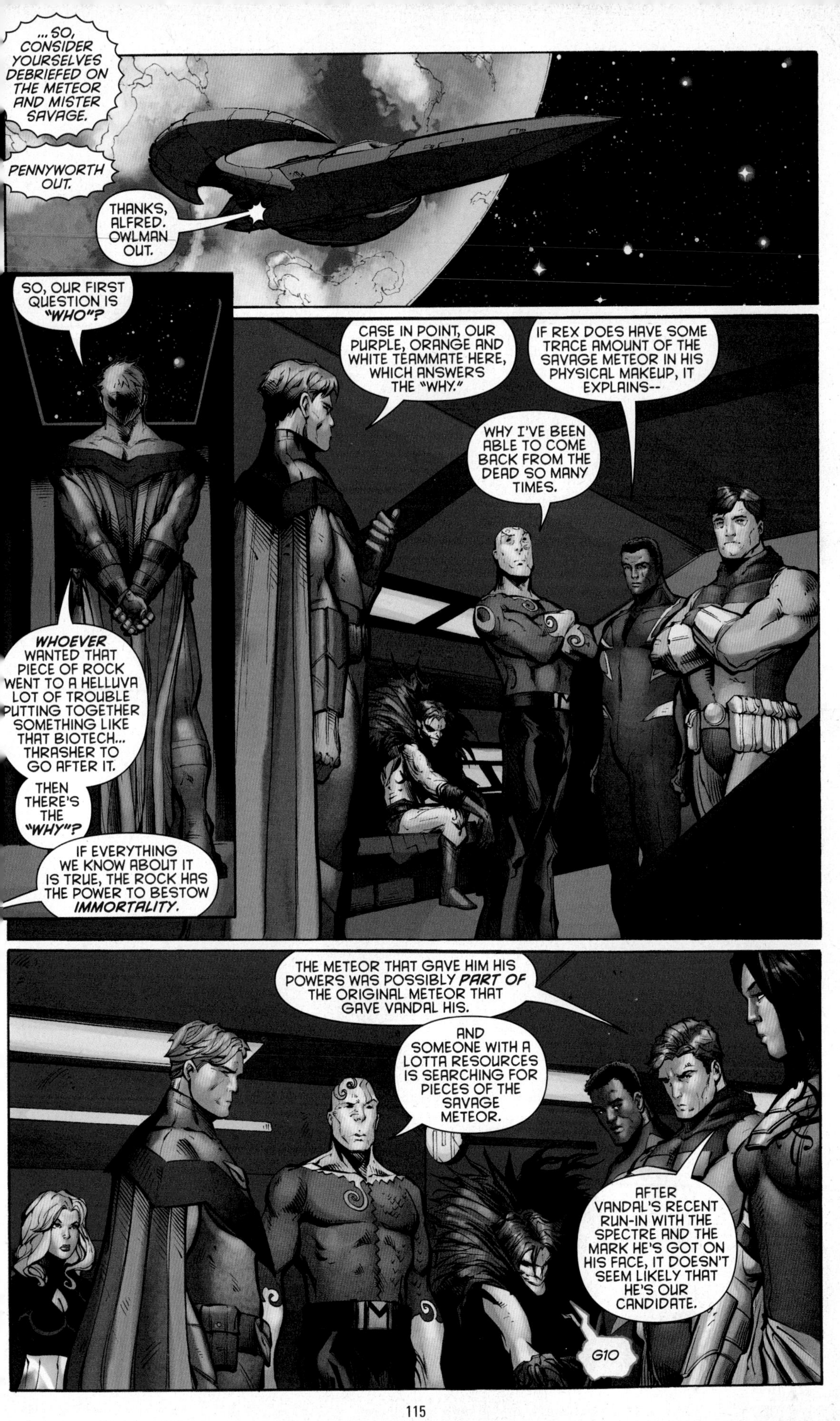
...SO, CONSIDER YOURSELVES DEBRIEFED ON THE METEOR AND MISTER SAVAGE.
PENNYWORTH OUT.
THANKS, ALFRED. OWLMAN OUT.
SO, OUR FIRST QUESTION IS "WHO"?
WHOEVER WANTED THAT PIECE OF ROCK WENT TO A HELLUVA LOT OF TROUBLE PUTTING TOGETHER SOMETHING LIKE THAT BIOTECH... THRASHER TO GO AFTER IT.
THEN THERE'S THE "WHY"?
IF EVERYTHING WE KNOW ABOUT IT IS TRUE, THE ROCK HAS THE POWER TO BESTOW IMMORTALITY.
CASE IN POINT, OUR PURPLE, ORANGE AND WHITE TEAMMATE HERE, WHICH ANSWERS THE "WHY."
IF REX DOES HAVE SOME TRACE AMOUNT OF THE SAVAGE METEOR IN HIS PHYSICAL MAKEUP, IT EXPLAINS--
WHY I'VE BEEN ABLE TO COME BACK FROM THE DEAD SO MANY TIMES.
THE METEOR THAT GAVE HIM HIS POWERS WAS POSSIBLY PART OF THE ORIGINAL METEOR THAT GAVE VANDAL HIS.
AND SOMEONE WITH A LOTTA RESOURCES IS SEARCHING FOR PIECES OF THE SAVAGE METEOR.
AFTER VANDAL'S RECENT RUN-IN WITH THE SPECTRE AND THE MARK HE'S GOT ON HIS FACE, IT DOESN'T SEEM LIKELY THAT HE'S OUR CANDIDATE.
G10

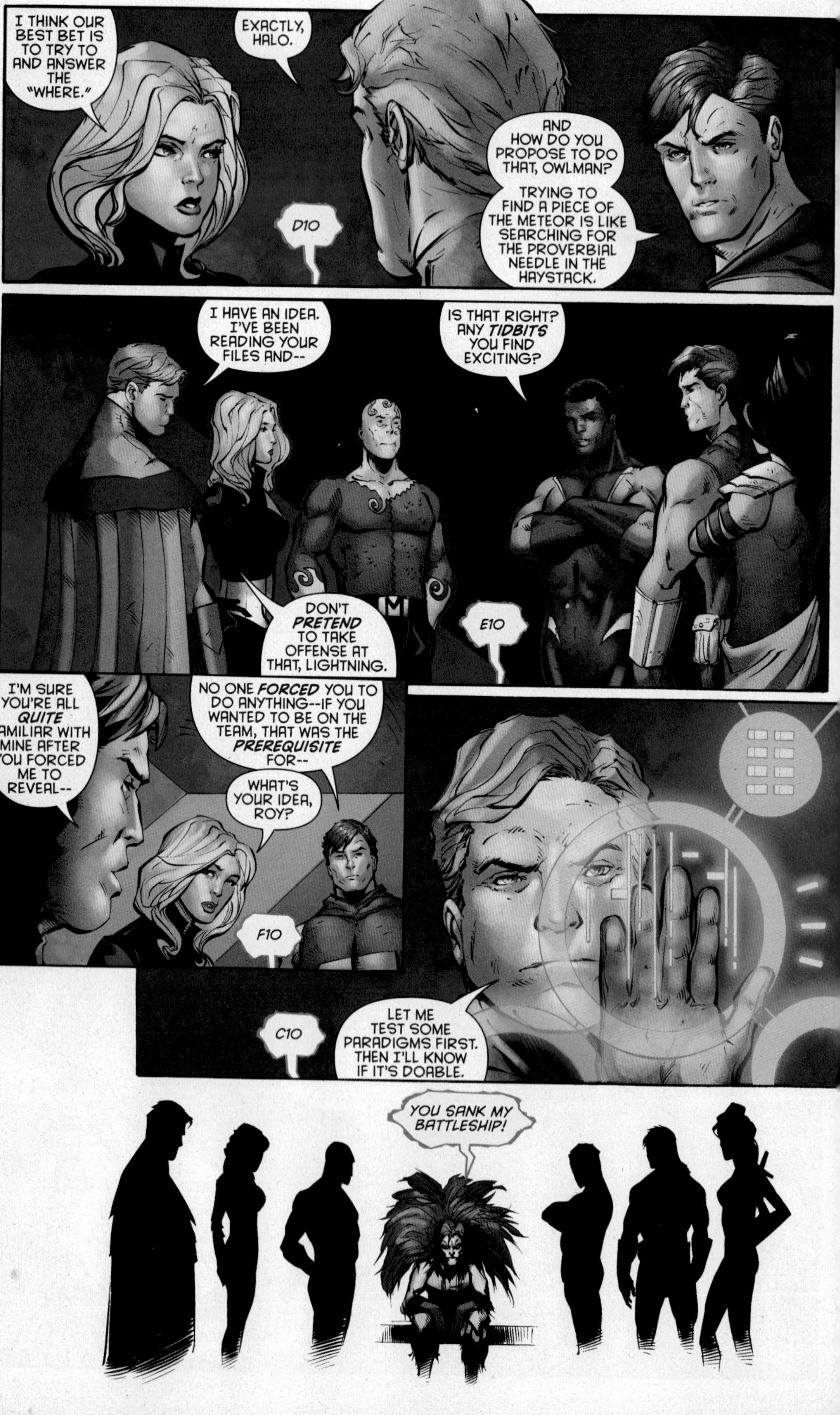
I THINK OUR BEST BET IS TO TRY TO AND ANSWER THE "WHERE."
EXACTLY, HALO.
AND HOW DO YOU PROPOSE TO DO THAT, OWLMAN?
TRYING TO FIND A PIECE OF THE METEOR IS LIKE SEARCHING FOR THE PROVERBIAL NEEDLE IN THE HAYSTACK.
D10
I HAVE AN IDEA. I'VE BEEN READING YOUR FILES AND--
IS THAT RIGHT? ANY TIDBITS YOU FIND EXCITING?
DON'T PRETEND TO TAKE OFFENSE AT THAT, LIGHTNING.
E10
I'M SURE YOU'RE ALL QUITE FAMILIAR WITH MINE AFTER YOU FORCED ME TO REVEAL--
NO ONE FORCED YOU TO DO ANYTHING--IF YOU WANTED TO BE ON THE TEAM, THAT WAS THE PREREQUISITE FOR--
WHAT'S YOUR IDEA, ROY?
F10
LET ME TEST SOME PARADIGMS FIRST. THEN I'LL KNOW IF IT'S DOABLE.
C10
YOU SANK MY BATTLESHIP!

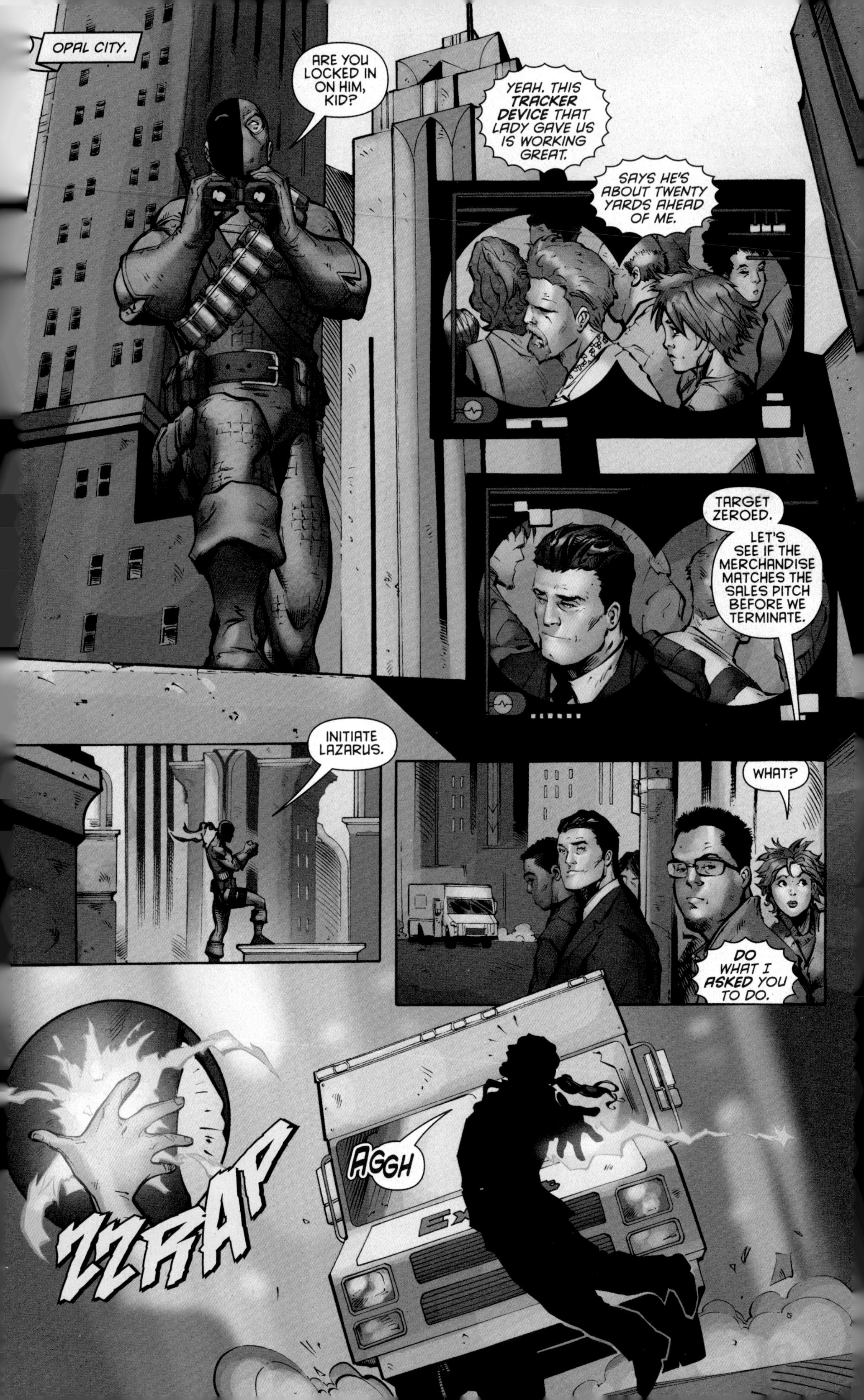

OPAL CITY.
ARE YOU LOCKED IN ON HIM, KID?
YEAH. THIS TRACKER DEVICE THAT LADY GAVE US IS WORKING GREAT.
SAYS HE'S ABOUT TWENTY YARDS AHEAD OF ME.
TARGET ZEROED.
LET'S SEE IF THE MERCHANDISE MATCHES THE SALES PITCH BEFORE WE TERMINATE.
INITIATE LAZARUS.
WHAT?
DO WHAT I ASKED YOU TO DO.
AGGH
ZZRAP

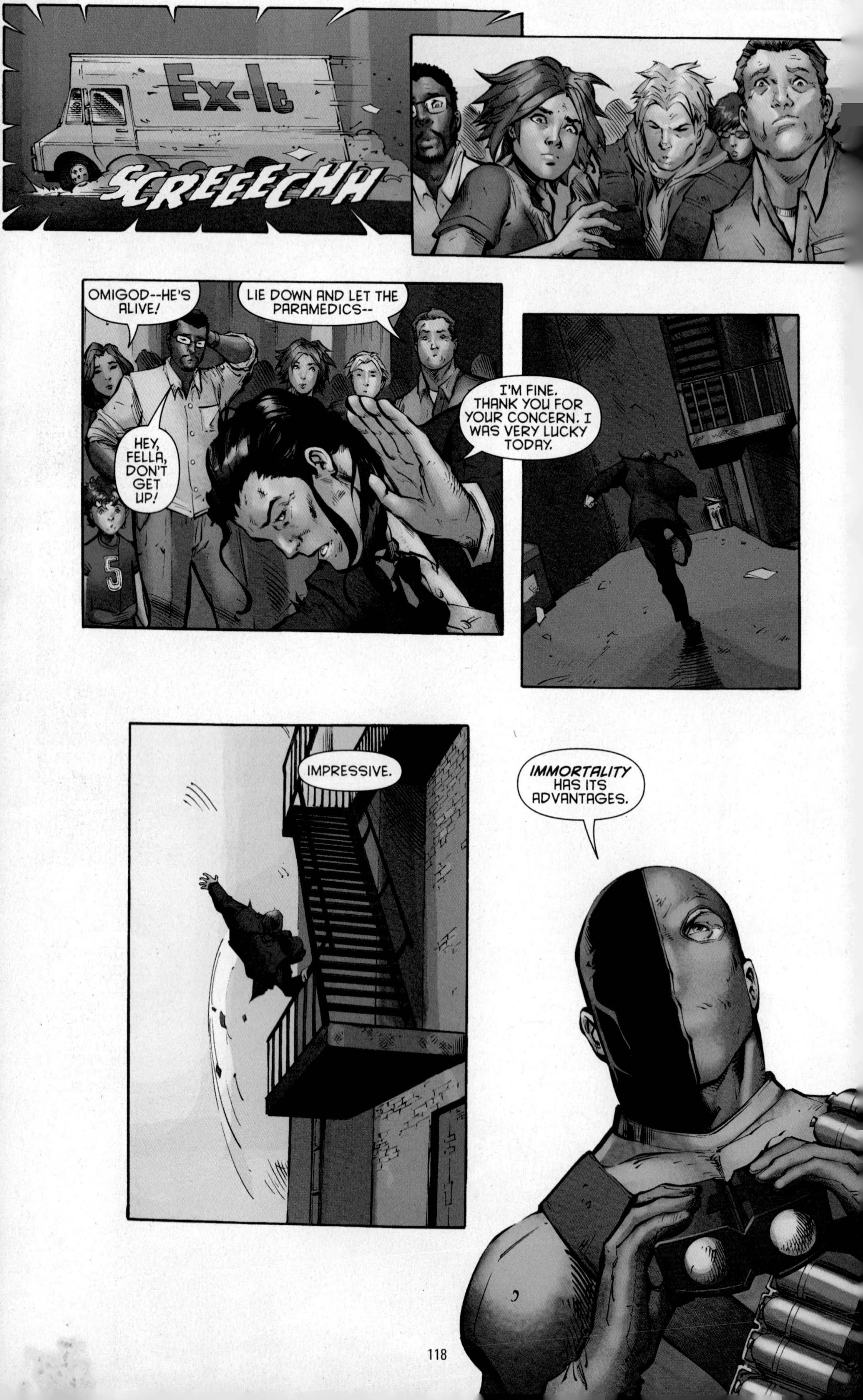
Ex-It
SCREEECHH
OMIGOD--HE'S ALIVE!
LIE DOWN AND LET THE PARAMEDICS--
HEY, FELLA, DON'T GET UP!
I'M FINE. THANK YOU FOR YOUR CONCERN. I WAS VERY LUCKY TODAY.
IMPRESSIVE.
IMMORTALITY HAS ITS ADVANTAGES.

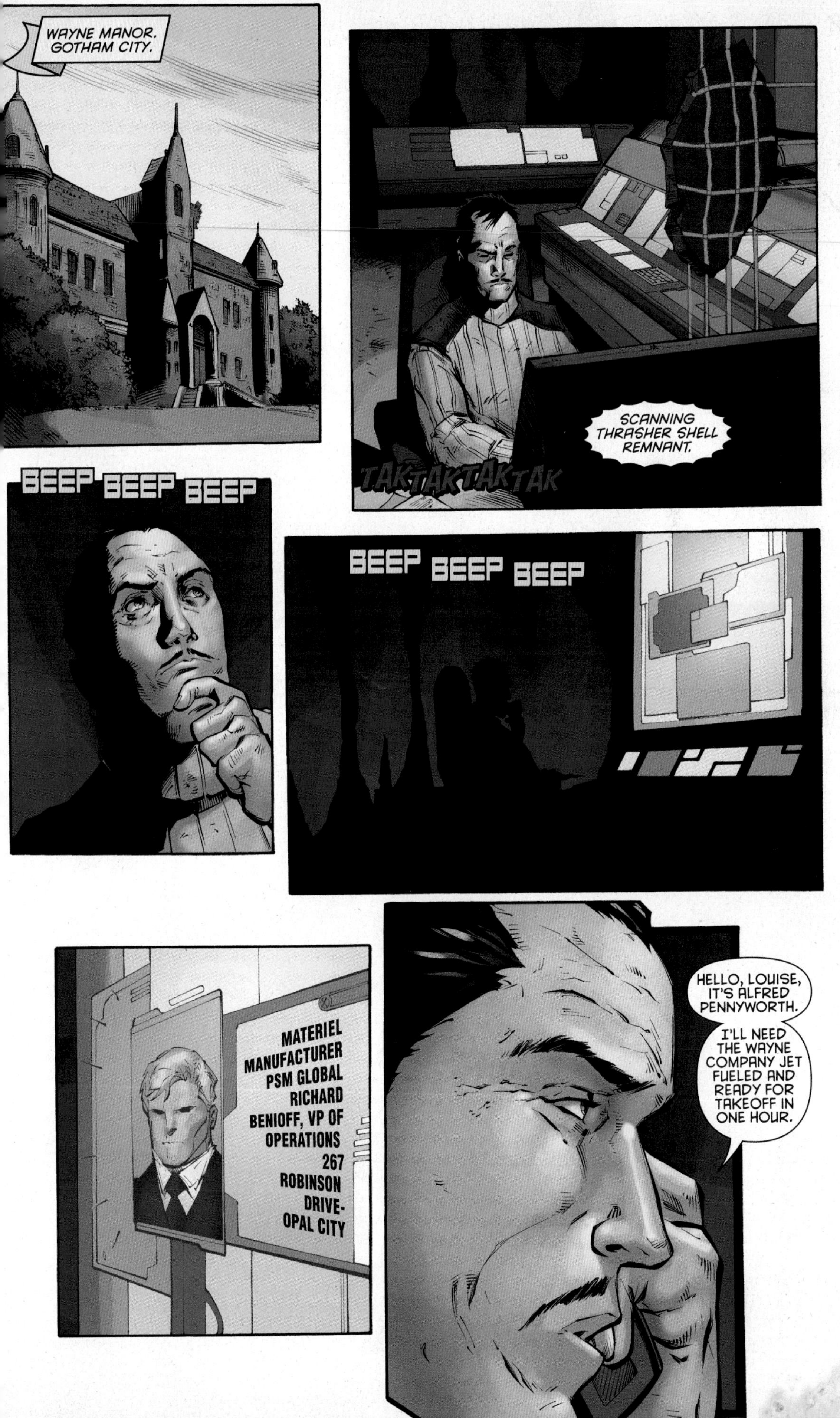
WAYNE MANOR. GOTHAM CITY.
SCANNING THRASHER SHELL REMNANT.
TAKTAKTAKTAK
BEEP BEEP BEEP
BEEP BEEP BEEP
MATERIEL MANUFACTURER PSM GLOBAL RICHARD BENIOFF, VP OF OPERATIONS 267 ROBINSON DRIVE- OPAL CITY
HELLO, LOUISE, IT'S ALFRED PENNYWORTH.
I'LL NEED THE WAYNE COMPANY JET FUELED AND READY FOR TAKEOFF IN ONE HOUR.

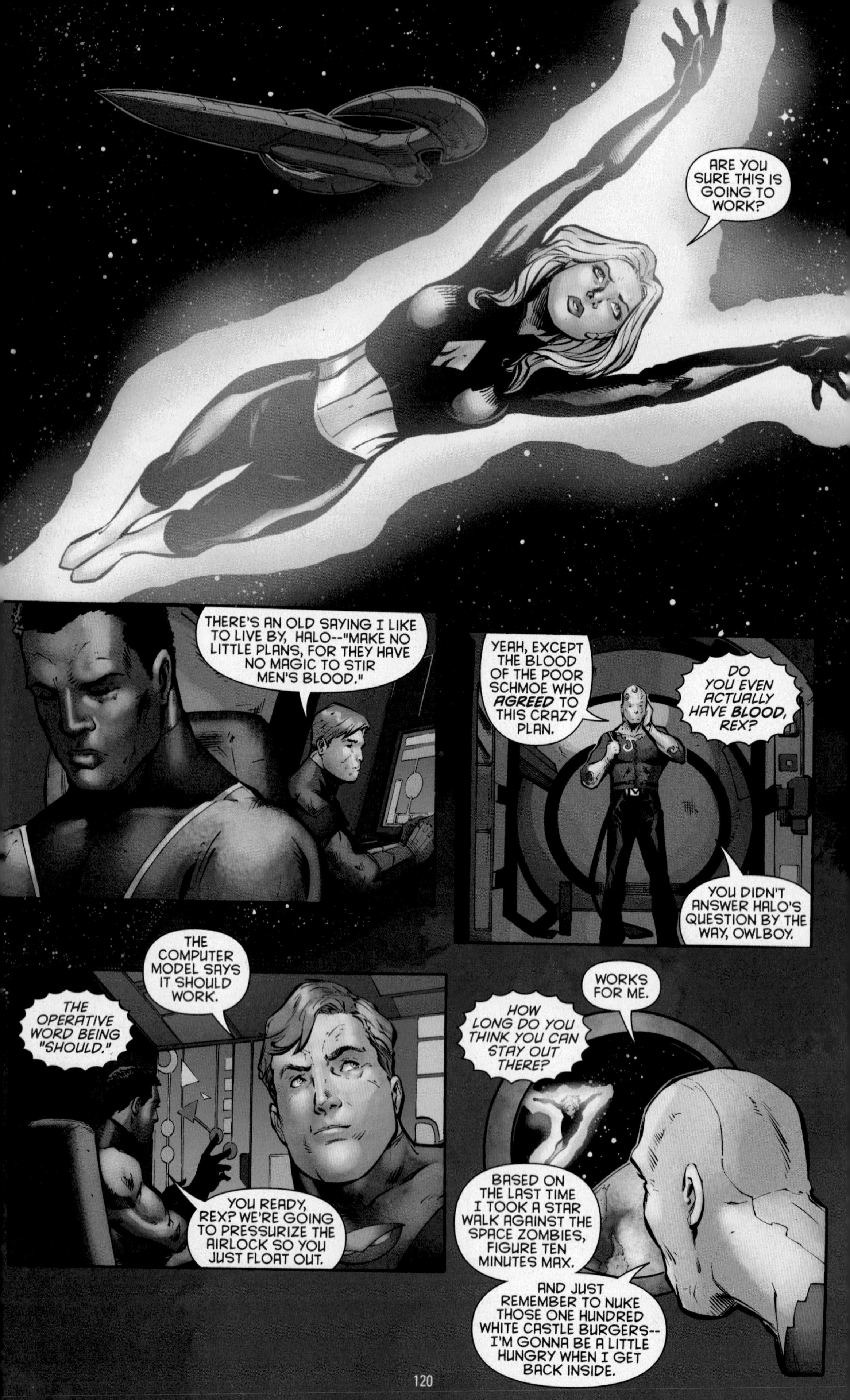
ARE YOU SURE THIS IS GOING TO WORK?
THERE'S AN OLD SAYING I LIKE TO LIVE BY, HALO--"MAKE NO LITTLE PLANS, FOR THEY HAVE NO MAGIC TO STIR MEN'S BLOOD."
YEAH, EXCEPT THE BLOOD OF THE POOR SCHMOE WHO AGREED TO THIS CRAZY PLAN.
DO YOU EVEN ACTUALLY HAVE BLOOD, REX?
YOU DIDN'T ANSWER HALO'S QUESTION BY THE WAY, OWLBOY.
THE COMPUTER MODEL SAYS IT SHOULD WORK.
THE OPERATIVE WORD BEING "SHOULD."
YOU READY, REX? WE'RE GOING TO PRESSURIZE THE AIRLOCK SO YOU JUST FLOAT OUT.
WORKS FOR ME.
HOW LONG DO YOU THINK YOU CAN STAY OUT THERE?
BASED ON THE LAST TIME I TOOK A STAR WALK AGAINST THE SPACE ZOMBIES, FIGURE TEN MINUTES MAX.
AND JUST REMEMBER TO NUKE THOSE ONE HUNDRED WHITE CASTLE BURGERS--I'M GONNA BE A LITTLE HUNGRY WHEN I GET BACK INSIDE.

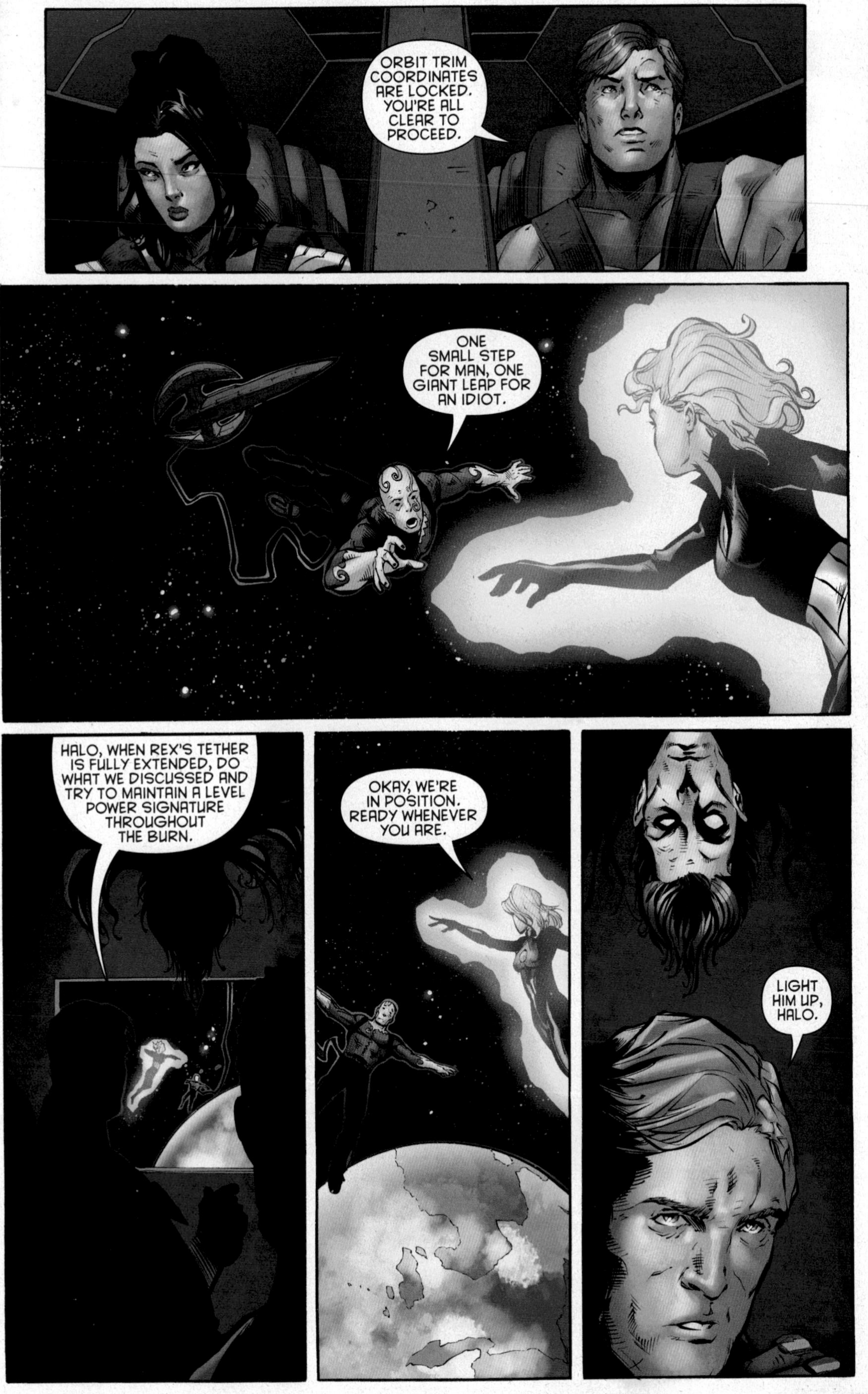
ORBIT TRIM COORDINATES ARE LOCKED. YOU'RE ALL CLEAR TO PROCEED.
ONE SMALL STEP FOR MAN, ONE GIANT LEAP FOR AN IDIOT.
HALO, WHEN REX'S TETHER IS FULLY EXTENDED, DO WHAT WE DISCUSSED AND TRY TO MAINTAIN A LEVEL POWER SIGNATURE THROUGHOUT THE BURN.
OKAY, WE'RE IN POSITION. READY WHENEVER YOU ARE.
LIGHT HIM UP, HALO.

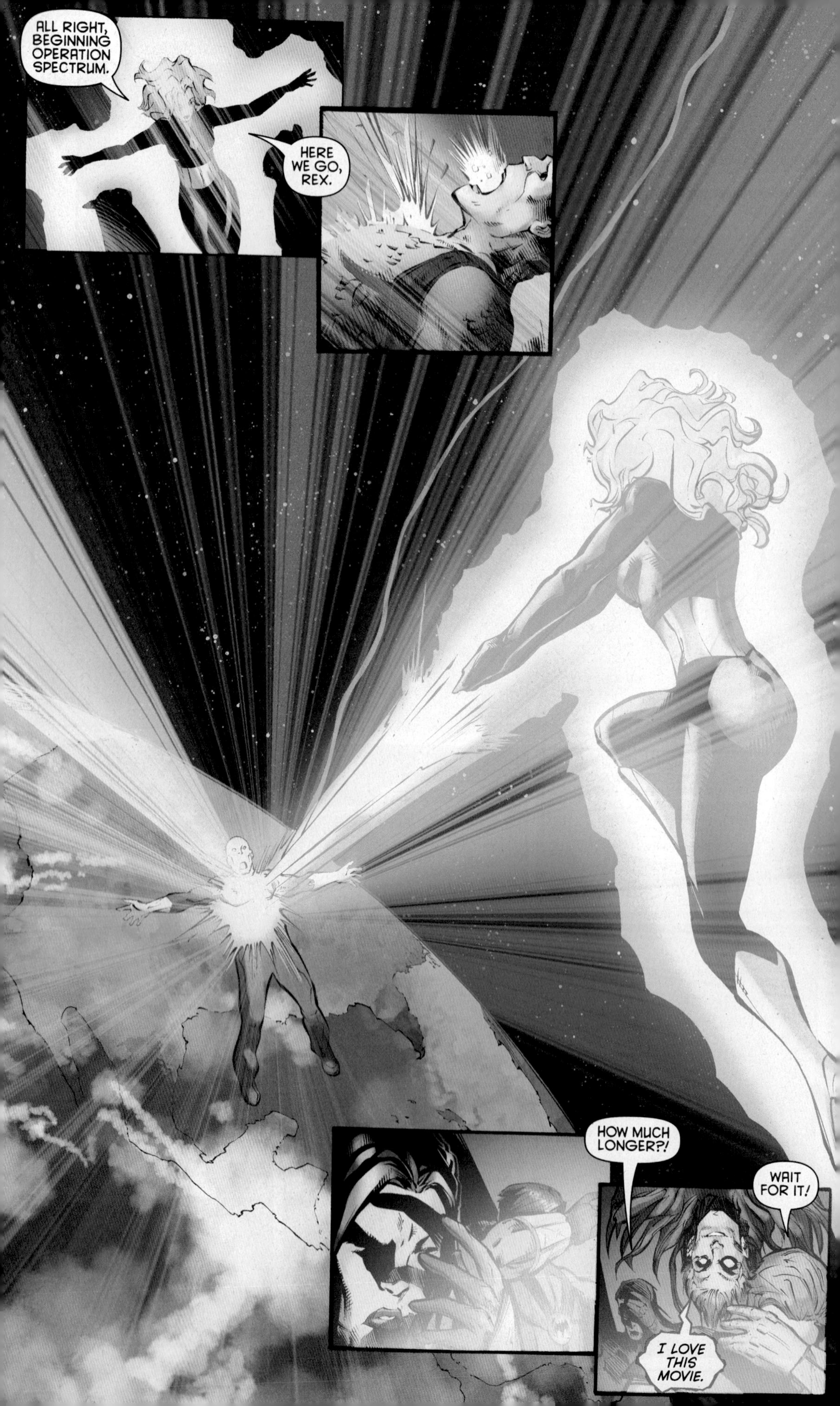
ALL RIGHT, BEGINNING OPERATION SPECTRUM.
HERE WE GO, REX.
HOW MUCH LONGER?!
WAIT FOR IT!
I LOVE THIS MOVIE.

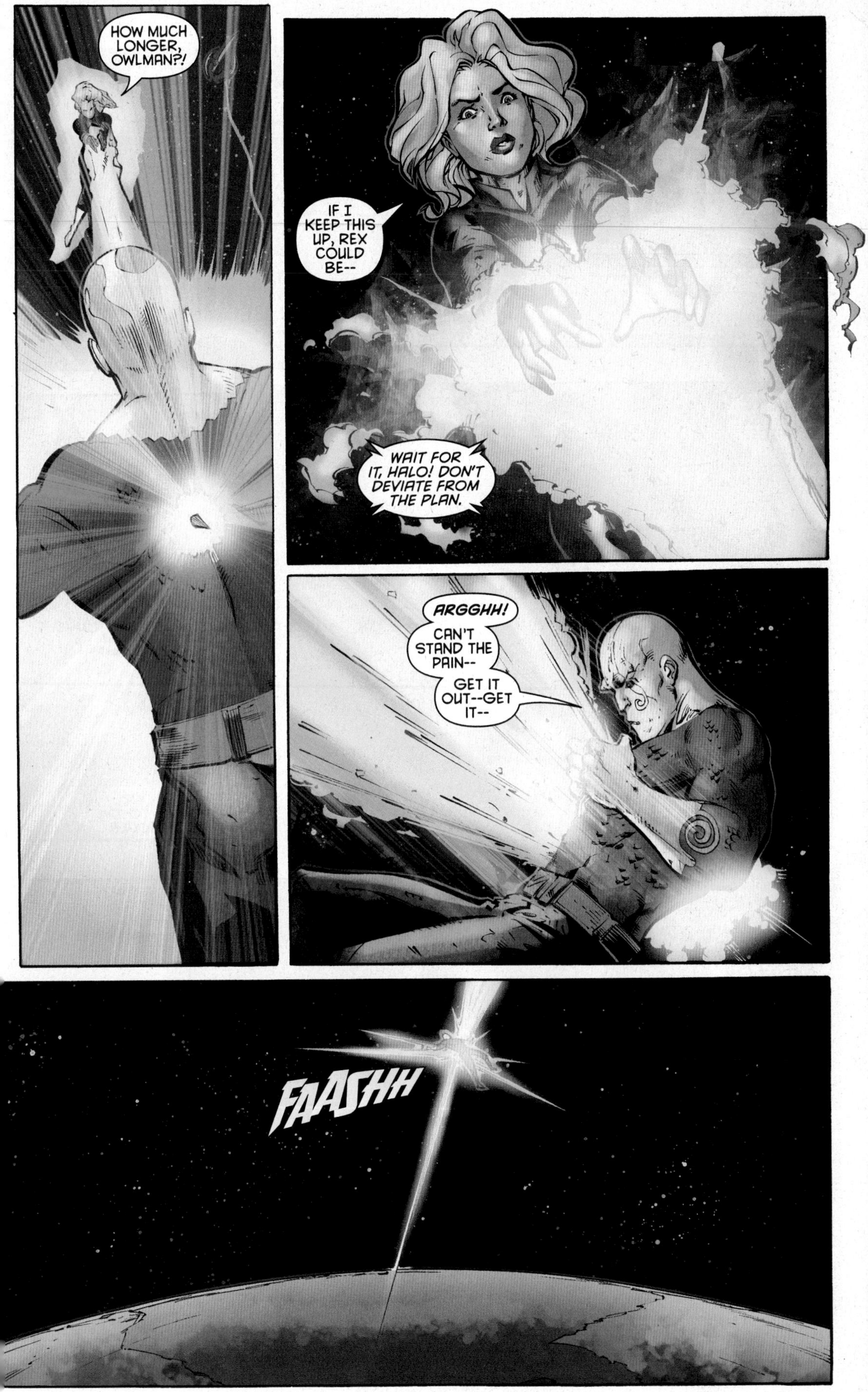
HOW MUCH LONGER, OWLMAN?!
IF I KEEP THIS UP, REX COULD BE--
WAIT FOR IT, HALO! DON'T DEVIATE FROM THE PLAN.
ARGGHH!
CAN'T STAND THE PAIN--
GET IT OUT--GET IT--
FAASHH

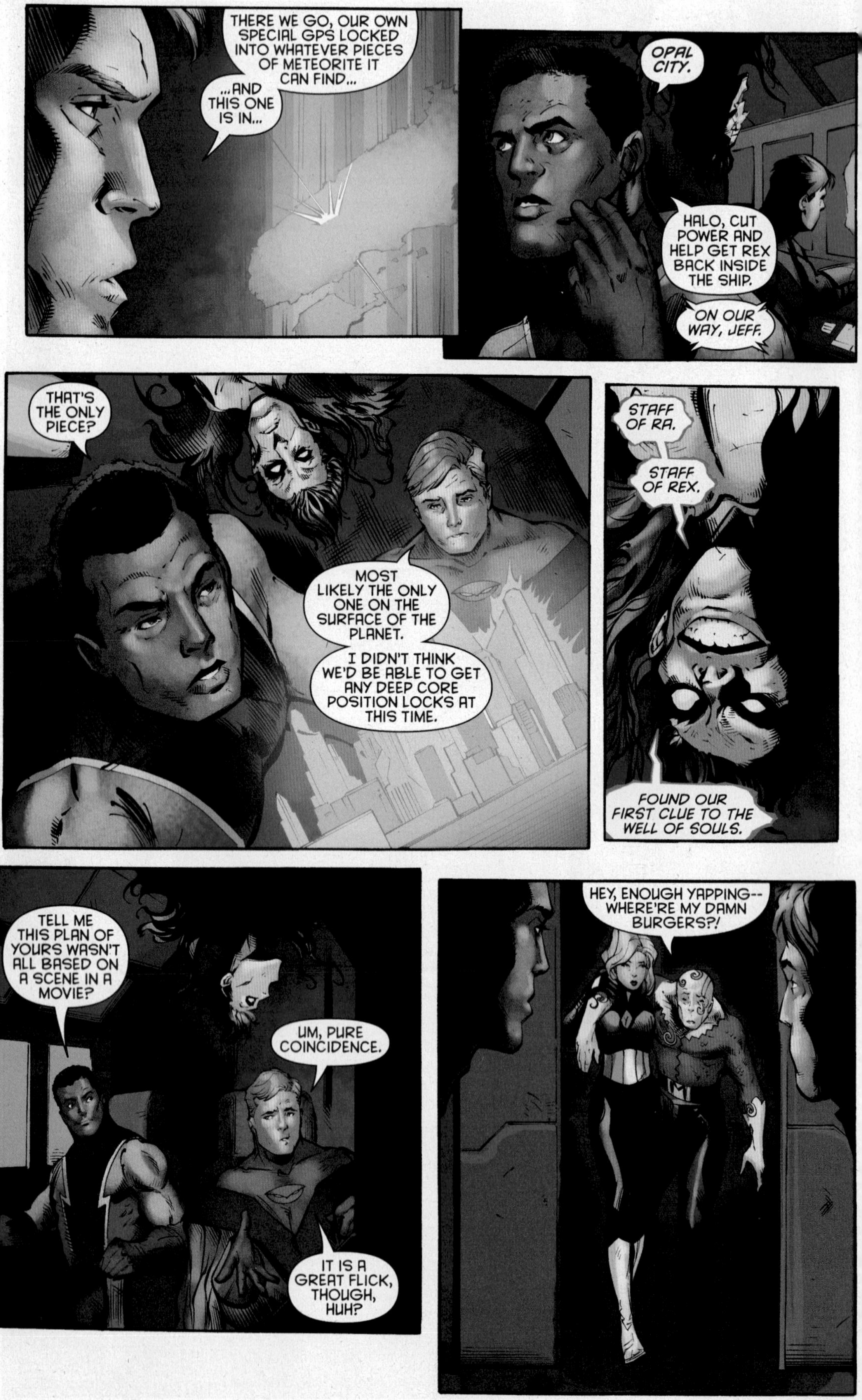

THERE WE GO, OUR OWN SPECIAL GPS LOCKED INTO WHATEVER PIECES OF METEORITE IT CAN FIND...
...AND THIS ONE IS IN...
OPAL CITY.
HALO, CUT POWER AND HELP GET REX BACK INSIDE THE SHIP.
ON OUR WAY, JEFF.
THAT'S THE ONLY PIECE?
MOST LIKELY THE ONLY ONE ON THE SURFACE OF THE PLANET.
I DIDN'T THINK WE'D BE ABLE TO GET ANY DEEP CORE POSITION LOCKS AT THIS TIME.
STAFF OF RA.
STAFF OF REX.
FOUND OUR FIRST CLUE TO THE WELL OF SOULS.
TELL ME THIS PLAN OF YOURS WASN'T ALL BASED ON A SCENE IN A MOVIE?
UM, PURE COINCIDENCE.
IT IS A GREAT FLICK, THOUGH, HUH?
HEY, ENOUGH YAPPING-- WHERE'RE MY DAMN BURGERS?!

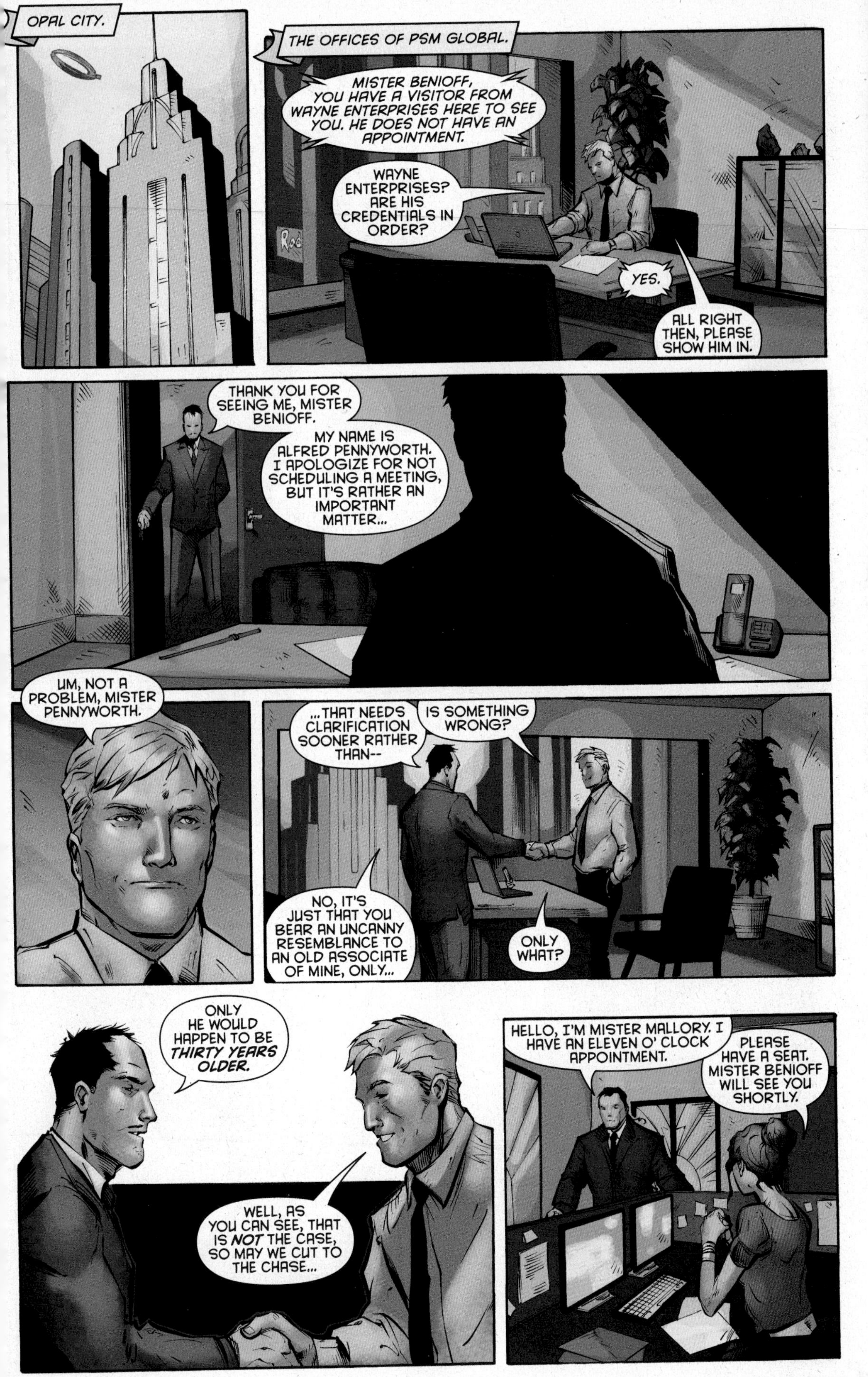

OPAL CITY.
THE OFFICES OF PSM GLOBAL.
MISTER BENIOFF, YOU HAVE A VISITOR FROM WAYNE ENTERPRISES HERE TO SEE YOU. HE DOES NOT HAVE AN APPOINTMENT.
WAYNE ENTERPRISES? ARE HIS CREDENTIALS IN ORDER?
YES.
ALL RIGHT THEN, PLEASE SHOW HIM IN.
THANK YOU FOR SEEING ME, MISTER BENIOFF.
MY NAME IS ALFRED PENNYWORTH. I APOLOGIZE FOR NOT SCHEDULING A MEETING, BUT IT'S RATHER AN IMPORTANT MATTER...
UM, NOT A PROBLEM, MISTER PENNYWORTH.
...THAT NEEDS CLARIFICATION SOONER RATHER THAN--
IS SOMETHING WRONG?
NO, IT'S JUST THAT YOU BEAR AN UNCANNY RESEMBLANCE TO AN OLD ASSOCIATE OF MINE, ONLY...
ONLY WHAT?
ONLY HE WOULD HAPPEN TO BE THIRTY YEARS OLDER.
WELL, AS YOU CAN SEE, THAT IS NOT THE CASE, SO MAY WE CUT TO THE CHASE...
HELLO, I'M MISTER MALLORY. I HAVE AN ELEVEN O' CLOCK APPOINTMENT.
PLEASE HAVE A SEAT. MISTER BENIOFF WILL SEE YOU SHORTLY.

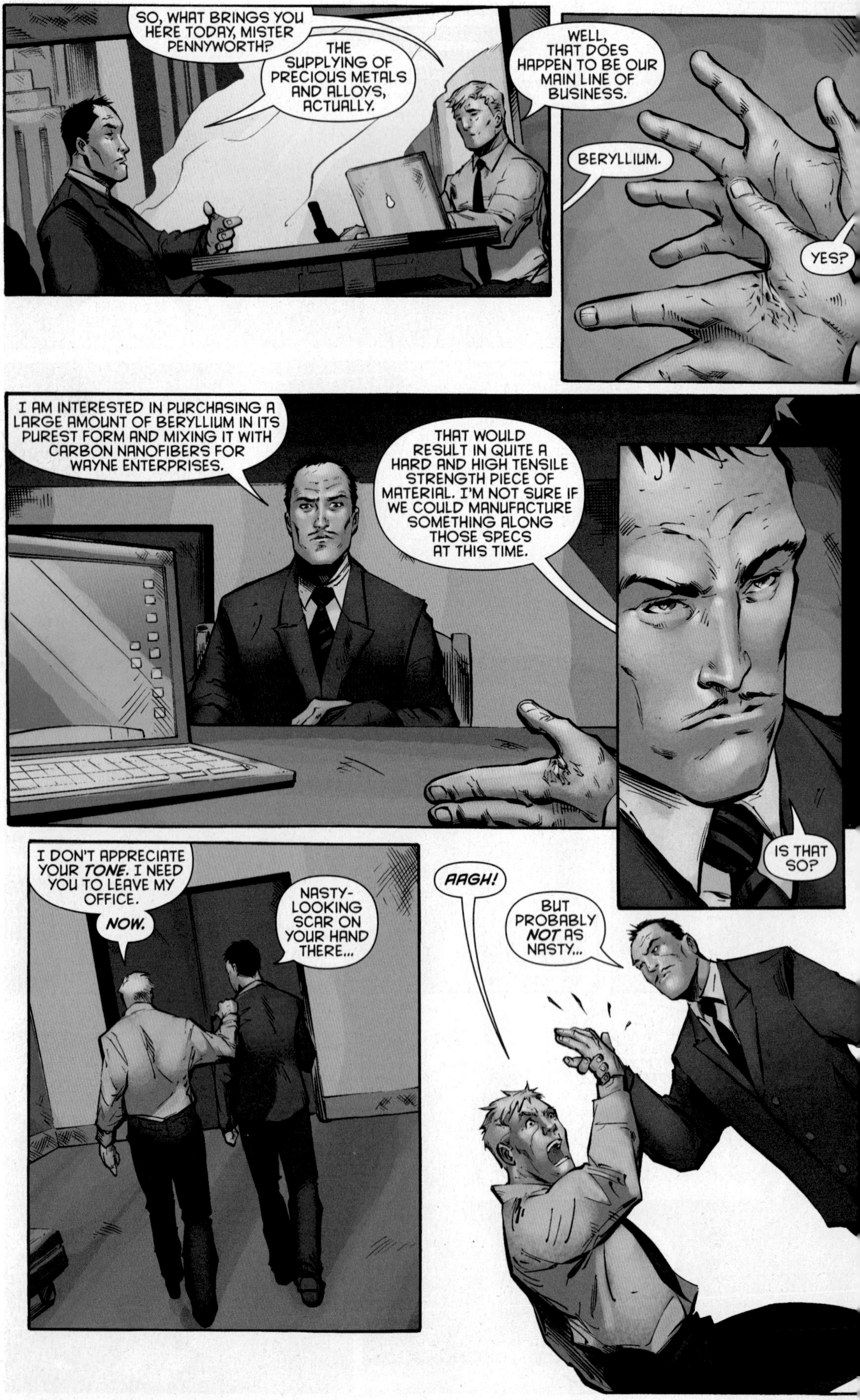
SO, WHAT BRINGS YOU HERE TODAY, MISTER PENNYWORTH?
THE SUPPLYING OF PRECIOUS METALS AND ALLOYS, ACTUALLY.
WELL, THAT DOES HAPPEN TO BE OUR MAIN LINE OF BUSINESS.
BERYLLIUM.
YES?
I AM INTERESTED IN PURCHASING A LARGE AMOUNT OF BERYLLIUM IN ITS PUREST FORM AND MIXING IT WITH CARBON NANOFIBERS FOR WAYNE ENTERPRISES.
THAT WOULD RESULT IN QUITE A HARD AND HIGH TENSILE STRENGTH PIECE OF MATERIAL. I'M NOT SURE IF WE COULD MANUFACTURE SOMETHING ALONG THOSE SPECS AT THIS TIME.
IS THAT SO?
I DON'T APPRECIATE YOUR *TONE*. I NEED YOU TO LEAVE MY OFFICE.
NOW.
NASTY-LOOKING SCAR ON YOUR HAND THERE...
AAGH!
BUT PROBABLY *NOT* AS NASTY...

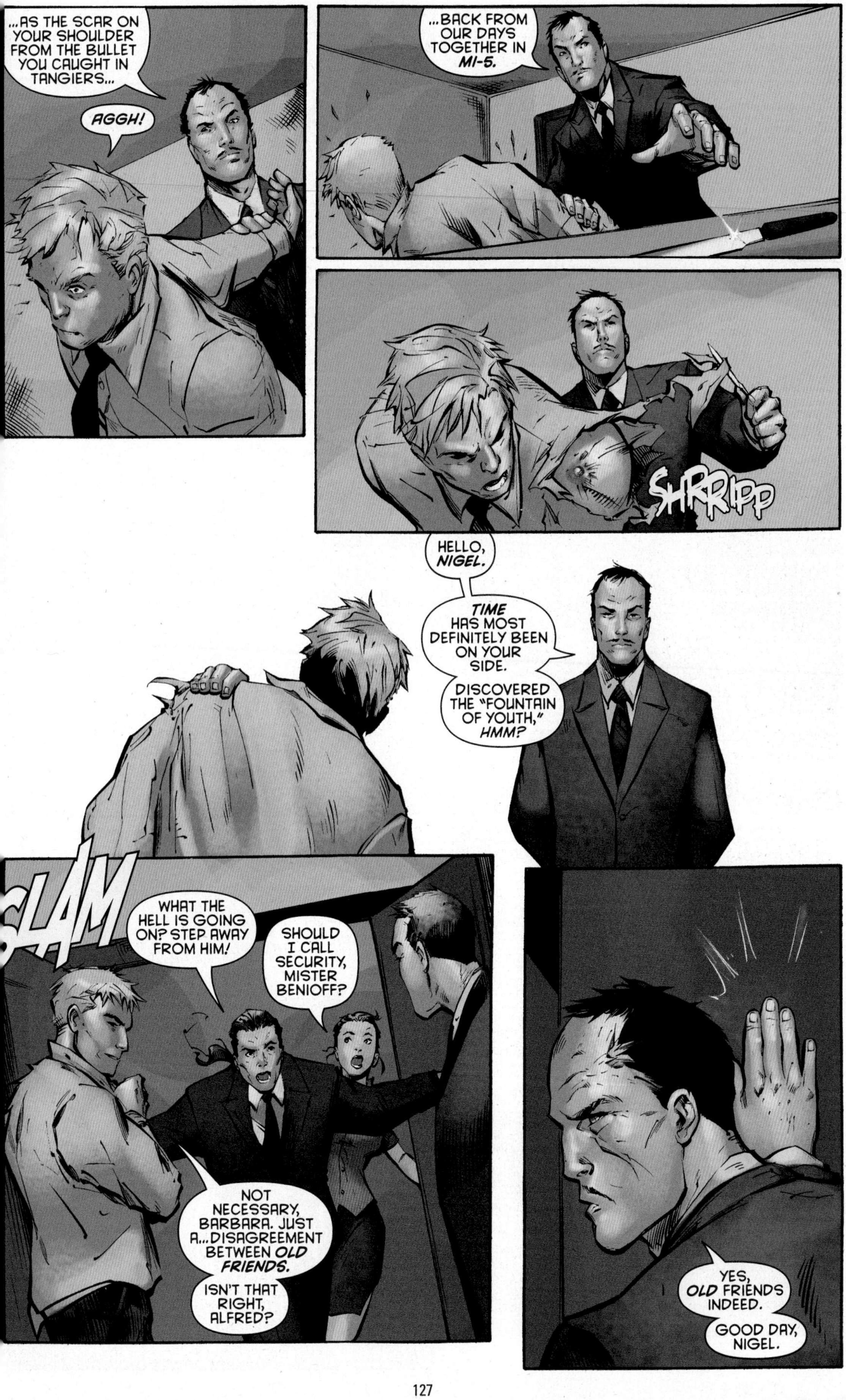
...AS THE SCAR ON YOUR SHOULDER FROM THE BULLET YOU CAUGHT IN TANGIERS...
AGGH!
...BACK FROM OUR DAYS TOGETHER IN MI-5.
SHRRIPP
HELLO, NIGEL.
TIME HAS MOST DEFINITELY BEEN ON YOUR SIDE.
DISCOVERED THE "FOUNTAIN OF YOUTH," HMM?
SLAM
WHAT THE HELL IS GOING ON? STEP AWAY FROM HIM!
SHOULD I CALL SECURITY, MISTER BENIOFF?
NOT NECESSARY, BARBARA. JUST A...DISAGREEMENT BETWEEN OLD FRIENDS.
ISN'T THAT RIGHT, ALFRED?
YES, OLD FRIENDS INDEED.
GOOD DAY, NIGEL.

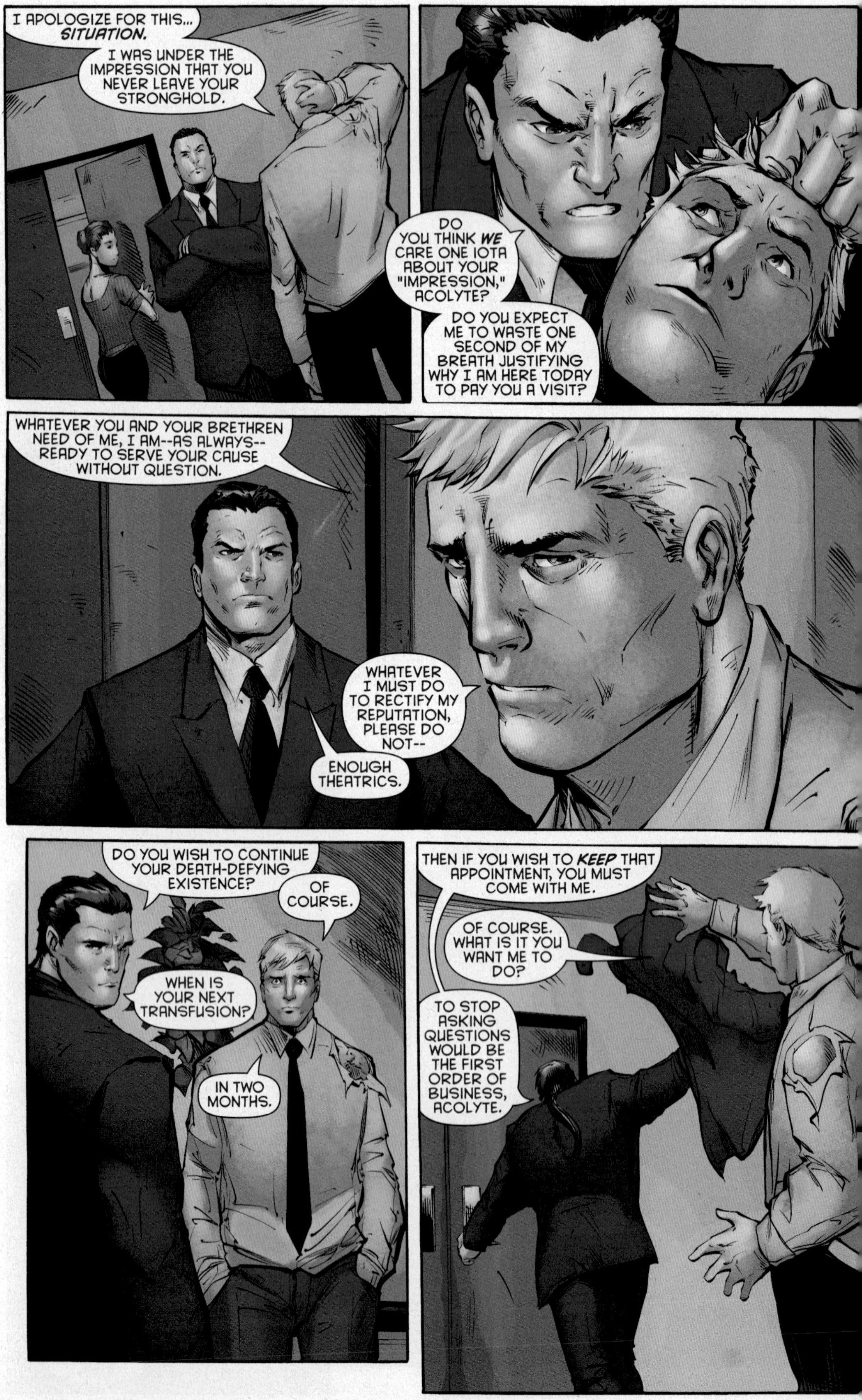

I APOLOGIZE FOR THIS... *SITUATION.*
I WAS UNDER THE IMPRESSION THAT YOU NEVER LEAVE YOUR STRONGHOLD.
DO YOU THINK *WE* CARE ONE IOTA ABOUT YOUR "IMPRESSION," ACOLYTE?
DO YOU EXPECT ME TO WASTE ONE SECOND OF MY BREATH JUSTIFYING WHY I AM HERE TODAY TO PAY YOU A VISIT?
WHATEVER YOU AND YOUR BRETHREN NEED OF ME, I AM--AS ALWAYS--READY TO SERVE YOUR CAUSE WITHOUT QUESTION.
WHATEVER I MUST DO TO RECTIFY MY REPUTATION, PLEASE DO NOT--
ENOUGH THEATRICS.
DO YOU WISH TO CONTINUE YOUR DEATH-DEFYING EXISTENCE?
OF COURSE.
WHEN IS YOUR NEXT TRANSFUSION?
IN TWO MONTHS.
THEN IF YOU WISH TO *KEEP* THAT APPOINTMENT, YOU MUST COME WITH ME.
OF COURSE. WHAT IS IT YOU WANT ME TO DO?
TO STOP ASKING QUESTIONS WOULD BE THE FIRST ORDER OF BUSINESS, ACOLYTE.

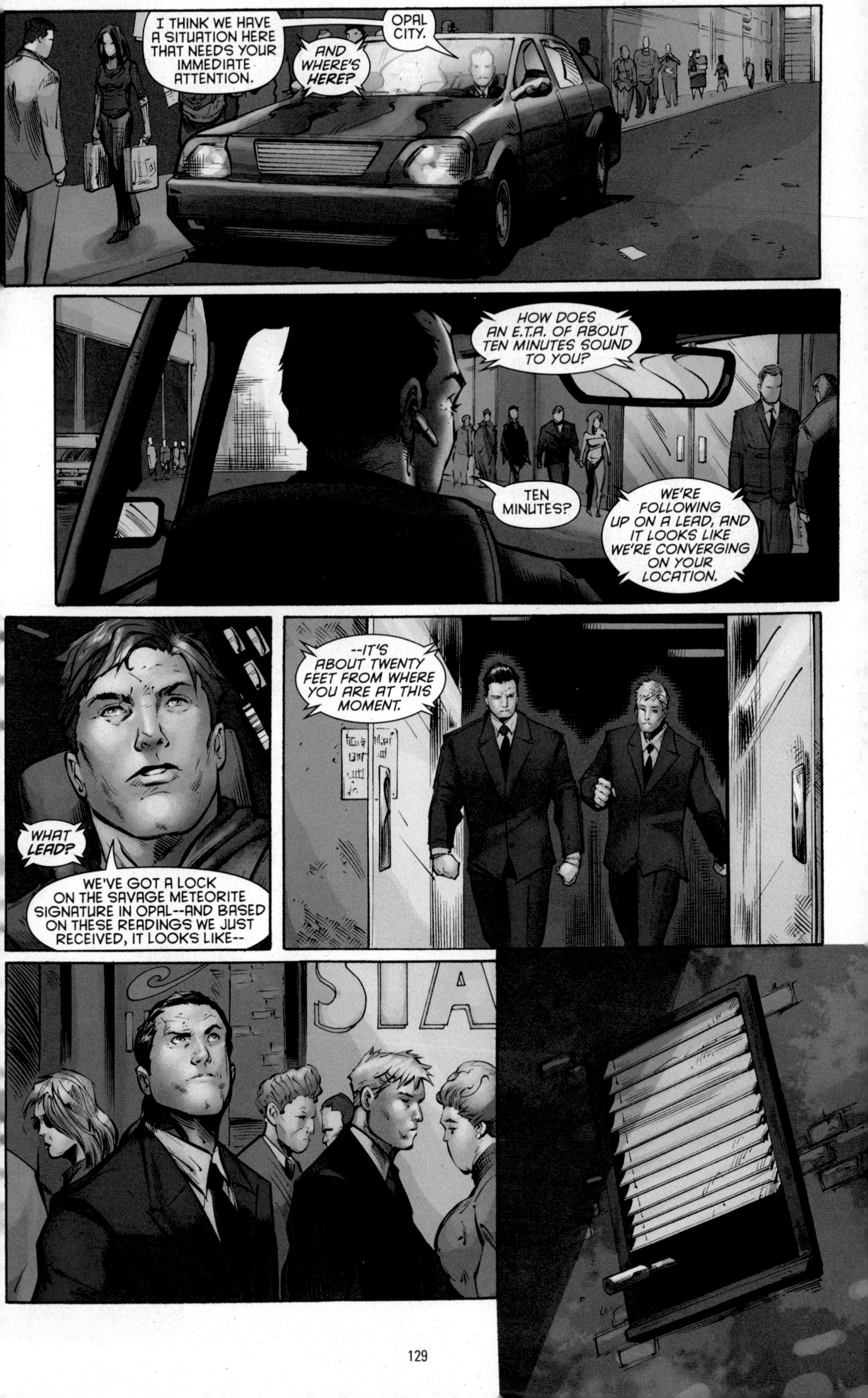
I THINK WE HAVE A SITUATION HERE THAT NEEDS YOUR IMMEDIATE ATTENTION.
AND WHERE'S HERE?
OPAL CITY.
HOW DOES AN E.T.A. OF ABOUT TEN MINUTES SOUND TO YOU?
TEN MINUTES?
WE'RE FOLLOWING UP ON A LEAD, AND IT LOOKS LIKE WE'RE CONVERGING ON YOUR LOCATION.
WHAT LEAD?
WE'VE GOT A LOCK ON THE SAVAGE METEORITE SIGNATURE IN OPAL--AND BASED ON THESE READINGS WE JUST RECEIVED, IT LOOKS LIKE--
--IT'S ABOUT TWENTY FEET FROM WHERE YOU ARE AT THIS MOMENT.

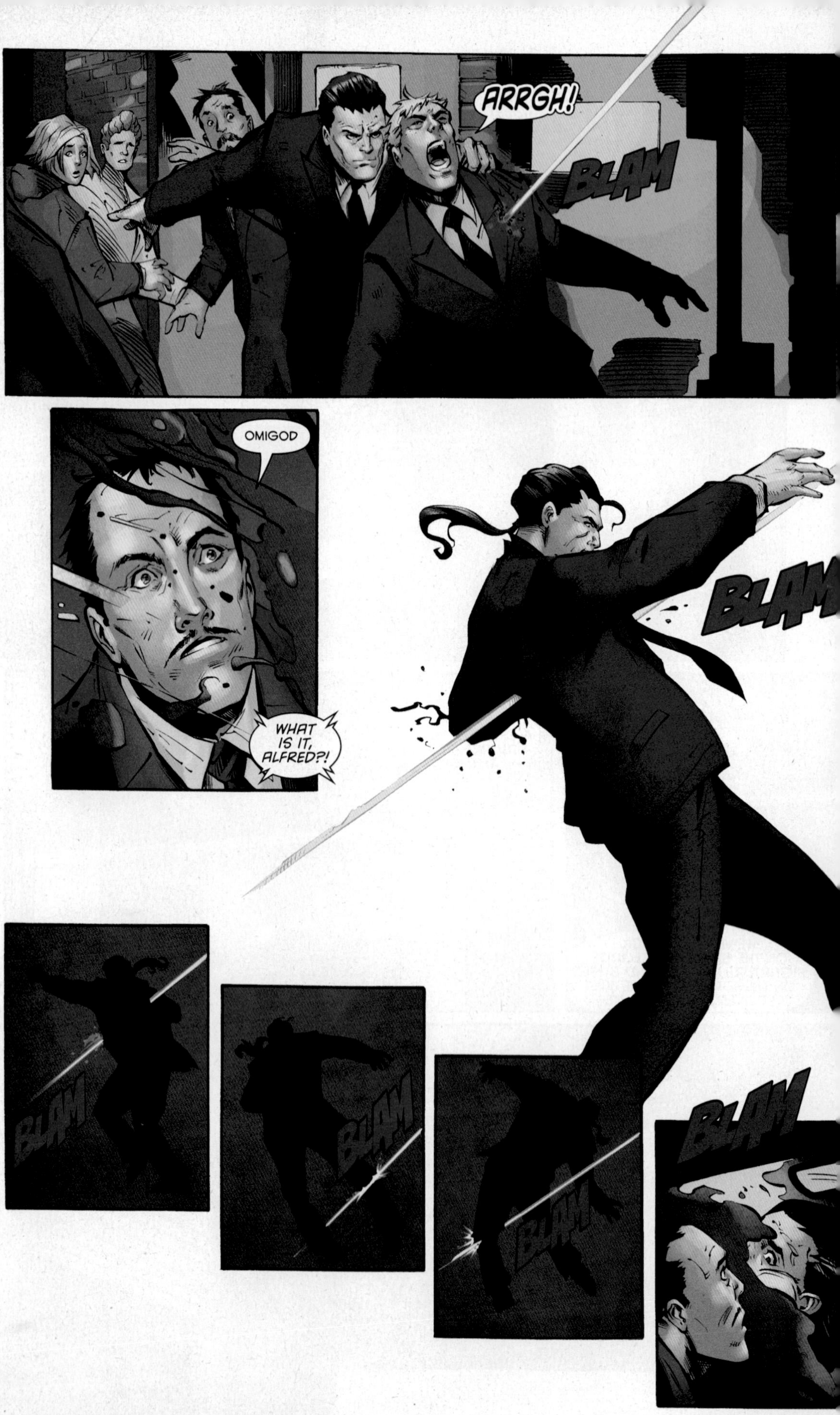
ARRGH!
BLAM
OMIGOD
WHAT IS IT, ALFRED?!
BLAM
BLAM
BLAM
BLAM
BLAM

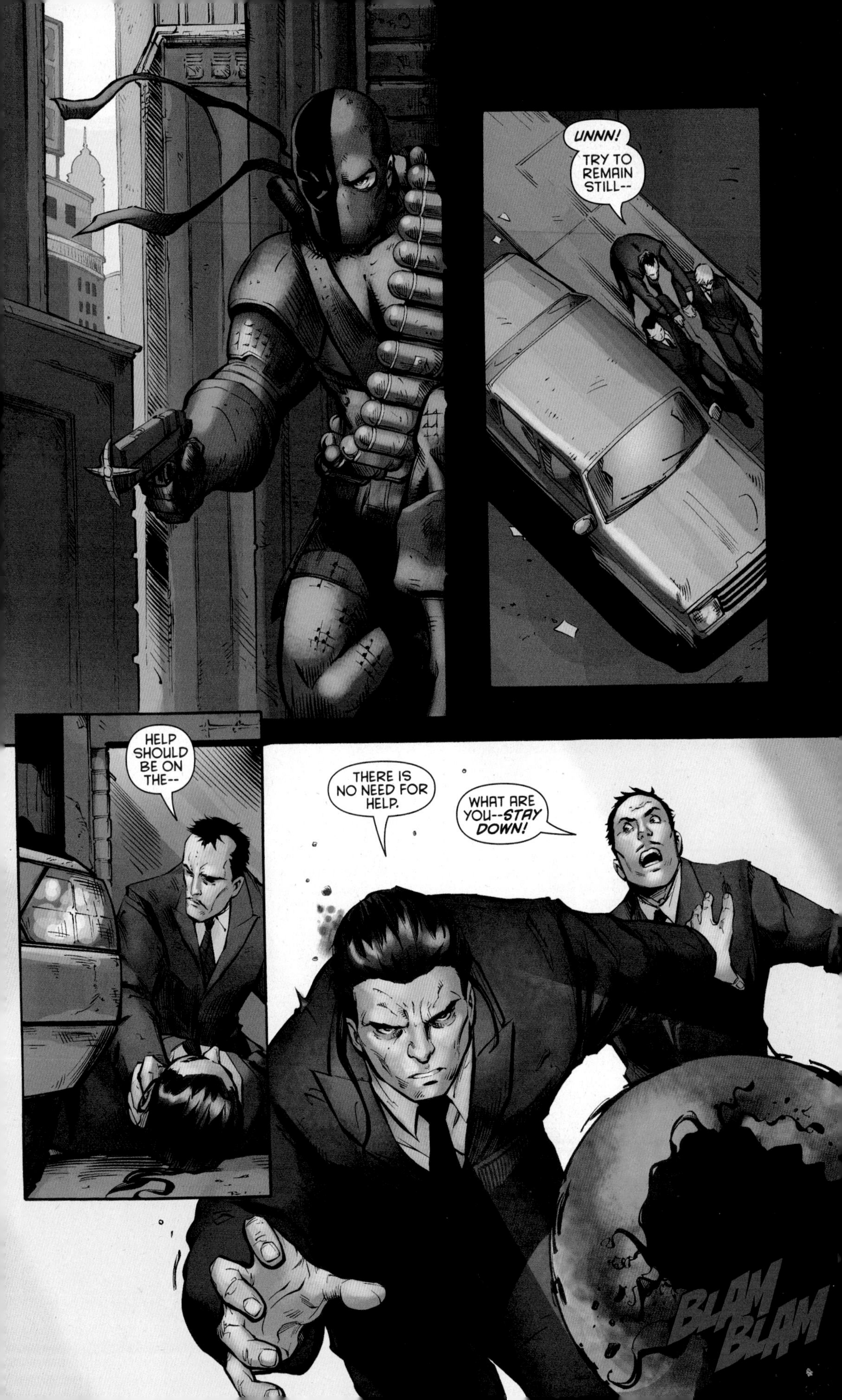
UNNN!
TRY TO REMAIN STILL--
HELP SHOULD BE ON THE--
THERE IS NO NEED FOR HELP.
WHAT ARE YOU--STAY DOWN!
BLAM BLAM

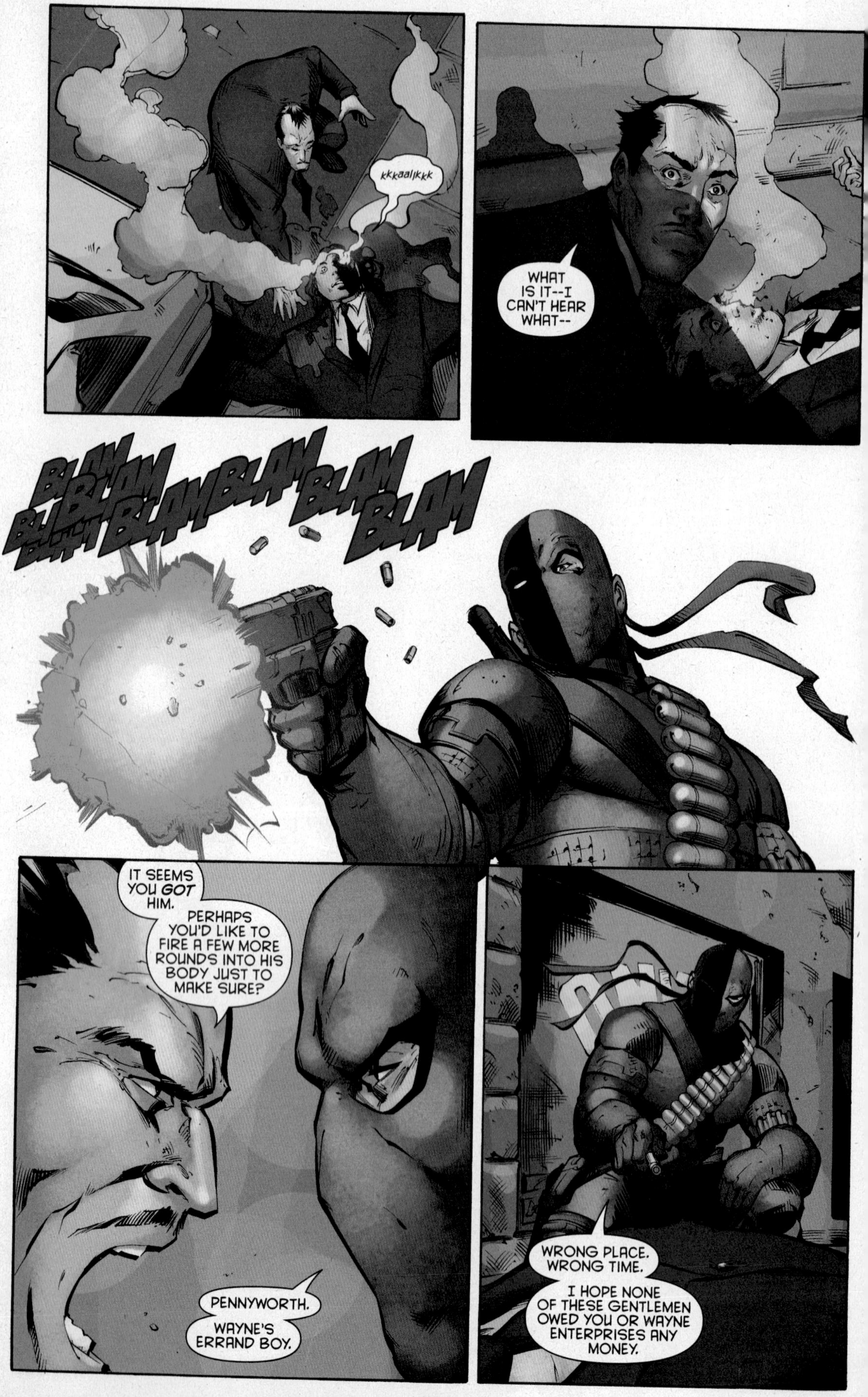
kkkaalikkk
WHAT IS IT--I CAN'T HEAR WHAT--
BLAM BLAM BLAM BLAM BLAM BLAM BLAM BLAM
IT SEEMS YOU GOT HIM.
PERHAPS YOU'D LIKE TO FIRE A FEW MORE ROUNDS INTO HIS BODY JUST TO MAKE SURE?
PENNYWORTH.
WAYNE'S ERRAND BOY.
WRONG PLACE. WRONG TIME.
I HOPE NONE OF THESE GENTLEMEN OWED YOU OR WAYNE ENTERPRISES ANY MONEY.

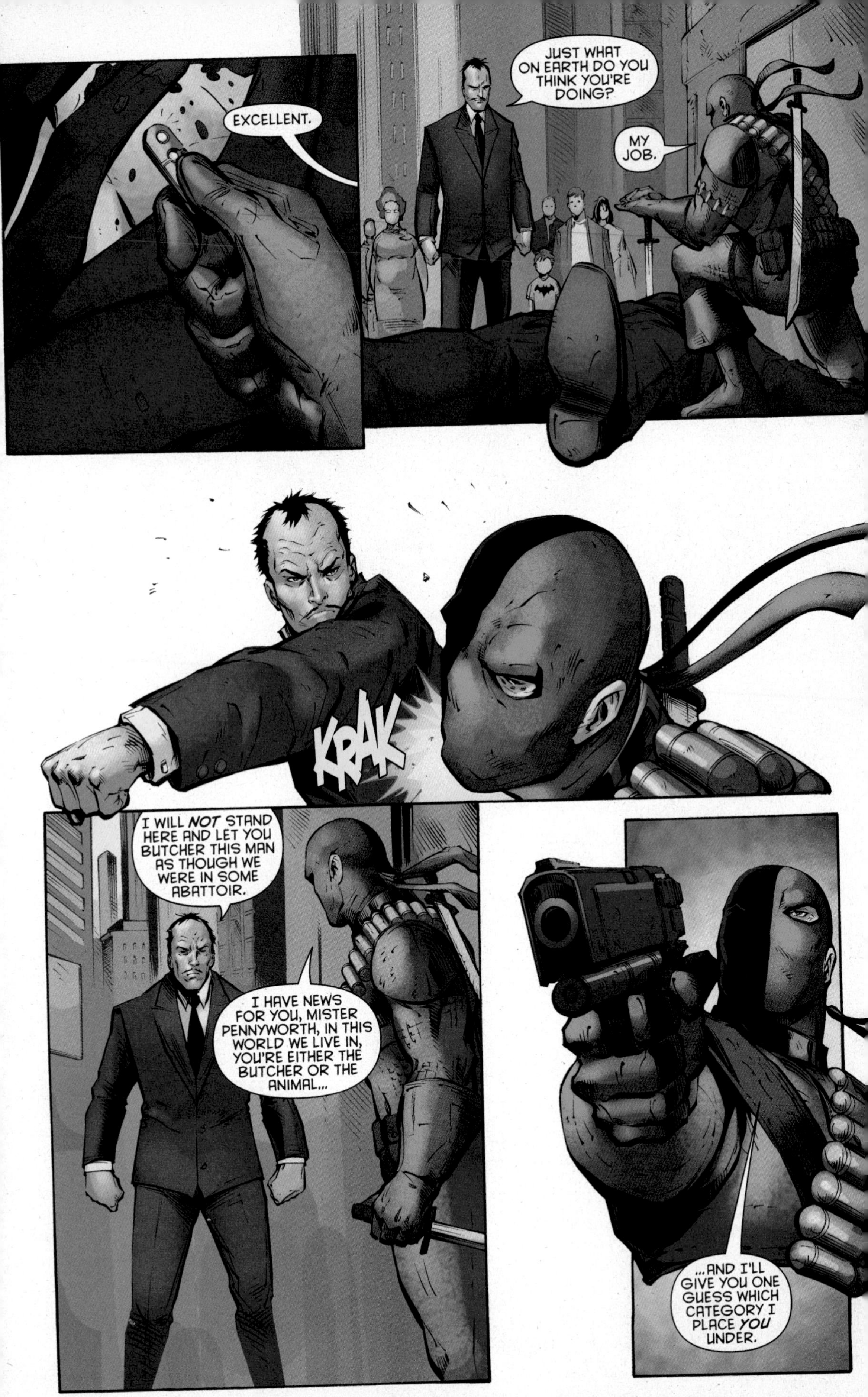
EXCELLENT.
JUST WHAT ON EARTH DO YOU THINK YOU'RE DOING?
MY JOB.
KRAK
I WILL NOT STAND HERE AND LET YOU BUTCHER THIS MAN AS THOUGH WE WERE IN SOME ABATTOIR.
I HAVE NEWS FOR YOU, MISTER PENNYWORTH, IN THIS WORLD WE LIVE IN, YOU'RE EITHER THE BUTCHER OR THE ANIMAL...
...AND I'LL GIVE YOU ONE GUESS WHICH CATEGORY I PLACE YOU UNDER.

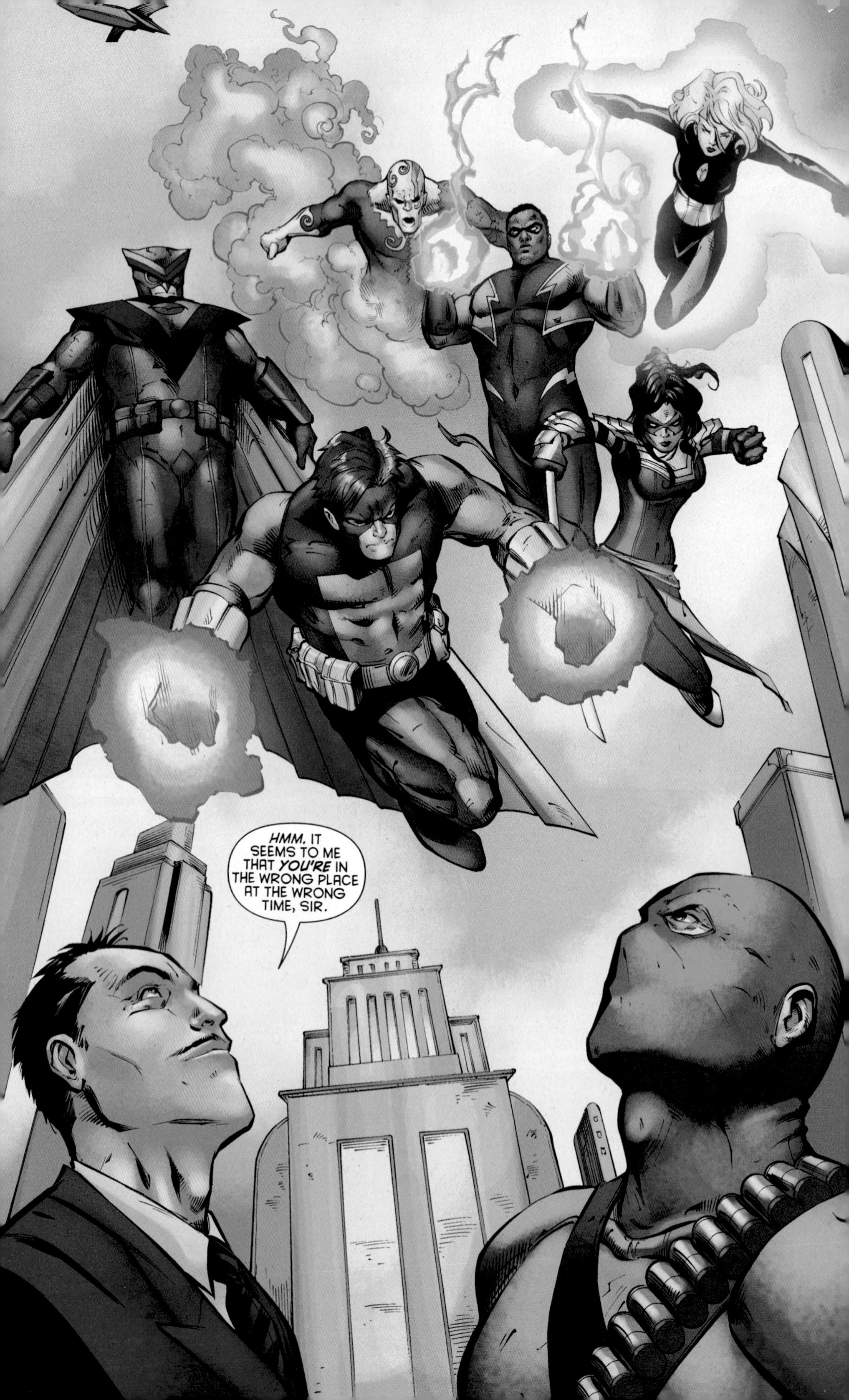
HMM. IT SEEMS TO ME THAT YOU'RE IN THE WRONG PLACE AT THE WRONG TIME, SIR.

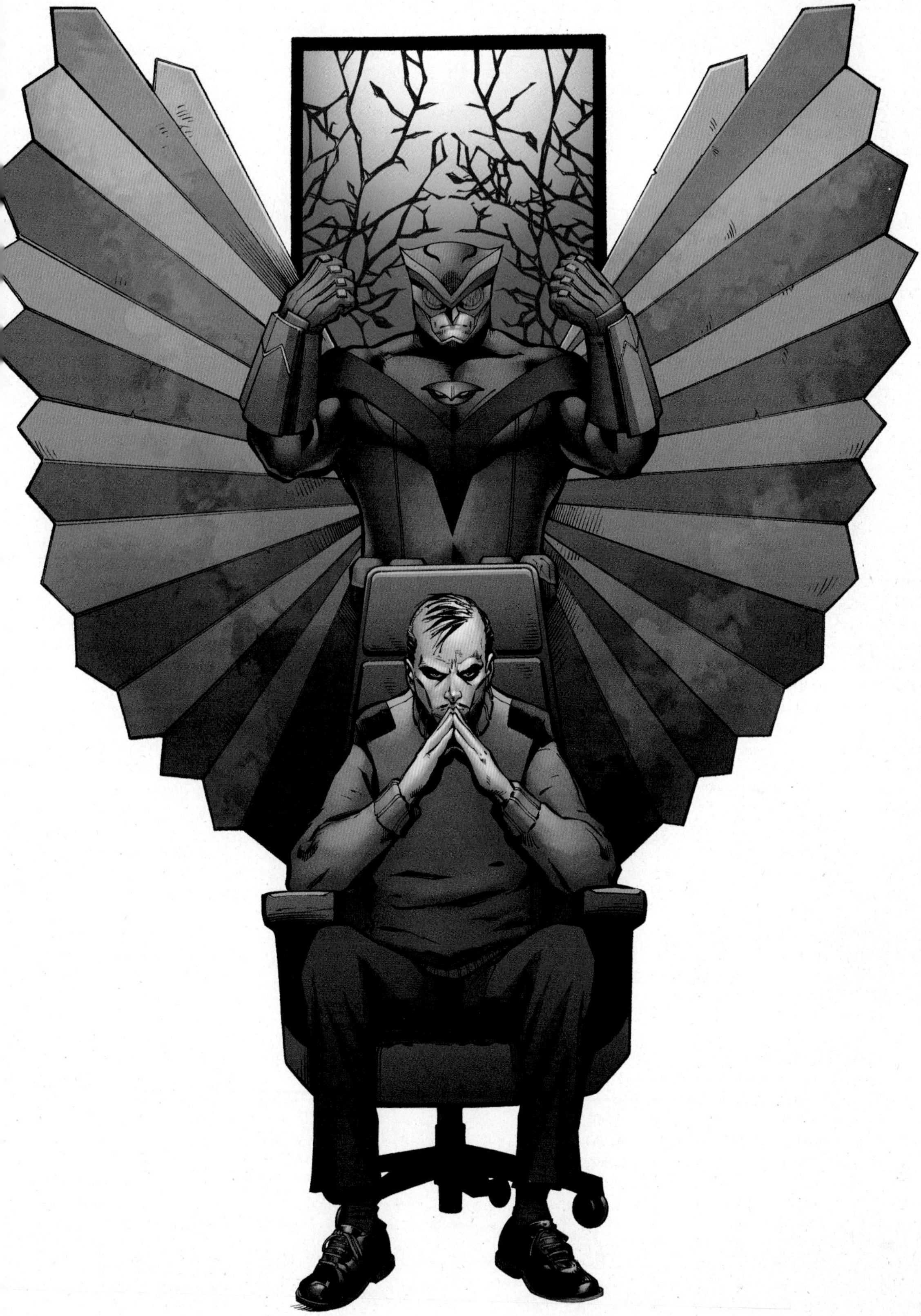

"Epic purpose is not to be feared
or shunned. It is to be embraced."

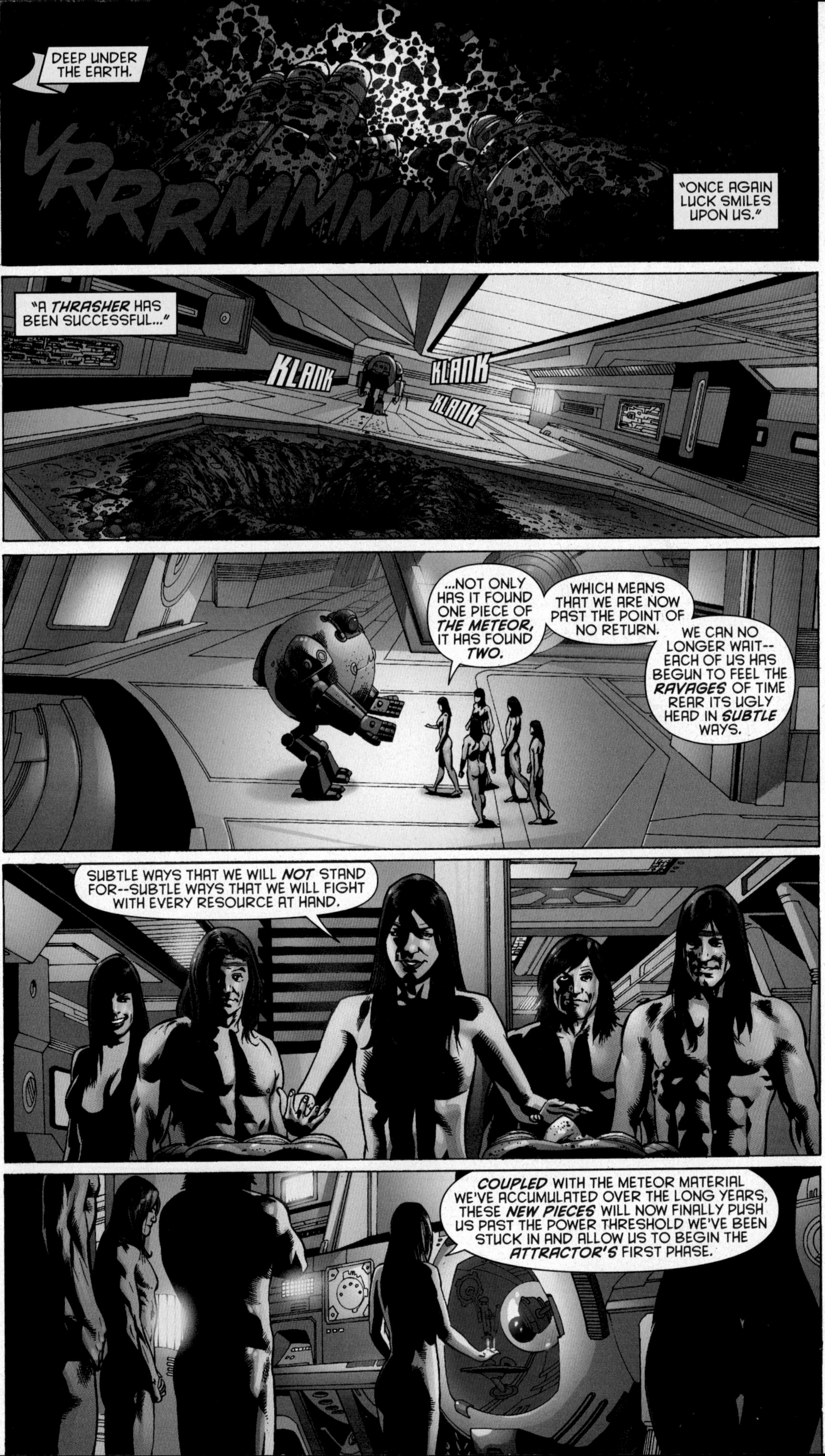
DEEP UNDER THE EARTH.
VRRRMMMMM
"ONCE AGAIN LUCK SMILES UPON US."
"A THRASHER HAS BEEN SUCCESSFUL..."
KLANK
KLANK
KLANK
...NOT ONLY HAS IT FOUND ONE PIECE OF THE METEOR, IT HAS FOUND TWO.
WHICH MEANS THAT WE ARE NOW PAST THE POINT OF NO RETURN.
WE CAN NO LONGER WAIT--EACH OF US HAS BEGUN TO FEEL THE RAVAGES OF TIME REAR ITS UGLY HEAD IN SUBTLE WAYS.
SUBTLE WAYS THAT WE WILL NOT STAND FOR--SUBTLE WAYS THAT WE WILL FIGHT WITH EVERY RESOURCE AT HAND.
COUPLED WITH THE METEOR MATERIAL WE'VE ACCUMULATED OVER THE LONG YEARS, THESE NEW PIECES WILL NOW FINALLY PUSH US PAST THE POWER THRESHOLD WE'VE BEEN STUCK IN AND ALLOW US TO BEGIN THE ATTRACTOR'S FIRST PHASE.

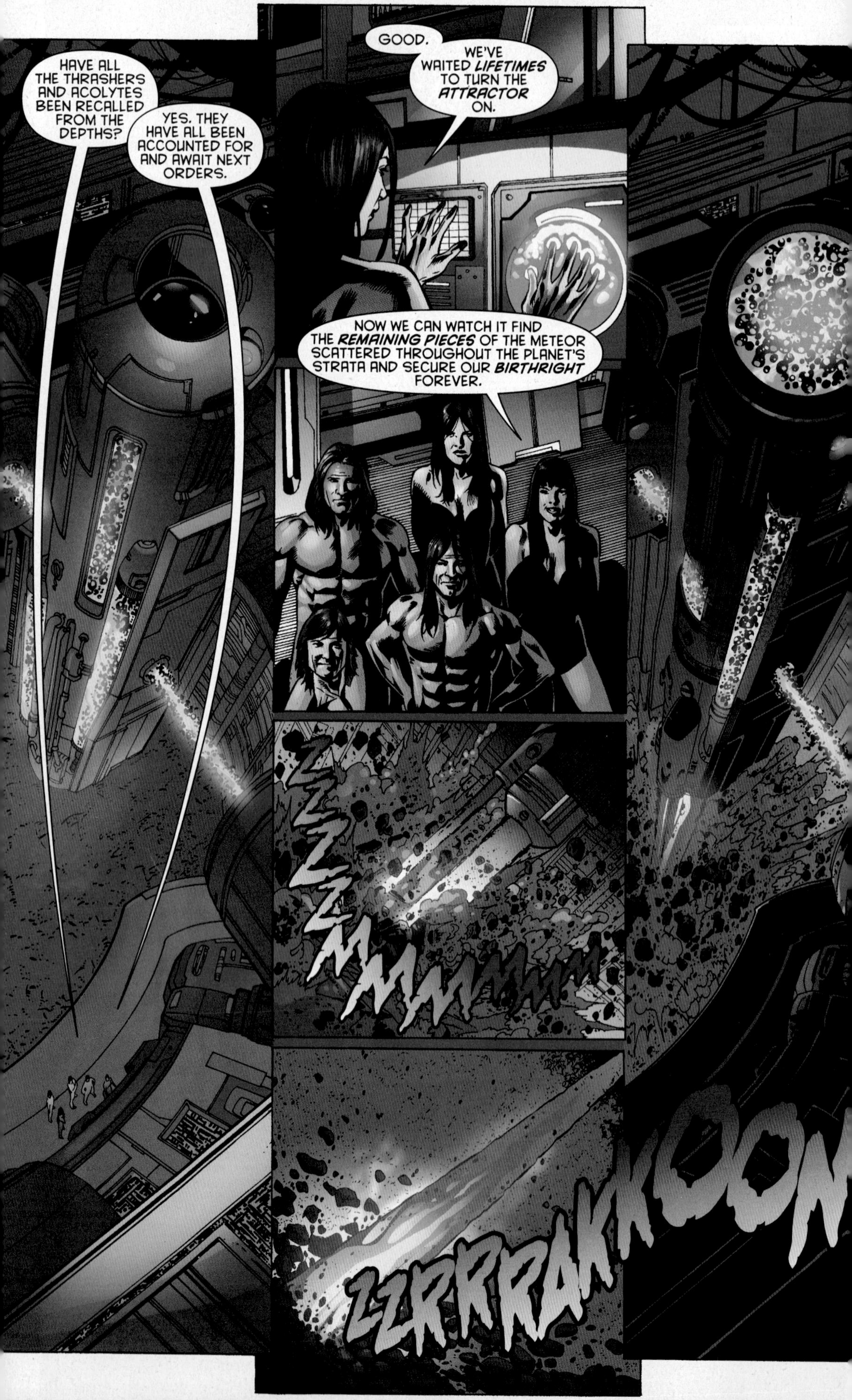

HAVE ALL THE THRASHERS AND ACOLYTES BEEN RECALLED FROM THE DEPTHS?
YES. THEY HAVE ALL BEEN ACCOUNTED FOR AND AWAIT NEXT ORDERS.
GOOD.
WE'VE WAITED *LIFETIMES* TO TURN THE *ATTRACTOR* ON.
NOW WE CAN WATCH IT FIND THE *REMAINING PIECES* OF THE METEOR SCATTERED THROUGHOUT THE PLANET'S STRATA AND SECURE OUR *BIRTHRIGHT* FOREVER.
ZZZZZMMMMMMMM
ZZRRRAKKOOOM

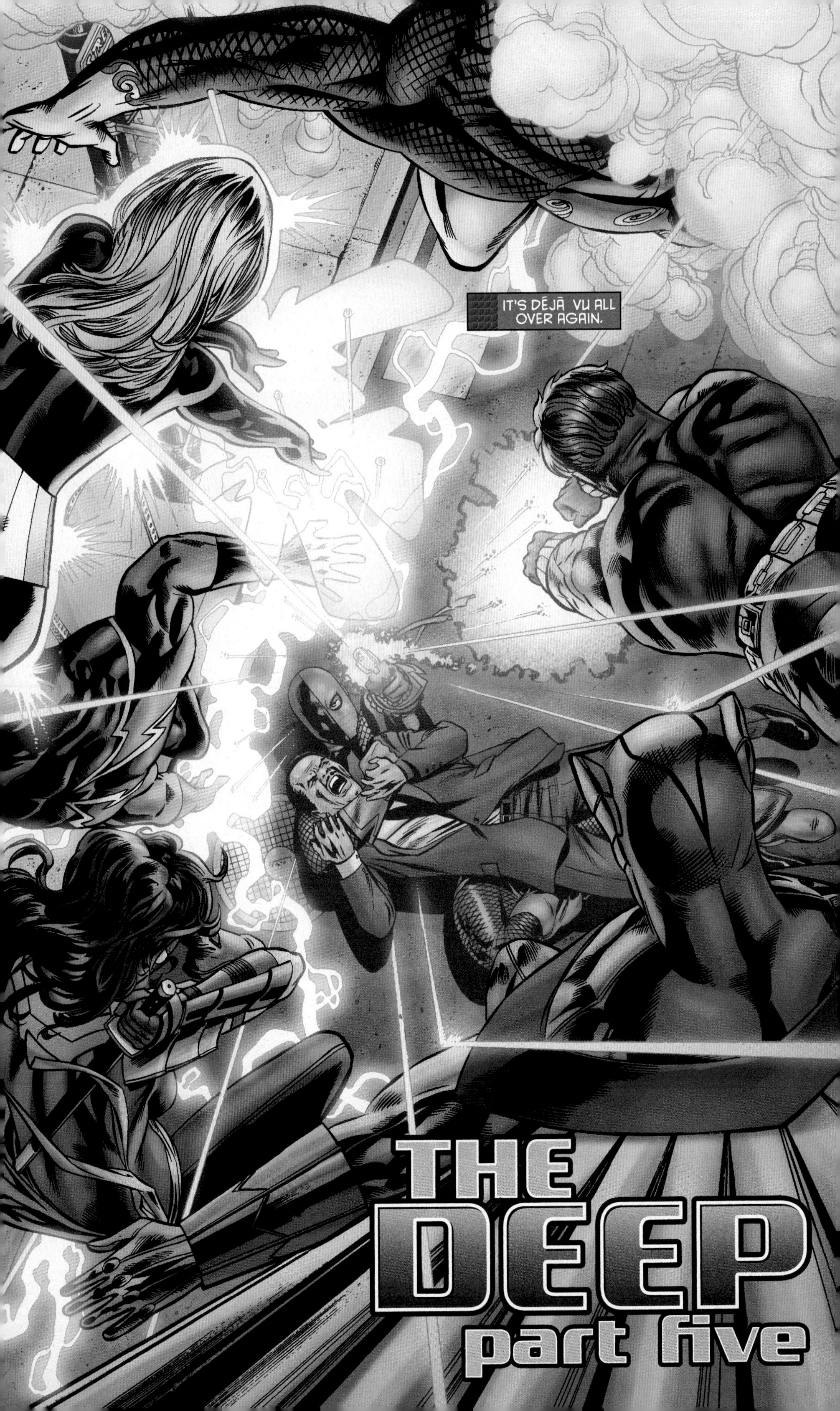

IT'S DÉJÀ VU ALL OVER AGAIN.
THE DEEP
part five

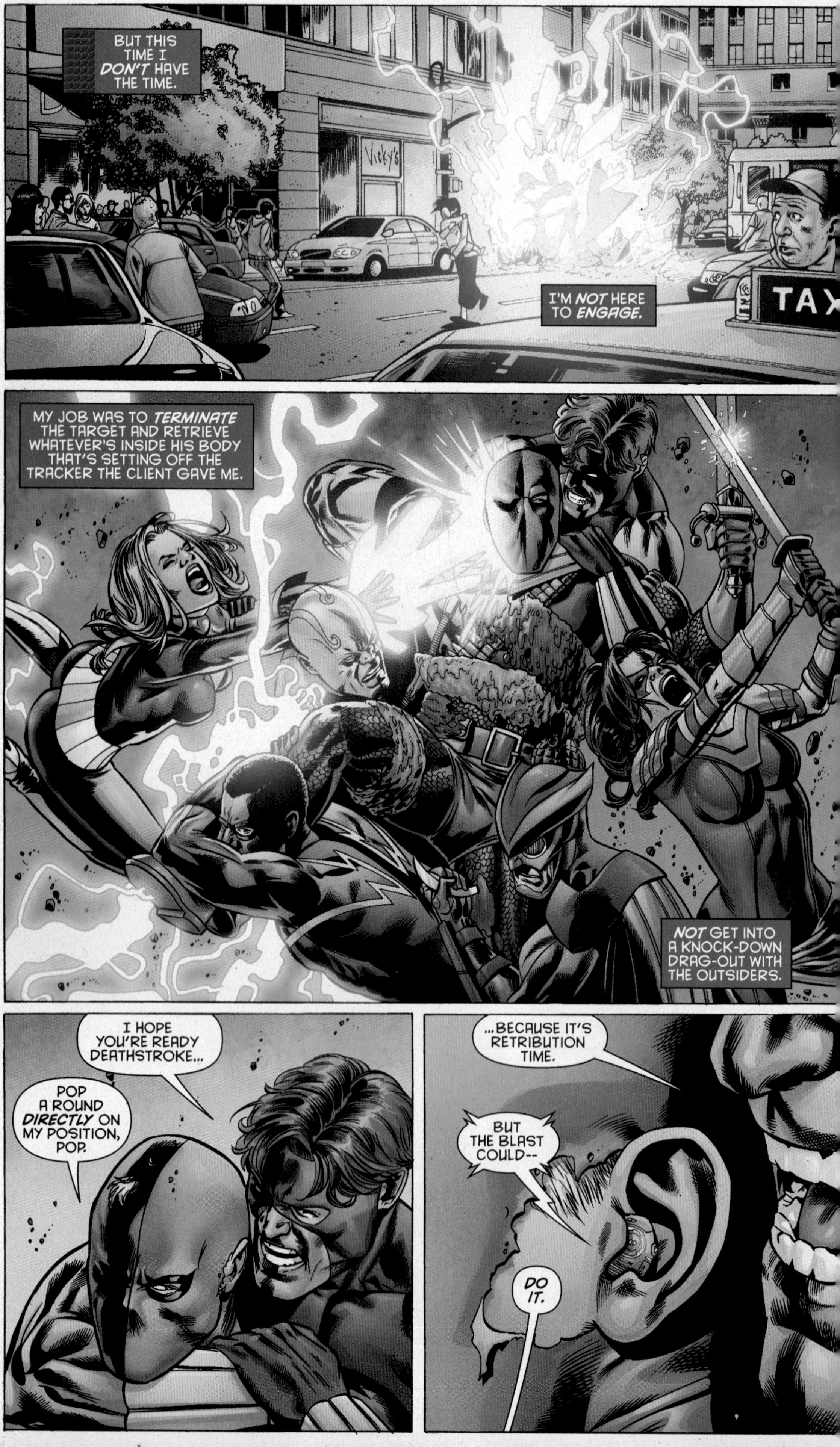

BUT THIS TIME I DON'T HAVE THE TIME.
Vicky's
TAX
I'M NOT HERE TO ENGAGE.
MY JOB WAS TO TERMINATE THE TARGET AND RETRIEVE WHATEVER'S INSIDE HIS BODY THAT'S SETTING OFF THE TRACKER THE CLIENT GAVE ME.
NOT GET INTO A KNOCK-DOWN DRAG-OUT WITH THE OUTSIDERS.
I HOPE YOU'RE READY DEATHSTROKE...
POP A ROUND DIRECTLY ON MY POSITION, POP.
...BECAUSE IT'S RETRIBUTION TIME.
BUT THE BLAST COULD--
DO IT.

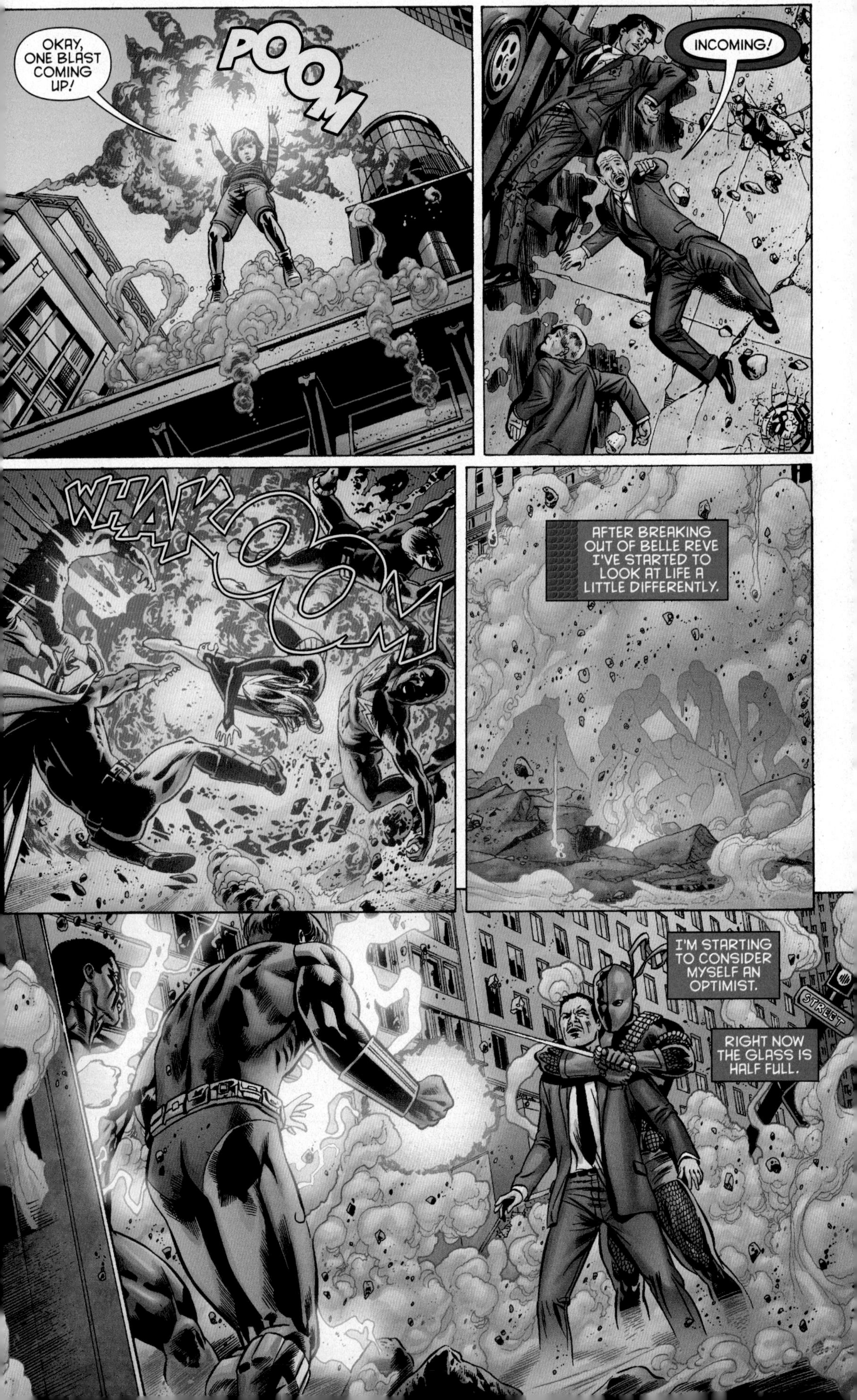
OKAY, ONE BLAST COMING UP!
POOM
INCOMING!
WHAKOOOM
AFTER BREAKING OUT OF BELLE REVE I'VE STARTED TO LOOK AT LIFE A LITTLE DIFFERENTLY.
I'M STARTING TO CONSIDER MYSELF AN OPTIMIST.
STREET
RIGHT NOW THE GLASS IS HALF FULL.

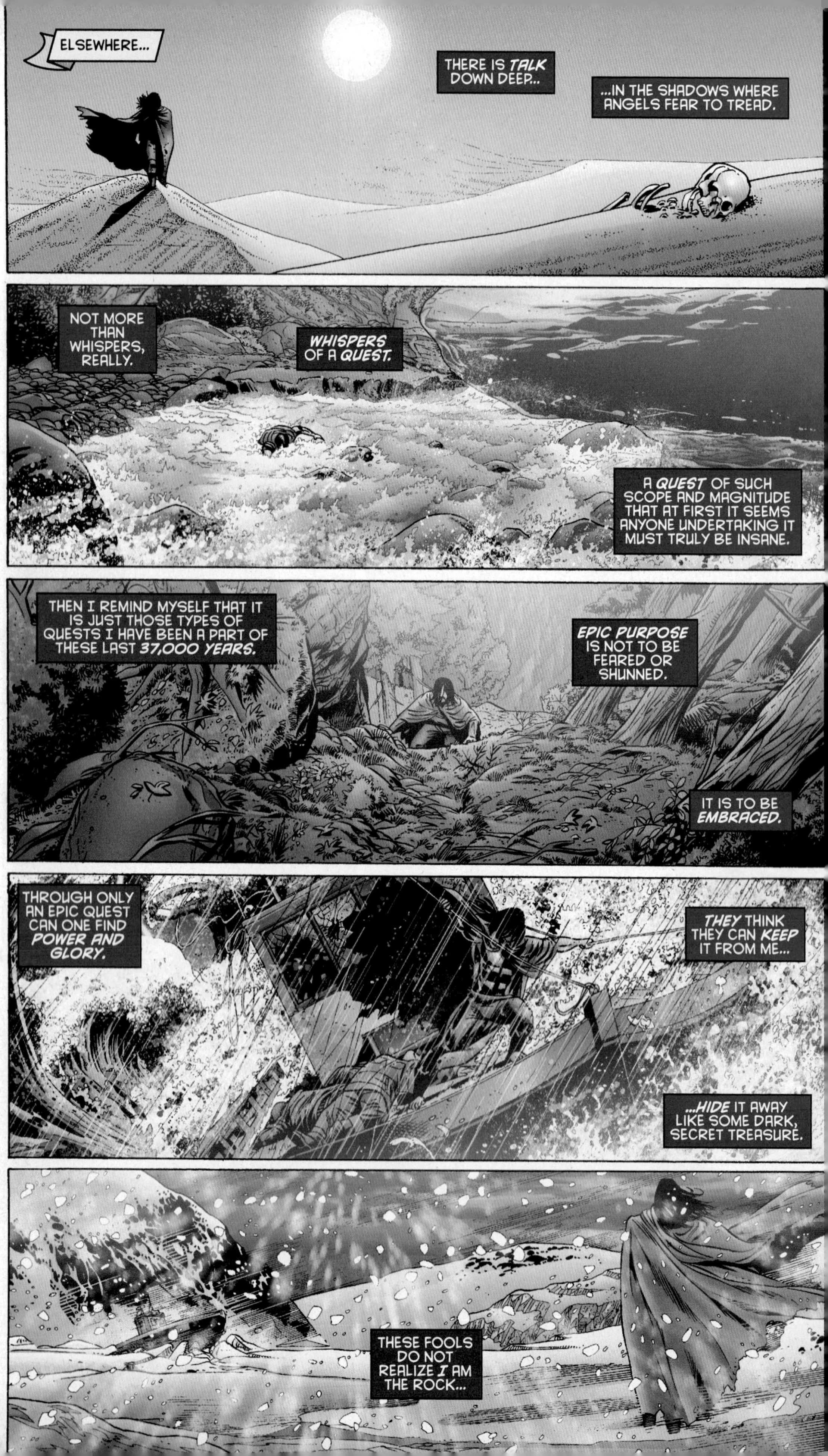
ELSEWHERE...
THERE IS TALK DOWN DEEP...
...IN THE SHADOWS WHERE ANGELS FEAR TO TREAD.
NOT MORE THAN WHISPERS, REALLY.
WHISPERS OF A QUEST.
A QUEST OF SUCH SCOPE AND MAGNITUDE THAT AT FIRST IT SEEMS ANYONE UNDERTAKING IT MUST TRULY BE INSANE.
THEN I REMIND MYSELF THAT IT IS JUST THOSE TYPES OF QUESTS I HAVE BEEN A PART OF THESE LAST 37,000 YEARS.
EPIC PURPOSE IS NOT TO BE FEARED OR SHUNNED.
IT IS TO BE EMBRACED.
THROUGH ONLY AN EPIC QUEST CAN ONE FIND POWER AND GLORY.
THEY THINK THEY CAN KEEP IT FROM ME...
...HIDE IT AWAY LIKE SOME DARK, SECRET TREASURE.
THESE FOOLS DO NOT REALIZE I AM THE ROCK...

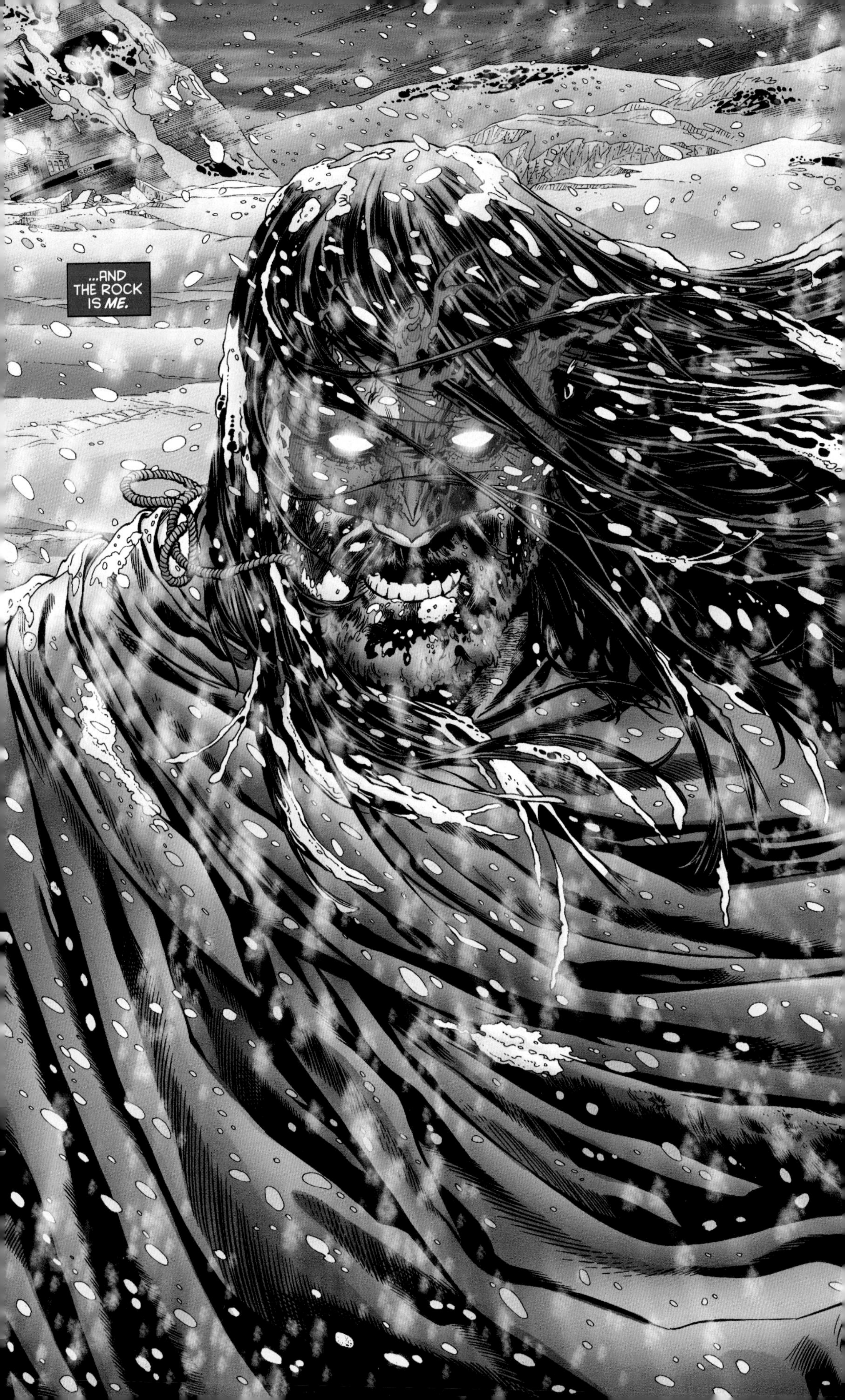
...AND THE ROCK IS *ME.*

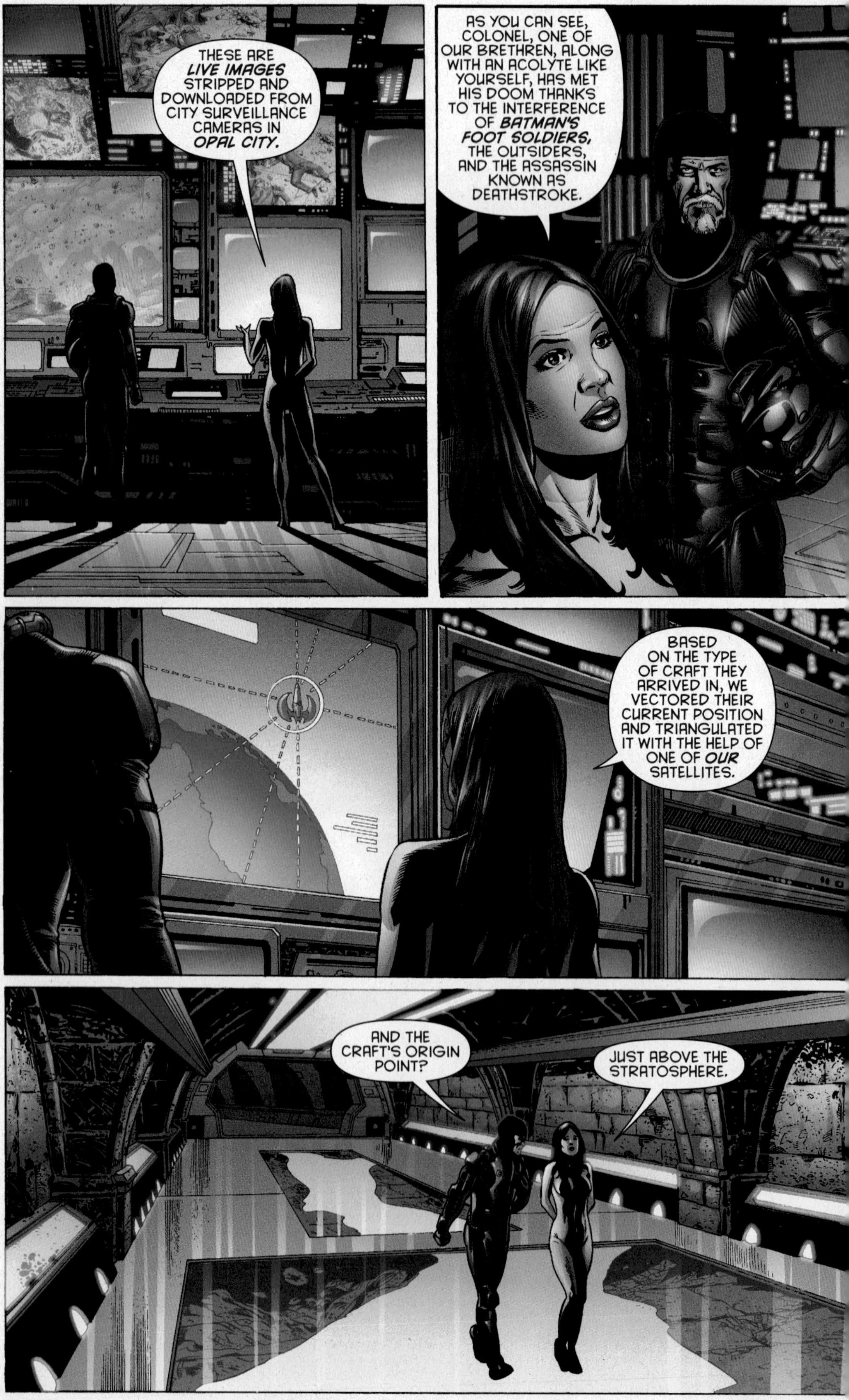
THESE ARE LIVE IMAGES STRIPPED AND DOWNLOADED FROM CITY SURVEILLANCE CAMERAS IN OPAL CITY.
AS YOU CAN SEE, COLONEL, ONE OF OUR BRETHREN, ALONG WITH AN ACOLYTE LIKE YOURSELF, HAS MET HIS DOOM THANKS TO THE INTERFERENCE OF BATMAN'S FOOT SOLDIERS, THE OUTSIDERS, AND THE ASSASSIN KNOWN AS DEATHSTROKE.
BASED ON THE TYPE OF CRAFT THEY ARRIVED IN, WE VECTORED THEIR CURRENT POSITION AND TRIANGULATED IT WITH THE HELP OF ONE OF OUR SATELLITES.
AND THE CRAFT'S ORIGIN POINT?
JUST ABOVE THE STRATOSPHERE.

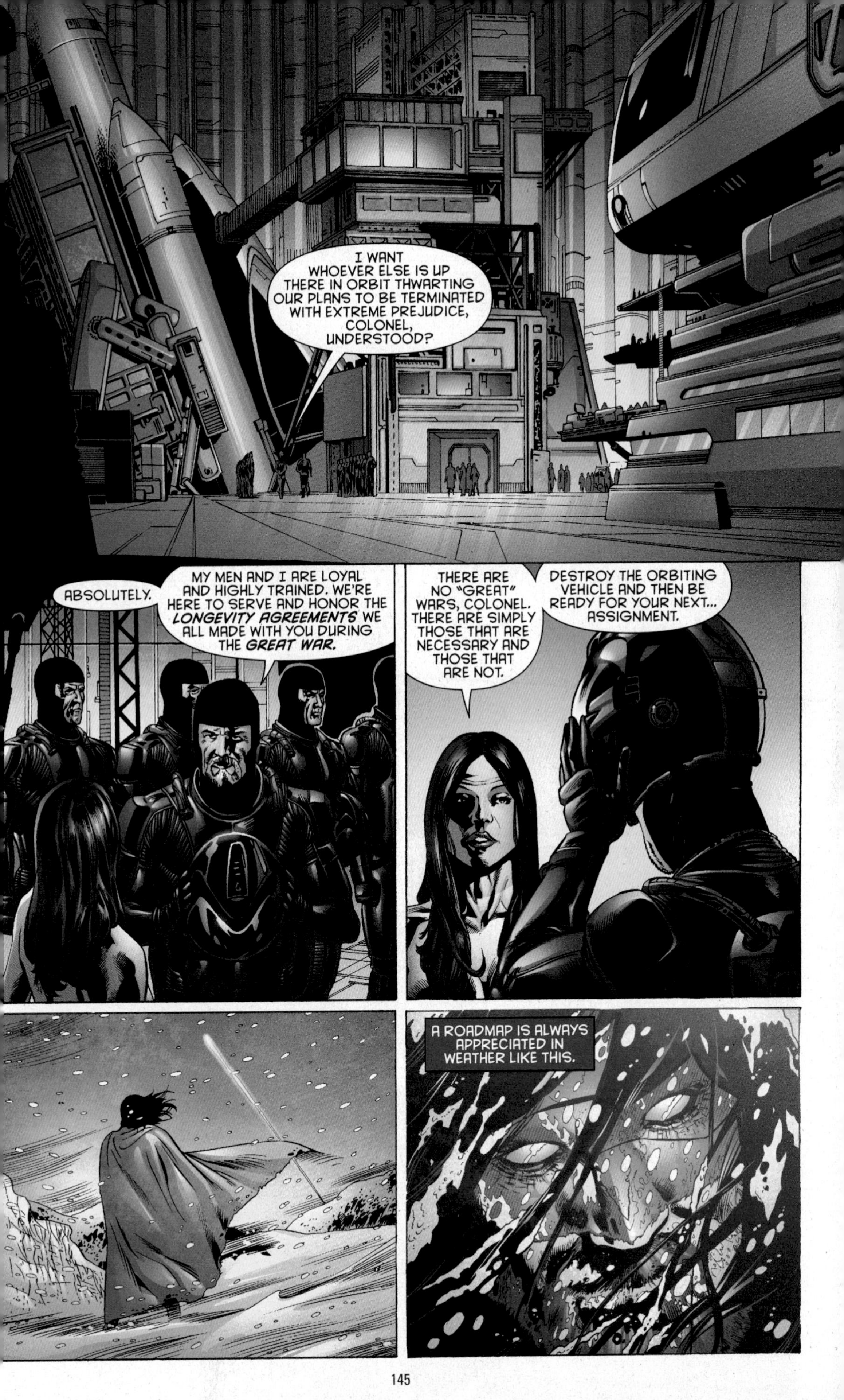
I WANT WHOEVER ELSE IS UP THERE IN ORBIT THWARTING OUR PLANS TO BE TERMINATED WITH EXTREME PREJUDICE, COLONEL, UNDERSTOOD?
ABSOLUTELY.
MY MEN AND I ARE LOYAL AND HIGHLY TRAINED. WE'RE HERE TO SERVE AND HONOR THE *LONGEVITY AGREEMENTS* WE ALL MADE WITH YOU DURING THE *GREAT WAR.*
THERE ARE NO "GREAT" WARS, COLONEL. THERE ARE SIMPLY THOSE THAT ARE NECESSARY AND THOSE THAT ARE NOT.
DESTROY THE ORBITING VEHICLE AND THEN BE READY FOR YOUR NEXT... ASSIGNMENT.
A ROADMAP IS ALWAYS APPRECIATED IN WEATHER LIKE THIS.

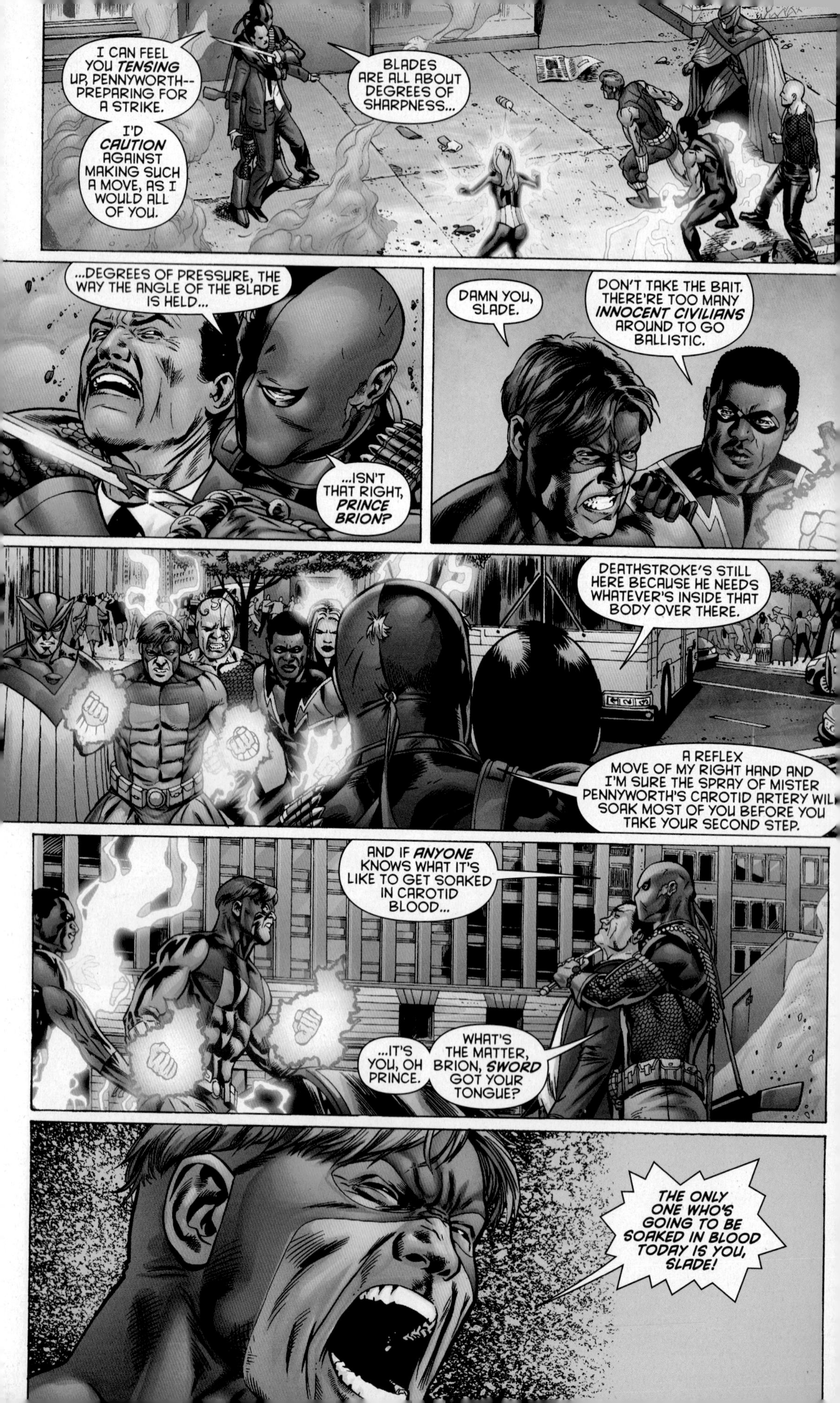
I CAN FEEL YOU TENSING UP, PENNYWORTH-- PREPARING FOR A STRIKE.
I'D CAUTION AGAINST MAKING SUCH A MOVE, AS I WOULD ALL OF YOU.
BLADES ARE ALL ABOUT DEGREES OF SHARPNESS...
...DEGREES OF PRESSURE, THE WAY THE ANGLE OF THE BLADE IS HELD...
...ISN'T THAT RIGHT, PRINCE BRION?
DAMN YOU, SLADE.
DON'T TAKE THE BAIT. THERE'RE TOO MANY INNOCENT CIVILIANS AROUND TO GO BALLISTIC.
DEATHSTROKE'S STILL HERE BECAUSE HE NEEDS WHATEVER'S INSIDE THAT BODY OVER THERE.
A REFLEX MOVE OF MY RIGHT HAND AND I'M SURE THE SPRAY OF MISTER PENNYWORTH'S CAROTID ARTERY WIL SOAK MOST OF YOU BEFORE YOU TAKE YOUR SECOND STEP.
AND IF ANYONE KNOWS WHAT IT'S LIKE TO GET SOAKED IN CAROTID BLOOD...
...IT'S YOU, OH PRINCE.
WHAT'S THE MATTER, BRION, SWORD GOT YOUR TONGUE?
THE ONLY ONE WHO'S GOING TO BE SOAKED IN BLOOD TODAY IS YOU, SLADE!

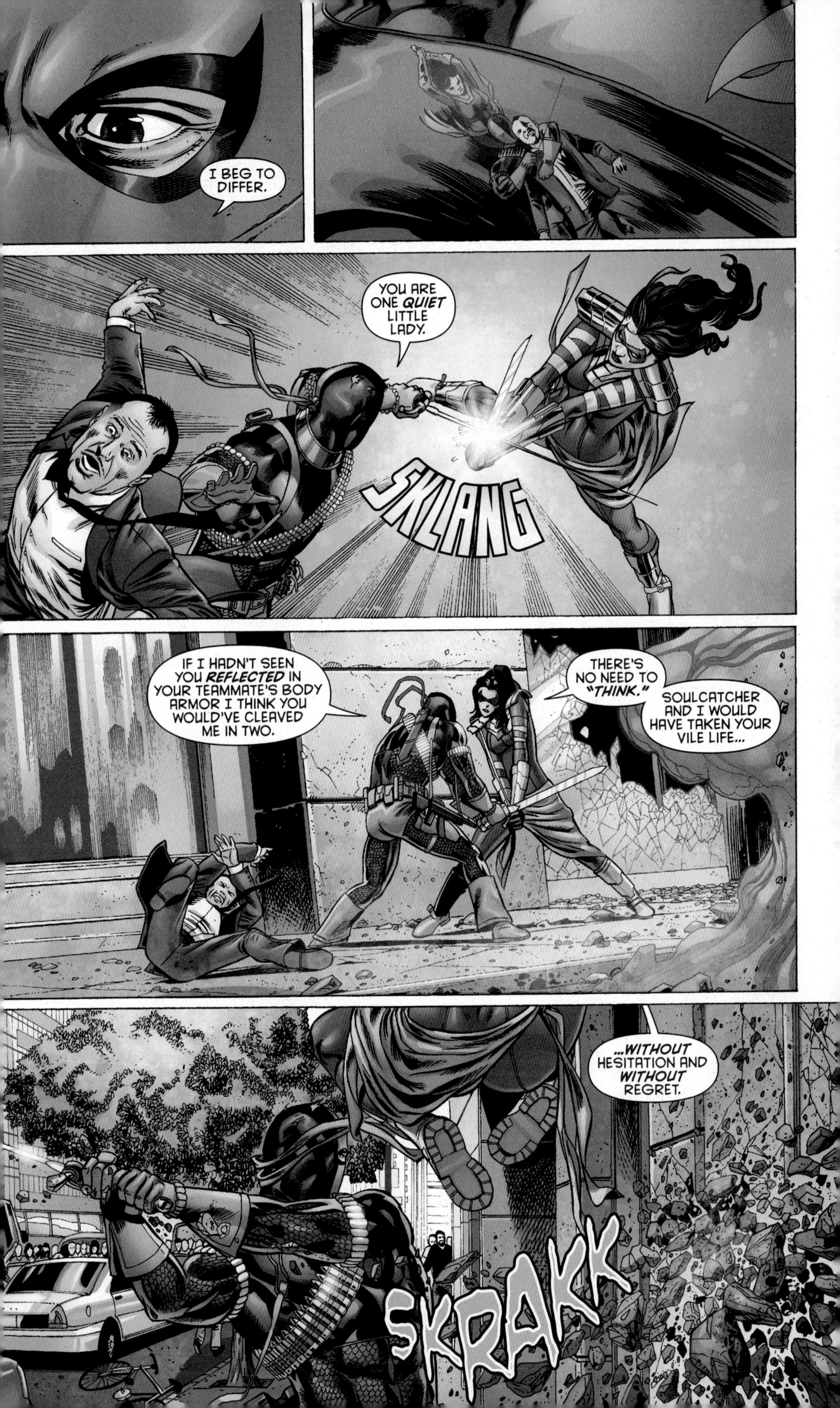
I BEG TO DIFFER.
YOU ARE ONE QUIET LITTLE LADY.
SKLANG
IF I HADN'T SEEN YOU REFLECTED IN YOUR TEAMMATE'S BODY ARMOR I THINK YOU WOULD'VE CLEAVED ME IN TWO.
THERE'S NO NEED TO "THINK."
SOULCATCHER AND I WOULD HAVE TAKEN YOUR VILE LIFE...
...WITHOUT HESITATION AND WITHOUT REGRET.
SKRAKK

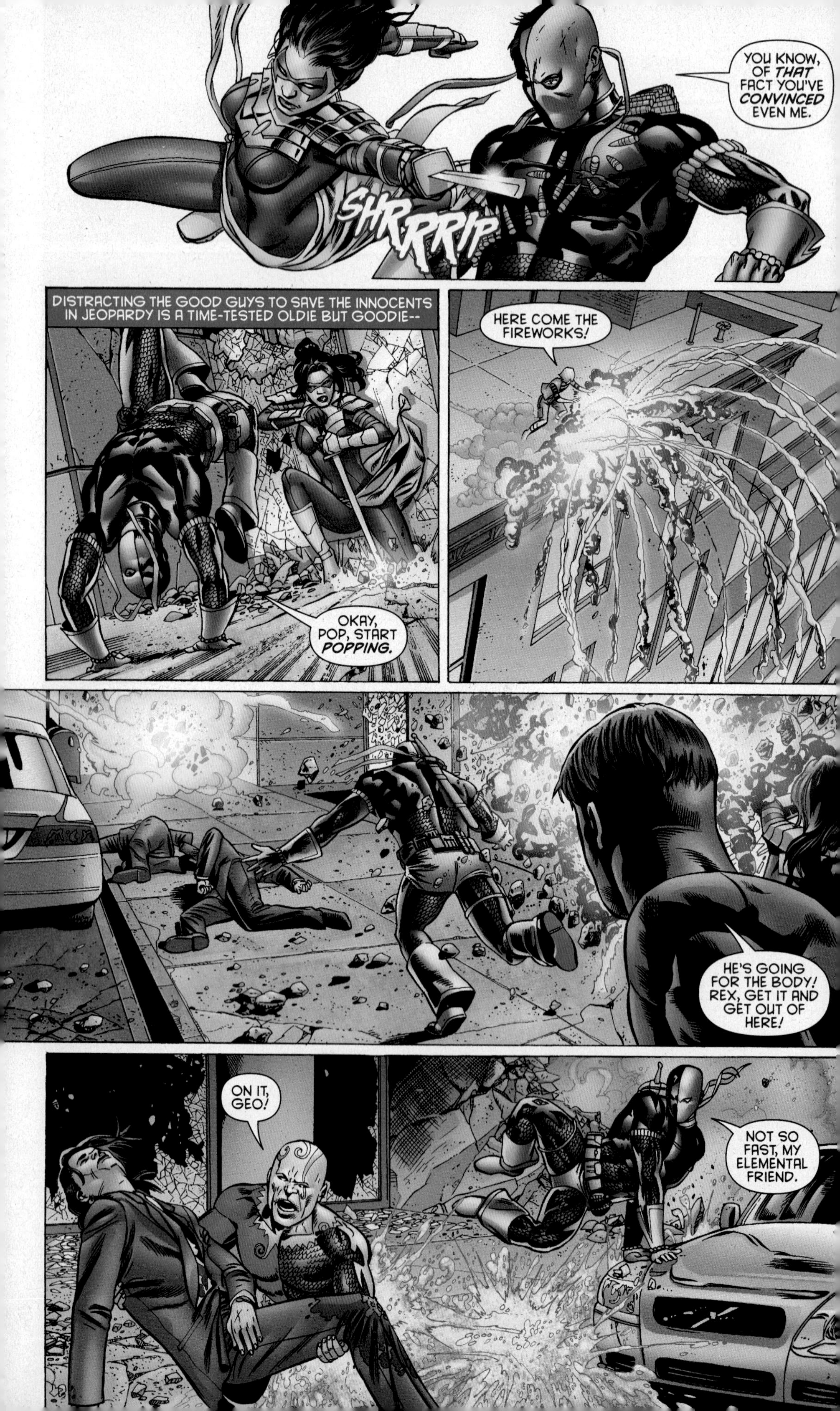
YOU KNOW, OF THAT FACT YOU'VE CONVINCED EVEN ME.
SHRRRIP
DISTRACTING THE GOOD GUYS TO SAVE THE INNOCENTS IN JEOPARDY IS A TIME-TESTED OLDIE BUT GOODIE--
OKAY, POP, START POPPING.
HERE COME THE FIREWORKS!
HE'S GOING FOR THE BODY! REX, GET IT AND GET OUT OF HERE!
ON IT, GEO!
NOT SO FAST, MY ELEMENTAL FRIEND.

OWLMAN! HALO! INTERCEPT THE EXPLOSIVE CHARGES BEFORE THEY HIT THE STREET!

YOU'RE NOT GETTING HIM, SLADE!

DON'T WORRY...

...I ONLY WANT A *PIECE* OF HIM!

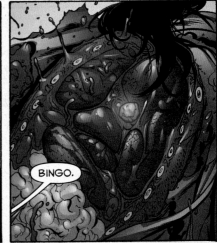

BINGO.

WHOOM WHOOM WHOOM WHOOM WHOOM WHOOM

KEEP UP THE COMMOTION, KID.

A FEW MORE SECONDS IS ALL I--

YOU'RE NOT GOING ANYWHERE, SLADE!

FORGET HIM, DAMN IT!

INNOCENT PEOPLE NEED SAVING, GEO-FORCE!

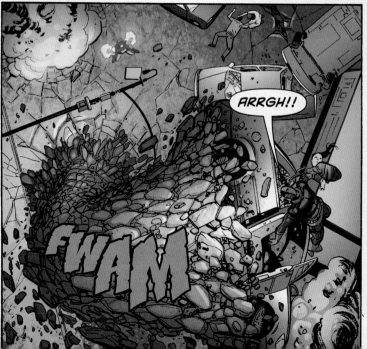
ARRGH!!

FWAM

SKOOM

STAY DOWN!

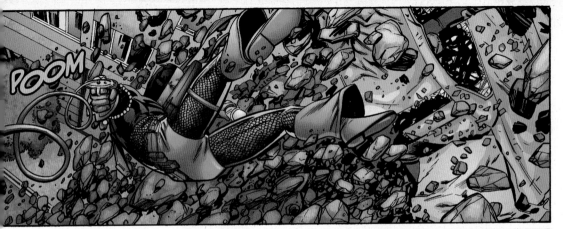

POOM

WHAT THE HELL ARE YOU DOING, GEO?!?

SHUT UP! I NEED TO FOCUS!

PRIORITY, MAN! KEEPING THESE PEOPLE OUT OF HARM'S WAY IS OUR DUTY! NOTHING'S MORE IMPORTANT THAN THAT!

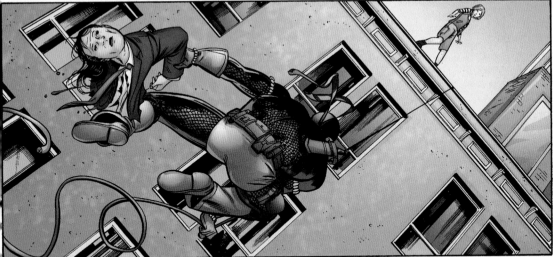

SHLLLLUK

GOT IT!

FAP

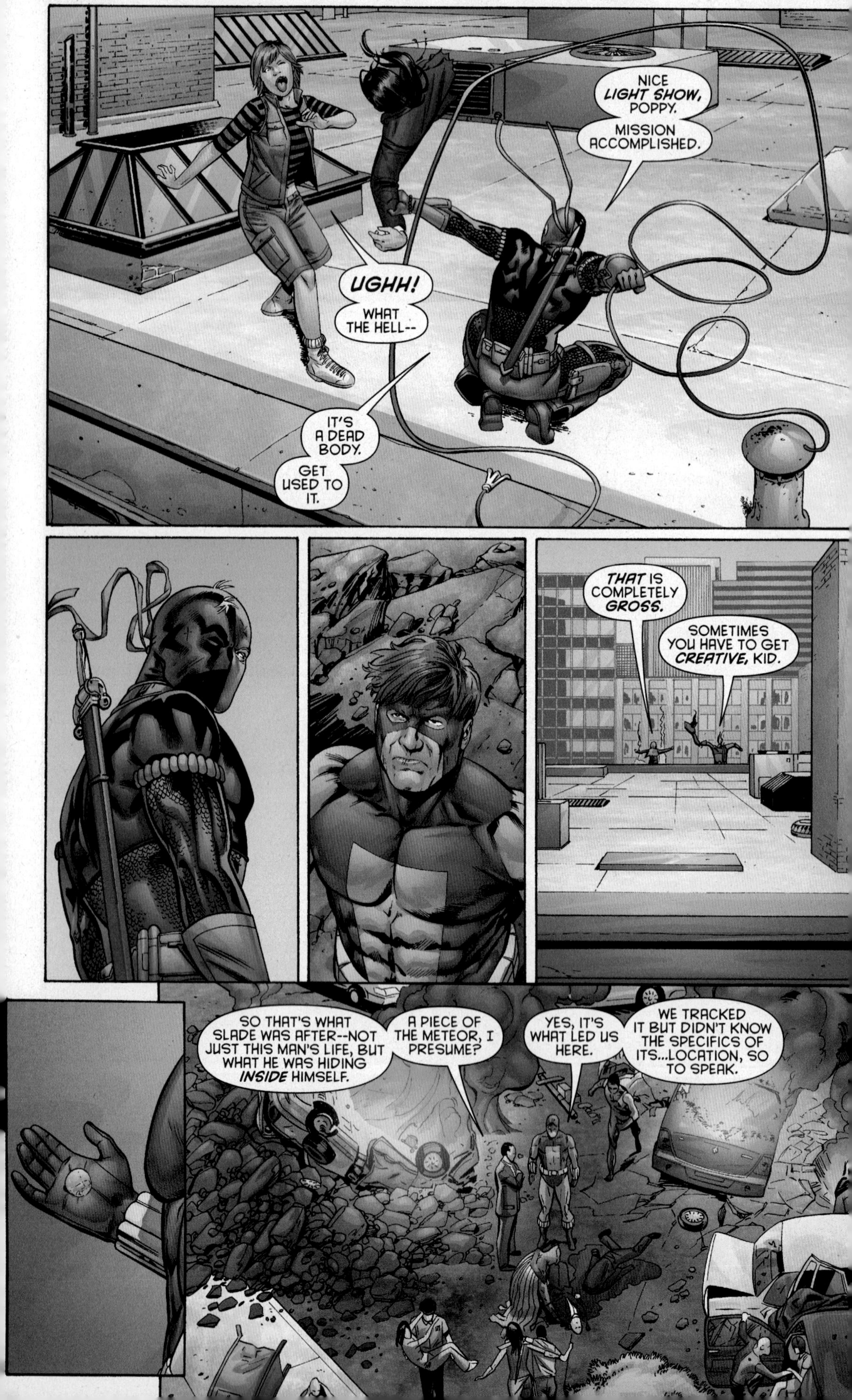
NICE LIGHT SHOW, POPPY.
MISSION ACCOMPLISHED.
UGHH!
WHAT THE HELL--
IT'S A DEAD BODY.
GET USED TO IT.
THAT IS COMPLETELY GROSS.
SOMETIMES YOU HAVE TO GET CREATIVE, KID.
SO THAT'S WHAT SLADE WAS AFTER--NOT JUST THIS MAN'S LIFE, BUT WHAT HE WAS HIDING INSIDE HIMSELF.
A PIECE OF THE METEOR, I PRESUME?
YES, IT'S WHAT LED US HERE.
WE TRACKED IT BUT DIDN'T KNOW THE SPECIFICS OF ITS...LOCATION, SO TO SPEAK.

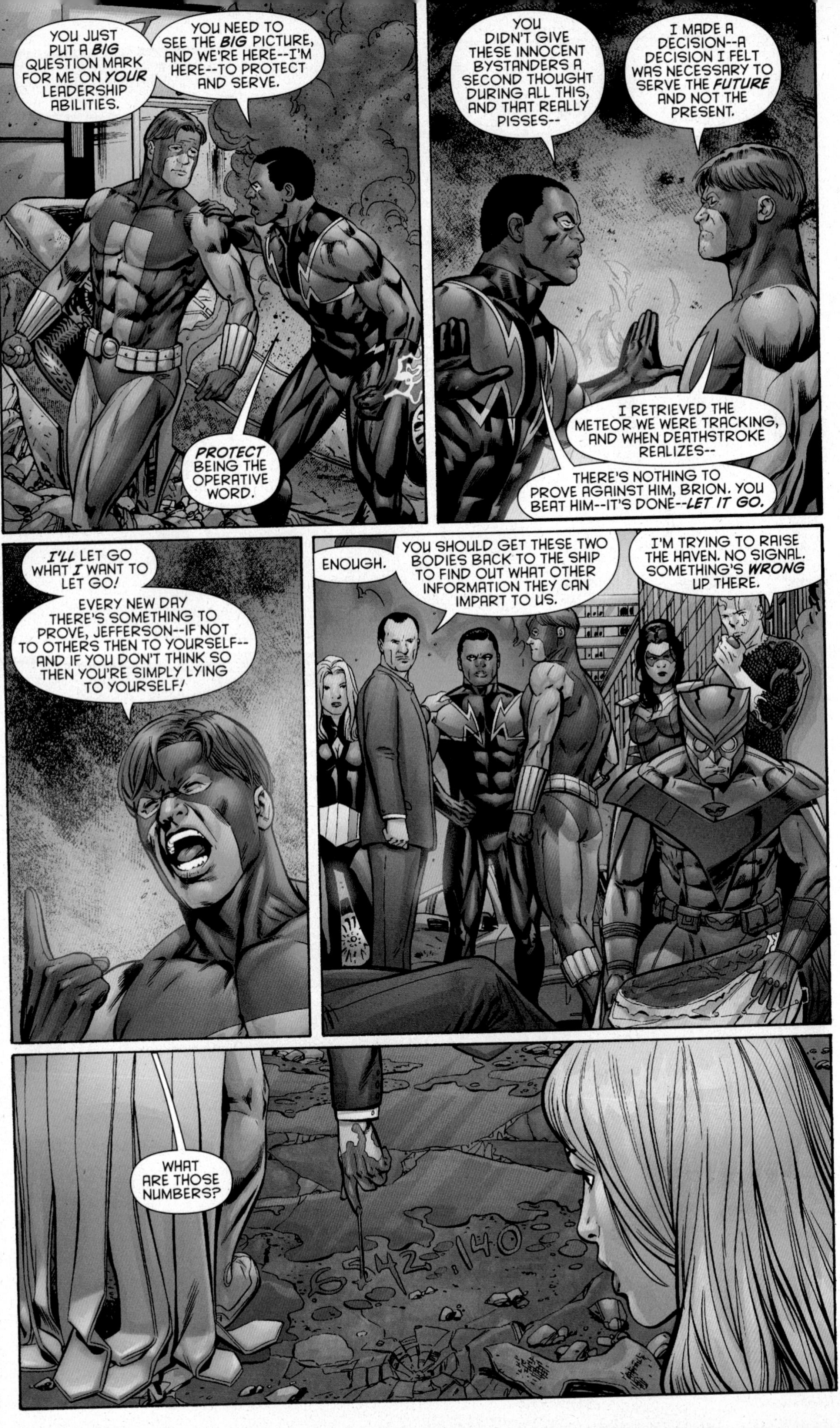
YOU JUST PUT A BIG QUESTION MARK FOR ME ON YOUR LEADERSHIP ABILITIES.
YOU NEED TO SEE THE BIG PICTURE, AND WE'RE HERE--I'M HERE--TO PROTECT AND SERVE.
PROTECT BEING THE OPERATIVE WORD.
YOU DIDN'T GIVE THESE INNOCENT BYSTANDERS A SECOND THOUGHT DURING ALL THIS, AND THAT REALLY PISSES--
I MADE A DECISION--A DECISION I FELT WAS NECESSARY TO SERVE THE FUTURE AND NOT THE PRESENT.
I RETRIEVED THE METEOR WE WERE TRACKING, AND WHEN DEATHSTROKE REALIZES--
THERE'S NOTHING TO PROVE AGAINST HIM, BRION. YOU BEAT HIM--IT'S DONE--LET IT GO.
I'LL LET GO WHAT I WANT TO LET GO!
EVERY NEW DAY THERE'S SOMETHING TO PROVE, JEFFERSON--IF NOT TO OTHERS THEN TO YOURSELF--AND IF YOU DON'T THINK SO THEN YOU'RE SIMPLY LYING TO YOURSELF!
ENOUGH.
YOU SHOULD GET THESE TWO BODIES BACK TO THE SHIP TO FIND OUT WHAT OTHER INFORMATION THEY CAN IMPART TO US.
I'M TRYING TO RAISE THE HAVEN. NO SIGNAL. SOMETHING'S WRONG UP THERE.
WHAT ARE THOSE NUMBERS?
6542.140

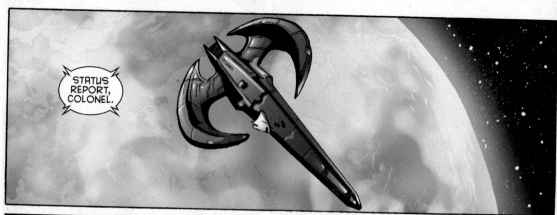

STATUS REPORT, COLONEL.

GOOD NEWS AND BAD.

GOOD NEWS IS, WE'VE DOCKED AND ARE COMMENCING OUR PURGE OPS.

BAD NEWS IS, THE SHIP'S SHAPED LIKE A BAT SYMBOL SO WE'RE MOST LIKELY GONNA BE FACING CAPES.

KEEP ME APPRISED OF THE SITUATION.

COLONEL, SO FAR WE'VE SEEN NO EVIDENCE OF--

YARRGH!

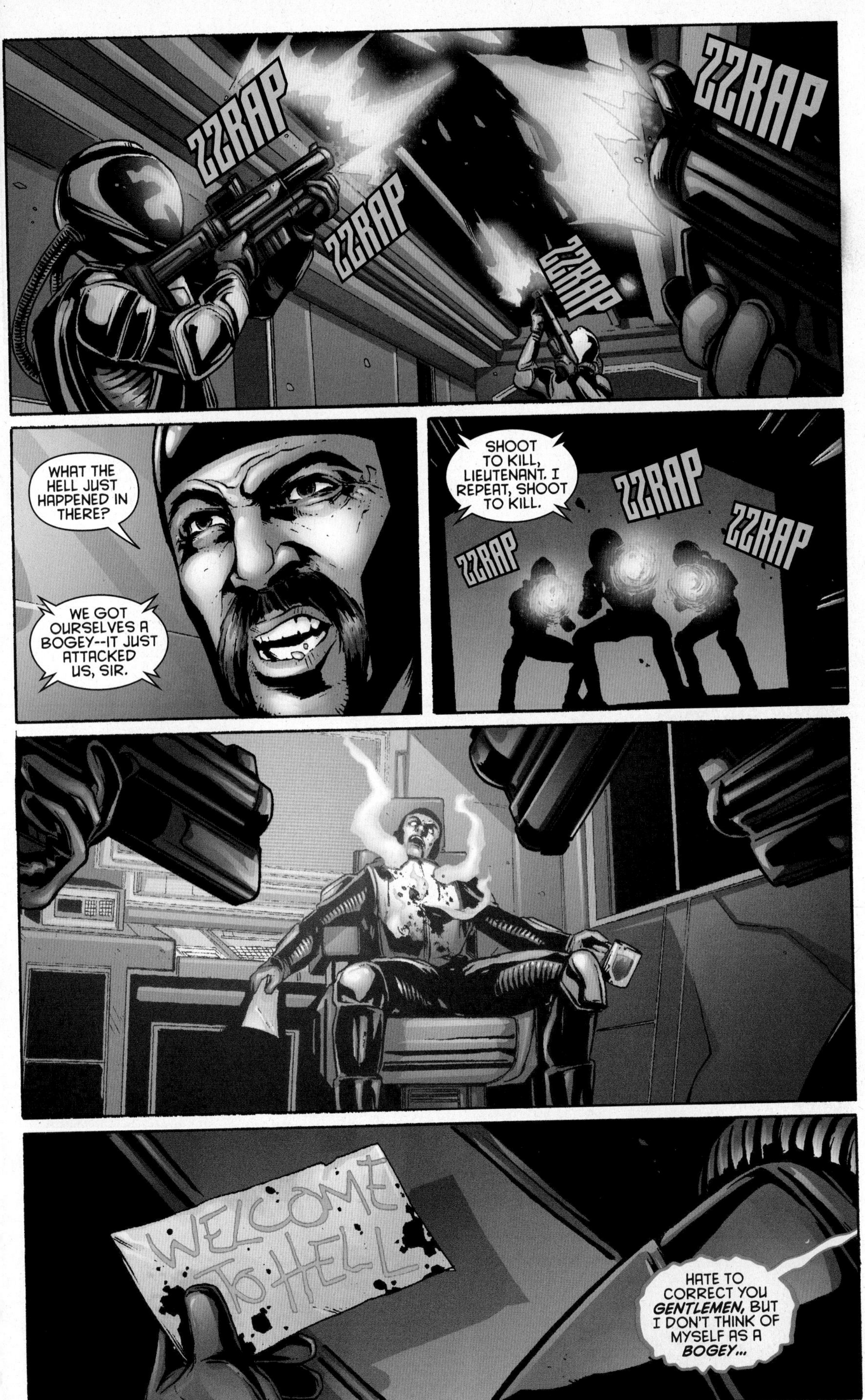
ZZRAP
ZZRAP
ZZRAP
ZZRAP
WHAT THE HELL JUST HAPPENED IN THERE?
WE GOT OURSELVES A BOGEY--IT JUST ATTACKED US, SIR.
SHOOT TO KILL, LIEUTENANT. I REPEAT, SHOOT TO KILL.
ZZRAP
ZZRAP
ZZRAP
WELCOME TO HELL
HATE TO CORRECT YOU *GENTLEMEN,* BUT I DON'T THINK OF MYSELF AS A *BOGEY...*

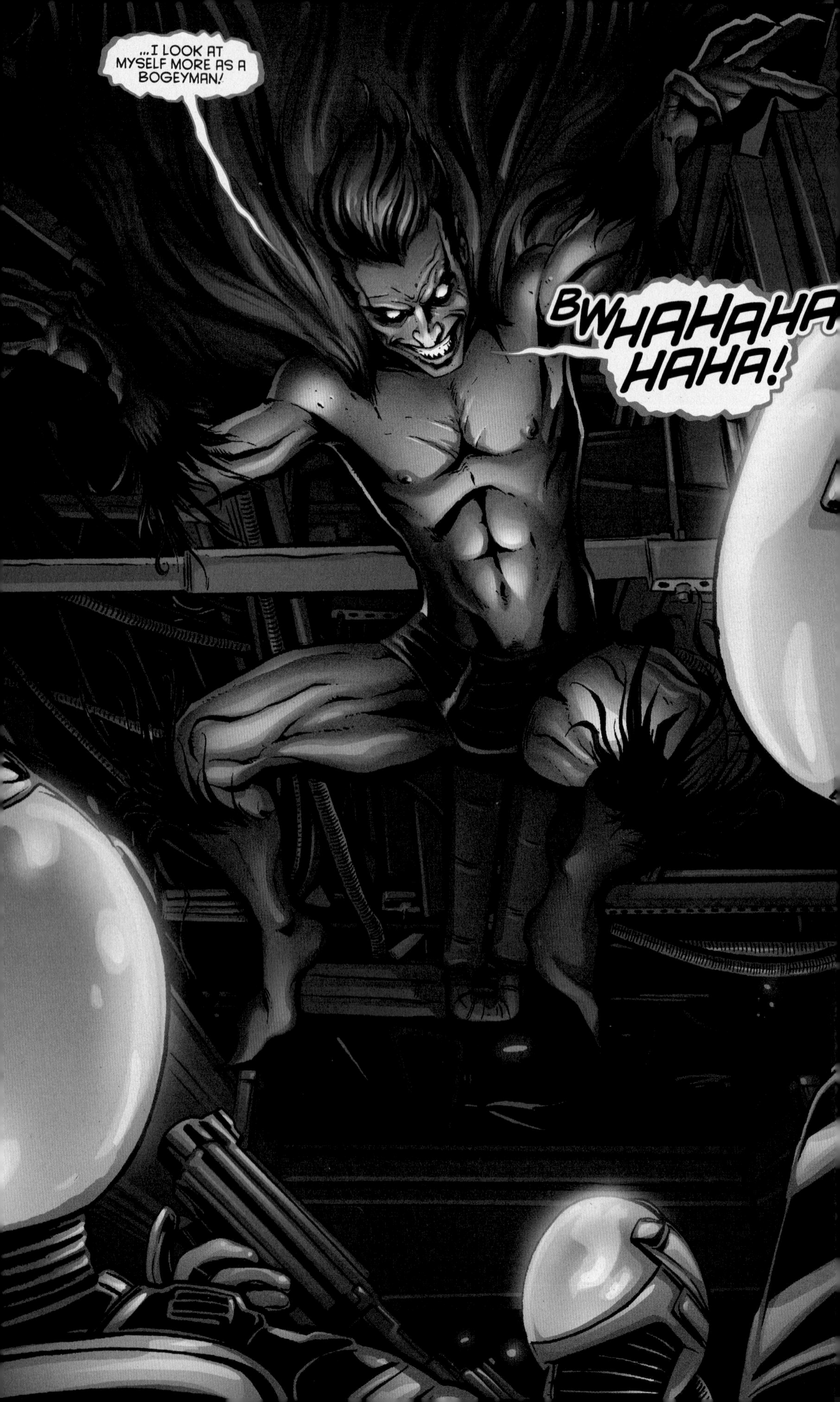
...I LOOK AT MYSELF MORE AS A BOGEYMAN!
BWHAHAHA HAHA!

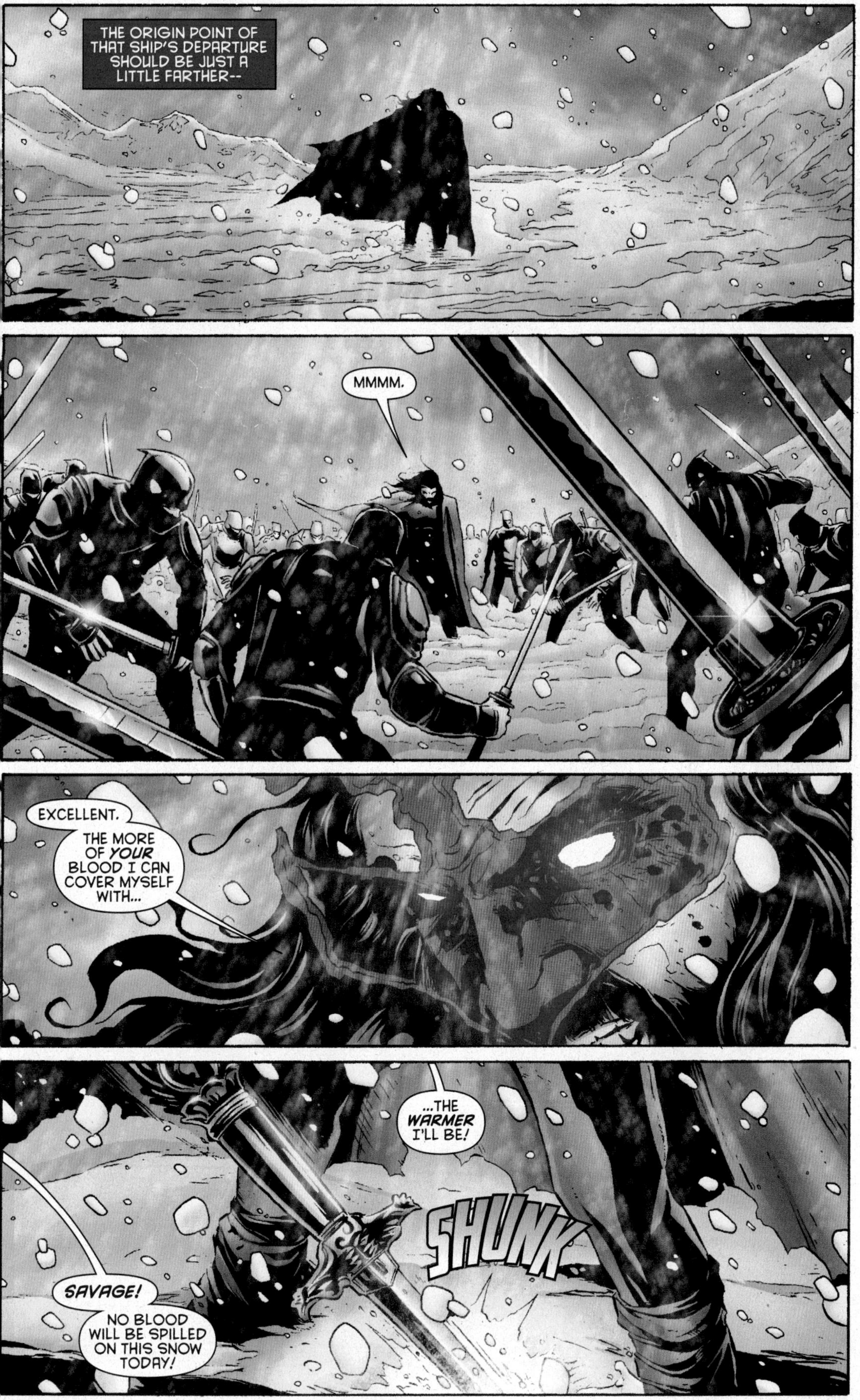
THE ORIGIN POINT OF THAT SHIP'S DEPARTURE SHOULD BE JUST A LITTLE FARTHER--
MMMM.
EXCELLENT.
THE MORE OF YOUR BLOOD I CAN COVER MYSELF WITH...
...THE WARMER I'LL BE!
SHUNK
SAVAGE!
NO BLOOD WILL BE SPILLED ON THIS SNOW TODAY!

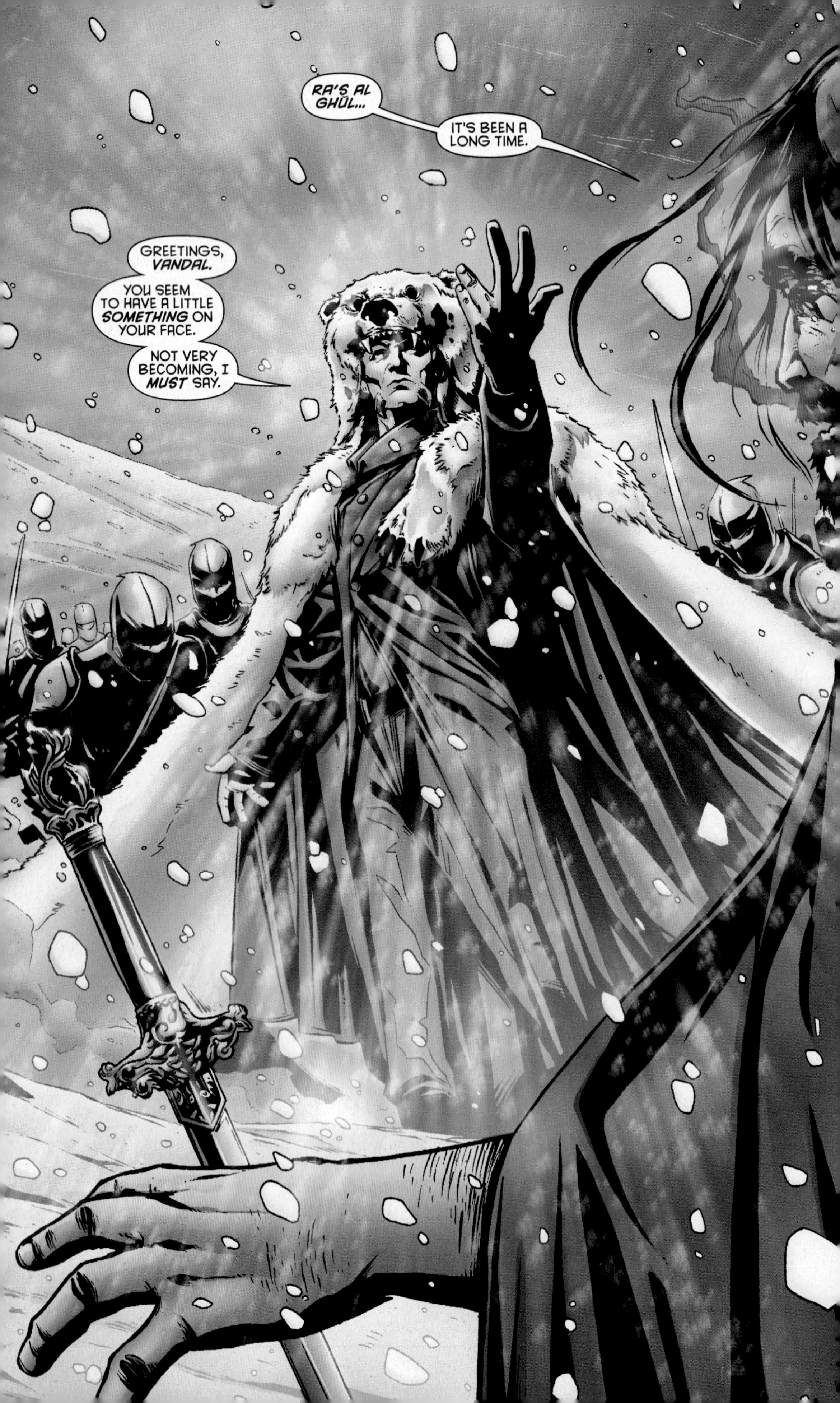
RA'S AL GHŪL...
IT'S BEEN A LONG TIME.
GREETINGS, VANDAL.
YOU SEEM TO HAVE A LITTLE SOMETHING ON YOUR FACE.
NOT VERY BECOMING, I MUST SAY.

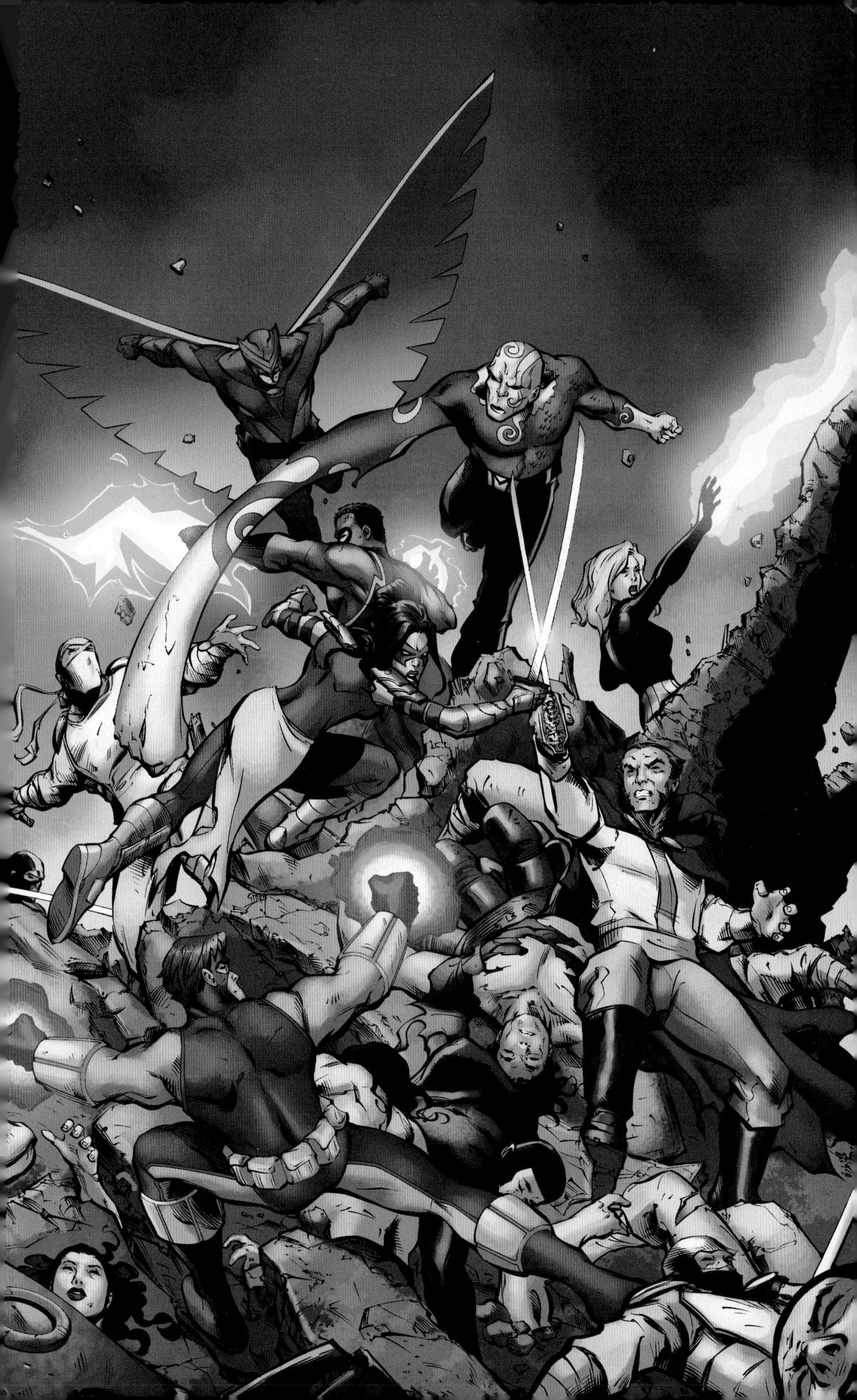

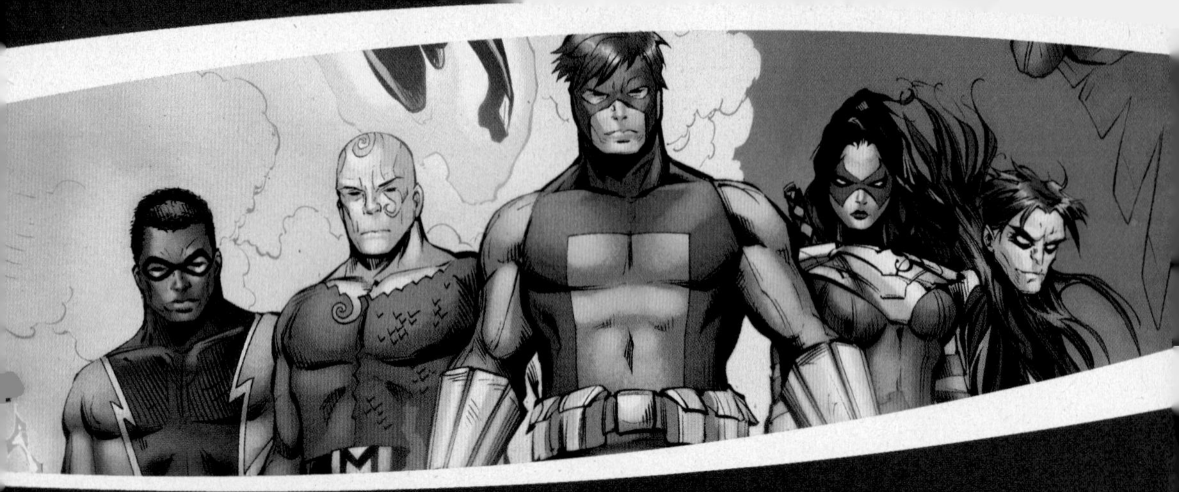

"Pain is what reminds us we're alive."

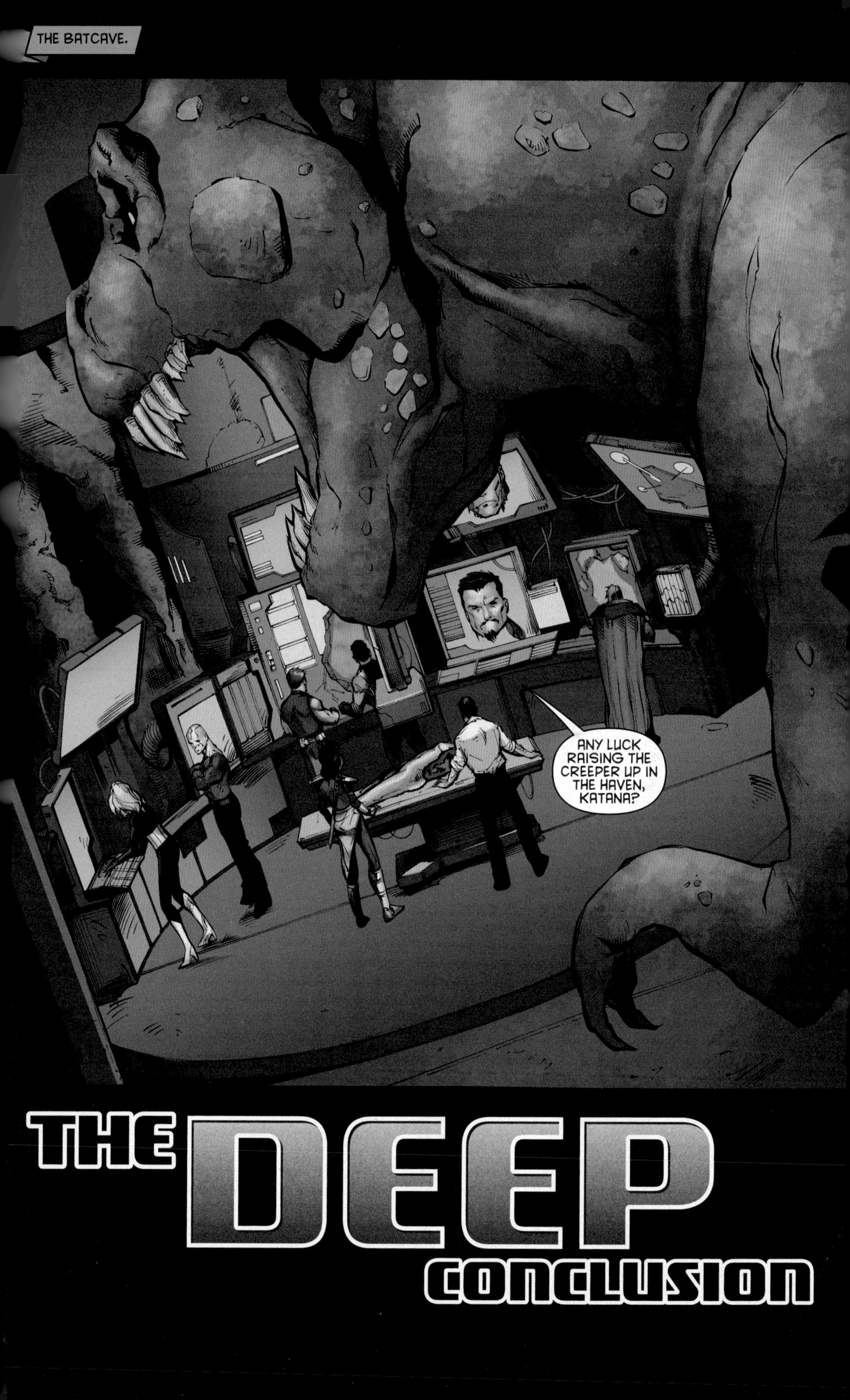
THE BATCAVE.
ANY LUCK RAISING THE CREEPER UP IN THE HAVEN, KATANA?
THE DEEP
CONCLUSION

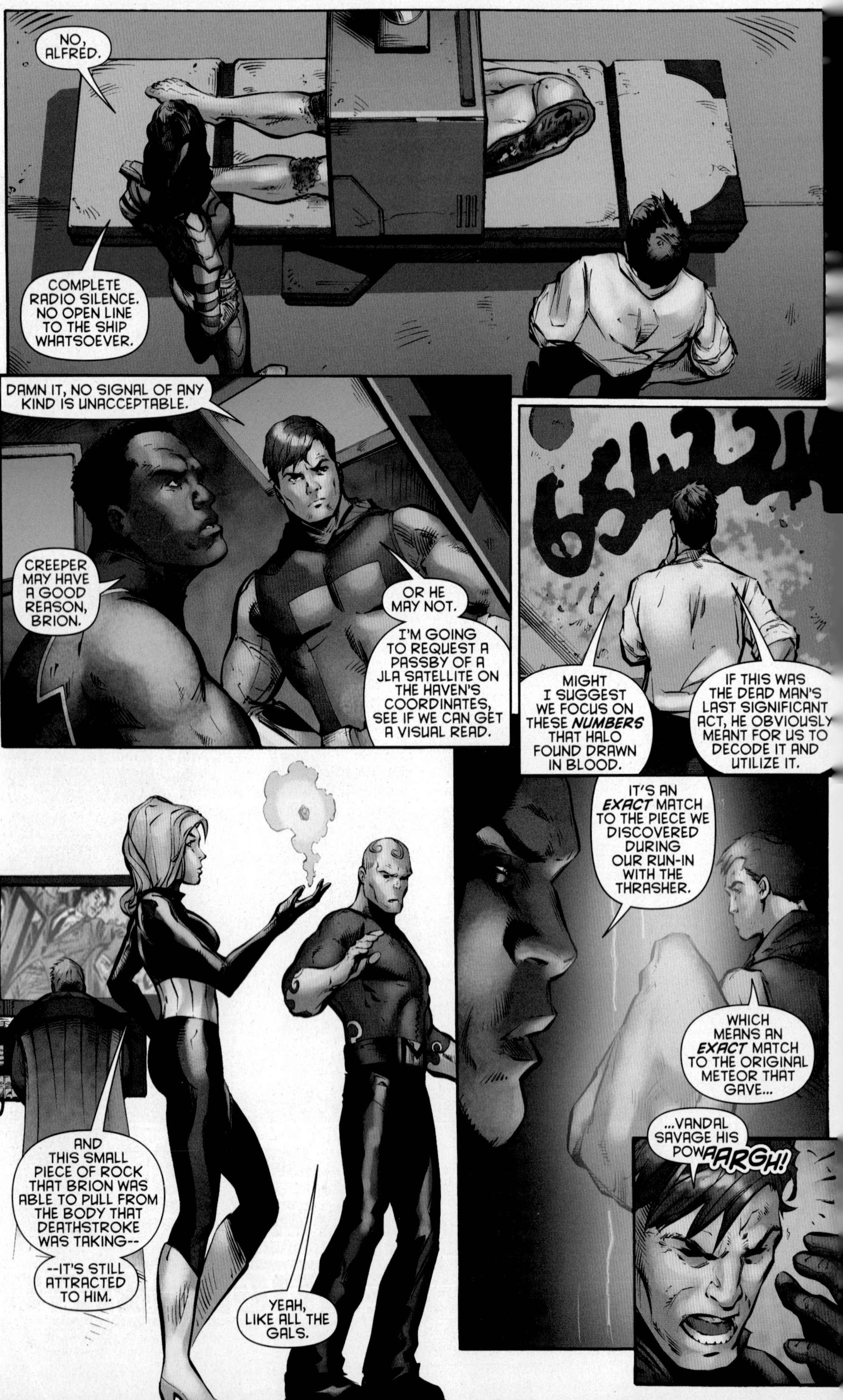
NO, ALFRED.
COMPLETE RADIO SILENCE. NO OPEN LINE TO THE SHIP WHATSOEVER.
DAMN IT, NO SIGNAL OF ANY KIND IS UNACCEPTABLE.
CREEPER MAY HAVE A GOOD REASON, BRION.
OR HE MAY NOT.
I'M GOING TO REQUEST A PASSBY OF A JLA SATELLITE ON THE HAVEN'S COORDINATES, SEE IF WE CAN GET A VISUAL READ.
MIGHT I SUGGEST WE FOCUS ON THESE NUMBERS THAT HALO FOUND DRAWN IN BLOOD.
IF THIS WAS THE DEAD MAN'S LAST SIGNIFICANT ACT, HE OBVIOUSLY MEANT FOR US TO DECODE IT AND UTILIZE IT.
AND THIS SMALL PIECE OF ROCK THAT BRION WAS ABLE TO PULL FROM THE BODY THAT DEATHSTROKE WAS TAKING--
--IT'S STILL ATTRACTED TO HIM.
YEAH, LIKE ALL THE GALS.
IT'S AN EXACT MATCH TO THE PIECE WE DISCOVERED DURING OUR RUN-IN WITH THE THRASHER.
WHICH MEANS AN EXACT MATCH TO THE ORIGINAL METEOR THAT GAVE...
...VANDAL SAVAGE HIS POWAARGH!

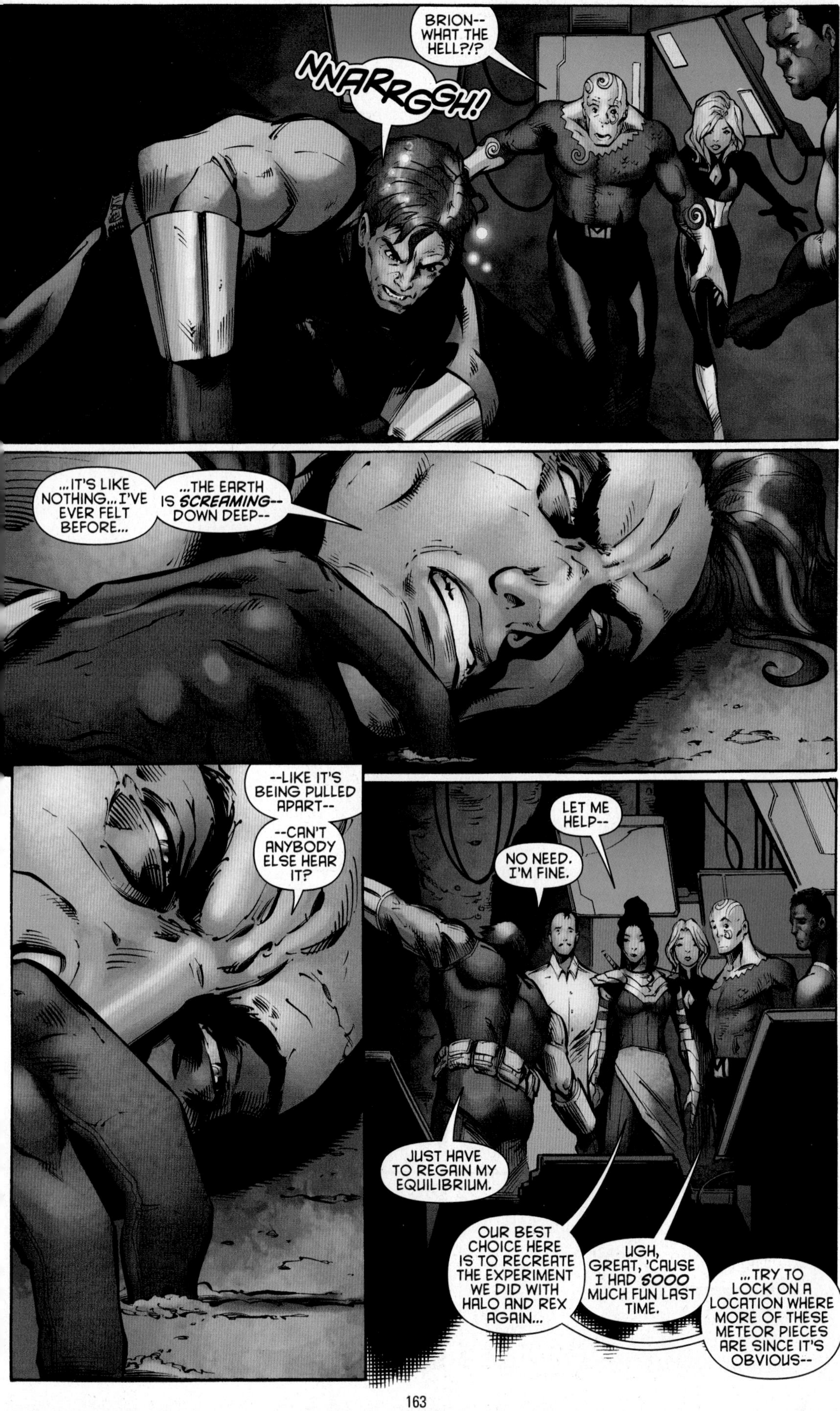
BRION-- WHAT THE HELL?!?
NNARRGGH!
...IT'S LIKE NOTHING...I'VE EVER FELT BEFORE...
...THE EARTH IS SCREAMING-- DOWN DEEP--
--LIKE IT'S BEING PULLED APART--
--CAN'T ANYBODY ELSE HEAR IT?
LET ME HELP--
NO NEED. I'M FINE.
JUST HAVE TO REGAIN MY EQUILIBRIUM.
OUR BEST CHOICE HERE IS TO RECREATE THE EXPERIMENT WE DID WITH HALO AND REX AGAIN...
UGH, GREAT, 'CAUSE I HAD SOOO MUCH FUN LAST TIME.
...TRY TO LOCK ON A LOCATION WHERE MORE OF THESE METEOR PIECES ARE SINCE IT'S OBVIOUS--

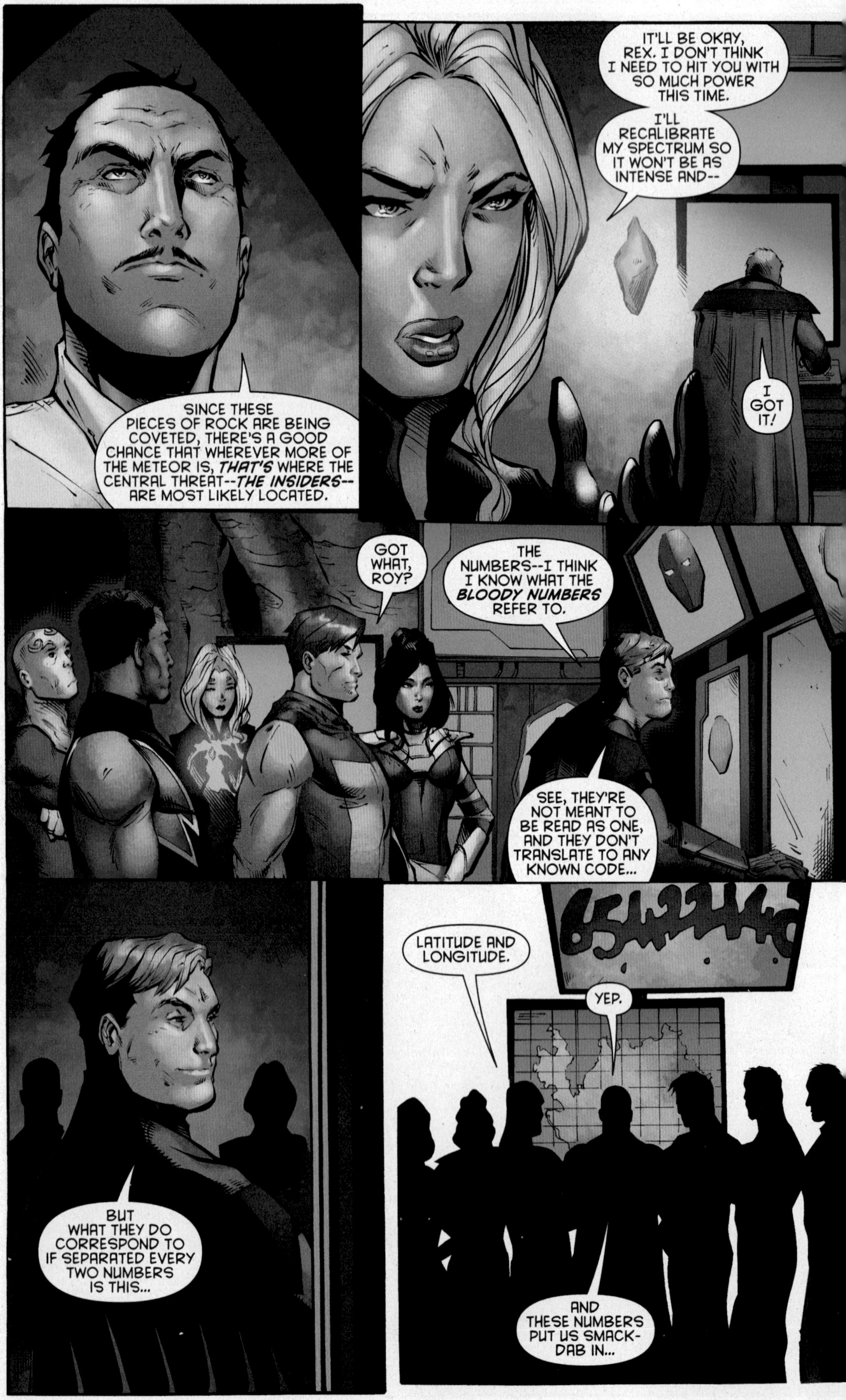
SINCE THESE PIECES OF ROCK ARE BEING COVETED, THERE'S A GOOD CHANCE THAT WHEREVER MORE OF THE METEOR IS, THAT'S WHERE THE CENTRAL THREAT--THE INSIDERS--ARE MOST LIKELY LOCATED.
IT'LL BE OKAY, REX. I DON'T THINK I NEED TO HIT YOU WITH SO MUCH POWER THIS TIME.
I'LL RECALIBRATE MY SPECTRUM SO IT WON'T BE AS INTENSE AND--
I GOT IT!
GOT WHAT, ROY?
THE NUMBERS--I THINK I KNOW WHAT THE BLOODY NUMBERS REFER TO.
SEE, THEY'RE NOT MEANT TO BE READ AS ONE, AND THEY DON'T TRANSLATE TO ANY KNOWN CODE...
BUT WHAT THEY DO CORRESPOND TO IF SEPARATED EVERY TWO NUMBERS IS THIS...
LATITUDE AND LONGITUDE.
YEP.
AND THESE NUMBERS PUT US SMACK-DAB IN...

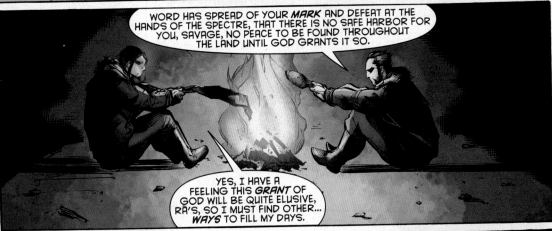

WORD HAS SPREAD OF YOUR *MARK* AND DEFEAT AT THE HANDS OF THE SPECTRE, THAT THERE IS NO SAFE HARBOR FOR YOU, SAVAGE, NO PEACE TO BE FOUND THROUGHOUT THE LAND UNTIL GOD GRANTS IT SO.

YES, I HAVE A FEELING THIS *GRANT* OF GOD WILL BE QUITE ELUSIVE, RA'S, SO I MUST FIND OTHER... *WAYS* TO FILL MY DAYS.

SO, ARE WE GOING TO PLAY COY, PRETEND WE HAVEN'T BOTH HEARD THE WHISPERS--DANCE AROUND THE REASON WE BOTH FIND OURSELVES HERE--WHILE *THOSE BELOW* OUR FEET GO ABOUT FINALIZING THEIR PLANS?

AND JUST WHAT DO *YOU* KNOW ABOUT THESE PLANS?

THOUGH OUR PATHS HAVE NEVER CROSSED, I DO KNOW *THEY* ARE NOT FOND OF *SHARING IMMORTALITY.*

THROUGH THE YEARS THEY HAVE TAKEN GREAT PAINS TO SEEK OUT AND OBLITERATE LAZARUS PITS ACROSS THE GLOBE, WHICH, AS YOU KNOW, I TEND TO HOLD NEAR AND DEAR TO MY HEART.

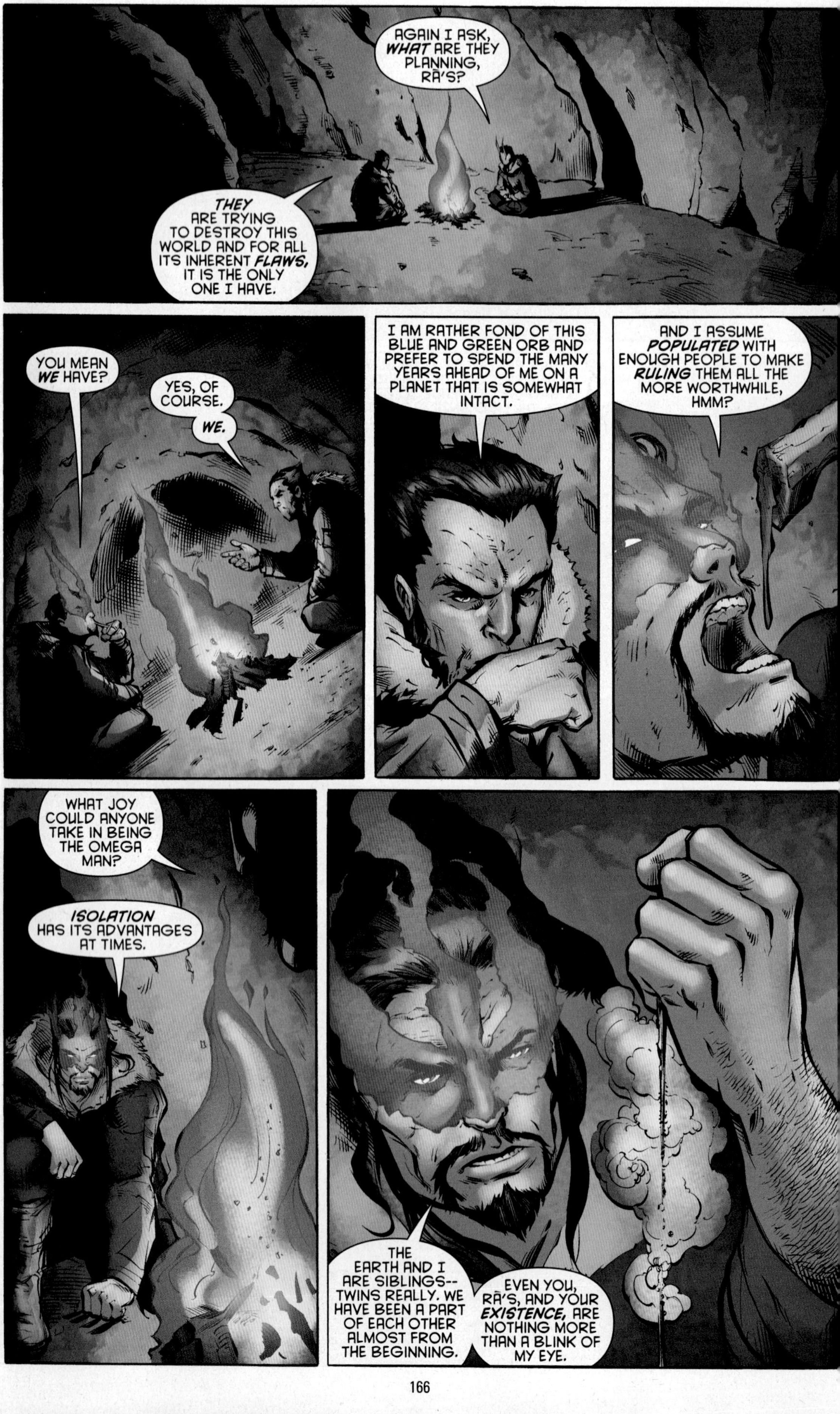
AGAIN I ASK, WHAT ARE THEY PLANNING, RA'S?
THEY ARE TRYING TO DESTROY THIS WORLD AND FOR ALL ITS INHERENT FLAWS, IT IS THE ONLY ONE I HAVE.
YOU MEAN WE HAVE?
YES, OF COURSE.
WE.
I AM RATHER FOND OF THIS BLUE AND GREEN ORB AND PREFER TO SPEND THE MANY YEARS AHEAD OF ME ON A PLANET THAT IS SOMEWHAT INTACT.
AND I ASSUME POPULATED WITH ENOUGH PEOPLE TO MAKE RULING THEM ALL THE MORE WORTHWHILE, HMM?
WHAT JOY COULD ANYONE TAKE IN BEING THE OMEGA MAN?
ISOLATION HAS ITS ADVANTAGES AT TIMES.
THE EARTH AND I ARE SIBLINGS-- TWINS REALLY. WE HAVE BEEN A PART OF EACH OTHER ALMOST FROM THE BEGINNING.
EVEN YOU, RA'S, AND YOUR EXISTENCE, ARE NOTHING MORE THAN A BLINK OF MY EYE.

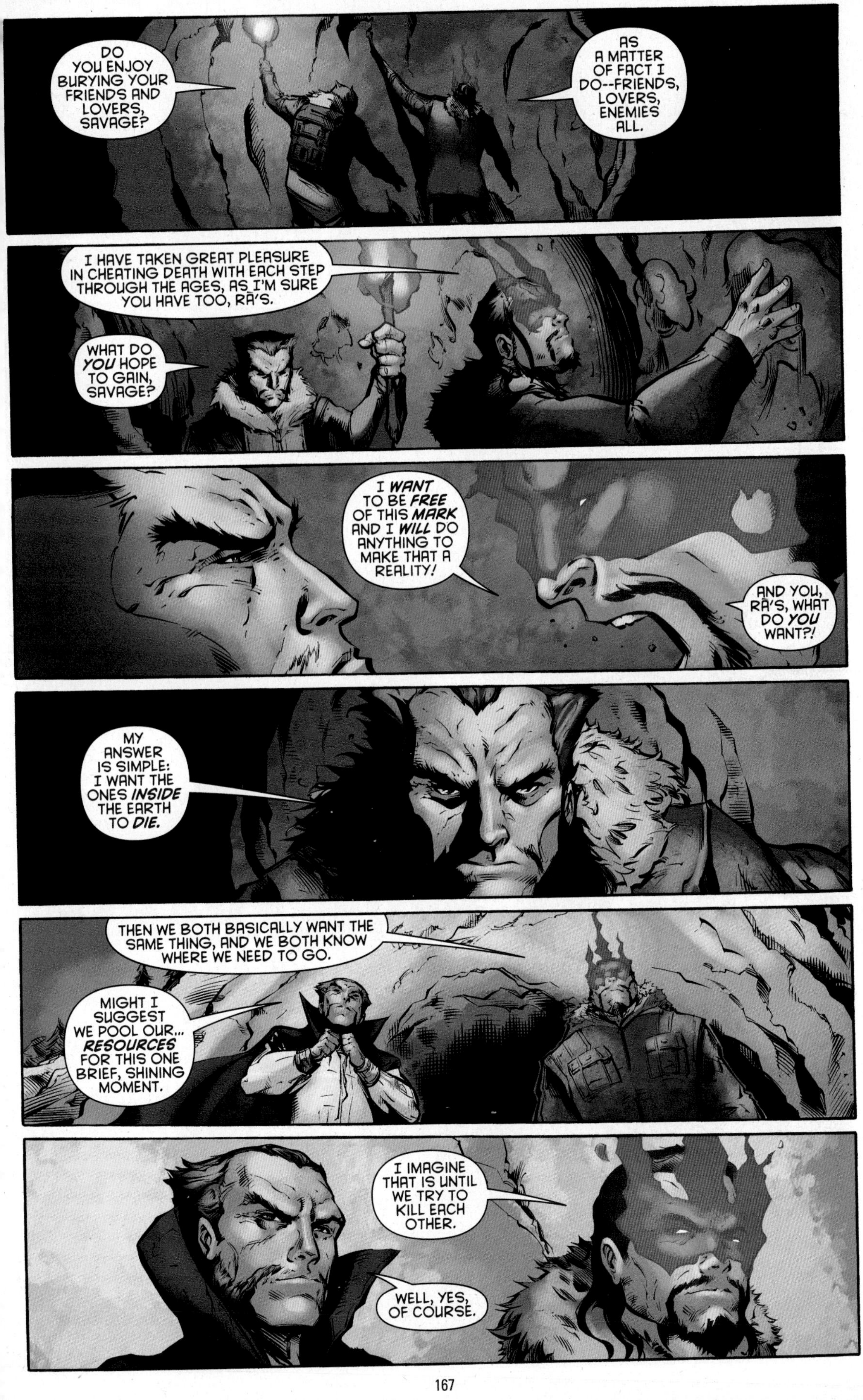
DO YOU ENJOY BURYING YOUR FRIENDS AND LOVERS, SAVAGE?
AS A MATTER OF FACT I DO--FRIENDS, LOVERS, ENEMIES ALL.
I HAVE TAKEN GREAT PLEASURE IN CHEATING DEATH WITH EACH STEP THROUGH THE AGES, AS I'M SURE YOU HAVE TOO, RA'S.
WHAT DO *YOU* HOPE TO GAIN, SAVAGE?
I *WANT* TO BE *FREE* OF THIS *MARK* AND I *WILL* DO ANYTHING TO MAKE THAT A REALITY!
AND YOU, RA'S, WHAT DO *YOU* WANT?!
MY ANSWER IS SIMPLE: I WANT THE ONES *INSIDE* THE EARTH TO *DIE.*
THEN WE BOTH BASICALLY WANT THE SAME THING, AND WE BOTH KNOW WHERE WE NEED TO GO.
MIGHT I SUGGEST WE POOL OUR... *RESOURCES* FOR THIS ONE BRIEF, SHINING MOMENT.
I IMAGINE THAT IS UNTIL WE TRY TO KILL EACH OTHER.
WELL, YES, OF COURSE.

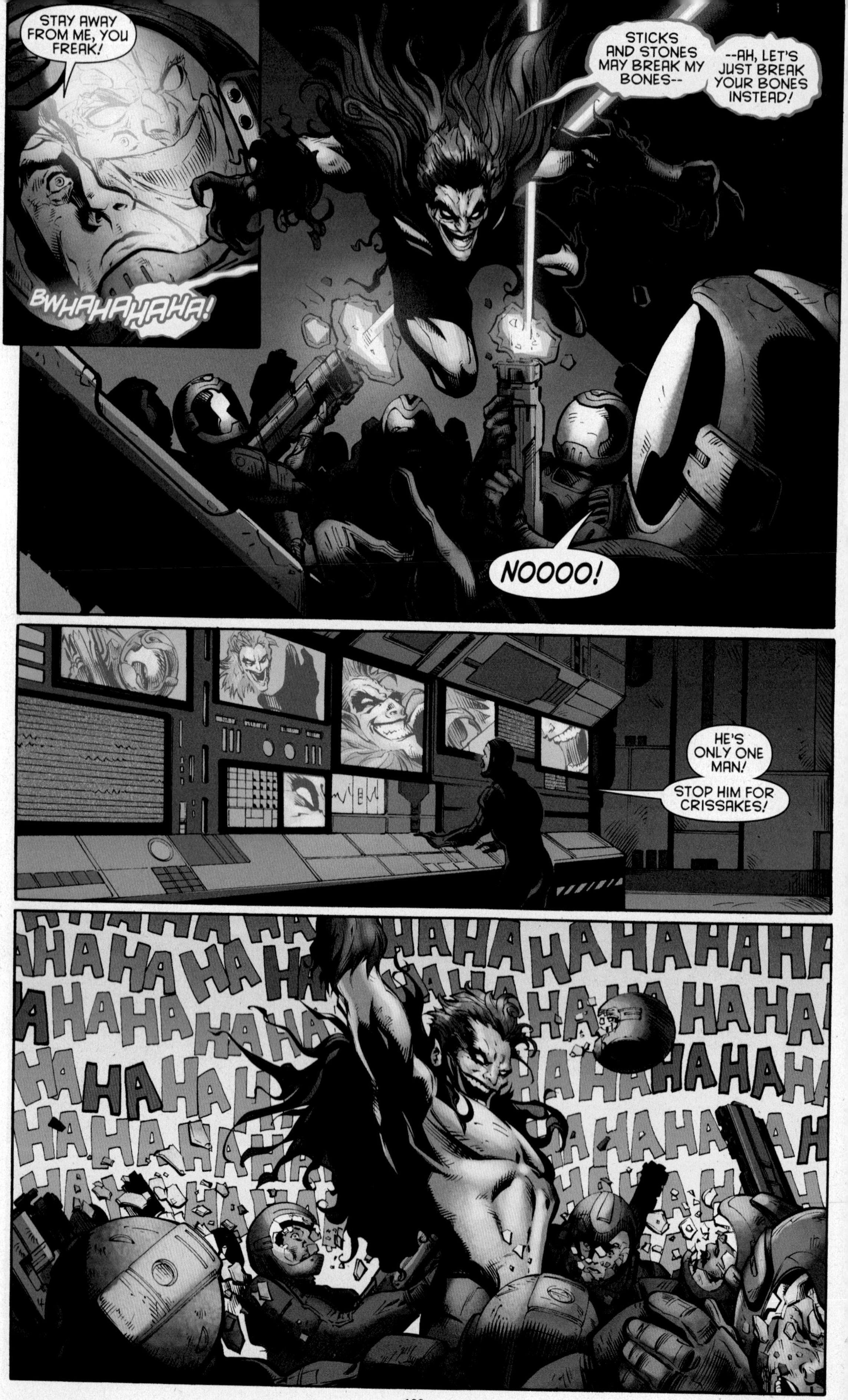
STAY AWAY FROM ME, YOU FREAK!
BWHAHAHAHAHA!
STICKS AND STONES MAY BREAK MY BONES--
--AH, LET'S JUST BREAK YOUR BONES INSTEAD!
NOOOO!
HE'S ONLY ONE MAN!
STOP HIM FOR CRISSAKES!

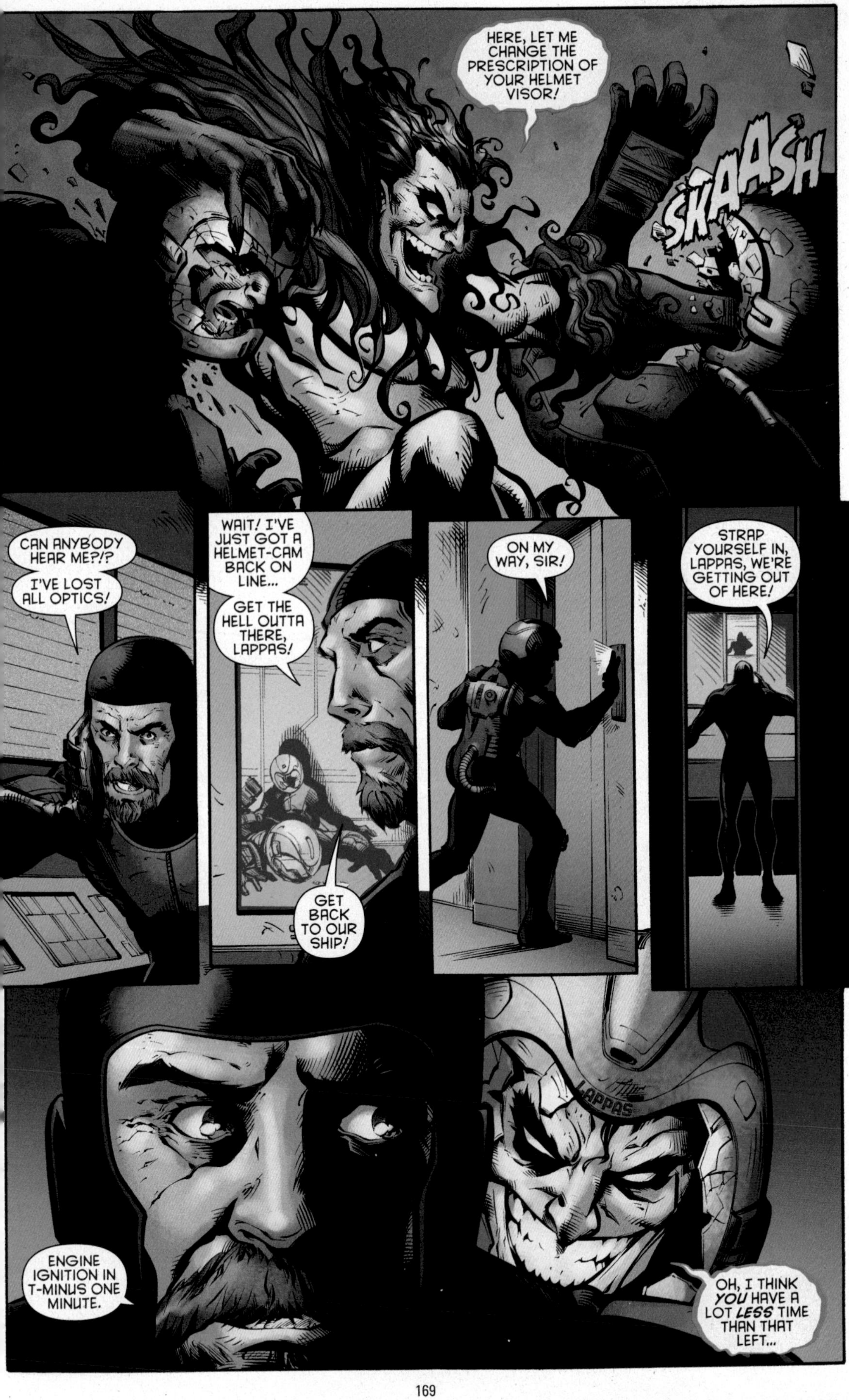
HERE, LET ME CHANGE THE PRESCRIPTION OF YOUR HELMET VISOR!
SKAASH
CAN ANYBODY HEAR ME?!?
I'VE LOST ALL OPTICS!
WAIT! I'VE JUST GOT A HELMET-CAM BACK ON LINE...
GET THE HELL OUTTA THERE, LAPPAS!
GET BACK TO OUR SHIP!
ON MY WAY, SIR!
STRAP YOURSELF IN, LAPPAS, WE'RE GETTING OUT OF HERE!
LAPPAS
ENGINE IGNITION IN T-MINUS ONE MINUTE.
OH, I THINK *YOU* HAVE A LOT *LESS* TIME THAN THAT LEFT...

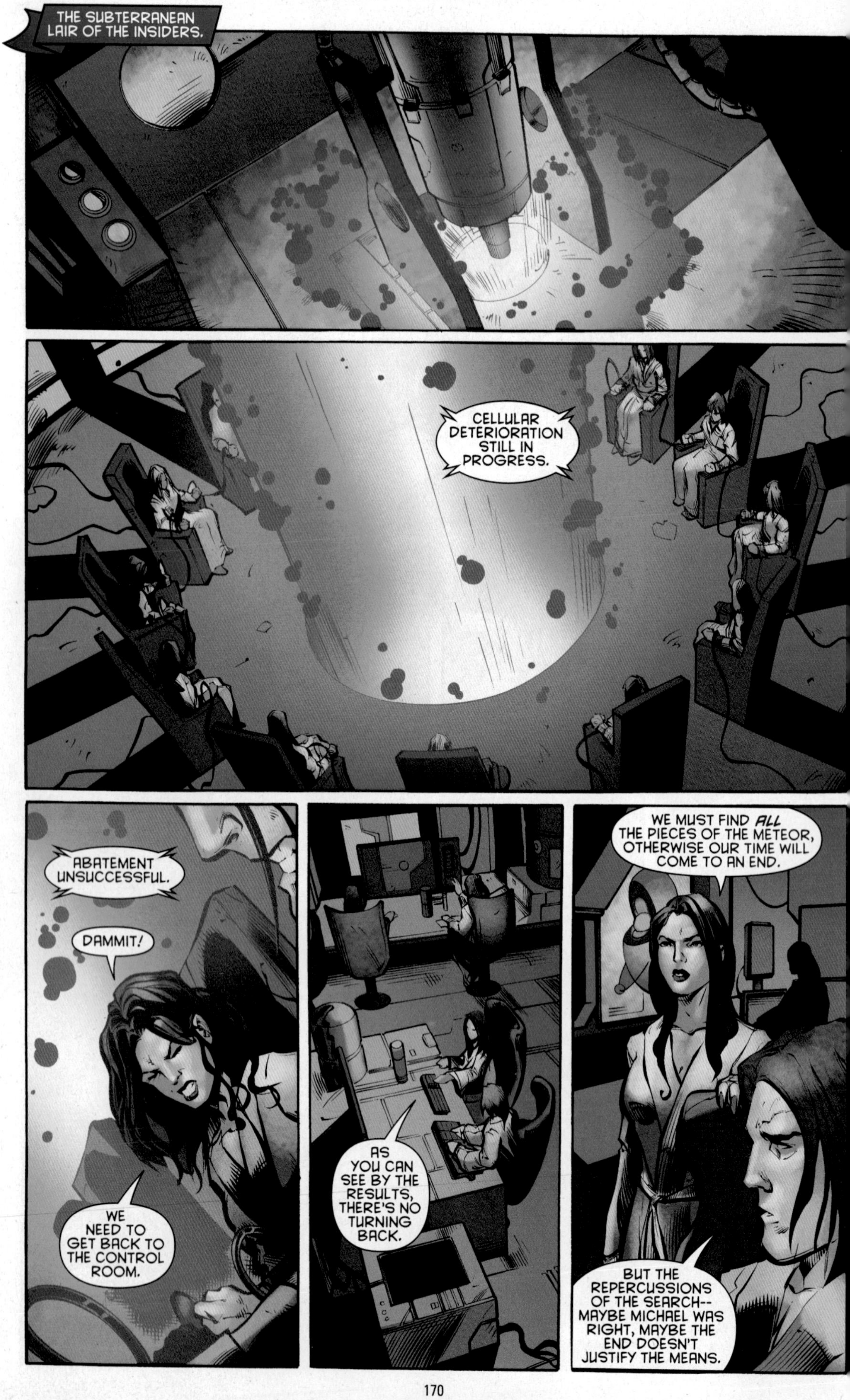
THE SUBTERRANEAN LAIR OF THE INSIDERS.
CELLULAR DETERIORATION STILL IN PROGRESS.
ABATEMENT UNSUCCESSFUL.
DAMMIT!
WE NEED TO GET BACK TO THE CONTROL ROOM.
AS YOU CAN SEE BY THE RESULTS, THERE'S NO TURNING BACK.
WE MUST FIND ALL THE PIECES OF THE METEOR, OTHERWISE OUR TIME WILL COME TO AN END.
BUT THE REPERCUSSIONS OF THE SEARCH-- MAYBE MICHAEL WAS RIGHT, MAYBE THE END DOESN'T JUSTIFY THE MEANS.

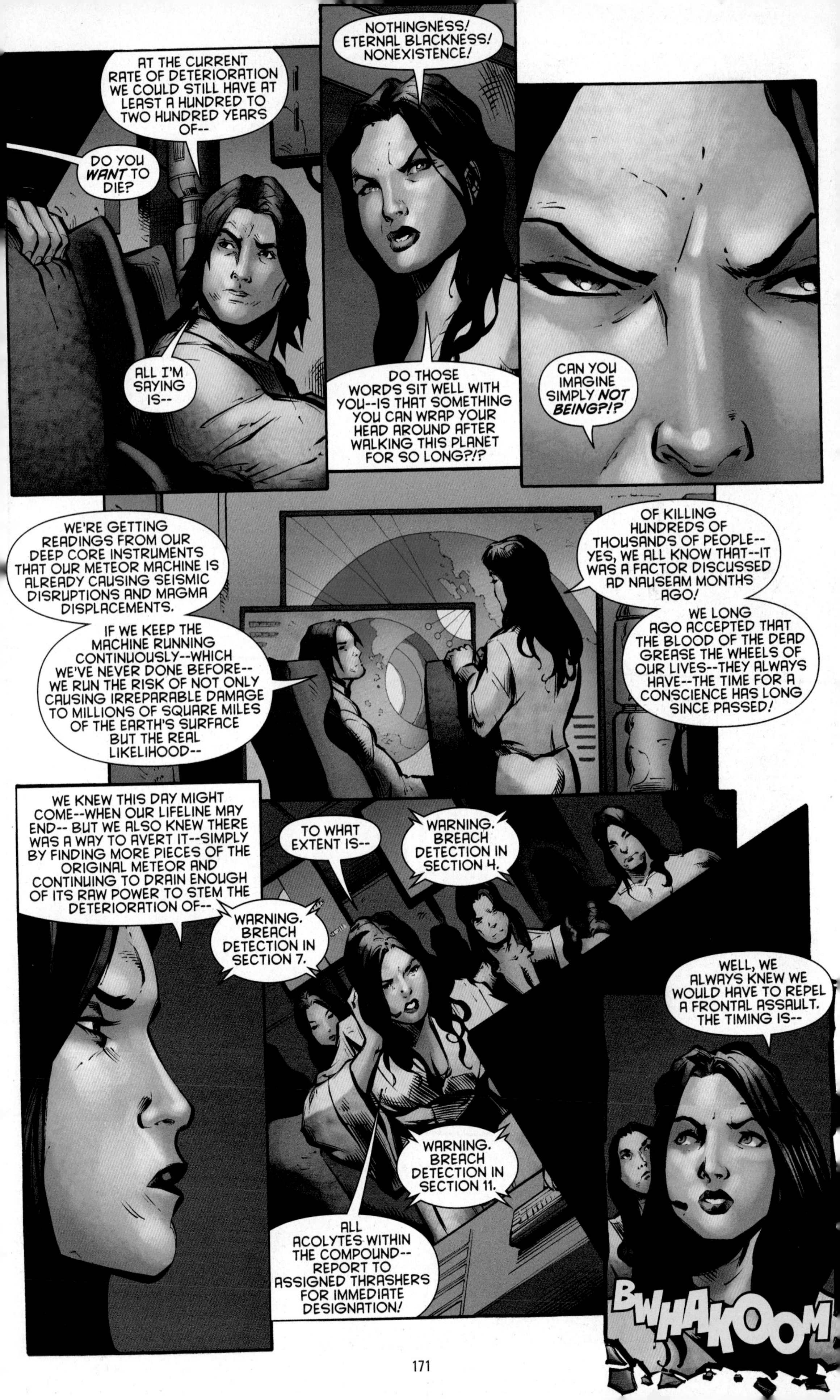

AT THE CURRENT RATE OF DETERIORATION WE COULD STILL HAVE AT LEAST A HUNDRED TO TWO HUNDRED YEARS OF--
DO YOU *WANT* TO DIE?
ALL I'M SAYING IS--
NOTHINGNESS! ETERNAL BLACKNESS! NONEXISTENCE!
DO THOSE WORDS SIT WELL WITH YOU--IS THAT SOMETHING YOU CAN WRAP YOUR HEAD AROUND AFTER WALKING THIS PLANET FOR SO LONG?!?
CAN YOU IMAGINE SIMPLY *NOT BEING?!?*
WE'RE GETTING READINGS FROM OUR DEEP CORE INSTRUMENTS THAT OUR METEOR MACHINE IS ALREADY CAUSING SEISMIC DISRUPTIONS AND MAGMA DISPLACEMENTS.
IF WE KEEP THE MACHINE RUNNING CONTINUOUSLY--WHICH WE'VE NEVER DONE BEFORE--WE RUN THE RISK OF NOT ONLY CAUSING IRREPARABLE DAMAGE TO MILLIONS OF SQUARE MILES OF THE EARTH'S SURFACE BUT THE REAL LIKELIHOOD--
OF KILLING HUNDREDS OF THOUSANDS OF PEOPLE--YES, WE ALL KNOW THAT--IT WAS A FACTOR DISCUSSED AD NAUSEAM MONTHS AGO!
WE LONG AGO ACCEPTED THAT THE BLOOD OF THE DEAD GREASE THE WHEELS OF OUR LIVES--THEY ALWAYS HAVE--THE TIME FOR A CONSCIENCE HAS LONG SINCE PASSED!
WE KNEW THIS DAY MIGHT COME--WHEN OUR LIFELINE MAY END-- BUT WE ALSO KNEW THERE WAS A WAY TO AVERT IT--SIMPLY BY FINDING MORE PIECES OF THE ORIGINAL METEOR AND CONTINUING TO DRAIN ENOUGH OF ITS RAW POWER TO STEM THE DETERIORATION OF--
WARNING. BREACH DETECTION IN SECTION 7.
TO WHAT EXTENT IS--
WARNING. BREACH DETECTION IN SECTION 4.
WARNING. BREACH DETECTION IN SECTION 11.
ALL ACOLYTES WITHIN THE COMPOUND--REPORT TO ASSIGNED THRASHERS FOR IMMEDIATE DESIGNATION!
WELL, WE ALWAYS KNEW WE WOULD HAVE TO REPEL A FRONTAL ASSAULT. THE TIMING IS--
BWHAKOOOM

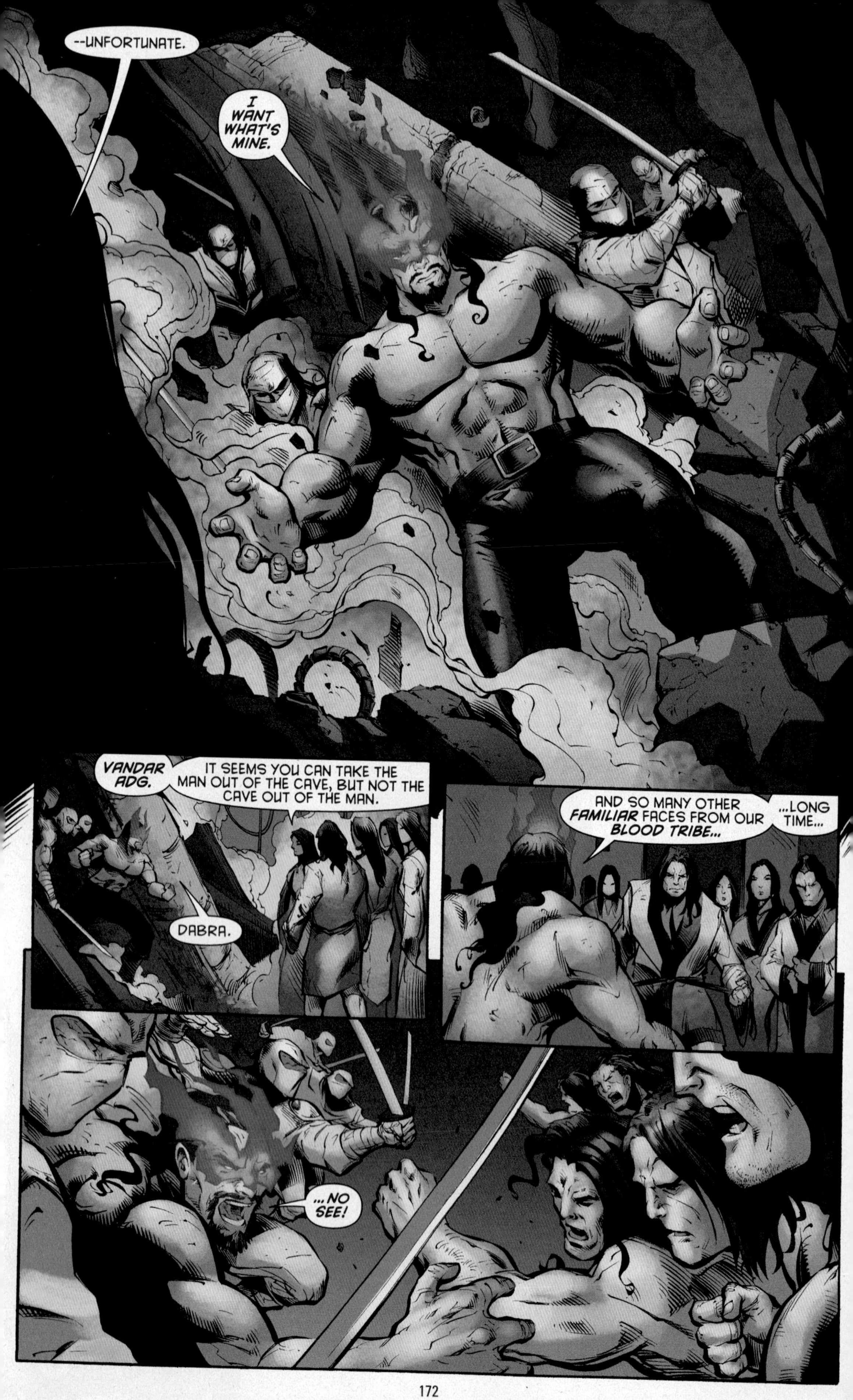
--UNFORTUNATE.
I WANT WHAT'S MINE.
VANDAR ADG.
IT SEEMS YOU CAN TAKE THE MAN OUT OF THE CAVE, BUT NOT THE CAVE OUT OF THE MAN.
DABRA.
AND SO MANY OTHER FAMILIAR FACES FROM OUR BLOOD TRIBE...
...LONG TIME...
...NO SEE!

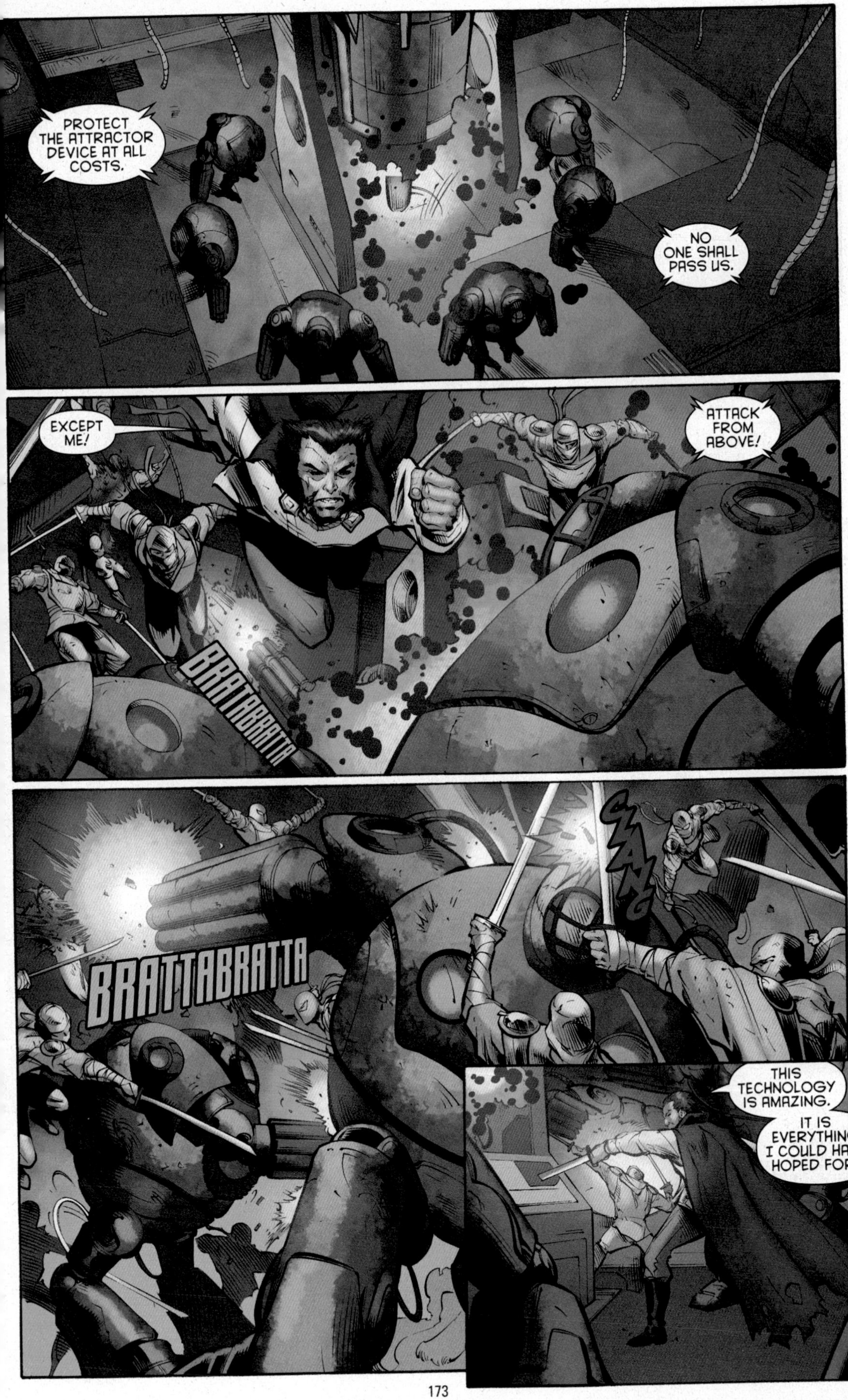
PROTECT THE ATTRACTOR DEVICE AT ALL COSTS.
NO ONE SHALL PASS US.
EXCEPT ME!
ATTACK FROM ABOVE!
BRATTABRATTA
CLANG
BRATTABRATTA
THIS TECHNOLOGY IS AMAZING.
IT IS EVERYTHING I COULD HAVE HOPED FOR!

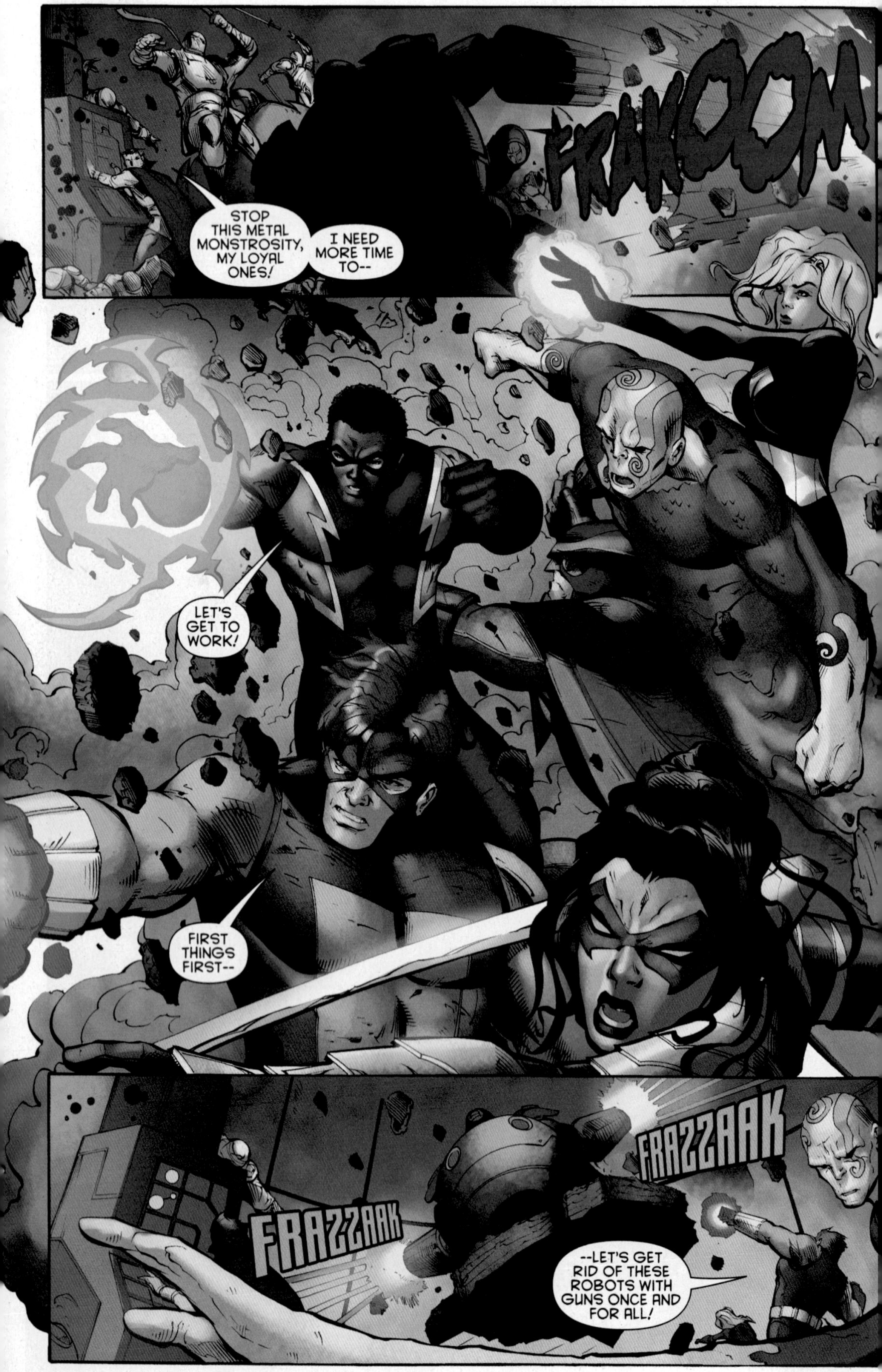
FRAKOOM
STOP THIS METAL MONSTROSITY, MY LOYAL ONES!
I NEED MORE TIME TO--
LET'S GET TO WORK!
FIRST THINGS FIRST--
FRAZZAAK
FRAZZAAK
--LET'S GET RID OF THESE ROBOTS WITH GUNS ONCE AND FOR ALL!

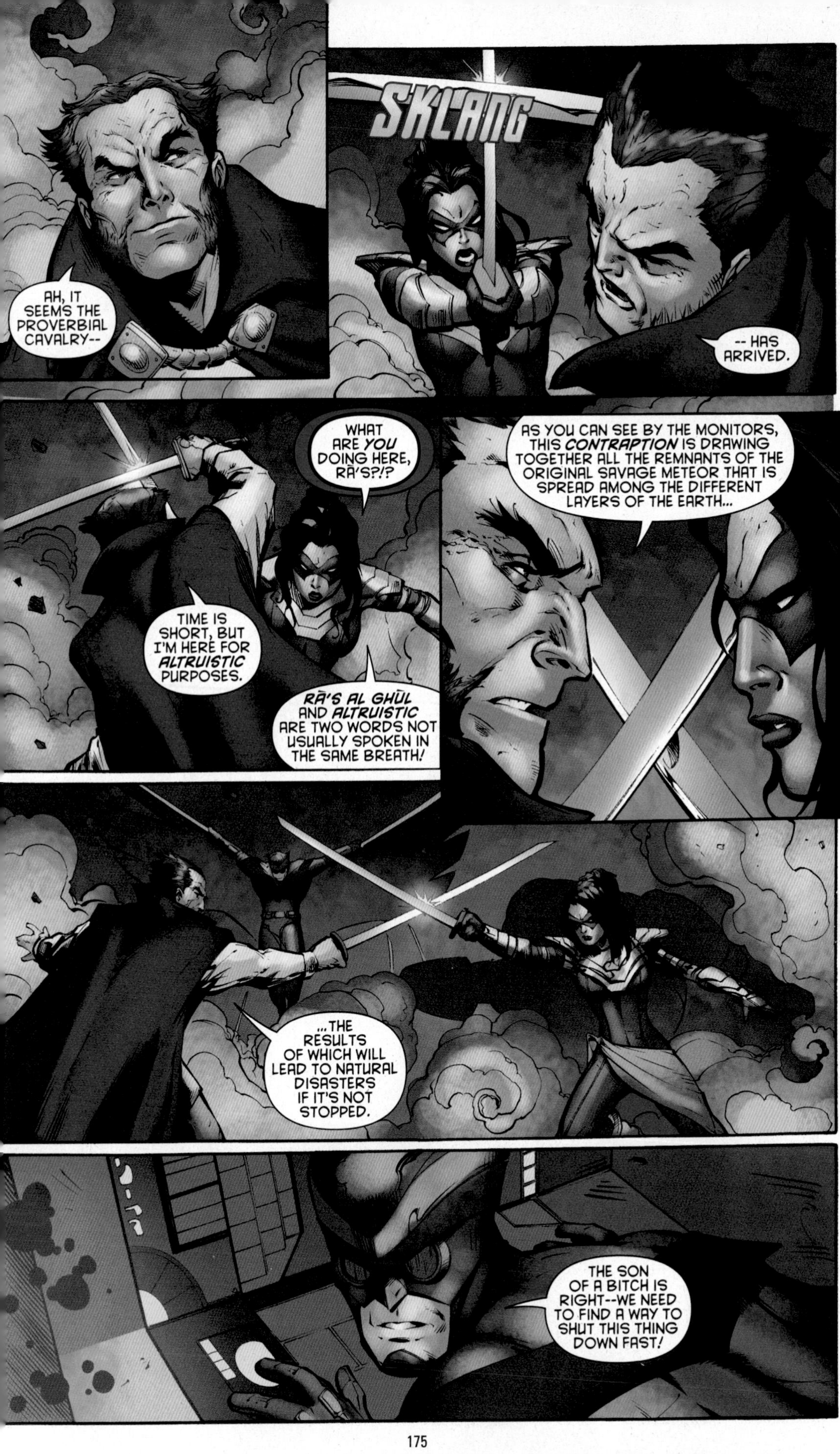
AH, IT SEEMS THE PROVERBIAL CAVALRY--
SKLANG
-- HAS ARRIVED.
WHAT ARE YOU DOING HERE, RA'S?!?
TIME IS SHORT, BUT I'M HERE FOR ALTRUISTIC PURPOSES.
RA'S AL GHUL AND ALTRUISTIC ARE TWO WORDS NOT USUALLY SPOKEN IN THE SAME BREATH!
AS YOU CAN SEE BY THE MONITORS, THIS CONTRAPTION IS DRAWING TOGETHER ALL THE REMNANTS OF THE ORIGINAL SAVAGE METEOR THAT IS SPREAD AMONG THE DIFFERENT LAYERS OF THE EARTH...
...THE RESULTS OF WHICH WILL LEAD TO NATURAL DISASTERS IF IT'S NOT STOPPED.
THE SON OF A BITCH IS RIGHT--WE NEED TO FIND A WAY TO SHUT THIS THING DOWN FAST!

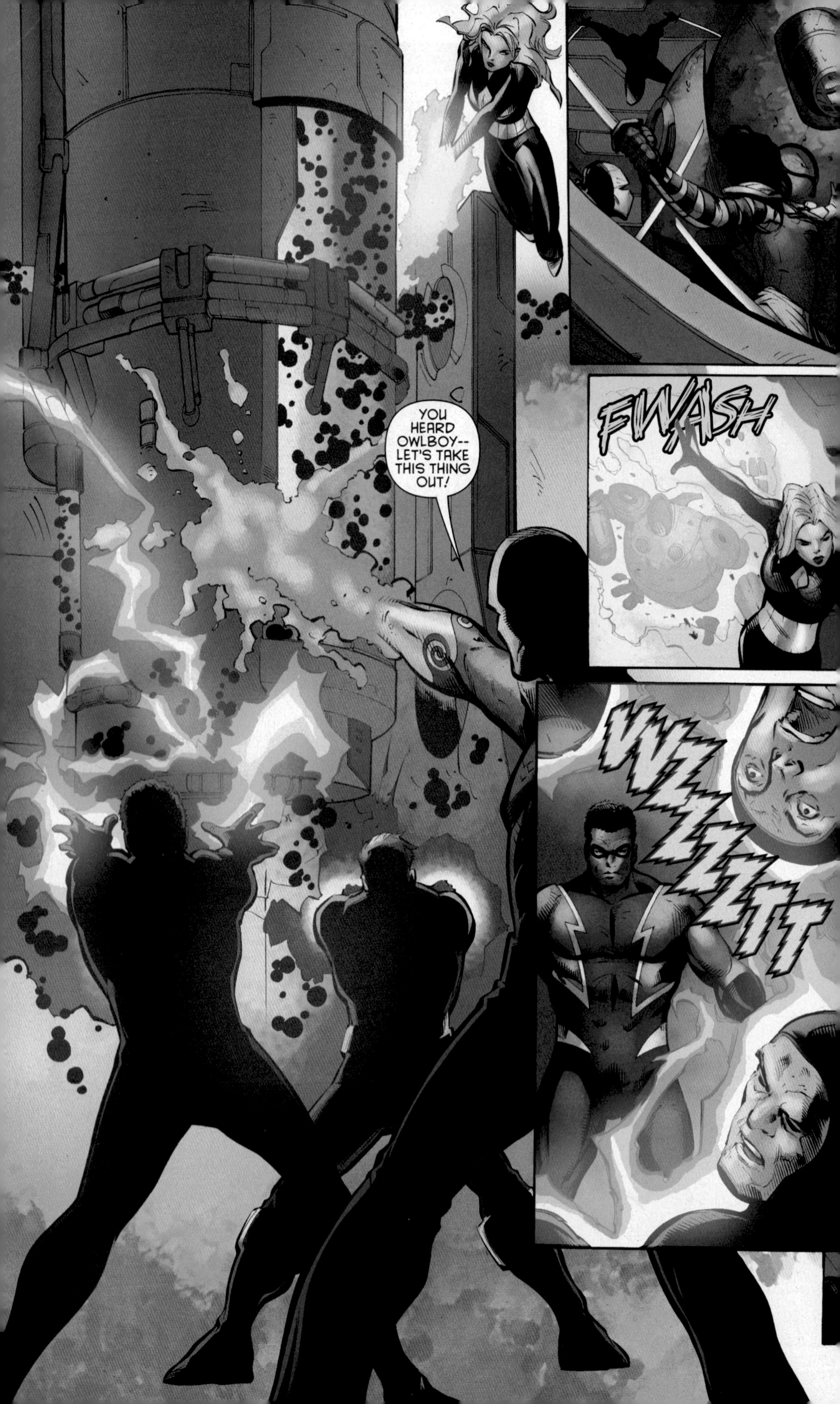

YOU HEARD OWLBOY-- LET'S TAKE THIS THING OUT!
FWASH
VVZZZZTT

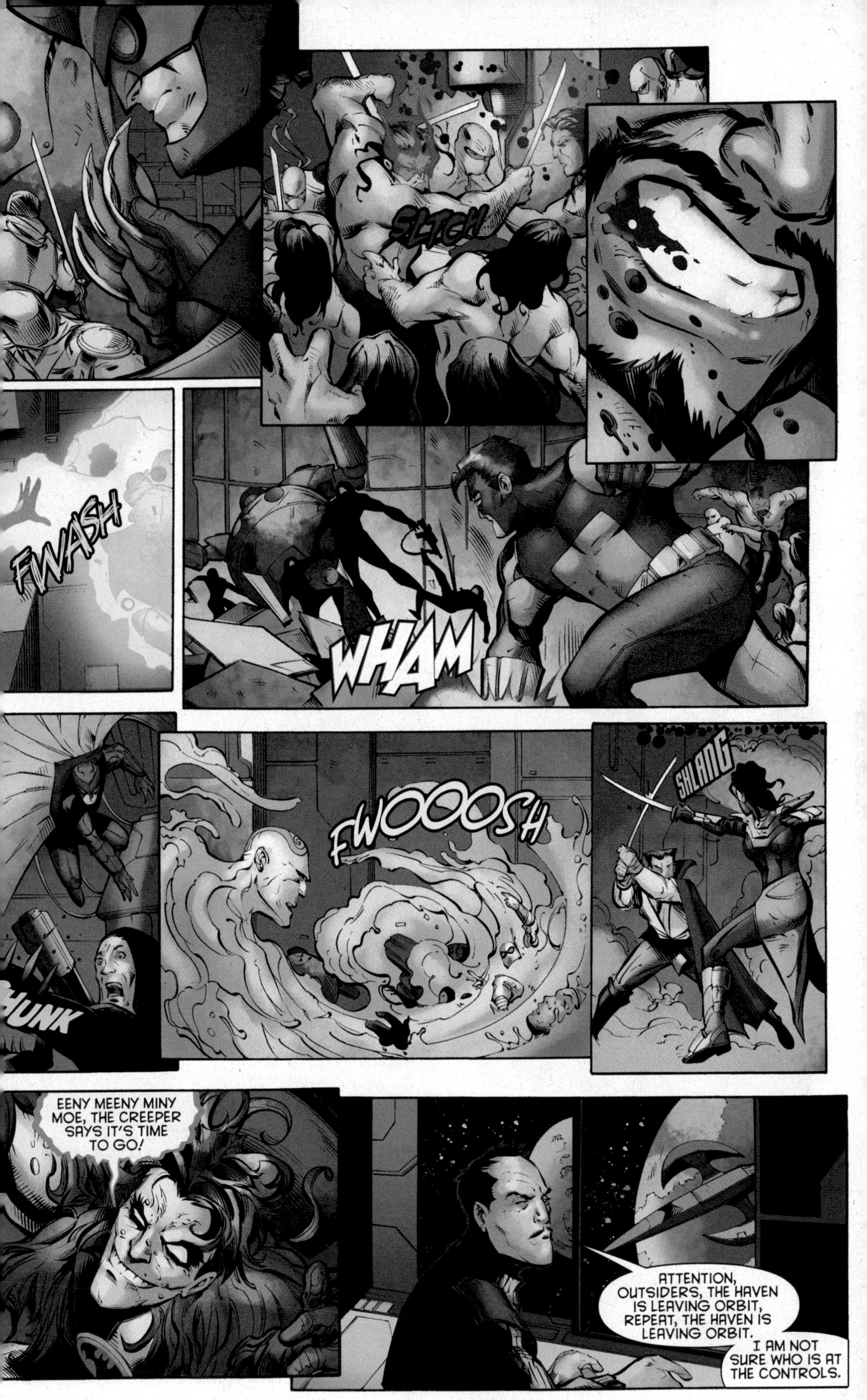
SLTCH
FWASH
WHAM
SHLANG
FWOOOSH
THUNK
EENY MEENY MINY MOE, THE CREEPER SAYS IT'S TIME TO GO!
ATTENTION, OUTSIDERS, THE HAVEN IS LEAVING ORBIT, REPEAT, THE HAVEN IS LEAVING ORBIT.
I AM NOT SURE WHO IS AT THE CONTROLS.

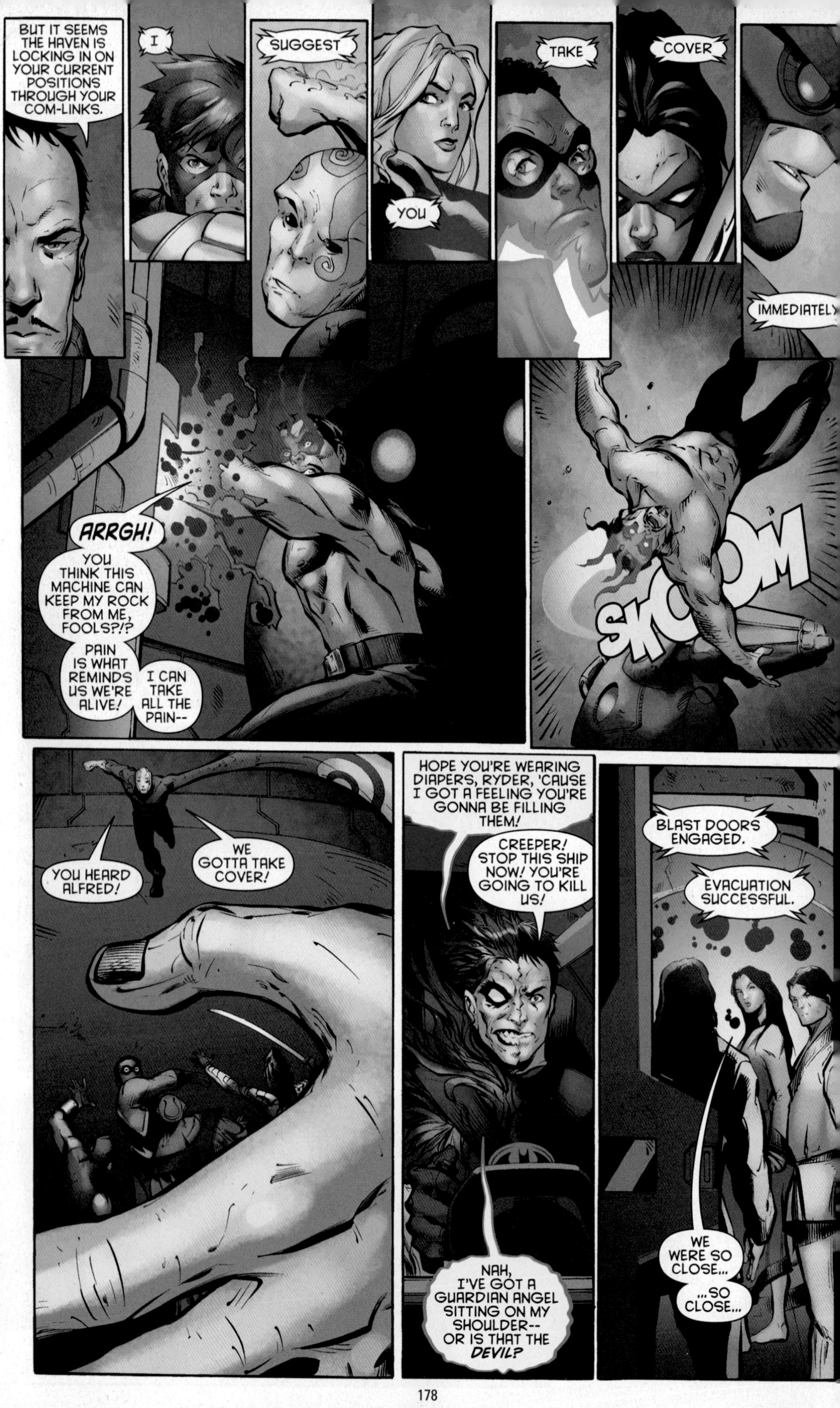
BUT IT SEEMS THE HAVEN IS LOCKING IN ON YOUR CURRENT POSITIONS THROUGH YOUR COM-LINKS.
I
SUGGEST
YOU
TAKE
COVER
IMMEDIATELY
ARRGH!
YOU THINK THIS MACHINE CAN KEEP MY ROCK FROM ME, FOOLS?!?
PAIN IS WHAT REMINDS US WE'RE ALIVE!
I CAN TAKE ALL THE PAIN--
SKOOOM
YOU HEARD ALFRED!
WE GOTTA TAKE COVER!
HOPE YOU'RE WEARING DIAPERS, RYDER, 'CAUSE I GOT A FEELING YOU'RE GONNA BE FILLING THEM!
CREEPER! STOP THIS SHIP NOW! YOU'RE GOING TO KILL US!
NAH, I'VE GOT A GUARDIAN ANGEL SITTING ON MY SHOULDER-- OR IS THAT THE *DEVIL?*
BLAST DOORS ENGAGED.
EVACUATION SUCCESSFUL.
WE WERE SO CLOSE...
...SO CLOSE...

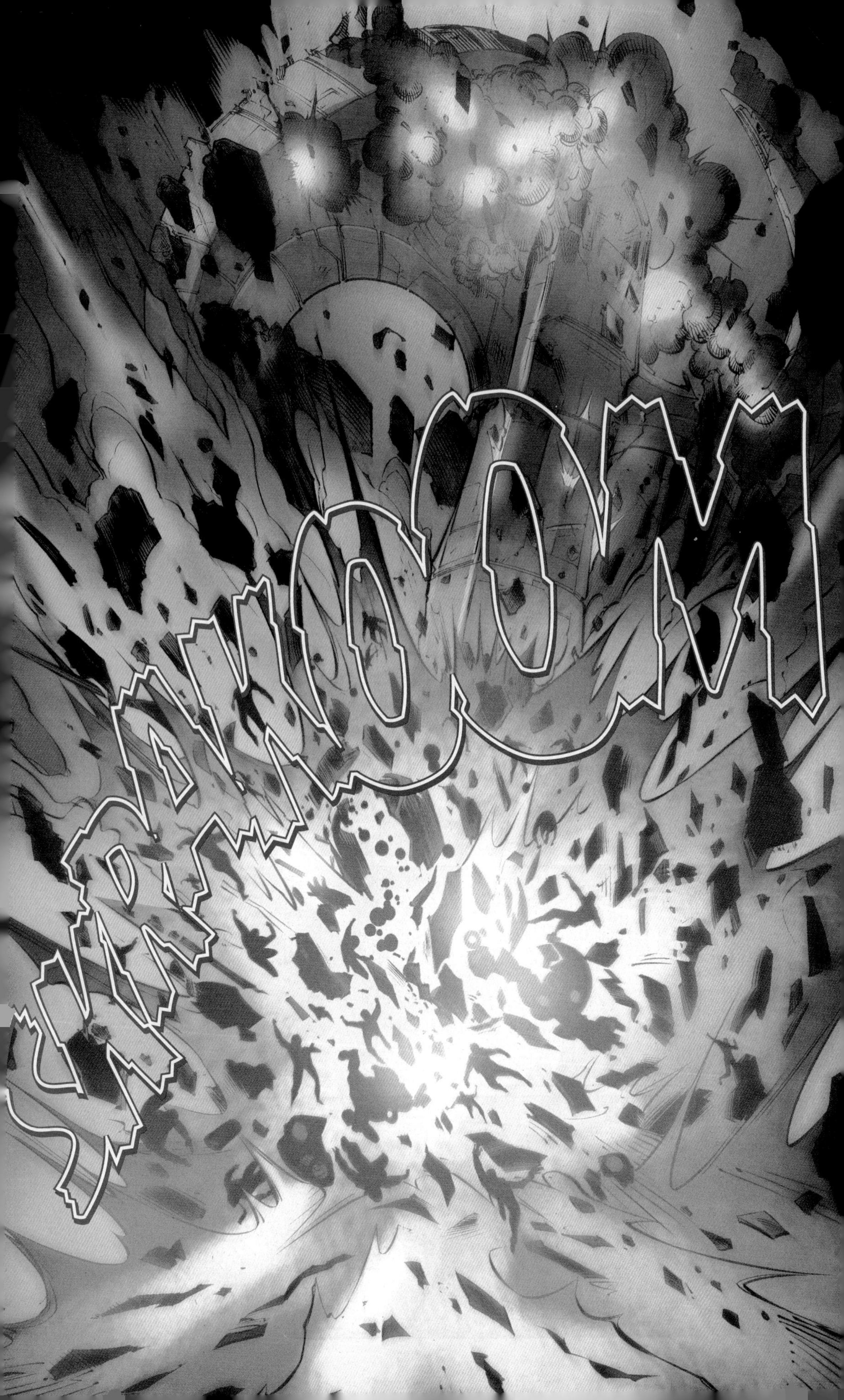

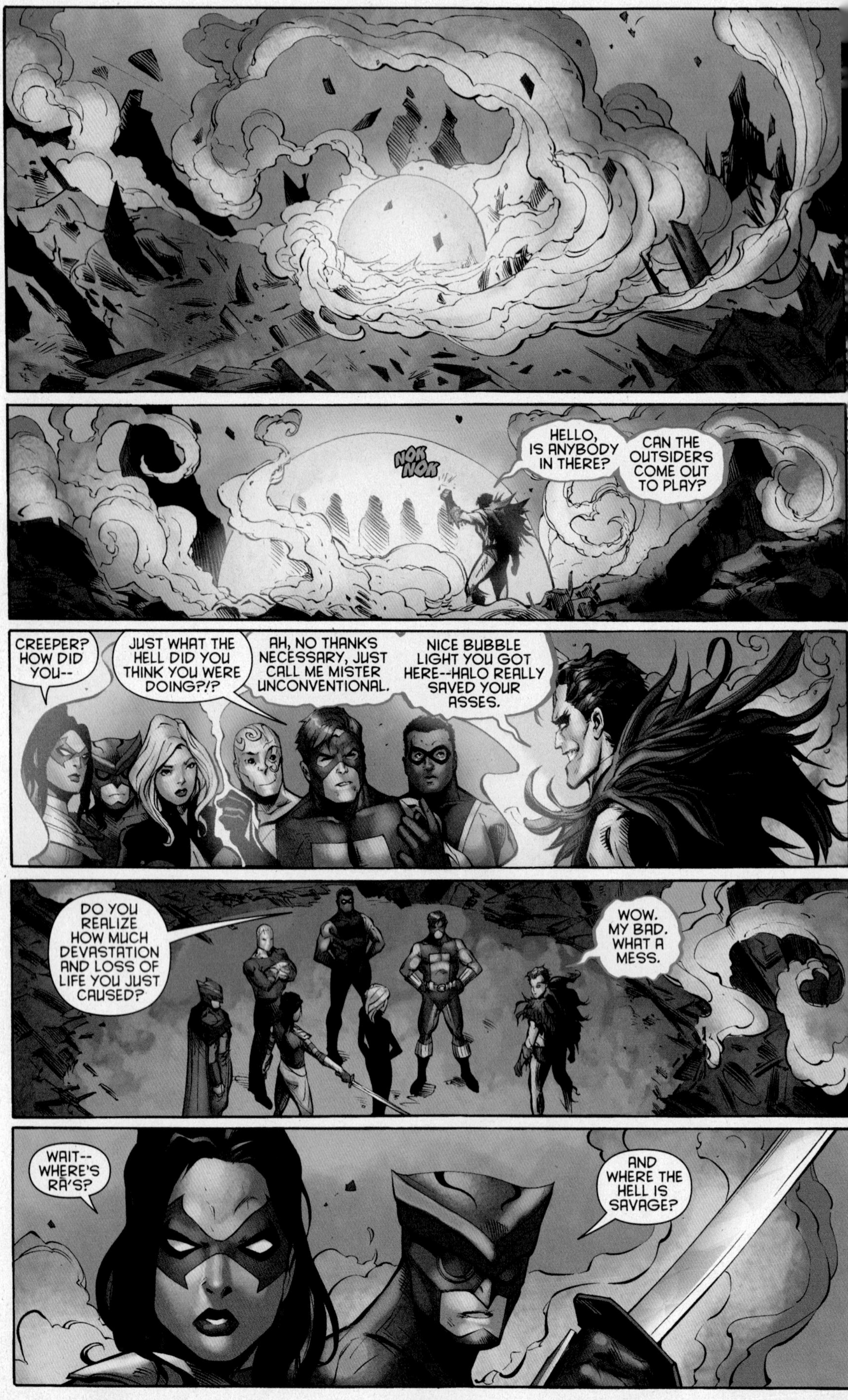
NOK NOK
HELLO, IS ANYBODY IN THERE?
CAN THE OUTSIDERS COME OUT TO PLAY?
CREEPER? HOW DID YOU--
JUST WHAT THE HELL DID YOU THINK YOU WERE DOING?!?
AH, NO THANKS NECESSARY, JUST CALL ME MISTER UNCONVENTIONAL.
NICE BUBBLE LIGHT YOU GOT HERE--HALO REALLY SAVED YOUR ASSES.
DO YOU REALIZE HOW MUCH DEVASTATION AND LOSS OF LIFE YOU JUST CAUSED?
WOW. MY BAD. WHAT A MESS.
WAIT-- WHERE'S RA'S?
AND WHERE THE HELL IS SAVAGE?

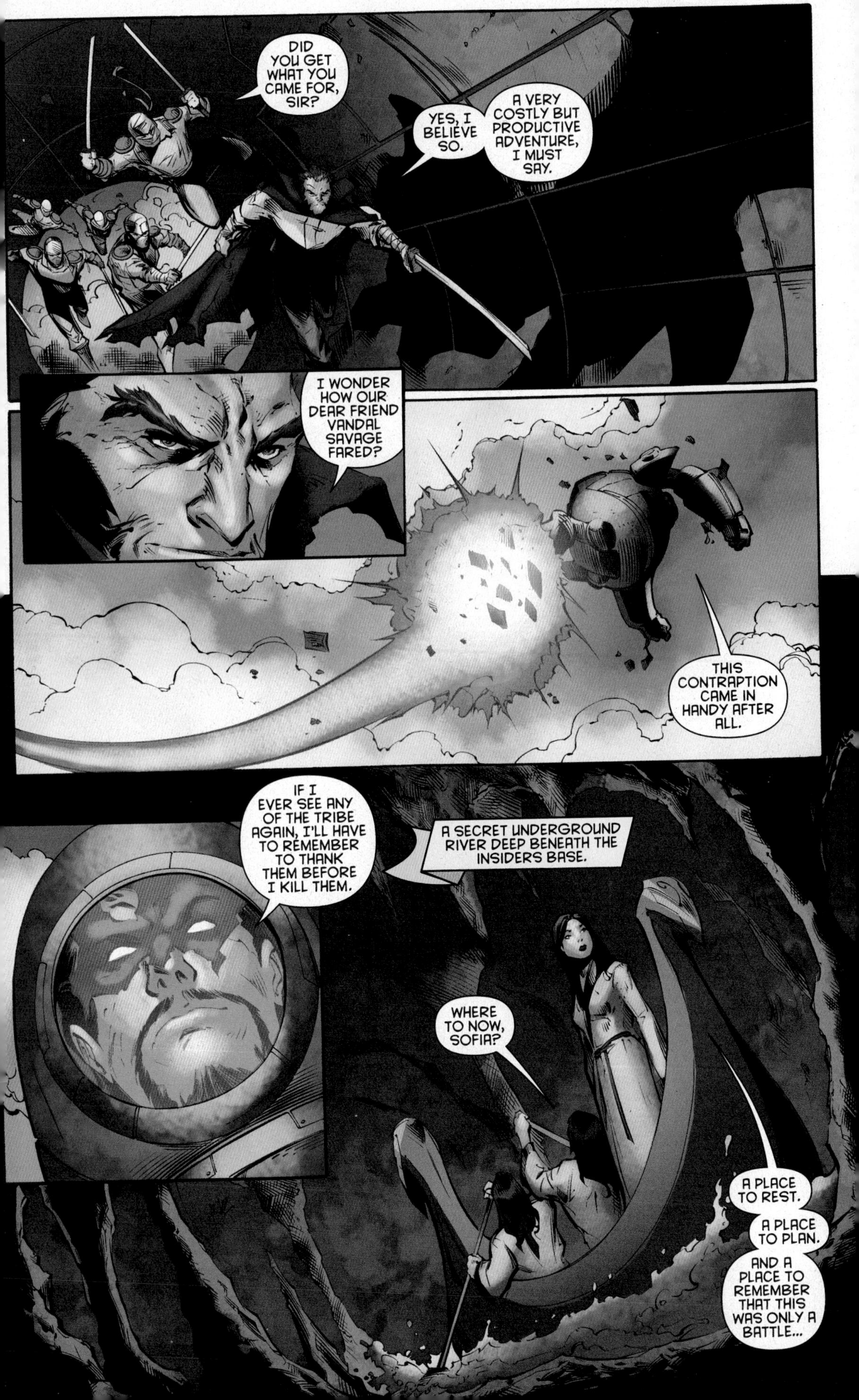
DID YOU GET WHAT YOU CAME FOR, SIR?
YES, I BELIEVE SO.
A VERY COSTLY BUT PRODUCTIVE ADVENTURE, I MUST SAY.
I WONDER HOW OUR DEAR FRIEND VANDAL SAVAGE FARED?
THIS CONTRAPTION CAME IN HANDY AFTER ALL.
IF I EVER SEE ANY OF THE TRIBE AGAIN, I'LL HAVE TO REMEMBER TO THANK THEM BEFORE I KILL THEM.
A SECRET UNDERGROUND RIVER DEEP BENEATH THE INSIDERS BASE.
WHERE TO NOW, SOFIA?
A PLACE TO REST.
A PLACE TO PLAN.
AND A PLACE TO REMEMBER THAT THIS WAS ONLY A BATTLE...

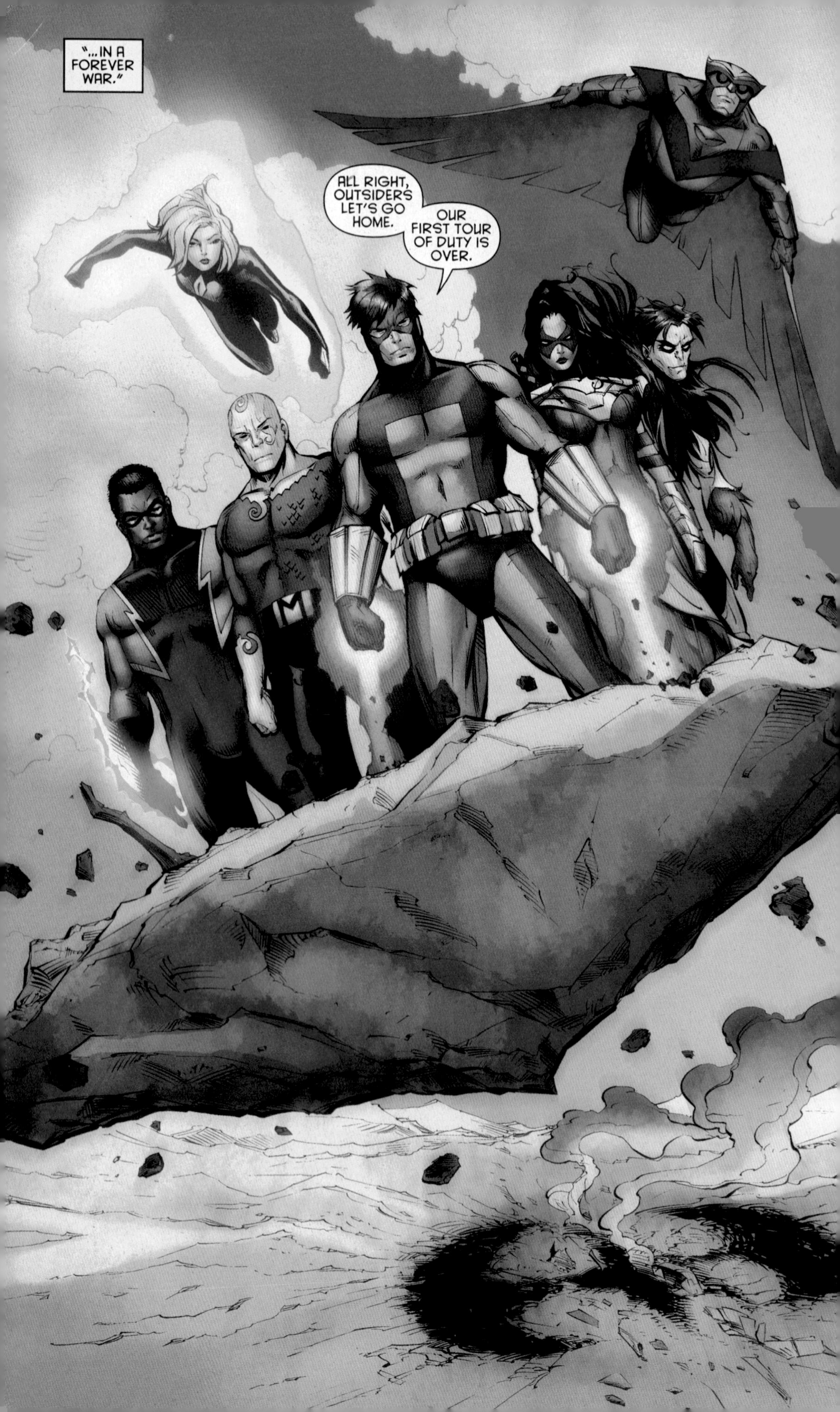
"...IN A FOREVER WAR."
ALL RIGHT, OUTSIDERS LET'S GO HOME.
OUR FIRST TOUR OF DUTY IS OVER.

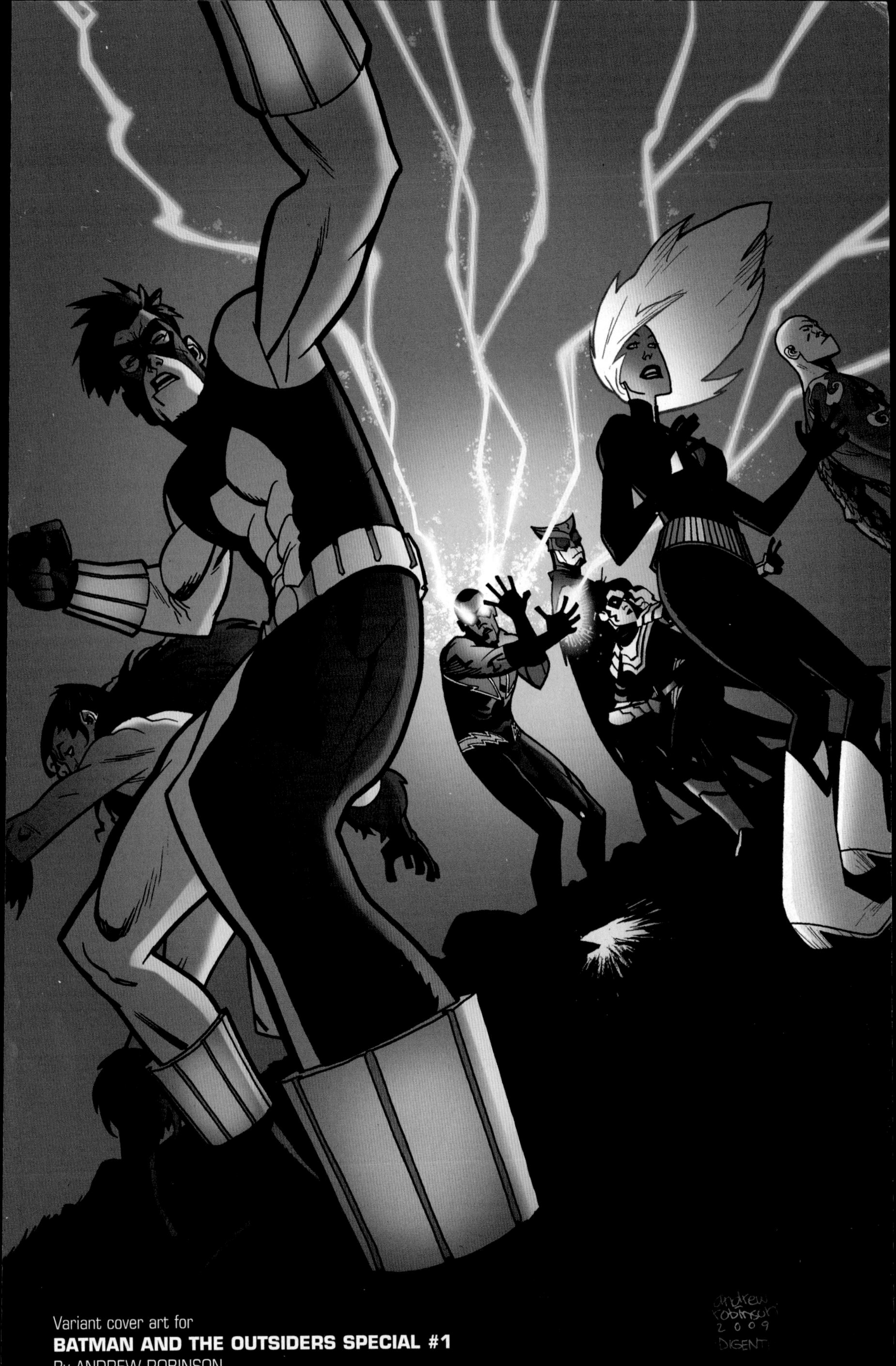

Variant cover art for
BATMAN AND THE OUTSIDERS SPECIAL #1
By ANDREW ROBINSON

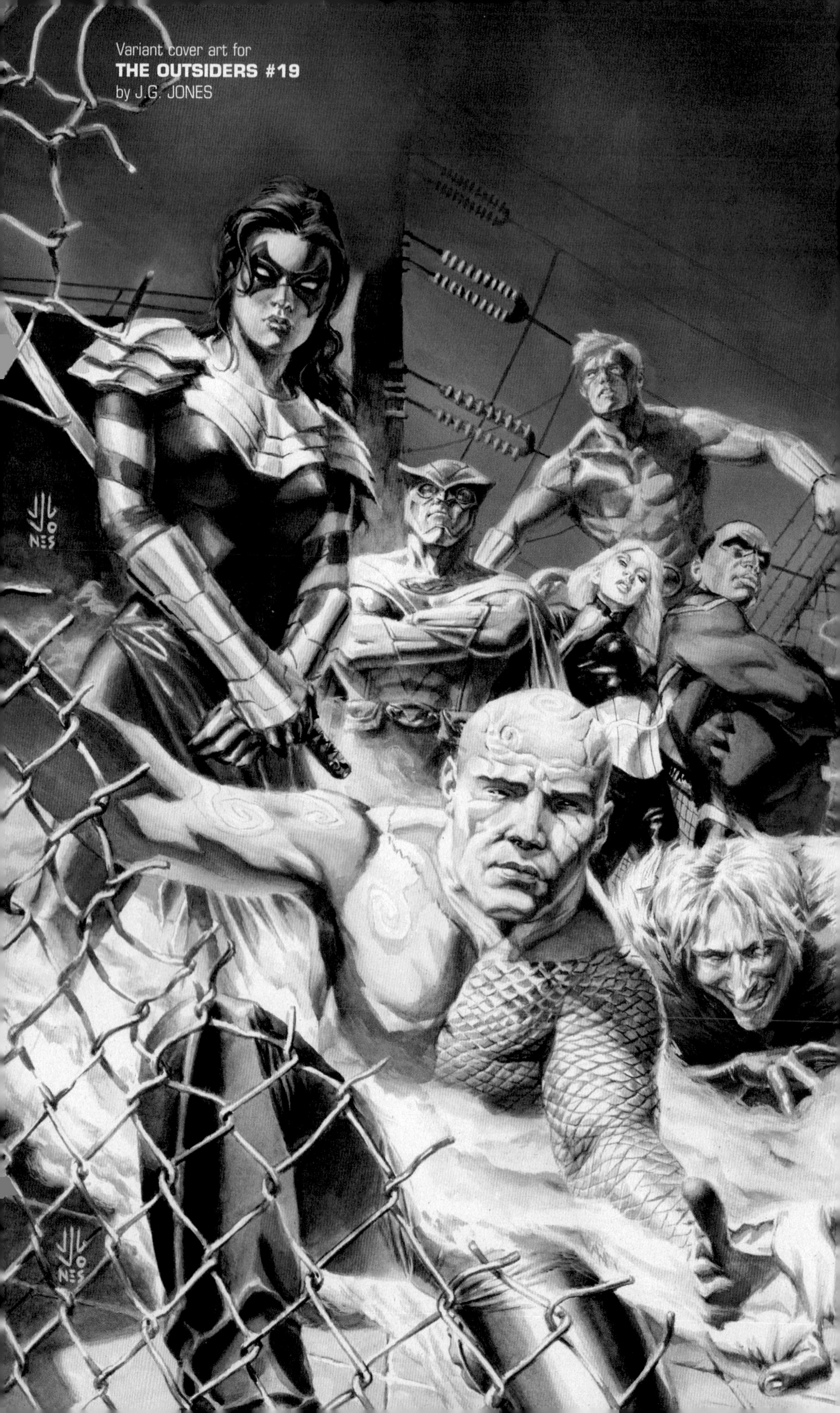

Variant cover art for
THE OUTSIDERS #19
by J.G. JONES

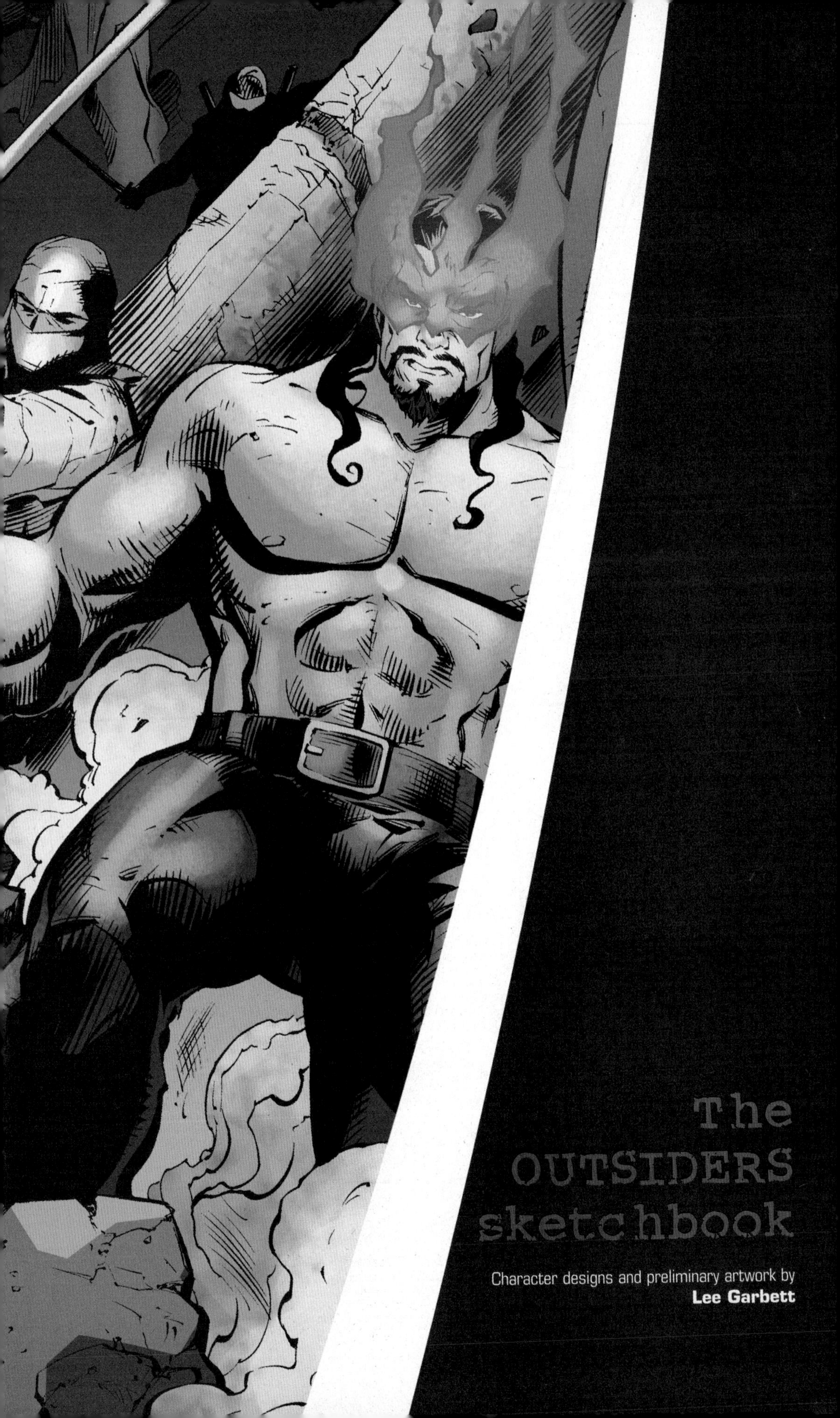

The OUTSIDERS sketchbook

Character designs and preliminary artwork by
Lee Garbett

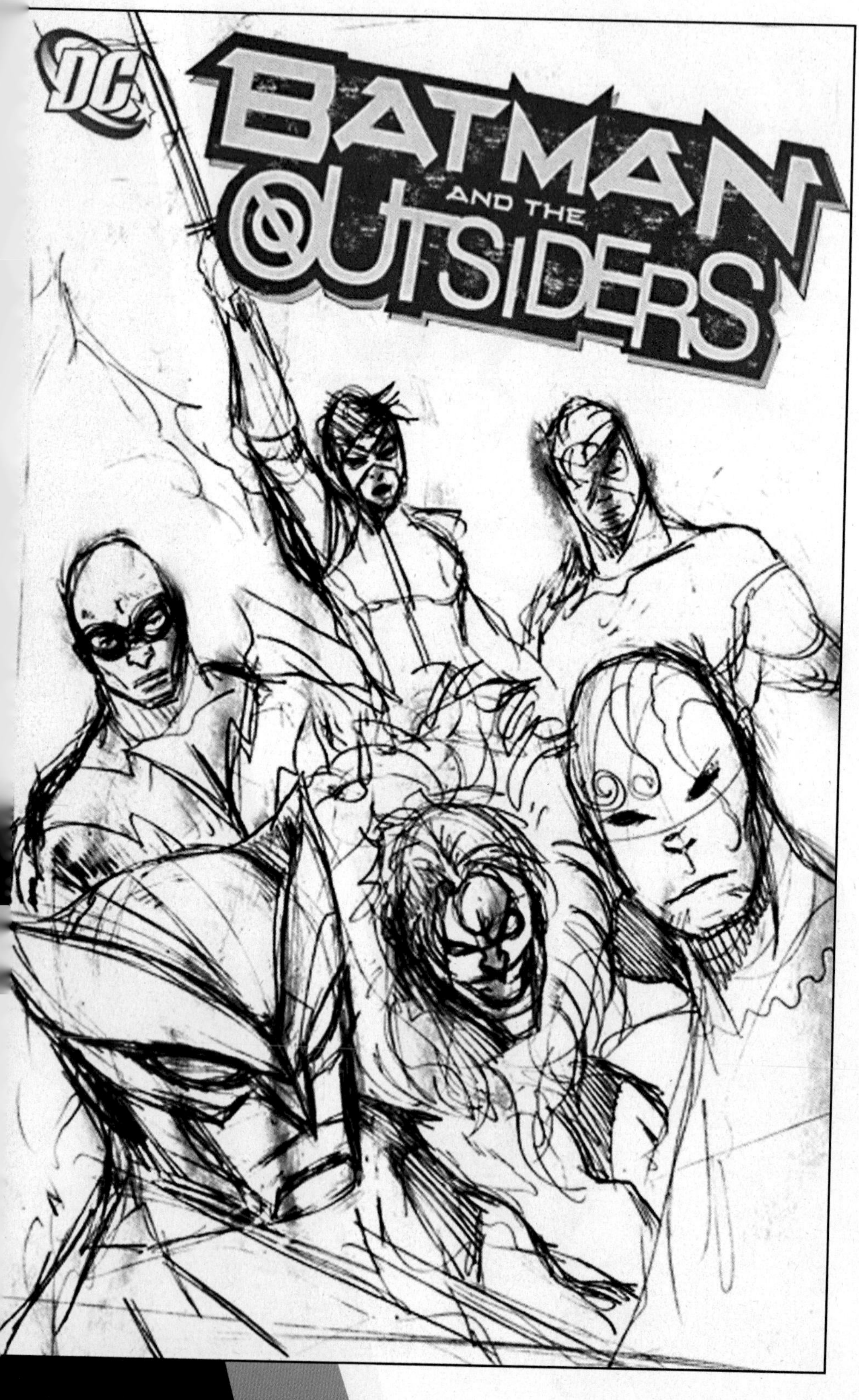
DC
BATMAN
AND THE
OUTSIDERS

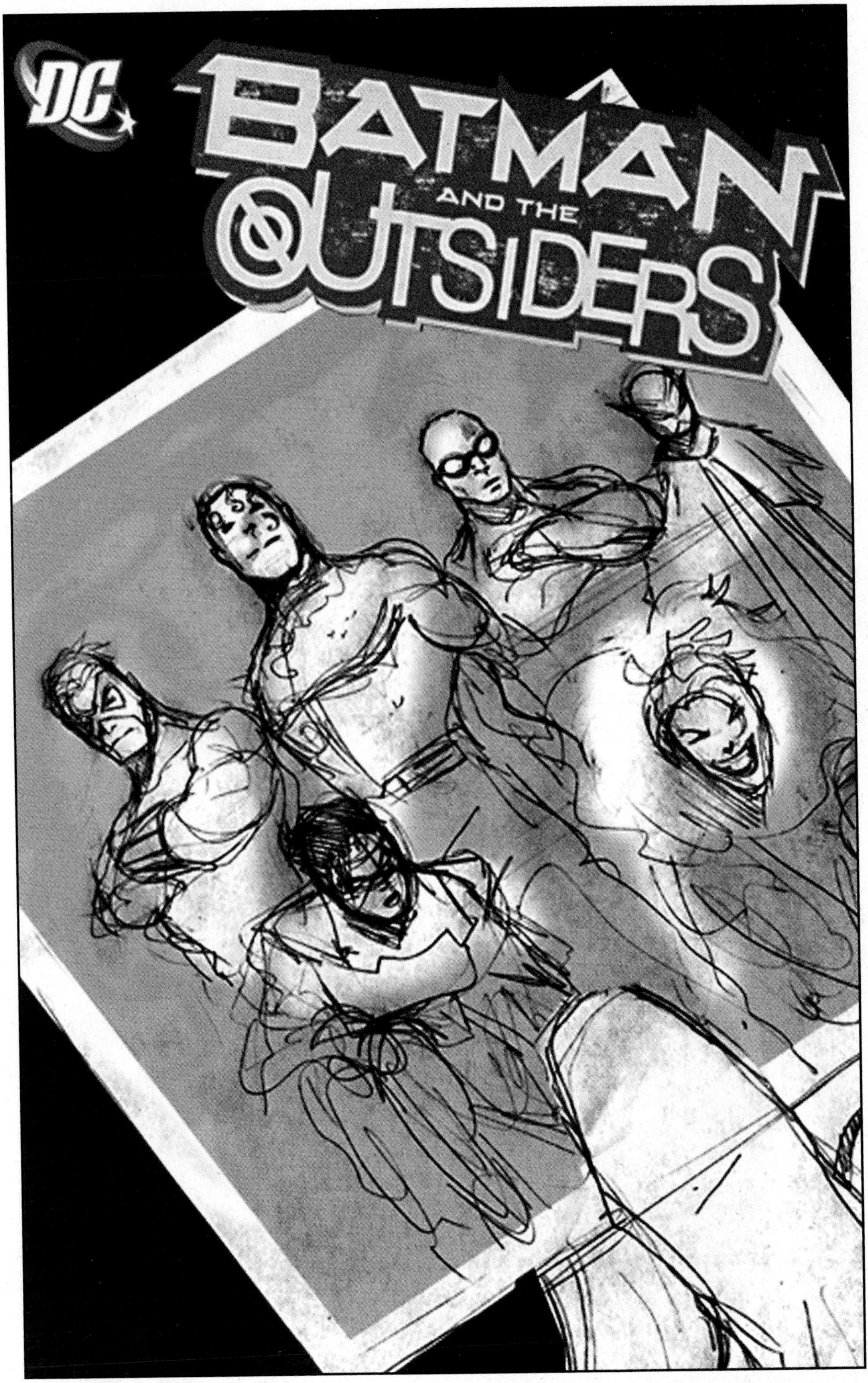
DC
BATMAN
AND THE
OUTSIDERS

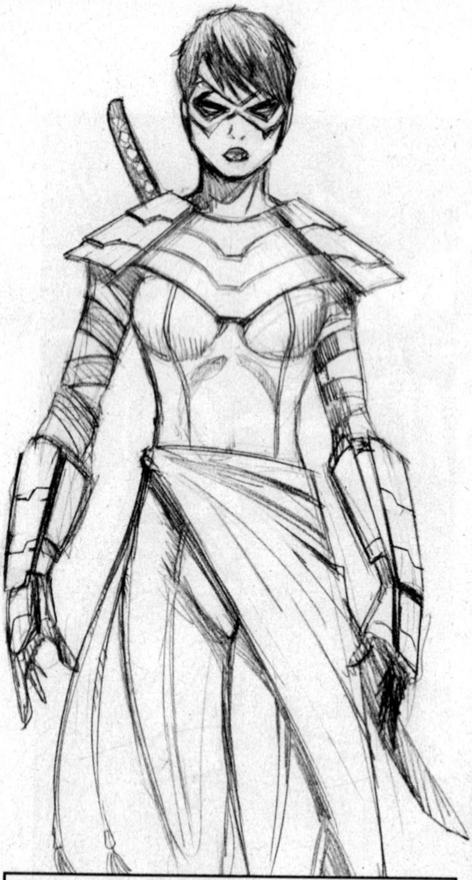
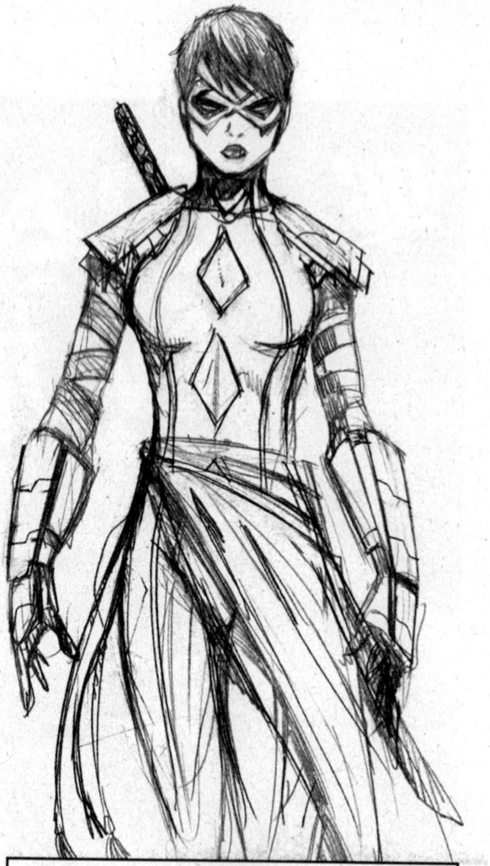
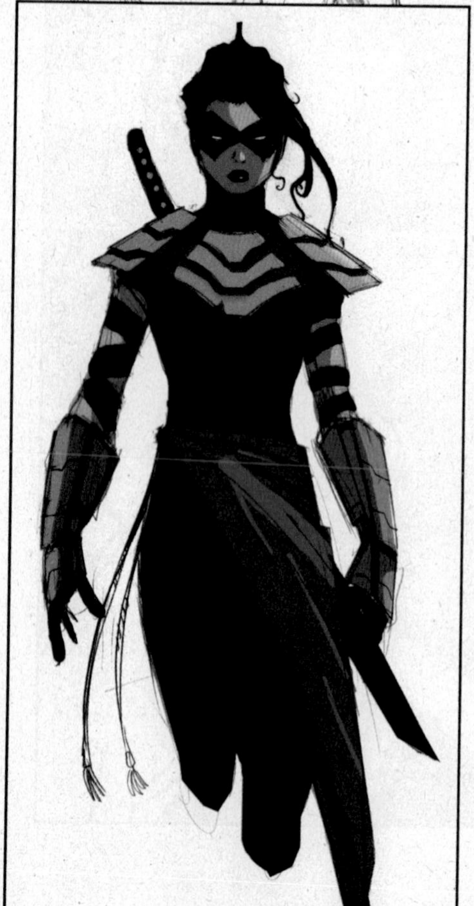
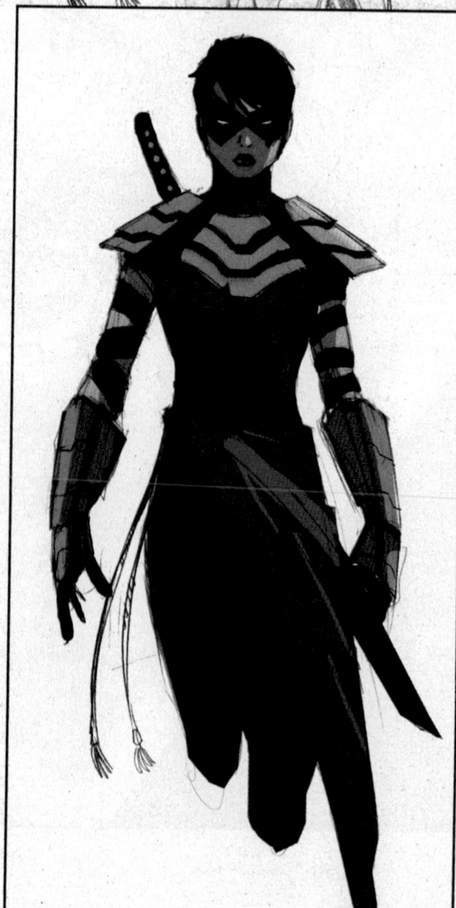

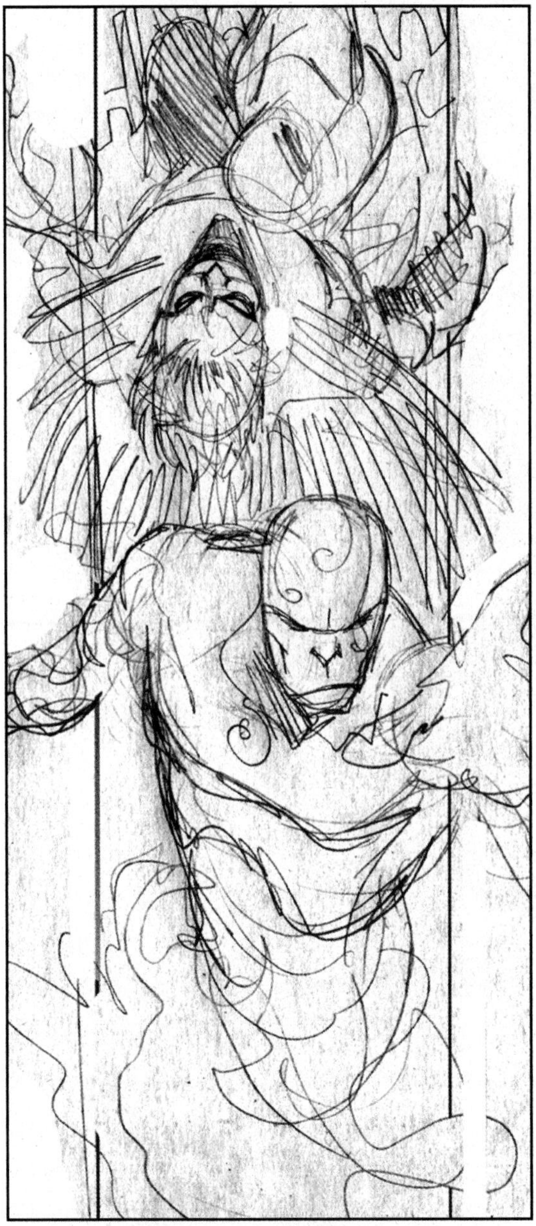

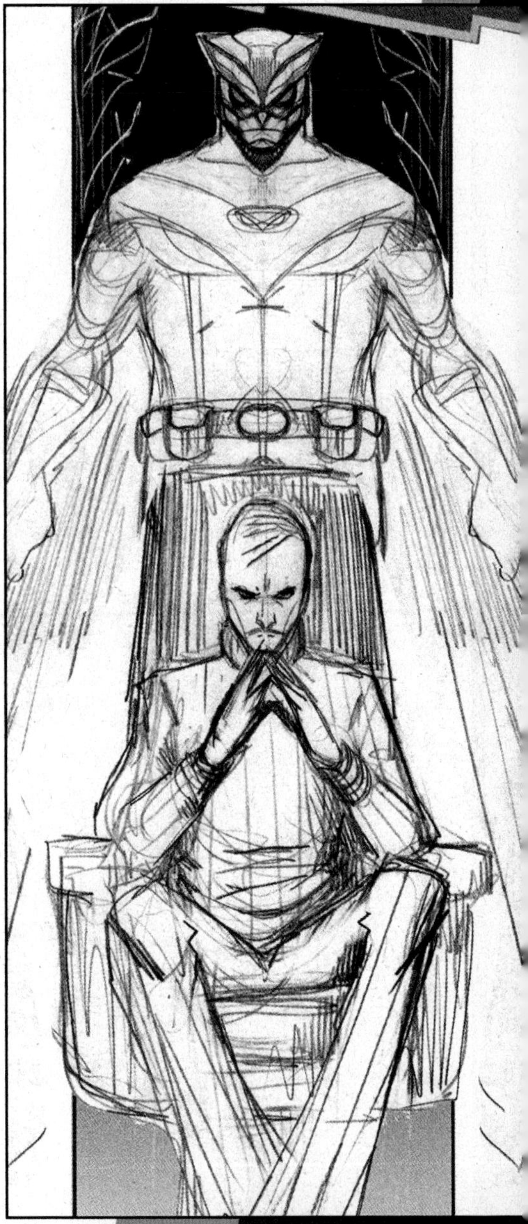

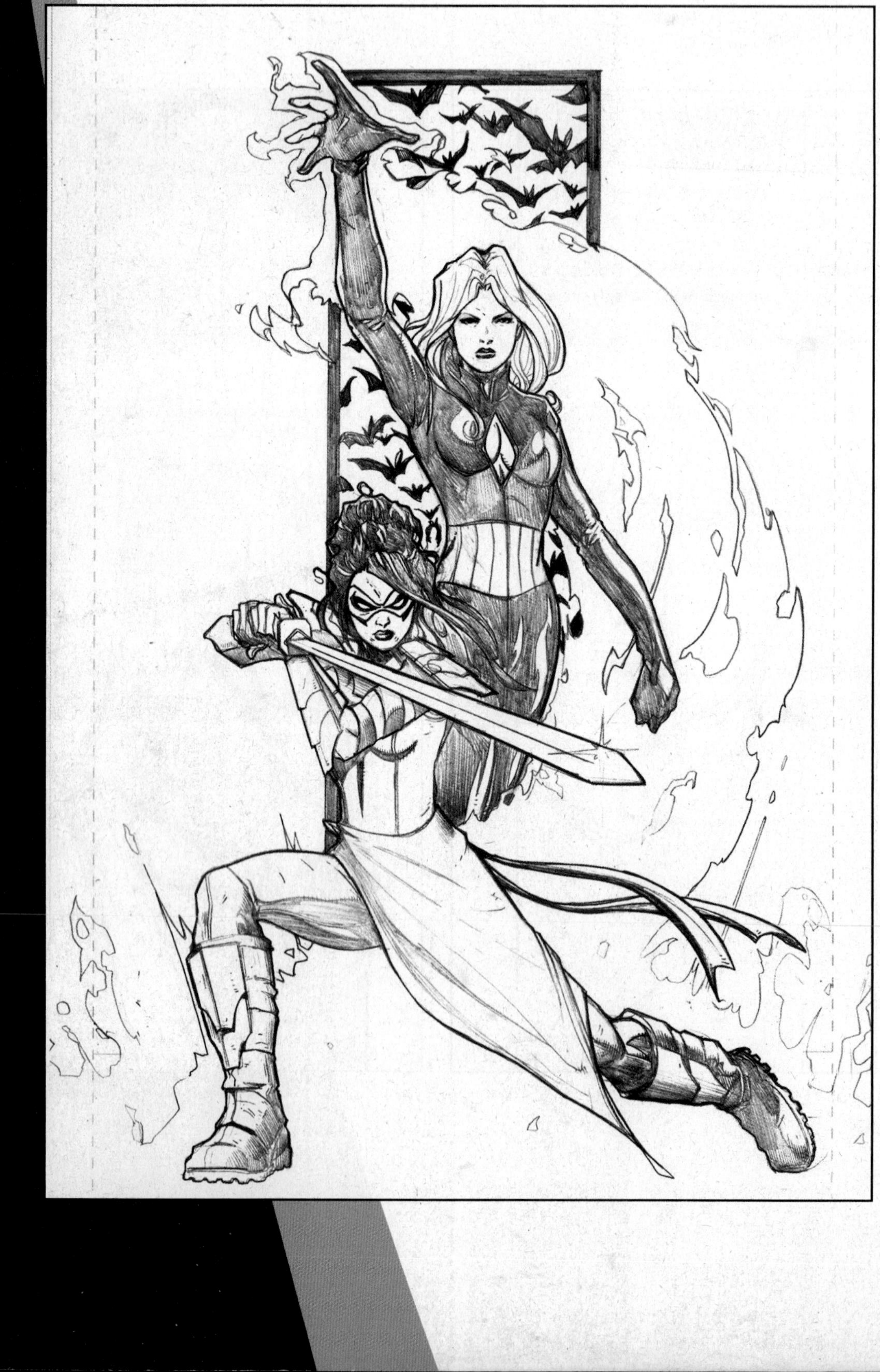

MORE CLASSIC TALES OF THE DARK KNIGHT

BATMAN: HUSH
VOLUME ONE

JEPH LOEB
JIM LEE

BATMAN: HUSH
VOLUME TWO

JEPH LOEB
JIM LEE

BATMAN:
THE LONG HALLOWEEN

JEPH LOEB
TIM SALE

BATMAN:
DARK VICTORY

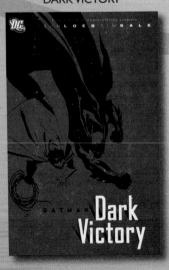

JEPH LOEB
TIM SALE

BATMAN:
HAUNTED KNIGHT

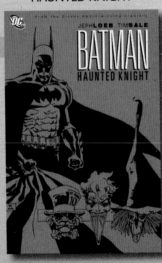

JEPH LOEB
TIM SALE

BATMAN:
YEAR 100

PAUL POPE